Heaven's Genuine &
COUNTERFEIT MINISTRY

Linwood Jackson, Jr.

PUBLISHED BY FIDELI PUBLISHING, INC.

© Copyright 2018, Linwood Jackson, Jr.

All Rights Reserved.

No part of this book may be reproduced, stored in a retrieval system, or transmitted by any means, electronic, mechanical, photocopying, recording, or otherwise, without written permission from the author.

ISBN: 978-1-948638-98-2

For information, email the author at
LinwoodJackson@hotmail.com

Published by
Fideli Publishing, Inc.
www.FideliPublishing.com

Contents

1. The Word of Reconciliation 1
2. The Song Of Our Confidence 11
3. The Arm Of Assurance 19
4. His Blessed Mercy 26
5. Love's Laws 31
6. The Law Of Faith 40
7. The Will Of The Father 50
8. A Profitable Hope By Faith 61
9. By The River Jordan 70
10. The Inward Voice Of The Gospel 82
11. His Pledge For Our Faithfulness 93
12. The Law Of His Faith 98
13. The Word Of His Patience 106
14. Believest Thou This? 114
15. Behold The Lamb 121
16. I Come to Do Thy Will 131
17. He Whose Right It Is 141
18. Your Most Holy Faith 149
19. The Current Cleansing 162
20. O House Of Aaron 175
21. To Escape The Seat Of Lies 187
22. Purify Before The Time 198
23. They Should Make An Image 207
24. The Law Of Truth And Peace 215

25.	The Heart Of The Serpent 223
26.	A Fearful Disposition 232
27.	Stedfast Unto The End 240
28.	Vash'ti The Queen 250
29.	That Beast Of The Earth 260
30.	Ha'man 270
31.	The Will And Nature Of The Beast 278
32.	The Gravity Of The Earth, And The Agitation Awaiting It 287
33.	The Earth And The Sea 295
34.	Dinah And She'chem 308
35.	The Fall Of The Glory Of All Kingdoms 320
36.	Mischievous Betrayers 332
37.	Judas And The Chief Of The Jews 342
38.	With Respect Of Persons 352
39.	By A Statute For Ever 362
40.	The Times Of Refreshing 372
41.	The First To Be Rewarded 381
42.	Of Thieves And Robbers 393
43.	Deprivation's Compromise 404

Introduction

1. Says the LORD, "I will make a new covenant with the house of Israel and with the house of Judah: not according to the covenant that I made with their fathers in the day when I took them by the hand to lead them out of the land of Egypt; because they continued not in my covenant, and I regarded them not, saith the Lord. For this is the covenant that I will make with the house of Israel after those days, saith the Lord; I will put my laws into their mind, and write them in their hearts: and I will be to them a God, and they shall be to me a people: and they shall not teach every man his neighbour, and every man his brother, saying, Know the Lord: for all shall know me, from the least to the greatest."[1]

2. It is crucial that the one professing faith in the Christ of God know the voice and covenant of God attached to the doctrine of His Son. From the moment the blood of this Christ met the air, a new government of personal religion came into existence for the one believing on "the LORD God of the Hebrews,"[2] for it says, "He taketh away the first, that he may establish the second."[3] The first covenant was that bond made between the LORD and the literal nation of Israel, for Moses said, "The LORD made not this covenant with our fathers, but with us."[4] This covenant found no place, or had no involvement, with Abraham, Isaac, and Jacob, for to them rested their own covenant, even "the covenant which he made with Abraham,"[5] which covenant "was confirmed before of God in Christ."[6]

---

1 Hebrews 8:8-11
2 Exodus 3:18
3 Hebrews 10:9
4 Deuteronomy 5:3
5 1 Chronicles 16:16
6 Galatians 3:17

3. The LORD swore by Himself repeatedly; "because he could swear by no greater, he sware by himself";[7] that the covenant that governed the nation of Israel would not last for ever. He blatantly confessed, concerning the will that He had established in Abraham's name, "My name shall be great among the Gentiles,"[8] and, "In the place where it was said unto them, Ye are not my people, there it shall be said unto them, Ye are the sons of the living God. Then shall the children of Judah and the children of Israel be gathered together, and appoint themselves one head."[9] His "Christ is the head of the church,"[10] even as it is written, "I will set up one shepherd over them, and he shall feed them, even my servant David; he shall feed them, and he shall be their shepherd."[11] Thus, for this cause it is written, "The Lamb which is in the midst of the throne shall feed them."[12]

4. The Lamb in the midst of the LORD's throne should move the mind to remember what Christ said: "Ye believe in God, believe also in me."[13] The throne of the Lamb and of the Spirit is "the throne of grace."[14] "The kingdom of Christ and of God"[15] is that word and instruction of the Lamb found at "the right hand of the throne of the Majesty in the heavens."[16] This is why the apostle counsels, "Our fellowship is with the Father, and with his Son."[17] Thus, the Lamb in the midst of the LORD's throne fulfills the saying, "We have an advocate with the Father, Jesus Christ the righteous."[18] And so the inquiring mind must ask, "An advocate for what?" And upon asking such a thing, the answer

---

7   Hebrews 6:13
8   Malachi 1:11
9   Hosea 1:10,11
10   Ephesians 5:23
11   Ezekiel 34:23,24
12   Revelation 7:17
13   John 14:1
14   Hebrews 4:16
15   Ephesians 5:5
16   Hebrews 8:1
17   1 John 1:3
18   1 John 2:1

is given, "Repentance toward God, and faith toward our Lord Jesus Christ,"[19] that "we shall be also in the likeness of his resurrection."[20]

5. Due to religious error against the name of the LORD God, humanity needed a sacrifice for the wall that man's obstinacy had willingly erected between their spirit and the LORD's. Because of the strange taint born within Adam, man is naturally "fallen and dead"[21] within the moral and mental realms of their existence. Before knowledge of religious error entered into the atmosphere of the soul, the immutable laws of God were written upon the heart of Eden's host, but spiritual negligence caused a break from the mind of God to occur in His thinking and feeling creation, which break we have inherited from our first parents. The soul needs to intelligently understand from whence it is fallen that it may stimulate the spirit to give life to the heart, and it is from the instruction of the Faith of Jesus that every heart is to be made warm for the conscious reception of their character defects, that in rightly observing self, they may observe that which is without corruption through the lens of the LORD's doctrine of love and godliness. It is for this reason that the law of the Lamb and the ten laws of the throne of the Majesty cannot, and should not be separated, from our personal religion.

6. Remember how the LORD Himself has said, "I will put My laws in their mind,"[22] for the inquiring one must ask, "What laws?" Says Scripture, "With the mind I myself serve the law of God."[23] Again the Spirit says, "I will write my laws on their heart,"[24] and again it must be asked, "What laws are to be written on the heart?" Says Scripture, "Christ may dwell in your hearts by faith,"[25] and, "Let the word of Christ dwell in you richly in all wisdom."[26] It is plain to see that the heart of the spirit of the mind is to hold both the Ten Commandments

---

19 Acts 20:21
20 Romans 5:5
21 2 Samuel 1:4
22 Hebrews 8:10
23 Romans 7:25
24 Hebrews 8:10
25 Ephesians 3:17
26 Colossians 3:16

of God and the law of His Son's name. Thus, "by the law of faith,"[27] the humble believer, by an experimental faith in "the law of Christ,"[28] will confess, "I delight in the law of God after the inward man."[29] The true and honest servant of God's Man will "be strengthened with might by his Spirit in the inner man,"[30] for as Scripture says, "Thou desirest truth in the inward parts,"[31] it is to be understood that the "wisdom" spoken of is specific, for "wisdom strengtheneth the wise."[32]

7. This is why the active believer should know that "through knowledge shall the just be delivered."[33] By way of "the law of the Spirit of life in Christ,"[34] the believer is to receive within himself or herself the precepts of the Spirit's wisdom from actively carrying out His instruction by faith. It is through Spirit's doctrine that the heart will sorrow after a godly manner, and as it realizes that it is indeed a violator of the commandments of God, the eye and hand of faith will boldly extended to the hand of His High Priest for knowledge of forgiveness to receive the righteousness of His God. The soul needs to understand the intimate and personal reason behind its aching heart, for its void is caused by a separation from the knowledge and intention of the living God, and if that heart is without right consolation, being left to its self, it will feign a form of comfort that is most injurious to both self and to others. It is the law of the Faith of Christ that is to bring the heart to acknowledge its emptiness, for by acknowledging this will, the heart will be given health to daily maintain and advance an honest conversation with self and God's voice.

8. This is the new covenant of God that is under the supervision of His Son's intercession and His Spirit's name. That old covenant "sanctifieth to the purifying of the flesh,"[35] yet that new covenant rati-

---

27   Romans 3:27
28   Galatians 6:2
29   Romans 7:22
30   Ephesians 3:16
31   Psalms 51:6
32   Ecclesiastes 7:19
33   Proverbs 11:9
34   Romans 8:2
35   Hebrews 9:13

fied by faith on the virtue of the blood of God's Man is ordained to "purge your conscience from dead works to serve the living God."[36] The covenant that ultimately mattered to the LORD was that promise conferred to Abraham's person for his faithfulness, thus "the scripture, foreseeing that God would justify the heathen through faith, preached before the gospel unto Abraham."[37] That blessed to Abraham's name was that promise to fulfill the Spirit's will and doctrine in the believer by an experimental faith on the Father's commandment, and that blessed of Aaron by the law of Moses was a figurative representation of what should become of the believer after faith's exercise had seized their heart and mind. Thus it is written, "Abraham believed God, and it was imputed unto him for righteousness,"[38] and this is written that every believer might hear, "We through the Spirit wait for the hope of righteousness by faith."[39]

9. It is through "his righteousness"; the righteousness of His Christ; "for the remission of sins that are past,"[40] that humanity receives a second probation to uphold every divine and holy commandment of heaven "through the forbearance of God."[41] The first covenant was without the Spirit and righteousness of God "with all spiritual blessings,"[42] but gave righteousness through that "which stood only in meats and drinks, and divers washings, and carnal ordinances, imposed on them."[43] These things were "a figure for the time then present, in which were offered both gifts and sacrifices, that could not make him that did the service perfect, as pertaining to the conscience,"[44] yet now, with His Christ being head over "a more excellent ministry, by how

---

36 Hebrews 9:14
37 Galatians 3:8
38 James 2:23
39 Galatians 5:5
40 Romans 3:25
41 Romans 3:25
42 Ephesians 1:3
43 Hebrews 9:10
44 Hebrews 9:9

much also he is the mediator of a better covenant"[45] to "purge your conscience from dead works to serve the living God."[46]

10. The believer must now know that full contact with the LORD's Spirit through the law of His doctrine means a fresh opportunity to be "written not with ink, but with the Spirit of the living God; not in tables of stone, but in fleshy tables of the heart."[47] The old and tangible religion is passed away. That done within the flesh by fear of routine or tradition or superstition is of no weight or value any longer. The reformer declares, "I serve with my spirit in the gospel of his Son,"[48] "for we know that the law is spiritual,"[49] and that the LORD has now made it a point for every believer to "be filled with the knowledge of his will in all wisdom and spiritual understanding."[50] It is the living God's wisdom and knowledge; obtained from obeying the voice of the Faith of His Spirit; that will secure a rescuing of our spiritual understanding from corrupt manners. The power of the gospel is to fulfill the word, "He shall redeem their soul from deceit and violence,"[51] for it is the soul and spirit that is to be regenerated for the final gathering when "the Son of man shall come in the glory of his Father."[52]

11. This is why the one who allows himself or herself to feel after the LORD's Son should not disconnect their mind from personal communion with His Spirit. "Your love in the Spirit"[53] only increases through "fellowship of the Spirit,"[54] which fellowship is "the love of God, and the communion of the Holy Ghost,"[55] and this love and communion resulting in the bestowal of "the grace of the Lord."[56] It is for this reason that we should always remember the counsel, "Come

---

45	Hebrews 8:6
46	Hebrews 9:14
47	2 Corinthians 3:3
48	Romans 1:9
49	Romans 7:14
50	Colossians 1:9
51	Psalms 72:14
52	Matthew 16:27
53	Colossians 1:8
54	Philippians 2:1
55	2 Corinthians 13:14
56	2 Corinthians 13:14

now, and let us reason together,"[57] and, "His delight is in the law of the LORD; and in his law doth he meditate day and night,"[58] and, "Grow in grace, and in the knowledge of our Lord and Saviour Jesus Christ."[59]

12. From "the Spirit of grace"[60] comes "the grace of life,"[61] and because "the Spirit is life because of righteousness,"[62] out of this same Spirit pours "abundance of grace,"[63] which is "the gift of righteousness."[64] This is how the Spirit will fulfill the promise, "All will know Me,"[65] for with the power of His grace joined to our confidence in the virtue of His sacrifice, every man or woman, girl or boy, who applies themselves to the Spirit's commandment of life and godliness will be created into a new creature. This living creature of the Spirit is His product by way of faithful observance and application given to the precepts of His doctrine, for the laws of our High Priest rest both in the heart and mind of such individuals strengthened by knowledge of His mediation's new covenant promise.

13. This is why the LORD anciently said, "Let there be light,"[66] for as creation is representative of "the beginning of the gospel"[67] on the dreary surface of the heart, so too "God, who commanded the light to shine out of darkness, hath shined in our hearts, to give the light of the knowledge of the glory of God in the face of Jesus Christ."[68] Paul is connecting the creation of the world to the renewing of the heart, for he heard by Christ Himself the vocation given him in relation to this praise, which phrase is as He says, "To open their eyes, and to turn them from darkness to light, and from the power of Satan unto God, that they may receive forgiveness of sins, and inheritance among

---

57 Isaiah 1:18
58 Psalm 1:2
59 2 Peter 3:18
60 Hebrews 10:29
61 1 Peter 3:7
62 Romans 8:10
63 Romans 5:17
64 Romans 5:17
65 Jeremiah 31:34
66 Genesis 1:3
67 Philippians 4:15
68 2 Corinthians 4:6

them which are sanctified by faith that is in me."[69] God's Priest would have every spirit sanctified, or purified, by that will and doctrine of His LORD's Spirit, for the believer is to be "sanctified by God the Father,"[70] and "being sanctified by the Holy Ghost,"[71] is to receive grace and showers of mercies to aid in the conversion of their inward person to reverence His Ten Commandments.

---

69 Acts 26:18
70 Jude 1:1
71 Romans 15:16

1

The Word Of Reconciliation

1. The counsel of our Father is, "This is my beloved Son: hear him."[72] The covenant of old simply said, "Obey my voice,"[73] and now the new covenant ratified by His Son continues the trend, saying, "Hear the voice of the Son of God."[74] Of old, it was that "from his right hand went a fiery law for them,"[75] and similarly it would be accomplished again, for this same God prophesied, "A law shall proceed from me,"[76] for which cause His Christ says, "I proceeded forth and came from God."[77] "I came down from heaven,"[78] says God's Man, for as the LORD did anciently send His throne's Standard by His own hand, so again in like manner He sent His Son's name for a law and covenant to establish His throne's new will. What our Father hoped to accomplish by the hand of Moses He will accomplish by the hand of His current High Priest, for as the Father operated of old with man by that earthly

---

72 Mark 9:7
73 Jeremiah 7:23
74 John 5:25
75 Deuteronomy 33:2
76 Isaiah 51:4
77 John 8:42
78 John 6:38

tabernacle, so too His Christ is now ordained to commune with man by that heavenly Sanctuary.

2. After His Christ should "receive power, and riches, and wisdom, and strength, and honour, and glory, and blessing,"[79] and after the Father should have "put all things under his feet...to be head over all things to the church,"[80] then said the Father to His Son, "Thy throne, O God,"[81] for remember, "he hath by inheritance obtained a more excellent name,"[82] being now "an high priest over the house of God."[83] God's spiritual Israel will hear and consent to His voice, and He today speaks through the name of His High Priest, for Christ said, "Heareth my word, and believeth on him that sent me."[84] Who sent this Christ? Scripture teaches, "Jesus returned in the power of the Spirit."[85] This Christ was "declared to be the Son of God with power,"[86] for God "anointed Jesus of Nazareth with the Holy Ghost and with power."[87] It was the power of the LORD His Father that lifted up Christ on earth and even resurrected Him from the dead, therefore the reformer "should believe on him that raised up Jesus our Lord from the dead."[88]

3. "The Spirit of him that raised up Jesus from the dead"[89] is given when there is a personal acknowledgement of the Sprit's voice of instruction. "All men should honour the Son, even as they honour the Father,"[90] therefore He says, "Hear the voice of the Son of God,"[91] and, "Heareth my word, and believeth on him that sent me."[92] Because the believer is counseled to now turn the eye of their faith to the Spirit's

---

79 Revelation 5:12
80 Ephesians 1:22
81 Hebrews 1:8
82 Hebrews 1:4
83 Hebrews 10:21
84 John 5:24
85 Luke 4:14
86 Romans 1:4
87 Acts 10:38
88 Romans 4:24
89 Romans 8:11
90 John 5:23
91 John 5:25
92 John 5:24

doctrine, Scripture counsels, "Walk, even as he walked,"[93] and Christ declares, "As the Father gave me commandment, even so I do."[94] Paul once wrote, "They walked not uprightly according to the truth of the gospel,"[95] for the believer is to order their conversation after the Spirit's counsel and doctrine as Christ does in the presence of the LORD His God, which is why He says, "If ye keep my commandments, ye shall abide in my love; even as I have kept my Father's commandments, and abide in his love."[96] Moses therefore told the truth when he said, "Him shall ye hear in all things,"[97] for Christ says, "I am the way, the truth, and the life."[98]

4. No longer can the believer come to God by the manners of the flesh; "having begun in the Spirit, are ye now made perfect by the flesh?"[99] It is for this reason that our Priest says, "No man cometh unto the Father, but by me."[100] For as through Christ's proverb we now commune with the living God, it must also be heard, "God hath given to us eternal life, and this life is in his Son."[101] "These things I say, that ye might be saved,"[102] says our salvation's Captain; that is, "that ye might have life";[103] for we are to confidently pray, "Deliver me from every evil work."[104] All that is in and of the Father is transferred to His Son's intercession "in the fullness of the blessing of the gospel of Christ."[105] God's Christ is "the mediator of the new covenant,"[106] "he is the mediator of a better covenant, which was established upon better promises,"[107] for it is yet His

---

93 1 John 2:6
94 John 14:32
95 Galatians 2:14
96 John 15:10
97 Acts 3:22
98 John 14:6
99 Galatians 3:3
100 John 14:6
101 1 John 5:11
102 John 5:34
103 John 5:40
104 2 Timothy 4:18
105 Romans 15:29
106 Hebrews 12:24
107 Hebrews 8:6

purpose to "bring us to God,"[108] to the end we may know the benefit of confidence in His name, "being sanctified by the Holy Ghost."[109]

5. The voice of our Father does not compel self-obedience to the Ten Commandments within the believer, but rather God has currently spoken by the law of His Son to those who would be faithful to obey them by faith according to the aim of His sacrifice. For this cause His Son says, "Every one which seeth Son, and believeth on him, may have everlasting life,"[110] or, "Whoso eateth my flesh, and drinketh my blood, hath eternal life,"[111] for the end of our Priest's name love towards His LORD and Father's voice, "and this is love, that we walk after his commandments."[112] To see and believe is to eat and drink, and both similarly result in an abundance of life. The flesh of Christ is as He says, "My flesh is meat,"[113] and the meat of Christ is as He says, "The bread that I will give is my flesh,"[114] and as for bread and meat, we read, "They continued steadfastly in the apostles' doctrine and fellowship, and in breaking bread,"[115] and, "Breaking bread from house to house, did eat their meat."[116] They that eat the doctrine of Christ and drink His blood; "for the life of the flesh is in the blood"[117] and gives power to the experience; will hear, "He that eateth my flesh, and drinketh my blood, dwelleth in me, and I in him,"[118] for then "God dwelleth in him, and he in God."[119]

6. God in the faithful is Christ in the believer, "and we know that he abideth in us, by the Spirit which he hath given us,"[120] for in the voice of

---

108 1 Peter 3:18
109 Romans 15:16
110 John 6:40
111 John 6:54
112 2 John 1:6
113 John 6:55
114 John 6:51
115 Acts 2:42
116 Acts 2:46
117 Leviticus 17:11
118 John 6:56
119 1 John 4:15
120 1 John 3:24

Christ is eternal life, and "God hath given to us eternal life."[121] To "be filled with all the fullness of God"[122] is to "be filled with the Spirit,"[123] and "hereby know we that we dwell in him, and he in us, because he hath given us of his Spirit."[124] We do know that "the Spirit is truth"[125] and that "the Spirit is life,"[126] for it is that from receiving and exercising faith on the Spirit's commandment; which commandment is "the word of truth, the gospel of your salvation";[127] and obeying those commandments of justification to obtain newness of heart and mind, the Spirit of Christ will be delivered to purify the soul temple to procure wisdom to the spirit after obeying those precepts. The Spirit is life for the reformer because His Faith leads into the science of heaven's righteousness, for the LORD testifies, "My righteousness shall not be abolished."[128] This is how we may know that creative redemption's doctrine is the praise of the Spirit's name and power for every active believer, for by heaven's new covenant Faith, every student of the Spirit's higher education sings, "All thy commandments are righteousness."[129]

7. Christ says, "As the living Father hath sent me, and I live by the Father: so he that eateth me, even he shall live by me."[130] As Christ lived on this earth under the wings of His Father's Spirit, so the Christian reformer is to live under the wings of the LORD's Priest not to unlawfully work the image of the Father, but by the aid of the same Spirit through the same commandment that strengthened the spirit of our High Priest, we are "to be conformed to the image of his Son"[131] to honor the image of the Father through a faith sanctified by a tried love in hope of His intercession. Christ says, "I am in the Father,"[132] and the hope of the believer is, "Ye in me, and

---

121 1 John 5:11
122 Ephesians 3:19
123 Ephesians 5:18
124 1 John 4:13
125 1 John 5:6
126 Romans 8:10
127 Ephesians 1:13
128 Isaiah 51:6
129 Psalm 119:172
130 John 6:57
131 Romans 8:29
132 John 14:11

I in you,"[133] for as Christ is in the Father, so too the believer should also rest in the same Father if they are in His Christ's Faith, and for this cause it is said, "Our fellowship is with the Father, and with his Son,"[134] and, "We also joy in God through our Lord Jesus."[135] The Holy Ghost is given of God to them that obey His voice of counsel,[136] that is, to them that obey the voice of His saying, which judgment is the present covenant of reconciliation to retain His moral image. Thus, as this Christ lived by His Father, so too the believer must maintain their conversation by the doctrine that shaped His peculiar stature; this is why it says, "If the Spirit of him that raised up Jesus from the dead dwell in you, he that raised up Christ from the dead shall also quicken your mortal bodies by his Spirit."[137]

8. Christ is that Priest and Officer of the new covenant over the LORD's heavenly House, and being equal in name with His God, He is the Physician of the deranged character of the human form. He does currently stand before the ark of His LORD's testament, even the ark that is in heaven, which ark Moses reproduced on earth as a copy of what exists above the earth. The ark on earth held the Ten Commandments and that in heaven does hold the same; yet now those precepts are under jurisdiction of a new covenant will, for the old was maintained on earth while the new is translated to heaven. The knowledge of God's Son is the true foundation of the new covenant promise, and is also the eternal life for what is inside of that ark. "Hear Him," says His Father, because the voice of Christ is the only voice to hear concerning redemption, justification, sanctification, regeneration, reform, and righteousness, which voice of old God illustrated through the book of the law, the book of the old covenant. Christ stands before the Ten Commandments as Priest over the Ten Commandments and Lord over the law of inward deliverance. His faith entails both the Law of God and the law of the Faith of His Spirit.

---

133   John 14:20
134   1 John 1:3
135   Romans 5:11
136   Acts 5:32
137   Romans 8:11

9. As Christ lived by His Father, so too the Christian is to hear every word of His doctrine to have in them His testimony and His Father's name. "The name of God and his doctrine"[138] are born by the obedient, for "here are they that keep the commandments of God, and the faith of Jesus."[139] Only by faith in the blessings of the new covenant may the believer progress to "the stature of the fullness of Christ,"[140] because by obedience to His instruction, the reformer is to receive "his Spirit in the inner man,"[141] to the end that the character of God would be perfected in their heart. Therefore, it has happened that the LORD sent out a law to the earth, called, "The law of Christ,"[142] and by this judgment we know why it says, "Thy law is the truth,"[143] for it says, "The truth is in Jesus,"[144] that is, the truth is magnified by "the doctrine of Christ."[145]

10. "The truth of God"[146] is hidden within "the faith of God"[147] revealing the hope of the image of God through "the knowledge of the Son of God."[148] This knowledge is that revelation of God called, "The gospel of Christ,"[149] and "it is the power of God"[150] revealing "the righteousness of God,"[151] to the end that by the revelation of Jesus' name, the believer would turn to worship "the Creator, who is blessed for ever,"[152] that is, "The God and Father of our Lord Jesus Christ, which is blessed for evermore."[153] It is for this cause that the believer does "joy in God through our Lord";[154] as it says, "Alive unto God through

---

138   1 Timothy 6:1
139   Revelation 14:12
140   Ephesians 4:13
141   Ephesians 3:16
142   Galatians 6:2
143   Psalms 119:142
144   Ephesians 4:21
145   2 John 1:9
146   Romans 3:7
147   Romans 3:3
148   Ephesians 4:13
149   Romans 1:16
150   Romans 1:16
151   Romans 1:17
152   Romans 1:25
153   1 Peter 1:3
154   Romans 5:1

Jesus";[155] for "we have peace with God through our Lord,"[156] meaning, the believer is filled with "peace, and joy in the Holy Ghost,"[157] to know and love the name of the living God. And besides the reception of the Holy Ghost by our faith on the virtue of the sacrifice of His Christ, there is a reception of rest, even as it is said, "We which have believed do enter into rest."[158] If the truth of God is the revelation of the name and glory of His Spirit, then it is a fact that the revelation of the power of God is found memorialized "in a certain place of the seventh day on this wise."[159]

11. The professed believer of Christ should not be void of the "seal of the righteousness of the faith."[160] Christ says, "I am come in my Father's name,"[161] and, "I have declared unto them thy name,"[162] and, "I love the Father,"[163] which is why He says, "Holy Father, keep through thine own name those whom thou hast given me."[164] Because he believed God, Abraham "received the sign of circumcision, a seal of the righteousness of the faith,"[165] and it is an example for those who should believe on Christ's law of regeneration in this age, for Christ has said of His faithful, "I will write upon him the name of my God,"[166] which is "his Father's name written in their foreheads."[167] It is because the name of the Father needs to be sealed within the believer that the Holy Ghost is given through Christ's Faith. Therefore, by our faithful exercise in the commandment of His mediation, we now "rejoice in the hope of the glory of God,"[168] for by this commandment we are heirs; by

---

155 Romans 6:11
156 Romans 5:1
157 Romans 14:7
158 Hebrews 4:3
159 Hebrews 4:3,4
160 Romans 4:11
161 John 5:43
162 John 17:26
163 John 14:31
164 John 17:11
165 Romans 4:11
166 Revelation 3:12
167 Revelation 14:1
168 Romans 5:2

our tried faith; of the Spirit's benevolence, even as Abraham who was called to be the heir of the world, that "through the righteousness of faith"[169] we should "believe on him that raised up our Lord."[170]

12. In the beginning it is said, "God blessed the seventh day, and sanctified it,"[171] and, "The LORD God commanded the man"[172] after He "took the man, and put him into the garden."[173] Since the beginning, His Sabbath has been joined to a covenant and specific commandments of that covenant, and it is yet no different at this time. In every dispensation, the LORD has provided His chosen with His Sabbath and covenant for the time in which they live, along with commandments advancing obedience to that Sabbath law, and currently the Spirit counsels, "Keep my commandments."[174] After there is belief on His Son's voice, and after strength is found in God's promise, it will be heard of God, "I sware unto thee, and entered into covenant with thee";[175] "then washed I thee with water...and put a jewel on thy forehead, and earrings in thine ears."[176]

13. If any one is without His Father, our Priest says, "My word hath no place in you,"[177] and, "Ye have not his word abiding in you";[178] "ye have not the love of God in you."[179] The voice of God's Son is the Father's manner of love, for through Christ "was manifested the love of God toward us,"[180] in that "he loved us"[181] "when we were enemies,"[182]

---

169 Romans 4:13
170 Romans 4:24
171 Genesis 2:3
172 Genesis 2:16
173 Genesis 2:15
174 John 14:15
175 Ezekiel 16:8
176 Ezekiel 16:9-11
177 John 8:37
178 John 5:38
179 John 5:42
180 1 John 4:9
181 1 John 4:10
182 Romans 5:10

"and sent his Son to be the propitiation for our sins."[183] If the believer "dwelleth in love";[184] that is, in "the kindness and love of God our Saviour toward man";[185] "we know that he abideth in us,"[186] and that we rest in Him "by the Spirit which he hath given us."[187] That which is our aid for mental and moral recovery is our consistent faith in the Faith consecrated through the mediation of God's Man, even that law of "the victory through our Lord Jesus,"[188] for the believer is to hear the voice of the Son of God and obey the doctrine of Christ that they may retain the name and Spirit of the Father for sanctification. Our compliance with this sanctification is the means whereby we may love the name of the LORD His God, which name is expressed by the law of His seventh-day Sabbath, "for this is the love of God, that we keep his commandments."[189]

14. By the blessings of the new covenant, the believer is to serve the LORD God by His Faith. There can be no true worship of the Father without reverence to that which declares the name and power of God, which is why the Spirit counsels, "Fear God, and give glory to him...that made heaven, and earth, and the sea, and the fountains of waters,"[190] for it is known, "In six days the LORD made heaven and earth, the sea, and all that in them is, and rested the seventh day: wherefore the LORD blessed the Sabbath day, and hallowed it."[191] That which declares the authority of God regulates the commandments of God, and the fourth commandment is that precept which maintains life and reconciliation in the Faith of salvation's science.

---

183 1 John 4:10
184 1 John 4:16
185 Titus 3:4
186 1 John 3:24
187 1 John 3:24
188 1 Corinthians 15:57
189 1 John 5:3
190 Revelation 14:7
191 Exodus 20:11

2

The Song Of Our Confidence

1. Says the Spirit, "This is my beloved Son: hear him,"[192] for His Christ says, "He that believeth on me, believeth not on me, but on him that sent me,"[193] that is, "The Father which sent me."[194]

2. The counsel of the Father is to hear the will of His Son whom He has anointed Priest and Savior of His intention. Thus, it is well to remember how His Christ says, "He gave me commandment, what I should say,"[195] for His Father, concerning Him, prophesied of old, "I have put my spirit upon him"[196] "and the isles shall wait for his law."[197] Herein the Spirit makes mention of "the law of Christ"[198] for obedience towards the ten laws of the Father's throne. It was because "they would not walk in his ways, neither were they obedient unto his law,"[199] that

---

192 Mark 9:7
193 John 12:44
194 John 12:45
195 John 12:49
196 Isaiah 42:1
197 Isaiah 42:4
198 Galatians 6:2
199 Isaiah 42:24

the Father declared, "Sing unto the LORD a new song,"[200] and, "Give glory unto the LORD,"[201] for the Father would send forth a proper commandment to know Him by, which is why His Christ says, "He that seeth me seeth him that sent me."[202]

3. This is why our Father said to His Christ, "I will preserve thee, and give thee for a covenant of the people."[203] "This before spake of the resurrection of Christ, that his soul was not left in hell, neither his flesh did see corruption. This Jesus hath God raised up"[204] "who is set on the right hand of the throne of the Majesty."[205] Christ being by the throne of the Father means that He is joined to Him "that created the heavens, and stretched them out; he that spread forth the earth, and that which cometh out of it,"[206] for which cause the saying should not be forgotten, "He had rested from all his work which God created and made."[207] Now "God, who created all things by Jesus Christ,"[208] He is that LORD who blessed and sanctified His Sabbath, for it says, "He had rested" from that "which God created and made." As His Angel created and made, it was the Spirit of the Father that brought all things to be, for "through faith we understand that the worlds were framed by the word of God,"[209] and that without creation's Spirit there "was not anything made that was made."[210]

4. The Father blessed His Sabbath as the true Memorial of His name, therefore through His Spirit He declared, "Let them give glory unto the LORD,"[211] that is, Let all remain "subject to the law

---

200   Isaiah 42:10
201   Isaiah 42:12
202   John 12:45
203   Isaiah 49:8
204   Acts 2:31,32
205   Hebrews 8:1
206   Isaiah 42:5
207   Genesis 2:3
208   Ephesians 3:9
209   Hebrews 11:3
210   John 1:3
211   Isaiah 42:12

of God,"[212] "obedient unto his law,"[213] for it says, "Fear God, and give glory to him."[214] He that brought all things to be by the power of His voice said to His Son, "I the LORD have called thee in righteousness, and will hold thine hand";[215] for it says, "All thy commandments are righteousness,"[216] and, "My righteousness shall not be abolished";[217] therefore said the Father, "A sceptre of righteousness is the sceptre of thy kingdom."[218] The voice of God is regulated by the voice of His Son through the reign of His Son's priesthood. To believe on the Son is to trust on the Father's name, and if there is communion with the Father's Faith, then we know that we do have "the Spirit of truth, which proceedeth from the Father."[219] So then "hear what the Spirit saith,"[220] for "God is a Spirit,"[221] and the words of Christ are that "which God gave unto him."[222] For this cause we know that it is the Father who says, "Wait for his law,"[223] for then we shall know the laws of the Father's throne, to love them.

5. The Father promises to hold the hand of His Christ, which is why His Man says, "And am set down with my Father in his throne."[224] The throne of the Son, "by reason of the glory that excelleth,"[225] magnifies the throne of His Father. Again, concerning the Father honoring His own name by His Son's ministry, "There came a voice from heaven, saying, I have";[226] for Christ had before said, "Father, glorify thy

---

212 Romans 8:7
213 Isaiah 42:24
214 Revelation 14:7
215 Isaiah 42:6
216 Psalms 119:172
217 Isaiah 51:6
218 Hebrews 1:8
219 John 15:26
220 Revelation 2:11
221 John 4:24
222 Revelation 1:1
223 Isaiah 42:4
224 Revelation 3:21
225 2 Corinthians 3:10
226 John 12:28

name";[227] "and will glorify it again,"[228] continued His Father. The name of the Father was to be glorified a second time, which is why He said, "A law shall proceed from me,"[229] and why Christ says, "He gave me a commandment,"[230] because "whosoever believeth on him shall not be ashamed."[231] Thus, the Spirit that speaks to the churches is of God the Father, for in every right church, the Father and the Son are to hold authority, and the Father is to receive praise by the name of His Son, as it says, "Unto him be glory in the church by Christ."[232] Every faithful church is bound to the LORD by that new song of hope and perfection to be sung, for the Father states, "The former things are come to pass, and new things do I declare,"[233] therefore He did "magnify the law,"[234] that is, the voice of Him who was to proceed from His Spirit, for it says, "Thou hast magnified thy word above all thy name."[235]

6. Says the Father, "Sing ye unto her, A vineyard of red wine,"[236] that is, "Announce to the House, 'Thou wast slain, and hast redeemed us to God by thy blood.'"[237] This is the Spirit's doctrine, for it is that Christ says, "He that believeth on me, believeth not on me, but on him that sent me,"[238] and, "I am come in my Father's name."[239]

7. The true worshipper will serve the Father due to the revelation made known of Him to their conscience by their personal examination of the knowledge and doctrine of His Son. The name of God cannot be reached but through the will of His Son and Sprit. It is the word of His patience, or rather, the word of the labor and works of His Christ, that

---

227 John 12:28
228 John 12:28
229 Isaiah 51:4
230 John 12:49
231 Romans 9:33
232 Ephesians 3:21
233 Isaiah 42:9
234 Isaiah 42:21
235 Psalms 138:2
236 Isaiah 27:2
237 Revelation 5:9
238 John 12:44
239 John 5:43

is to magnify the Father's name, that is to bring the believer to hear and obey the counsel, "Fear God, and keep his commandments."[240]

8. Christ says, "If I be lifted up from the earth, will draw all men unto me,"[241] yet said this same Jesus, "No man can come to me, except the Father which hath sent me draw him,"[242] and "this spake he of the Spirit, which they that believe on him should receive."[243] From "believing ye might have life through his name,"[244] for "the Spirit is life,"[245] and to them "that believe on the name of the Son of God,"[246] "know that ye have eternal life,"[247] for the Father promised, "Israel shall be saved in the LORD with an everlasting salvation."[248] "This life is in his Son,"[249] and the fullness of the Godhead that is in His name is transferred by faith on His voice to the believer, seeing as how "he became the author of eternal salvation unto all them that obey him."[250] For this cause the Scripture says, "Let him trust in the name of the LORD, and stay upon his God,"[251] for it should be that "we are in him that is true, even in his Son Jesus Christ."[252]

9. Christ says to His faithful, "I will write upon him the name of my God,"[253] because He had once said, "I ascend unto my Father, and your Father; and to my God, and your God."[254] The name of His God is that "seal of the righteousness of the faith,"[255] that blessed Memorial of His LORD instituted at the beginning of creation for a witness to His righteousness, and as the Father said, "Hear Him," and as to the Son

---

240 Ecclesiastes 12:13
241 John 12:32
242 John 6:44
243 John 7:39
244 John 20:31
245 Romans 8:10
246 1 John 5:13
247 1 John 5:13
248 Isaiah 5:17
249 1 John 5:11
250 Hebrews 5:9
251 Isaiah 50:10
252 1 John 5:20
253 Revelation 3:12
254 John 20:17
255 Romans 4:11

He said, "Your throne O God,"[256] it is that now, through the law of His Son's mediation, God has given to every believer a continual season of blessing for inward health. If we actively believe on the virtue of the merits of His Christ, we are believers on the Spirit's Faith, and in so doing we are in fellowship with Him that is true and faithful to receive the end of that confidence, for "it pleased the Father that in him should all fullness dwell."[257]

10. God has made "a new and living way, which he hath consecrated for us"[258] to joy in His name, for He promised, "This is the covenant that I will make with the house of Israel."[259] Concerning the house of Israel, we know how it is said, "O house of Israel: bless the LORD, O house of Aaron."[260] For it was "that another priest should rise after the order of Melchis'edec, and not be called after the order of Aaron,"[261] because to God "after the similitude of Melchis'edec there ariseth another priest... after the power of an endless life."[262] The LORD's new covenant is made with the house of Aaron; that is, the "church of the firstborn"[263] within "the city of the living God, the heavenly Jerusalem";[264] because the LORD had said, "I the LORD will be their God, and my servant David a prince among them."[265] Through Christ, worship to the Father is had by the Faith on the Father's will, for the Father gives life and newness to the believer for the purpose of a healthy personal and devotional conversation, even as it says, "Sanctified by the Holy Ghost."[266]

11. But, says the Godhead, "Who hath believed our report?"[267] Before He said, "I will not leave you comfortless,"[268] is it not Him

---

256   Hebrews 1:8
257   Colossians 1:19
258   Hebrews 10:20
259   Hebrews 8:10
260   Psalms 135:19
261   Hebrews 7:11
262   Hebrews 7:15,16
263   Hebrews 12:23
264   Hebrews 12:22
265   Ezekiel 34:24
266   Romans 15:16
267   Isaiah 53:1
268   John 14:18

that said, "I, even I, am he that comforteth you,"[269] and, "The LORD hath comforteth his people, and will have mercy on the afflicted"?[270] "According to his mercy he saved us,"[271] says the apostle, but before that, He had said, "With great mercies will I gather thee,"[272] which is why it is said, "By the mercies of God...be ye transformed by the renewing of your mind."[273] As the believer advances from "obeying the truth through the Spirit,"[274] it was previously ordained that by His mercies they should "be renewed in knowledge,"[275] "created in righteousness and true holiness"[276] "after the image of him that created him,"[277] for He said, "Everyone that is called by my name...I have created him...I have formed him; yea, I have made him."[278] For this cause, our Father counsels, "I am the LORD, your Holy One, the creator of Israel, your King,"[279] which is why it is purposed of His Spirit for the Christian "to be conformed to the image of his Son."[280]

12. "To them that are sanctified by God the Father";[281] that is, "sanctified by the Holy Ghost";[282] "and preserved in Jesus Christ";[283] that is, "sanctified through the offering of the body of Jesus";[284] these are they whom the Spirit has created for Himself. The Father said of His Son, "He shall bring forth judgment unto truth,"[285] and we do know how it is said, "Thy law is the truth,"[286] for from out of the LORD's

---

269 Isaiah 51:12
270 Isaiah 49:13
271 Titus 3:5
272 Isaiah 54:7
273 Romans 12:1,2
274 1 Peter 1:22
275 Colossians 3:10
276 Ephesians 4:24
277 Colossians 3:10
278 Isaiah 43:7
279 Isaiah 43:15
280 Romans 8:29
281 Jude 1:1
282 Romans 15:16
283 Jude 1:1
284 Hebrews 10:10
285 Isaiah 42:3
286 Psalms 119:142

character shines the revelation of Christ, because "the truth is in Jesus."[287] Thus, "Ye are sanctified, but ye are justified in the name of the Lord Jesus, and by the Spirit of our God,"[288] confirms the apostle, therefore Christ counsels, "Let thine eyes observe my ways,"[289] and, "Keep my commandments, and live; and my law as the apple of thine eye."[290] The Faith of Jesus is that knowledge to awaken the heart to hear God's Priest confess, "I love the Father."[291] For this cause, the LORD and Father of this Christ "hath translated us into the kingdom of his Son"[292] that it should be fulfilled, "Bind up the testimony, seal the law among my disciples."[293] Thus, because He through His Spirit spoke beforehand of that law and doctrine that should produce newness of spirit by faith on its operation, "truly our fellowship is with the Father, and with his Son."[294]

---

287 Ephesians 4:21
288 1 Corinthians 6:11
289 Proverbs 23:6
290 Proverbs 7:2
291 John 14:31
292 Colossians 1:13
293 Isaiah 8:16
294 1 John 1:3

3

The Arm Of Assurance

1. "Hear ye him,"[295] says the Father of His Son, for it was spoken of old, "Him shall ye hear in all things whatsoever he shall say unto you."[296] Thus, the Father declared, "A law shall proceed from me,"[297] and by this law, "They shall sanctify my name, and sanctify the Holy One of Jacob,"[298] says the Spirit. For this cause the Father says, "Wait for his law,"[299] that is, the law of Him that should proceed from Him, for He that came from the Spirit said, "I proceeded forth and came from God,"[300] therefore the Scripture says, "Fulfill the law of Christ."[301] It is for this reason that the Spirit counsels, "Hear the law of the LORD,"[302] and, "Hear my voice,"[303] because it says, "His arm shall rule for him,"[304]

---

295 Matthew 17:5
296 Acts 3:22
297 Isaiah 51:4
298 Isaiah 29:23
299 Isaiah 42:4
300 John 8:42
301 Galatians 6:2
302 Isaiah 30:9
303 Isaiah 32:9
304 Isaiah 40:10

and, "On mine arm shall they trust,"[305] for it is written, "The Father loveth the Son, and hath given all things into his hand."[306]

2. Every thing concerning the LORD's name is now in the possession of this law of His Spirit, for the law that was given of God for man is now "a covenant of the people."[307] This is why, to know Him, the LORD established a judgment for us to learn of and do, saying, in reference to the commandment of His Son's mediation, "The isles shall wait for his law,"[308] that is, "I will give to Jerusalem one that bringeth good tidings."[309] This is why His Son says, "The LORD hath anointed me to preach good tidings,"[310] and again in another place, "He hath anointed me to preach the gospel."[311] There was to be a second charge of God encouraging obedience to the first; a second pledge of another commandment for them that would obey the Ten Commandments; a new covenant and decree for devotion; and this law was to be obeyed by all desiring to love the LORD. Through this law that was to be contained within the name of His High Priest; as it says, "A man shall be as an hiding place";[312] the saying was to be confirmed, "Thou shalt rejoice in the LORD, and shalt glory in the Holy One of Israel."[313] For our consolation, the Spirit moved John to observe the assembly honoring the Father through the name of His Son, to the end that we might receive courage to elevate our faith's activity on that name's order. This vision states: "Therefore are they before the throne of God, and serve him day and night in his temple: and he that sitteth on the throne shall dwell among them."[314]

---

305 Isaiah 51:5
306 John 3:35
307 Isaiah 49:8
308 Isaiah 42:4
309 Isaiah 41:27
310 Isaiah 61:1
311 Luke 4:18
312 Isaiah 32:2
313 Isaiah 41:16
314 Revelation 7:15

3. Christ came to this earth for two reason, and He says, "The zeal of thine house hath eaten me up";[315] "lo, I come to do thy will,"[316] and, "That he might deliver us from this present evil world,"[317] "Christ died for our sins,"[318] for the Father made a promise by Him, saying, "I will remember their sins no more."[319] Again, the Father, concerning His new covenant will, said, "I will be merciful to their unrighteousness,"[320] therefore in the confidence of Christ, the reformer may say, "Be merciful unto me: heal my soul";[321] "so shall I keep the testimony of thy mouth,"[322] and, "The law of thy mouth is better unto me than thousands of gold and silver."[323] Therefore, "to the law and to the testimony: if they speak not according to this word, it is because there is no light in them,"[324] for the Father has said, "Hear him";[325] that is, hear "the record that God gave of his Son";[326] because "he that hath received his testimony hath set to his seal that God is true."[327]

4. The law of Christ joins the believer to God by their faith in His mediation's operation, that by obeying the Faith of His Spirit, the Spirit of His intercession may fashion their conversation after the likeness of His Son's. This is why it is written, "Hear the law of the LORD,"[328] because from this law comes a judgment for the deliverance of the soul and spirit, as it says, "I give you good doctrine, forsake ye not my law."[329] That which proceeds from God is the word of Christ, which is the present voice of God for our conformity to His kind will, thus

---

315 Psalms 69:9
316 Hebrews 10:9
317 Galatians 1:4
318 1 Corinthians 15:3
319 Jeremiah 31:34
320 Hebrews 8:13
321 Psalms 41:4
322 Psalms 119:88
323 Psalms 119:72
324 Isaiah 8:20
325 Mark 9:7
326 1 John 5:10
327 John 3:33
328 Isaiah 30:9
329 Proverbs 4:2

fulfilling the Scripture, "A king shall reign in righteousness."[330] Through this will the Father promised, "My people shall dwell in a peaceable habitation...in quiet resting places,"[331] therefore He says to "the deaf that have ears,"[332] "Look upon Zion...thine eyes shall see the king in his beauty...thine eyes shall see Jerusalem a quiet habitation."[333] The believer is taken by the Father through their spirit into the heavenly reign of His Son, and by an exercised faith on the commandment of His Spirit is "come unto mount Si'on, and unto the city of the living God,"[334] "the city of our solemnities."[335]

5. The law of Christ came through the LORD's ten immutable laws, and it is this Faith that the believer is to hear, dress, and keep. The kingdom of Christ holds the ministration of righteousness for the active believer, for the mind of God has set the constitution of the faithful "above, where Christ sitteth on the right hand of God,"[336] for it is purposed that "there the glorious LORD will be unto us a place of broad rivers and streams."[337] As Scripture declares God's Christ "on the right hand of the throne of the Majesty,"[338] so this Man is ever connected to the name of His Father, even as it says, "Bless the LORD your God for ever and ever: and blessed be thy glorious name."[339] This is why He says, "I and my Father are one."[340]

6. This Christ did not cancel the authority of the name and power of the LORD His Father; which name and honor is revealed in the fourth commandment of His Sabbath; but rather He further magnified and hallowed that name, shedding light on its immutability. He Himself says of Himself, "I am come in my Father's name,"[341] therefore God the

---

330   Isaiah 32:1
331   Isaiah 32:18
332   Isaiah 43:8
333   Isaiah 33:17,20
334   Hebrews 12:22
335   Isaiah 33:20
336   Colossians 3:1
337   Isaiah 33:21
338   Hebrews 8:1
339   Nehemiah 9:5
340   John 10:30
341   John 5:43

Father has given all things concerning His name into the hands of His High Priest that by faith on this law of His Spirit, the doctrine of the Christ of God would bring all honest men and women to His throne to love His name by honoring the virtue of His Son, even as His Son says, "He that believeth on me, believeth not on me, but on him that sent me."[342] "On mine arm shall they trust,"[343] says the Father, for He did not plainly say, "On Me they will trust," but rather, "His arm shall rule for him,"[344] and concerning this arm, we know that it works for the good of the LORD's name, ensuring His host that He will be like "as the shadow of a great rock in a weary land."[345] That of old was a "shadow of things to come; but the body is of Christ,"[346] for we should know "that Rock was Christ."[347]

7. That which came of God is the foundation of the Faith that is to lead back to God, because Christ came to exalt the name of His Father and to establish a better way to reverence Him, for which cause the Father promised, "I will do a new thing...I will make a way in the wilderness, and rivers in the desert."[348] In Christ, the Father promised, "I will pour my spirit upon thy seed, and my blessing,"[349] because He said of this law, "I have put my spirit upon him."[350] This He said "in hope of eternal life, which God, that cannot lie, promised before the world began,"[351] which is why through Abraham he said, "I will bless them that bless thee,"[352] which promise was truly spoken of in confidence of the good to come by exercising faith on heaven's will. By training the heart through Abraham's peculiar brand of faith and determination, "the blessing of Abraham might come"[353] from obeying the voice of

---

342 John 12:44
343 Isaiah 51:5
344 Isaiah 40:10
345 Isaiah 32:2
346 Colossians 2:17
347 1 Corinthians 10:4
348 Isaiah 43:19
349 Isaiah 44:3
350 Isaiah 42:2
351 Titus 1:2
352 Genesis 12:3
353 Galatians 3:14

Christ; that is, "the promise of the Spirit through faith";[354] for by the power and wisdom of the Spirit, the believer is to be saved, delivered, recovered in heart and mind by "the renewing of the Holy Ghost,"[355] meaning that through faith, the inward person is "sanctified by God the Father,"[356] that is, "sanctified by the Holy Ghost."[357] The doctrine of Christ is to deliver the believer into the hands of the Father for purification, for the mind is to be delivered from slavery to self and the religious world, for "he will deliver it; and passing over he will preserve it."[358]

8. The inward parts of the heart are to be preserved by the Father and kept hidden from harm when nourished by the knowledge of His Son. The charge from out of the mouth of God's Spirit demands reverence to "the law of faith"[359] and to "the law of the Spirit of life."[360] It is the doctrine of Christ that teaches, "I am the LORD that doth sanctify you,"[361] for if it is the Father that does sanctify, and if there is a profession of Christ, wherefore is there justification in removing the heart from hearing the name and foundation of that sanctification? He of whom there is a profession of faith in God says with His Christ, "I love the Father,"[362] and the Father has commanded every willing soul to hear the depth of His Son's tone, for He says, "Whosoever will not hearken unto my words which he shall speak in my name, I will require it of him."[363] Thus, in response to this, what did His Son say? "Father, keep through thine own name those whom thou hast given me,"[364] He prays, for the glorious name of the LORD His Father is wrapped within "the glorious gospel of the blessed God."[365] It is for this reason that

---

354 Galatians 3:14
355 Titus 3:5
356 Jude 1:1
357 Romans 15:16
358 Isaiah 31:5
359 Romans 3:27
360 Romans 8:2
361 Exodus 31:13
362 John 14:31
363 Deuteronomy 18:19
364 John 17:11
365 1 Timothy 1:11

Christ says, "Keep My commandments. Even as I have heard and have obeyed My Father, hear Me as I have heard and obeyed Him. For if any man will love Me, he will keep My words."[366]

9. The Spirit of the Father brings the believer into the kingdom and reign of His Son, for as He does sit on the right hand of the Father's throne, this Man rules His own throne for the praise of His Father's, even the "throne of grace."[367] Therefore "the Holy Ghost saith, To day if ye will hear his voice, harden not your hearts,"[368] for the Father says of His Son, "He shall be a priest upon his throne."[369] The Father has given us heaven's Faith and knowledge as an unbreakable and unchangeable golden rope of love and hope leading to Him, which is why He, concerning the commandment of His Son's intercession, counsels, "Wait for his law,"[370] that we may be obedient to the ten laws of His throne for the good of self, and of one another.

---

366 John 14:15; John 14:23
367 Hebrews 4:16
368 Hebrews 3:7,8
369 Zechariah 6:13
370 Isaiah 42:4

4

His Blessed Mercy

1. Says the Spirit, "And you, being dead in your sins, and in the uncircumcision of your flesh, hath he quickened together with him, having forgiven you all trespasses."[371]

2. What a blessed revelation of the mercy of God! His ways are beyond finite comprehension and His gift of love without mortal understanding. The plight of humanity is bound to the throne of the Father and the Son with an unbreakable chain of love, but who will believe the fact? "Thy faith hath saved thee,"[372] says the LORD's Priest to any one who will believe the fact. In His name rests mental and moral health and redemption, cure and justice, and as we are yet negligent in thought and feeling, this is the way that we are naturally desired of Him, just as sinful in thought and in feeling as we are. They who would believe "on him that justifieth the ungodly"[373] should turn heart and mind to full curiosity of this strange matter. The ungodly are to be made godly; the vile are to be cherished in the shadow of the Son to the glory of the Father; for by the law of His Christ's ministry,

---

371 Colossians 2:13
372 Luke 18:42
373 Romans 4:5

the dead who would know their pulse are made alive to die for a perfect life, that by mercy they may obtain the name of the Father and the image of His Son.

3. Truly the Spirit's tenderness is an unanswerable mystery, an endless happening continually unfolding the purpose of God through His admirable character. How may the ungodly wear perfection? How can the dead in spiritual trespass and error appear sinless? How can the mind of death endure a quickened spirit to receive forgiveness of error against the LORD? How can the dead receive forgiveness to find consciousness? Behold the mystery of God! "You, being dead in your sins, and in the uncircumcision of your flesh, hath he quickened together with him,"[374] and that regeneration by exercising faith on a most wonderful counsel to override the inherited and impaired human being. We are desired in uncircumcision, for how was the blessing of Abraham received? "Not in circumcision, but in uncircumcision."[375] "Te'rah, the father of Abraham...served other gods,"[376] and that man Abraham endured in uncircumcision through faith on the living God to believe every word of that God, for he believed the LORD and was blessed with the power of the seal of His wisdom.

4. This is why His Christ says, "It is your Father's good pleasure to give you the kingdom,"[377] and, "The Father himself loveth you, because ye have loved me, and have believed that I came out from God."[378] Abraham believed the LORD's promise and it was accounted to him for the reception of His righteousness, therefore the LORD loved him so much that He made a promise by his name, that they which posses the mind of Abraham should inherit the promise of the LORD's Spirit, for He said, "He that shall come forth of thine own bowels shall be thine heir."[379] Therefore "they which be of faith are blessed with faithful Abraham,"[380] "and if ye be Christ's, then are ye

---

374 Colossians 2:3
375 Romans 4:11
376 Joshua 24:2
377 Luke 12:32
378 John 16:27
379 Genesis 15:4
380 Galatians 3:9

Abrahams seed, and heirs according to the promise,"[381] that is, "The promise of the Spirit through faith."[382]

5. Through the Faith of Christ; that is, through "the knowledge of the Son of God";[383] the believer is to know their ungodliness by the revelation of His person upon the spirit of their conscience, that they would then turn to repent to God for the Law and Order that they have broken, clinging to "the blood of his cross."[384] The mercy of God has so reached unlimited bounds that they who would be whole will be transformed in mind by active faith on the hope of His will, delivering the heart of the penitent into the heavenly reign of His Christ to be purified by His Spirit. God has quickened together, with His Son, he or she who believes on and values the virtue of His sacrifice, to the end that he which was ungodly may appear perfect, and she who was possessed may have a right mind, because He says, "He that believeth in me, though he were dead, yet shall he live."[385]

6. So then believe the fact: "You, being dead in your sins, and in the uncircumcision of your flesh, hath he quickened together with him, having forgiven you all trespasses."[386] All is forgiven upon an active and personal reception of the hope behind salvation's law, for the Father promised, "I will be merciful to their unrighteousness, and their sins and their iniquities will I remember no more,"[387] leaving it that "he is faithful and just to forgive us our sins, and to cleanse us from all unrighteousness."[388] The LORD would have the believer come to Him in their original filthy garments; that is all we have to appear before Him in. For how else can He prove to us His good and kind intention? No one need believe they must be a certain way to receive the attention of the living God. Our LORD and Father would have the sorrowing and troubled mind come to Him in that condition.

---

381 Galatians 3:29
382 Galatians 3:14
383 Ephesians 4:13
384 Colossians 1:20
385 John 11:25
386 Colossians 2:13
387 Hebrews 8:12
388 1 John 1:9

His High Priest accepts nothing less than an ungodly condition, for "Christ Jesus came into the world to save sinners"[389] that they might have the opportunity to hear Him say to them, "I came not to call the righteous, but sinners to repentance."[390]

7. Again, believe the fact of the matter: "You hath he quickened, who were dead in trespasses and sins."[391] The uncircumcised is to be made circumcised by their faith on the hope of His intercession, while the professedly *circumcised* "shall pine away in their iniquity...and also in the iniquities of their fathers shall they pine away,"[392] says the Spirit. But what is the counsel? "Whosoever believeth in him should not perish."[393] None are to die in heart or mind by the law of Christ's creative grace, but by faith are to know that they are reconciled to God by the name of His Son to endure a mental and moral work of righteousness, even the renewing of their thoughts and feelings on heavenly things through sanctification of the Spirit. The LORD accepts every sorrowful soul through His Man, no matter who they should be or what they should have done. All are to be made clean by a living faith that follows after the conviction to know His name, and it is well for us to remember how He says, "Ye are clean through the word which I have spoken."[394]

8. "Repent ye therefore, and be converted,"[395] says the Spirit, because now is that time for the new mind in Christ to flourish. Let the weary confess to His High Priest, "Help thou mine unbelief,"[396] for the ministration of Christ is yet in service, and to such a heart the Lord of salvation's science will reply, "Hear the voice of the Son of God."[397] By faith in the virtue of the merits of this Man, the believer is brought to God and made to appear in His spotlessness in order

---

389 1 Timothy 1:15
390 Luke 5:32
391 Ephesians 2:1
392 Leviticus 26:29
393 John 3:15
394 John 15:3
395 Acts 3:19
396 Mark 9:24
397 John 5:25

for them to pick up reform's will and course. We are accepted of God in Christ while yet uncircumcised in heart, but only while also utterly penitent in soul and in spirit to obey the command, "Take away the filthy garments."[398]

---

[398] Zechariah 3:4

5

Love's Laws

1. God's love for man is without articulation. To paint any picture of the love of God would surely do injustice to that which cannot be captured by finite speech or imagination. The very precepts of Christ's Faith are established in Eden's garden, in that He says, "Whether is greater, he that sitteth at meat, or he that serveth?"[399] The blood of the Spirit that ratified the LORD's new covenant, before religious error against this same LORD came into existence, displayed the very foundation of His kingdom and glory. To Adam, the heart and character of God was openly displayed, and the demonstration of that affection is seen in how it says, "The LORD God planted,"[400] and, "Out of the ground made the LORD,"[401] and, "The LORD God took the man"[402] and said, "I will make him an help meet,"[403] and how out of the ground made He the animals, "and brought them unto Adam to see what he

---

399 Luke 22:27
400 Genesis 2:8
401 Genesis 2:9
402 Genesis 2:15
403 Genesis 2:18

would call them,"[404] then He made Adam a woman, "and brought her unto the man."[405]

2. He who has supreme and infinite power and wisdom, and whose voice "quickeneth the dead, and calleth those things which be not as though they were,"[406] is found on the sixth day of the earth's creation serving His creation, because He loves him. Herein is the character of God displayed for all who will see it, for in these things He says, "I have loved you, saith the LORD."[407] The LORD loved Adam, and He did work so hard for him because Adam confessed, "I will praise thee; for I am fearfully and wonderfully made.'[408] 'My substance was not hid from thee':[409] 'thine eyes did see my substance, yet being unperfect,'[410] when I was 'curiously wrought in the lowest parts of the earth.'"[411]

3. Adam was not created with any thing that we may not now have by faith on God's High Priest. He too, as we are, was made of the dust, therefore the source of his righteousness was not born with him or within him, but he had to receive the righteousness of God by faith, like as we do also. Being made from the earth, the LORD indeed would hold a special love towards him, for here was a soul that was spiritually naked and born without knowledge of the work of righteousness for the effect of righteousness, therefore the LORD would do all within His power to ensure the happiness of His son. It was then that "the LORD took the man" and "commanded the man, saying,"[412] "I, even I, am he that comforteth you."[413] Adam heard these words and confidently declared within himself, "I will hear what God the LORD will speak,"[414] and, "I will set no wicked thing before mine eyes."[415]

---

404 Genesis 2:19
405 Genesis 2:22
406 Romans 4:17
407 Malachi 1:2
408 Psalm 139:14
409 Psalm 139:15
410 Psalm 139:16
411 Psalms 139:15
412 Genesis 2:15,16
413 Isaiah 51:12
414 Psalms 85:8
415 Psalms 101:3

4. Even after creating man, the LORD still served him. It should be no new thing for us to observe, for Christ declared the future blessing that He would give to His faithful: "He shall gird himself, and make them to sit down to meat, and will come forth and serve them."[416] The God of creation and the One who walked the earth in sinful flesh bearing the LORD's glory, these carry a most striking similarity. It was God who made all things and then "brought them unto Adam to see what he would call them."[417] The LORD delighted in Adam so much that He bestowed confidence in him, insomuch that "whatsoever Adam called every living creature, that was the name thereof."[418] The love that God had for man in the beginning is no less withdrawn from us at this present day. All may confess, "He delivered me, because he delighted in me,"[419] should they remember the Christ that "gave himself for our sins, that he might deliver us"[420] into the Spirit's classroom to hear, "Let the word of Christ dwell in you richly in all wisdom."[421]

5. There are no words that may faithfully capture the LORD's love for every human being. A contrary understanding may cause us to reject the origin of our existence when supporting the stubbornness of our heart; we may believe these seductive and enticing words to withdraw from the LORD because of how sinful we may appear to ourselves; we may even hate ourselves to hurt ourselves because we cannot bring ourselves to believe that we are loved of God; yet remember how the LORD is toward man, how that in the beginning "the LORD hath loved him."[422] If we take hold of His love's commandment, to do it, like Adam, we will hear, "I have loved thee."[423]

6. Despite what we may believe, the actions of the LORD in the garden are a testimony to the length that He would go through just to save even one soul. How far is God willing to go for the creation that

---

416 Luke 12:37
417 Genesis 2:19
418 Genesis 2:19
419 Psalms 18:19
420 Galatians 1:4
421 Colossians 3:16
422 Isaiah 48:14
423 Revelation 3:9

He loves? It is written, "In this was manifested the love of God toward us, because that God sent his only begotten Son into the world, that we might live through him. Herein is love, not that we loved God, but that he loved us, and sent his Son to be the propitiation for our sins."[424] And what is that discourse from His mouth confessing to this love? It says, "The Son of man came not to be ministered unto, but to minister, and to give his life a ransom for many."[425] It is for this reason that it is time for us to personally know that "there is one God, and one mediator between God and men, the man Christ Jesus; who gave himself a ransom for all, to be testified in due time."[426]

7. The same God who did all things for Adam in the beginning, He is the same God who has again provided all things "now once in the end of the world...by the sacrifice of himself."[427] Therefore "beloved, if God so loved us, we ought also to love one another."[428] Concerning love, the Spirit defines the work of His servant to "love...and do good, and lend,"[429] for where it says, "Love one another,"[430] in reality the counsel is, "Edify one another."[431] The Spirit declares, "I have made, and I will bear; even I will carry, and deliver you,"[432] therefore "we then that are strong ought to bear the infirmities of the weak, and not to please ourselves...For even Christ pleased not himself,"[433] therefore the apostle counsels, "Fulfill the law of Christ,"[434] and, "Let every one of us please his neighbor for his good to edification."[435]

8. The Spirit's doctrine was established during and after the creation, and now it is ordained of God that the believer is "to be conformed to

---

424 1 John 4:9,10
425 Mark 10:45
426 1 Timothy 2:5,6
427 Hebrews 9:26
428 1 John 4:11
429 Luke 6:35
430 1 Thessalonians 4:9
431 1 Thessalonians 5:11
432 Isaiah 46:4
433 Romans 15:1-3
434 Galatians 6:2
435 Romans 15:2

the image of his Son,"[436] like as the earth conformed to the likeness of His person. If Christ is that Son of God, and if the knowledge of the Son of God is that instrument over creation, and if the Creator is the one who yet created and served His creation, then the image of Christ is the image of the Father, and if we love His Christ then we love the Creator, and if we love Him, it is that He says, "The Father himself loveth you, because ye have loved me."[437] The LORD created all things for the welfare of Adam, and even after Adam was formed and yet comfortable, the LORD still worked to provide Adam with no reason to fall away from delighting in His name. The LORD grew this and made that, He took this and brought that, He created a system in the earth for watering the soil so that all things could maintain life in case Adam fell to hunger, for He loved him, and He yet loves us with a benevolence that cannot be measured or broken.

9. So great is the love of God for fallen Adam that He said, "What man of you, having an hundred sheep, if he lose one of them, doth not leave the ninety and nine in the wilderness, and go after that which is lost, until he find it?"[438] Truly "God was in Christ, reconciling the world unto himself, not imputing their trespasses unto them,"[439] and by this work it was fulfilled, "With his stripes we are healed."[440] It is this Christ, who, "having obtained eternal redemption for us,"[441] "is even at the right hand of God, who also make the intercession for us."[442] The Creator did endure suffering by the slaying of His Spirit by men, and "Christ hath suffered for us in the flesh,"[443] that He may better emphasize to our dull eyes and fearfully benumbed hearts the thoughts of His Father concerning us, how that He says, "I have loved thee with an everlasting love."[444]

---

436   Romans 8:29
437   John 16:27
438   Luke 15:4
439   2 Corinthians 5:19
440   Isaiah 53:5
441   Hebrews 9:12
442   Romans 8:34
443   1 Peter 4:1
444   Jeremiah 31:3

10. The LORD loved man so much that God created his inward parts after His own likeness. As God created man and yet served him, so it would be that after sin man should be created after God through an experimental knowledge of His Son's person, to where He would serve penitent man as their High Priest to excel in the image of their God. Thus, it is now that Christ "is able to save them to uttermost that come unto God by him, seeing he ever liveth to make intercession for them."[445] The LORD ministered to Adam in the garden, and even while he was yet formed of the dust, the LORD treated him as if he were one of the angels and not made of the earth. So too even now it is the pleasure of Christ "to present you faultless before the presence of his glory with exceeding joy."[446] Adam maintained the life and righteousness of his God by faith in the commandment of God, and for the believer, the LORD has made His Christ "sin for us, who knew no sin; that we might be made the righteousness of God in him"[447] through salvation's commandment, for "we have received a commandment from the Father."[448]

11. It is through this Man's name "that the righteousness of the law might be fulfilled in us,"[449] and this righteousness secured by a doctrine of love that will never pass away. It is for this cause that the believer is counseled to bless, "knowing that ye are thereunto called, that ye should inherit a blessing."[450] As Adam obeyed the LORD, taking confidence on His operation to bless His name, he was then blessed of the LORD with the high privilege to name the animals, and was even blessed with a wife. It is for this cause that Christ has charged, "Give, and it shall be given unto you; good measure, pressed down, and shaken together, and running over...for with the same measure that ye mete withal it shall be

---

445 Hebrews 7:25
446 Jude 1:24
447 2 Corinthians 5:21
448 2 John 1:4
449 Romans 8:4
450 1 Peter 3:9

measured to you again."[451] For this cause it is written, "He who loveth God love his brother also."[452]

12. Again, the LORD has defined love, saying, "Love,"[453] "bless,"[454] "do good,"[455] "and pray for,"[456] for which cause the apostle says, "In lowliness of mind let each esteem other better than themselves."[457] Why, and for what reason, has the Spirit given this charge? The answer is because we see the living God, "who only hath immortality, dwelling in the light which no man can approach unto,"[458] as a servant to His own creation whom He formed from the dust of the earth. "Where is boasting then?"[459] This same Spirit did appear to the world acting through humanity's members, "and being found in fashion as a man, he humbled himself, and became obedient unto death."[460] He had no glory on earth, He had no fame, and, "There is no beauty that we should desire him,"[461] says the prophet, yet He was ordained to "taste death for every man."[462] Who, then, after carefully observing His character, would not care to lawfully "remember them that are in bonds, as bound with them; and them which suffer adversity, as being yourselves also in the body"?[463]

13. This is love, even benevolently ministering to the soul-benefit of one lesser advantaged in spirit should they care to help themselves. There is no boasting for the believer, for the living God ministered to man in both states of his existence; in both sinless and sinful; to the end we may, with the eye of our faith, look at Him and hear His advice: "If ye keep my commandments, ye shall abide in my love; even as I have kept

---

451 Luke 6:38
452 1 John 4:21
453 Matthew 5:44
454 Matthew 5:44
455 Matthew 5:44
456 Matthew 5:44
457 Philippians 2:3
458 2 Timothy 6:16
459 Romans 3:27
460 Philippians 2:8
461 Isaiah 53:2
462 Hebrews 2:9
463 Hebrews 13:3

my Father's commandments, and abide in his love."[464] The first Adam maintained the love of God and was rewarded with His righteousness, and the second Adam maintained the saying of His Father's Spirit and did also rest in the same righteousness. Christ did have no righteousness of His own while on earth, for He reports, "If I bear witness of myself, my witness is not true."[465] It is by "the righteousness of God which is by faith of Jesus Christ"[466] that the believer will be made perfect in His name, for there is no room for self-sufficiency in the Spirit's higher education. When "looking unto Jesus the author and finisher of our faith,"[467] we are beholding the LORD's character and the standard name for every sincere believer.

14. That which is seen of God, it is that which is given for us to do. "As we have therefore opportunity, let us do good unto all men, especially unto them who are of the household of faith";[468] "let brotherly love continue"[469] "and so fulfill the law of Christ."[470] It is for this cause that our High Priest counsels, "A new commandment I give unto you, That ye love one another; as I have loved you, that ye also love one another. By this shall all men know that ye are my disciples, if ye have love one to another."[471] This is why the apostle wrote to the churches, "The old commandment is the word which ye have heard from the beginning,"[472] for concerning them in this age, it was known, "Thou hast left thy first love."[473] What is our first love besides that which was first experienced and forgotten, even as it says, "All that believed were together, and had all things common."[474] "Neither was there any among them that lacked."[475]

464　John 15:10
465　John 5:31
466　Romans 3:22
467　Hebrews 12:2
468　Galatians 6:10
469　Hebrews 13:1
470　Galatians 6:2
471　John 13:34,35
472　1 John 2:7
473　Revelation 2:4
474　Acts 2:44
475　Acts 4:34

15. To keep us from experiencing the loss that the early Christian church knew, and still continues to experience, the LORD has given to us two laws to keep and dress "for the obedience of faith,"[476] and they are the law of His righteousness and the law of His Sabbath, to the end we may own a spirit of right "charity, which is the bond of perfectness."[477] Herein is how Adam maintained the righteousness of God, for he willingly allowed his heart to serve God, and allowed God to service him, neither doubting nor remaining partial in any commandment of God. Therefore it is written, "Be ye therefore followers of God, as dear children";[478] "as obedient children, not fashioning yourselves according to the former lusts in your ignorance."[479] For this reason our Priest counsels, "As I have obeyed our LORD and Father, so obey My voice and abide in My love,"[480] and as Adam obeyed and rested in the Spirit's righteousness, the example is for us to faithfully grow up in the knowledge of Christ that we may minister to one another as we have been cared for by the Godhead. The ministry that the Spirit held in the beginning did not change when He met sinful flesh, and it has not changed since He ascended to the Place of God to be in the presence of God. He has called every believer to observe His operation and to hear His voice.

---

476 Romans 16:26
477 Colossians 3:14
478 Ephesians 5:1
479 1 Peter 1:14
480 John 15:10

6

The Law Of Faith

1. The taint of sin within the soul temple has received unadulterated health, but who will believe this fact? "To whom is the arm of the LORD revealed?"[481] As by Adam "judgment came upon all men to condemnation; even so by the righteousness of one the free gift came upon all men unto justification of life."[482] It is "through the righteousness of faith"[483] that the spirit is recovered, for "if we believe on him"[484] "that justifieth the ungodly,"[485] even as him that "staggered not at the promise of God through unbelief,"[486] our faith will be "counted for righteousness."[487] But how can we be sure that this is so? How can we be sure that for us personal and devotional sin is conquered through our faith in the Spirit's will? It is written, "I will preserve thee, and give thee for a covenant of the people."[488] What is this that we have

---

481 Isaiah 53:1
482 Romans 5:18
483 Romans 4:13
484 Romans 4:24
485 Romans 4:5
486 Romans 4:20
487 Romans 4:5
488 Isaiah 49:8

just heard? Hear Him: "I have sworn by myself, the word is gone out of my mouth...and shall not return."[489] This is the word of God and the counsel of His Spirit, and the life of that instruction "is by one man, Jesus Christ."[490]

2. Listen to Him: "My covenant will I not break, nor alter the thing that is gone out of my lips. Once have I sworn by my holiness that I will not lie unto David."[491] What is it that "God, that cannot lie, promised before the world began"[492] to His Son David? It is written, "I shall give thee the heathen for thine inheritance,"[493] and, "As he saith in O'see, I will call them my people, which were not my people."[494] "There it shall be said unto them, Ye are the sons of the living God."[495] Therefore this Man, "after he had offered one sacrifice for sins for ever, sat down on the right hand of God; from henceforth expecting till his enemies be made his footstool,"[496] because it is "that the Gentiles should be fellow-heirs, and of the same body, and partakers of his promise in Christ by the gospel."[497] Thus, the LORD His God said, "David my servant shall be king over them,"[498] and, "I will make a covenant of peace with them."[499]

3. God has said these things, therefore they are as "written with a pen of iron, and with the point of a diamond."[500] The LORD has said that He will give His Son "for a covenant of the people, for a light of the Gentiles,"[501] and He has sworn and will not break the word that has passed from Him. God has promised the heathen as an inheritance for

---

489 Isaiah 45:23
490 Romans 5:15
491 Psalms 89:34,35
492 Titus 1:2
493 Psalms 2:8
494 Romans 9:25
495 Hosea 1:10
496 Hebrews 10:12,13
497 Ephesians 3:6
498 Ezekiel 37:24
499 Ezekiel 37:24,26
500 Jeremiah 17:1
501 Isaiah 42:6

His Son, and as "the scripture hath concluded all under sin,"[502] it serves to honestly comprehend that "there is none that doeth good, no, not one,"[503] for we who do believe in the virtue of His Son's name are that vile inheritance promised of the LORD to His Christ.

4. The promises of God are for us all who currently have air in our lungs and sickness flowing through our person. But will we believe on that which cannot be broken? Will we believe on Him that cannot lie over our pitiful inclinations and suppositions to disbelieve? "To whom sware he that they should not enter into his rest, but to them that believed not?"[504] "I sware in my wrath that they should not enter into my rest,"[505] said the LORD, for this word of condemnation is as sure as His word of hope, for there can be no unbelieving soul claiming the life of His Christ, just as there can be no believing soul who rejects the power and wisdom of His Spirit's voice. Sin against heaven, and against heaven's LORD and Spirit, is conquered through Christ not in a day, but rather, "By little and little I will drive them out from before thee, until thou be increased,"[506] says the Spirit, and to receive health without interruption, "Turn yourselves from your idols,"[507] He says.

5. Obedience is not without definitive action to relay the natural acceptance of the commandment embraced. Says the Spirit, "Having confidence in thy obedience I wrote unto thee, knowing that thou wilt also do more than I say."[508] The LORD does not doubt if any one person can obey Him, but it is us who maintain unnecessary thoughts about ourselves in relation to the image our perception has of Him and His Son. Who will lawfully awake to His manner of love and learning? Surely Paul spoke this word regarding obedience, but who was Paul? He was one brought into personal contact with God to "hear the voice

---

502 Galatians 3:22
503 Romans 3:12
504 Hebrews 3:18
505 Psalms 95:11
506 Exodus 23:30
507 Ezekiel 14:6
508 Philemon 1:21

of his mouth"[509] and "to be his witness unto all men."[510] So then his word belongs to whom? Hear from the mouth of the man himself: "The gospel which was preached of me is not after man. For I neither received it of man, neither was I taught it, but by the revelation of Jesus."[511] Therefore hear this man of God concerning His Christ: "Who gave himself for our sins."[512]

6. God has spoken the word, and that word tells of the fact that the sins of the spirit believing on the doctrine of God are passed away upon active belief, for "whosoever believeth in him shall receive remission of sins."[513] What does this mean? As the believer declares Christ their personal Savior and High Priest, obeying "from the heart that form of doctrine which was delivered"[514] them from communion with His name, it will be fulfilled, "Immediately her issue of blood stanched."[515] The error and plague of the heart ceases when once opened to the reception of the Spirit's doctrine, for sin is to cease that another industrious agent may take its place, for which cause it is said, "Where sin abounded, grace did much more abound."[516] As the penitent relinquish the idol meat of their heart by examining and doing the Spirit's will, immediately given to them is "the righteousness of God which is by faith of Jesus Christ,"[517] along with "abundance of grace"[518] to "fulfil all the good pleasure of his goodness, and the work of faith with power."[519]

7. Is it forgotten how one came to a man of God with a letter that said, "Recover him of his leprosy"?[520] And after he grew angry at the Spirit's simplicity, being familiar with false methods of healing and presumptuous hypocrites of medicine, what was the counsel given him

---

509 Acts 22:14
510 Acts 22:15
511 Galatians 1:11,12
512 Galatians 1:4
513 Acts 10:43
514 Romans 6:17
515 Luke 8:44
516 Romans 5:20
517 Romans 3:22
518 Romans 5:17
519 1 Thessalonians 1:11
520 2 Kings 5:3

at that time of his wrath? It was told him, "If the prophet had bid thee do some great thing, wouldest thou not have done it? how much rather then, when he saith to thee, Wash, and be clean?"[521] And after that he did obey the word and did wash and was blessed; for "his flesh came again like unto the flesh of a little child, and he was clean";[522] what then was his testimony after faith had come and worked? He said, "Now I know that there is no God in all the earth, but in Israel."[523] By faith, this stranger to the knowledge of God was made clean by depending on the word of the man of God to do as it had said, and for us the Son of God says, "Arise, go thy way: thy faith hath made thee whole."[524]

8. Surly the man of God became as intercessor between this foreigner and the LORD, and in receiving the word of the intercessor, "it was imputed unto him for righteousness,"[525] allowing him the opportunity to be taken of the Spirit and refreshed for his faith in the hope to appear. This lesson is for us. "There is one God, and one mediator between God and men, the man Christ Jesus; who gave himself a random for all,"[526] "specially of those that believe."[527] Wherefore "seest thou how faith wrought with his works, and by works was faith made perfect?"[528] This is the second time Paul has told us that it is Christ who has given Himself for ours sins, yet this time he introduces the fact of His role along with the fact of His name, for He "also maketh intercession for us."[529] Warfare with our heart is now pointless if our spirit is not engaged in recovering the inward parts by wrestling with the Spirit's commandment. "Where is boasting then? It is excluded. By what law? of works? Nay: but by the law of faith."[530] "For if Abraham were justified by works, he hath whereof to glory; but not before God."[531]

---

521   2 Kings 5:13
522   2 Kings 5:14
523   2 Kings 5:15
524   Luke 17:19
525   James 2:23
526   1 Timothy 2:5,6
527   1 Timothy 4:10
528   James 2:22
529   Romans 8:34
530   Romans 3:27
531   Romans 4:2

9. It was the law of works and of deeds that was to give birth to the law of experimental faith for the keeping of the LORD's ten laws, for of old this law; which law spoken of is that contained "written in the book of the law";[532] for by the priesthood of the Levites "the people received the law";[533] was "to bring us unto Christ, that we might be justified of faith."[534] Abraham received the law of circumcision not before he was justified by faith, but after he was made perfect by faith "he received the sign of circumcision, a seal of the righteousness of the faith which he had yet being uncircumcised."[535] Therefore "if the uncircumcision keep the righteousness so of the law";[536] that is, the praise "witnessed by the law and the prophets";[537] "shall not his uncircumcision be counted for circumcision?"[538] What then is that righteousness? It is even "the righteousness of faith,"[539] because "after that faith is come, we are no longer under a schoolmaster,"[540] but are become spirits quickened to newness of thought and feeling to experience "the kindness and love of God our Saviour toward man."[541]

10. The righteousness of that carnal law of works; which was "the ministration of death"[542] and "of condemnation";[543] was ever a labor of faith upheld by "the faith of Abraham"[544] if correctly executed. If the Jews could have discerned "the time of reformation"[545] through "meats and drinks, and diverse washings"[546] "that could not make him that did the service perfect, as pertaining to the conscience,"[547] knowledge of

---

532 Galatians 3:10
533 Hebrews 7:11
534 Galatians 3:24
535 Romans 4:11
536 Romans 2:26
537 Romans 3:21
538 Romans 2:26
539 Romans 4:11
540 Galatians 3:25
541 Titus 3:4
542 2 Corinthians 3:7
543 2 Corinthians 3:9
544 Romans 4:16
545 Hebrews 9:10
546 Hebrews 9:10
547 Hebrews 9:9

the dispensation to come would have intelligently cultivated their faith on the LORD's aim, but by stubborn unbelief, they missed His name. Thus, the Jews were quick to reiterate, because of an unlawful fondness to the tradition given them, "We have Abraham to our father,"[548] and what was Christ's response to this? "If ye were Abraham's children, ye would do the works of Abraham."[549] "Abraham believed God, and it was imputed to him for righteousness,"[550] but the Jews believed in "the law of commandments contained in ordinances,"[551] that righteousness "in the flesh made by hands,"[552] and believed, "Abraham was one, and he inherited the land: but we are many; the land is given us for inheritance."[553] None are made righteous by association, but the promise made by the Spirit in the name Abraham says, "I will bless them that bless thee."[554] Had the Jews kept the good manners of their fathers, they would have never ceased as a people from before the LORD, for He said of them, "This is Jerusalem: I have set it in the midst of the nations and countries,"[555] but as they left the faith of their favor, "She hath changed,"[556] says the Spirit.

11. It is therefore true, "If Abraham were justified by works, he hath whereof to glory; but not before God,"[557] for many would rather "glory in appearance, and not in heart."[558] The law of circumcision did not justify or sanctify Abraham, and the Jews were not cleansed by that law "which stood only in meats and drinks, and divers washings, and carnal ordinances, imposed on them."[559] Remember the saying, "Which are a shadow of things to come; but the body is of Christ."[560] Despite

---

548 Matthew 3:9
549 John 8:39
550 James 2:23
551 Ephesians 2:15
552 Ephesians 2:11
553 Ezekiel 33:24
554 Genesis 12:2
555 Ezekiel 5:5
556 Ezekiel 5:6
557 Romans 4:2
558 2 Corinthians 5:12
559 Hebrews 9:10
560 Colossians 2:17

whatever ritual or ceremony they performed, faith was ever the living principle that allowed the human soul to receive the health of God. The righteousness of the law and the righteousness of circumcision have always been driven by a faith that conforms the spirit to the Spirit's righteousness. The word of the Father promises that every believer of that law of His Spirit will be made the praise of the Spirit in the knowledge of His Son, but how? In the doctrine of Christ "the righteousness of God is revealed from faith to faith: as it is written, The just shall live by faith,"[561] that is, "By the law of faith."[562]

12. Our hardness of heart and terror of mind comes to an end by the counsel of Christ's mediation, for by faith in "his righteousness for the remission of sins that are passed,"[563] we become "the children of God by faith in Christ."[564] The example is set for us to understand that no thing done within our own power or understanding may remove error, for our Father only recognizes the fact that Christ "washed us from our sins in his own blood."[565] There is no thing within us that can purify us, for it is said that Christ did "sanctify the people with his own blood."[566] There is no thing that we may work within ourselves that may leave us "perfect, as pertaining to the conscience,"[567] for only faith in the virtue of the will of Christ's name may "purge your conscience from dead works to serve the living God."[568] So then what is the work of the believer? It is written, "To him that worketh not, but believeth on him that justifieth the ungodly, his faith is counted for righteousness."[569] Again, "Believe on him that raised up Jesus."[570]

13. Is it not written, "The Spirit of him that raised up Jesus"?[571] As the promise was made, and is to be kept by Abraham's name, so also it

---

561 Romans 1:17
562 Romans 3:27
563 Romans 3:25
564 Galatians 3:26
565 Revelation 1:5
566 Hebrews 13:12
567 Hebrews 9:9
568 Hebrews 9:14
569 Romans 4:5
570 Romans 4:24
571 Romans 8:11

was ratified by the name of God's Man for the believer to obtain "the promise of the Spirit through faith."[572] As faith in the name of Christ begins to conquer the fear within the heart, faith will be blessed of God with His Spirit's righteousness for the purpose of entering His presence for "the communion of the Holy Ghost."[573] It is that by faith we are "sealed with that holy Spirit of promise,"[574] even "the Holy Ghost, whom God hath given to them that obey him,"[575] for it is that "the love of God is shed abroad in our hearts by the Holy Ghost."[576] Thus, as faith has open intercourse with the human will, from "the Spirit of grace,"[577] by faith on the end of the sacrifice of Christ, they who believe on His office will be given "abundance of grace and of the gift of righteousness."[578]

14. For this cause, when the heart willingly becomes touched at the Spirit's doctrine, it will be fulfilled, "God hath sent forth the Spirit of his Son into your hearts."[579] Because "the Spirit is life,"[580] and since "he that hath the Son hath life,"[581] "we shall be saved by his life,"[582] that is, "He might deliver us from this present evil world"[583] "by the washing of regeneration, and renewing of the Holy Ghost."[584] All things are by faith on the Spirit's commandment, and by faith in this word of perfect reconciliation "that the name of our Lord Jesus Christ may be glorified in you, and ye in him,"[585] we will find our self welcomed in to the Spirit's righteousness to "know his will, and to see that Just One"[586] to "hear

---

572 Galatians 3:14
573 2 Corinthians 13:14
574 Ephesians 1:13
575 Acts 5:32
576 Romans 5:5
577 Hebrews 10:29
578 Romans 5:17
579 Galatians 4:6
580 Romans 8:10
581 1 John 5:12
582 Romans 5:10
583 Galatians 1:4
584 Titus 3:5
585 2 Thessalonians 1:12
586 Acts 22:14

the voice of his mouth."[587] It is of God "that Christ may dwell in your hearts by faith,"[588] to the end the believer "be strengthened with might by his Spirit in the inner man,"[589] for God would "have all men to be saved, and to come unto the knowledge of the truth."[590]

---

587 Acts 22:14
588 Ephesians 3:17
589 Ephesians 3:16
590 1 Timothy 2:4

7

The Will of The Father

1. It is the will of the Father that all who reverence Him remove their eyes from earth to know His heavenly Building, or else He would not have said, "Look unto me, and be ye saved."[591] To be saved of God is to be delivered or rescued by His Spirit, or rather, as the apostle once said, "The Lord shall deliver me from every evil work."[592] Indeed it is the will of the Father that, through the doctrine of His Christ, "he might redeem us from all iniquity,"[593] faithfully translating "us into the kingdom of his dear Son."[594] It is for this cause that "our conversation is in heaven,"[595] for our Priest confirms, "Not every one that saith unto me, Lord, Lord, shall enter into the kingdom of heaven; but he that doeth the will of my Father which is in heaven."[596] Entrance into the kingdom of God is not future. It is yet a living fact that God "hath in these last days spoken unto us by his Son, whom he hath appointed

---

591 Isaiah 45:22
592 2 Timothy 4:18
593 Titus 2:14
594 Colossians 1:13
595 Philippians 3:20
596 Matthew 7:21

heir of all things,"[597] and that the Spirit's kingdom is yet upheld by "the throne of grace,"[598] for the Father said to Him, "Thy throne, O God."[599]

2. Let it be known that the kingdom of God for the believer is not the kingdom of the Father, but is of the Son and High Priest of the Father, as His will is to have us "translated into the kingdom of his dear Son."[600] The base economy of God under the ancient Israelites was to establish the eternal economy of His Son in the Courts of heaven, "for the law having a shadow of good things to come, and not the very image of the things"[601] made none "perfect, as pertaining to the conscience."[602] It was ever the purpose of God to exemplify the foundation of hope for sinners of His name through vain customs and rites, for these did only "serve unto the example and shadow of heavenly things,"[603] "but the heavenly things themselves with better sacrifices than these."[604] The kingdom of the Spirit is the kingdom of Christ, and it is His kingdom and reign that the believer is to enter into. Because this is a living fact, the believer is not void of the LORD and Father of that Spirit, for it is His Spirit that does bring the heart to His Son, and seeing as how Christ "is set on the right hand of the throne of the Majesty in the heavens,"[605] it is that "our fellowship is with the Father, and with his Son."[606] This is why it today it says of His Christ, "He shall stand and feed in the strength of the LORD, in the majesty of the name of the LORD his God."[607]

3. Fellowship is had in this heavenly Place of God, and under the mediation of Christ within the current Room of His office, for there is no kingdom of Christ on earth, and His direct administration is not in the religious world. Christ Himself lets the one observing His doctrine

---

597   Hebrews 1:2
598   Hebrews 4:16
599   Hebrews 1:8
600   Colossians 1:13
601   Hebrews 10:1
602   Hebrews 9:9
603   Hebrews 8:5
604   Hebrews 9:23
605   Hebrews 8:1
606   1 John 1:3
607   Micah 5:4

contemplate the sayings, "The kingdom of heaven,"[608] and, "Your reward in heaven,"[609] and, "Your Father which is in heaven,"[610] and, "Thy kingdom come. Thy will be done in earth, as it is in heaven,"[611] and, "Seek ye first the kingdom of God, and his righteousness."[612] There is plainly a will for the reformer to learn of and do, and it is not found on earth or within the earth's religious institutions. It is for this reason that the apostle counsels, "Set your affection on things above, not on things on the earth."[613] Because it is the Father who exalted His Son after He had accepted His sacrifice "and set him at his own right hand in heavenly places,"[614] it is now our responsibility to know that "Christ is not entered into the holy places made with hands, which are the figures of the true; but into heaven itself, now to appear in the presence of God for us."[615]

4. It is the "inheritance in the kingdom of Christ and of God"[616] that every faithful believer should be concerned with. Christ does not say, "Enter this kingdom by My will," but rather He counsels us on the will of His Father, saying, "He that doeth the will of my Father."[617] The will and purpose is of the Father but the ministry belongs to Christ His High Priest, and as Christ is currently seated next to the throne of His Father, as mediator between the throne of God and the throne of grace for the throne of our heart, it is that by obeying to the will of the Father, all who would accept entrance into the kingdom of grace will be made whole, both personally and devotionally. It is "the mystery of his will, according to his good pleasure which he hath purposed in himself,"[618] that should consume our every thought. Entrance into the Spirit's dominion over the soul and spirit cannot commence without

---

608   Matthew 5:3
609   Matthew 5:12
610   Matthew 5:16
611   Matthew 6:10
612   Matthew 6:33
613   Colossians 3:2
614   Ephesians 1:20
615   Hebrews 9:24
616   Ephesians 5:5
617   Matthew 7:21
618   Ephesians 1:9

an education in the knowledge of the LORD's will, for every professor of Christ is counseled, "Be filled with the knowledge of his will in all wisdom and spiritual understanding."[619]

5. Christ confesses that if the one who believes on His name would do the will of His Father, then that individual would rest in the "riches of the glory of his inheritance in the saints."[620] Again, this Christ says, "If any man will do his will, he shall know the doctrine,"[621] and again, "This is the will of him that sent me, that every one which seeth the Son, and believeth on him, may have everlasting life."[622] What then is the will of the Father? It is written, "Believe on him whom he hath sent,"[623] but for what purpose? Says the Lord of this Faith, "I will give for the life of the world."[624] And what is this life of the world? It is said, "The life of the flesh is in the blood,"[625] and what is the blood of the religious world? It is said, "Meats offered to idols, and from blood, and from things strangled."[626] If the life of the world is found in such gross filth as idols and strangled commandments and doctrines, what then is this defilement that exists needing the Spirit's blood? It is said, "This is that spirit of an'tichrist, whereof ye have heard that it should come; and even now already is it in the world."[627]

6. The life of the religious world is that spirit within "the lusts of our flesh, fulfilling the desires of the flesh and of the mind,"[628] for it is written, "The whole world lieth in wickedness."[629] It is not the will of God that we remain in the spirit of the world, "for all that is in the world, the lust of the flesh, and the lust of the eyes, and the pride of life, is not of the Father, but is of the world."[630] Because God knows of

---

619 Colossians 1:9
620 Ephesians 1:18
621 John 7:17
622 John 6:40
623 John 6:29
624 John 6:51
625 Leviticus 17:11
626 Acts 15:29
627 1 John 4:3
628 Ephesians 2:3
629 1 John 5:19
630 1 John 2:16

the illness in man, He constructed a plan of hope against "the former conversation the old man, which is corrupt according to the deceitful lusts,"[631] and it is found in the saying, "I will give for the life of the world."[632] There is a gift of God for the one tired of the spirit of their flesh, exhausted by the nature of their unstable heart, and it is found in the doctrine of His Son "to declare his righteousness for the remission of sins."[633] The Spirit's righteousness is an education removing personal and spiritual error from the conscience, and with this righteousness is newness of life for our religious conversation, which is why "the Spirit is life."[634]

7. "For anguish of spirit, and for cruel bondage,"[635] the believer is given the righteousness of God the moment they strip themselves of pride and self-sufficiency. This is why our Priest says, "No man putteth a piece of a new garment upon an old; if otherwise, then both the new maketh a rent, and the piece that was taken out of the new agreeth not with the old."[636] Why does he say this? He counsels us to not only seek entrance into His kingdom, but to also learn of His Father's kind righteousness, and how is it that His virtue is imputed onto us for this end? He says, "He that doeth the will of my Father."[637] It is known of the living kingdom and ministry of Christ, "A sceptre of righteousness is the sceptre of thy kingdom,"[638] and, "Come boldly unto the throne of grace,"[639] for it is written, "Grace and truth came by Jesus Christ."[640] The mediation of Christ is one of righteousness' work and effect, for it is "the grace that is in Christ"[641] that is to perfect us after the image of God in righteousness through His righteousness.

---

631 Ephesians 4:22
632 John 6:51
633 Romans 3:25
634 Romans 8:10
635 Exodus 6:9
636 Luke 5:36
637 Matthew 7:21
638 Hebrews 1:8
639 Hebrews 4:16
640 John 1:17
641 2 Timothy 2:1

8. It is for this cause that Paul wrote, "An apostle of Jesus Christ by the will of God,"[642] and again, "An apostle of Jesus Christ by the commandment of God our Saviour."[643] He or she that would do the will of God is one that will accomplish the Spirit's commandment, which commandment, when consented to, encourages "charity out of a pure heart, and of a good conscience, and of faith unfeigned."[644] The Spirit's will is that which is after "the name of God and his doctrine,"[645] which, when assimilated into the stream of life flowing into the soul temple from the throne of God, produces the confession, "I have suffered loss"[646] "that I may know him."[647] That which is the will of God is that which says, "Fulfil the law of Christ,"[648] for it is "the light of the knowledge of the glory of God in the face of Jesus Christ"[649] that is to uplift the spirit to believe on the virtue of Christ, and this belief governed by doing that law of His virtue, and this doing is accomplished "if ye have faith, and doubt not."[650]

9. "This is the will of God, even your sanctification,"[651] but wherein is purification had or justified if there exists no living faith in God's Spirit to do just as He says? It is God who says, "I will work, and who shall let it?"[652] "I have made, and I will bear; even I will carry, and will deliver you."[653] Wherefore we are counseled, "Faithful is he that calleth you, who also will do it,"[654] and, "The Lord is faithful, who shall stablish you, and keep you from evil."[655] Do we believe on this as fact? Before sanctification begins, what is the only work of the believer? The Spirit

---

642   2 Timothy 1:1
643   1 Timothy 1:1
644   1 Timothy 1:5
645   1 Timothy 6:1
646   Philippians 3:8
647   Philippians 3:10
648   Galatians 6:2
649   2 Corinthians 4:6
650   Matthew 21:21
651   1 Thessalonians 4:3
652   Isaiah 43:13
653   Isaiah 46:4
654   1 Thessalonians 5:24
655   2 Thessalonians 3:3

says, "Believe on him whom he hath sent;"[656] that is, actively engage the mind on the saying of His voice; for the Father says, "Every one which seeth the Son, and believeth on him."[657] All that studiously believe "on him that justifieth the ungodly, his faith is counted for righteousness,"[658] and of such it will be reported, "This day is salvation come to this house, forsomuch as he also is a son of Abraham."[659]

10. The will of God is for the purification of every soul temple that confesses their conversation under the banner of His Chief Angel's name. Because it is the purpose of God that every believer maintains faith in His ministry's power to purify their inward parts, it is expected that every believing soul humble his or her spirit to receive knowledge of His Spirit's law for health and rejuvenation. It is the duty of the reformer to remain confident in "the promise of the Spirit by faith,"[660] for it is said, "The promise of life which is in Christ Jesus,"[661] or rather, "The grace that is in Christ,"[662] which grace is "the salvation which is in Christ."[663] "God hath given to us eternal life, and this life is in his Son,"[664] for it is that by faith in "the word of truth, the gospel of your salvation,"[665] the believer will "receive abundance of grace and of the gift of righteousness"[666] "to be conformed to the image of his Son."[667] It is the intention of the Spirit that after we have been convicted to offer faith in the testimony of soul's recovery by the example wrought by His Man, that "in the fulness of the blessings of the gospel of Christ,"[668] He

---

656 John 6:29
657 John 6:40
658 Romans 4:5
659 Luke 19:9
660 Galatians 3:14
661 2 Timothy 1:1
662 2 Timothy 2:1
663 2 Timothy 2:10
664 1 John 5:11
665 Ephesians 1:13
666 Romans 5:17
667 Romans 8:29
668 Romans 15:29

would "make you perfect in every good work to do his will, working in you that which is wellpleasing in his sight, through Christ."[669]

11. He or she that will do the will of God's Spirit will be blessed of Him with the power of His Spirit's wisdom for the health of their spirit. When once the soul believes on the counsel of its recovery, it is transferred into the kingdom of life and light to receive instruction "of the life that now is, and of that which is to come."[670] It is by hearing the word of God; that is, "The gospel preached,"[671] or, "The word preached"[672] that says, "Jesus Christ of the seed of David was raised from the dead"[673] "and declared the Son of God with power, according to the spirit of holiness,"[674] and is "gone into heaven, and is on the right hand of God"[675] "after the order of Melchis'edec";[676] that the soul will confess, "O wretched man that I am!"[677] "If thou, LORD, shouldest mark iniquities, O Lord, who shall stand?"[678] Yet, it is purposed of God that the believer "have as an anchor of the soul, both sure and steadfast,"[679] even "the righteousness of God which is by faith of Jesus Christ unto all and upon all them that believe."[680]

12. Them that would do the will of God are just in the sight of God to receive the benefits of His Son's mediation when exercising faith on the hope of that ministry. If any one would enter the kingdom of Christ to receive regeneration of heart and soul nourishment for their spirit, they should study after and do the will of the LORD's Spirit. Since the will of God concerning the body of His Son's understanding is, "Handle me, and see,"[681] whosoever should do so while depending on the Spirit's

---

669 Hebrews 13:21
670 1 Timothy 4:8
671 Hebrews 4:2
672 Hebrews 4:2
673 2 Timothy 2:8
674 Romans 1:4
675 1 Peter 3:22
676 Hebrews 7:21
677 Romans 7:25
678 Psalms 130:3
679 Hebrews 6:19
680 Romans 3:22
681 Luke 24:39

commandment to work the health that it decrees, "God dwelleth in him, and he in God."[682] No living soul will hear, "I never knew you,"[683] unless they "resist the truth,"[684] becoming "reprobate concerning the faith."[685] "He that hath the Son hath life,"[686] and if "the Spirit is life,"[687] "was Paul crucified for you? or were ye baptized in the name of Paul?"[688] None should be "led away with the error of the wicked"[689] to "heap to themselves teachers, having itching ears,"[690] for what is the counsel? "The anointing which ye have received of him abideth in you, and ye need not that any man teach you."[691]

13. Is this a lie? Does His Christ not plainly say, "If any man do the will of my Father,"[692] and, "If any man would will to do His will"?[693] Would God speak and have no power to follow? Would God ordain and occasion no thoughtful provision? He has said, "I will abundantly bless her provision,"[694] and, "I am come that they might have life, and that they might have it more abundantly."[695] Thus, herein is the faithful work of the sorrowing soul: "Arise, go thy way."[696] Them that had heard this charge, "as they went, they were cleansed,"[697] but what cleansed them? Christ spoke the word, but it could have been that "the word preached did not profit them, not being mixed with faith in them they heard it."[698] As these men heard the word, they were "not faithless, but believing."[699]

---

682   1 John 4:15
683   Matthew 7:24
684   2 Timothy 3:8
685   2 Timothy 3:8
686   1 John 5:12
687   Romans 8:10
688   1 Corinthians 1:13
689   2 Peter 3:17
690   2 Timothy 4:3
691   1 John 2:27
692   John 7:17
693   John 7:17
694   Psalms 132:15
695   John 10:10
696   Luke 17:19
697   Luke 17:14
698   Hebrews 4:2
699   John 20:27

From exercising faith in exactly what the word of Christ had said, the Spirit's righteousness conquered their illness, making them available to receive the power of God for restoration.

14. This example is for us. If a man or woman would enter into the only Place where refreshing and redemption transpire, it is to be done only by studiously investigating and believing on the Spirit's name and doctrine. What is the counsel? "Whosoever shall not receive the kingdom of God as a little child shall in no wise enter therein."[700] "Whosoever therefore shall humble himself as this little child, the same is greatest in the kingdom of heaven."[701] A little child will go to their father and say, "My head, my head,"[702] yet the one too adult, the one full of shame and too prideful to receive alleviation, would rather unnecessarily die in his or her condition. Wherefore "be not therefore ashamed of the testimony of our Lord...but be thou partakers of the afflictions of the gospel according to the power of God."[703] "Unto you it is given in the behalf of Christ, not only to believe on him, but also to suffer for his sake,"[704] "that believing ye might have life through his name."[705]

15. The reformer is charged of the Spirit to do the will of His LORD and Father, and this is why our Priest says, "I ascend unto my Father, and your Father; and to my God, and your God."[706] Christ is yet on the throne of His kingdom with the Father within His kingdom, and it is the LORD's intention that many would be justified; or cleansed and sanctified; by the Faith of His Christ that they may come into personal contact with His character, for He would have us "holy and without blame before him in love";[707] "sober, just, holy, temperate."[708] Therefore "let your conversation be as it be cometh the gospel of Christ"[709] and

---

700   Luke 18:17
701   Matthew 18:4
702   2 Kings 4:19
703   2 Timothy 1:8
704   Colossians 1:29
705   John 20:31
706   John 20:17
707   Ephesians 1:4
708   Titus 1:8
709   Philippians 1:27

"live soberly, righteously, and godly, in this present world."[710] It is the will of God that living faith is exercised to pronounce every soul righteous before His throne, for then it is evident that by humiliation the soul longs to join into fellowship with His Christ and High Priest. They who would enter the kingdom of grace do enter through that righteousness which is only by faith on the virtue of His Son's merits,[711] and upon entrance are blessed with the power of His Spirit to maintain the health of their eyes.

---

710   Titus 2:12
711   Hebrews 11:7

8

A Profitable Hope By Faith

1. The counsel for the reformer is, "Live according to God in the spirit";[712] "for he hath said, I will never leave thee, nor forsake thee."[713] Our Father says, "I will not leave thee, until I have done that which I have spoken to thee of,"[714] for it is written, "From all your filthiness, and from all your idols, will I cleanse you,"[715] and, "I will forgive their iniquity, and I will remember their sin no more."[716] Who will believe the fact contained in the voice of God? For, "I have spoken it, I have purposed it, and will not repent, neither will I turn back from it,"[717] says the LORD.

2. There is hope for the soul developing their spirit and faith in the doctrine of God's Son, and this is why "God sent forth his Son, made of a woman, made under the law, to redeem."[718] The LORD's Christ is that great sin offering who "hath given himself for us an offering and

---

712   1 Peter 4:6
713   Hebrews 13:5
714   Genesis 28:15
715   Ezekiel 36:25
716   Jeremiah 31:34
717   Jeremiah 4:28
718   Galatians 4:5

a sacrifice to God."[719] There is no longer cause for mental despair and internal anguish concerning the condition of our heart, for there today exists a course for wholeness by His mediation. Therefore "awake thou that sleepest, and arise from the dead";[720] that is, "being dead in your sins and the uncircumcision of your flesh";[721] "dead in trespasses and sins";[722] "and Christ shall give thee light."[723] It is ever a living fact that the active believer may be perfect in thought and feeling when cooperating with the Spirit's law, for He has said, "Be ye therefore perfect,"[724] wherefore "God commendeth his love toward us"[725] when saying, "My grace is sufficient for thee: for my strength is made perfect in weakness."[726]

3. The light of His grace is the law of His creative love, and since "the law is light,"[727] our assignment is in learning of and executing creation's law. The same power that brought all things into existence is that same power that will re-create the soul and mind into the likeness of the person of that power's voice. It is said of the name of God's Man, "All things were created by him, and for him: and he is before all things, and by him all things consist."[728] He who spoke all things into existence says, "Know that the Son of man hath power upon earth to forgive sins,"[729] therefore should the professor remain a thief, holding tightly to that error of heart which should be given to the One who owns that error by His soul and blood, having power over that same error by His voice? It is written, "Thou shalt not steal,"[730] yet who will steal back the confusion of their inward person when it has been buried with Christ to never have arisen with Him? If it is that the virtue of God's Faith is

---

719 Ephesians 5:2
720 Ephesians 5:14
721 Colossians 2:13
722 Ephesians 2:1
723 Ephesians 5:14
724 Matthew 5:48
725 Romans 5:8
726 2 Corinthians 12:9
727 Proverbs 6:23
728 Colossians 1:16,17
729 Luke 5:24
730 Exodus 20:15

believed on, then "if we be dead with Christ, we believe that we shall also live with him."[731] "He that is dead is freed from sin,"[732] "for this cause was the gospel preached to them that are dead";[733] that is, "dead in sins";[734] that the believing soul should "live according to God in the spirit."[735]

4. It is the purpose of grace's remedy for sin that the believer may become conscious of hope's medicine through active and experimental faith on the Spirit's will, for "where sin abounded, grace did much more abound."[736] The grace of God contained in the name of His Christ; which name is "the fullness of the godhead bodily,"[737] that is, "the fullness of God";[738] is given by faith in the merits of the sacrifice of Christ for the perfection of the soul's temple, for He said, "I will also save you from all your uncleannesses."[739] Therefore it is said, "According to his mercy he saved us,"[740] that is, "His abundant mercy,"[741] or rather, "abundance of peace so long as the moon endureth,"[742] and this being "abundance of grace and of the gift of righteousness."[743] If one would be made righteous then they need the gift of righteousness, which gift is the power of the Spirit's voice contained in showers of blessing, even showers of grace, which power brought all things to be and "effectually worketh also in you that believe."[744]

5. It is for this cause that as the word enters into the ear, "Their sins and their iniquities will I remember no more,"[745] it is the duty of

---

731   Romans 6:8
732   Romans 6:7
733   1 Peter 4:6
734   Ephesians 2:5
735   1 Peter 4:6
736   Romans 5:20
737   Colossians 2:9
738   Ephesians 3:19
739   Ezekiel 36:29
740   Titus 3:5
741   1 Peter 1:3
742   Psalms 72:7
743   Romans 5:17
744   1 Thessalonians 2:13
745   Hebrews 8:12

the hearer to confess, "Lord, to whom shall we go?"[746] "Whom have I in heaven but thee? and there is none upon earth that I desire beside thee."[747] The LORD's Christ is the complete sin offering for all who would believe on Him, for it is said, "Ye are complete in him,"[748] and, "God will redeem my soul from the power of the grave."[749] It is the soul and spirit that is to be redeemed and no thing else, for it is purposed of God "that the spirit may be saved in the day of the Lord Jesus."[750] For this cause it is written of the one that blatantly rejects submission to the counsel of God and to the influence of His Spirit, "The same soul will I destroy from among his people."[751] The soul is to be directly fed by the Spirit's hand through faith in the name of His Christ, to the end the heart would regain the warmth of life "that we should serve in newness of spirit."[752]

6. Seeing then that we are "justified by faith, we have peace with God through our Lord."[753] The voice of God has spoken it and the blood of His Man has made it officially eternal, that they who would hold Christ's name and commandment dear to their heart would receive the promise of His God's Spirit of to cleanse the conscience of their soul temple, ensuring perfect service to God, self, and to one another.

7. As Paul, upon one occasion, was brought into counsel for strange allegations against him, he confessed, "Men and brethren, I have lived in good conscience before God until this day,"[754] and after one was commanded to strike him for these words, he said, "Commandest me to be smitten contrary to the law?"[755] Why did Paul associate cleanliness of mind with the law of Moses?

---

746 John 6:68
747 Psalms 73:25
748 Colossians 2:10
749 Psalms 49:15
750 1 Corinthians 5:5
751 Leviticus 23:30
752 Romans 7:6
753 Romans 5:1
754 Acts 23:1
755 Acts 23:3

8. It is that law of types and shadows that brings light to the fact of the present heavenly dispensation. Within "the dispensation of the grace of God"[756] it is counseled, "Be filled with all the fullness of God,"[757] or rather, "Be filled with the Spirit."[758] Through the Levit'ical priesthood, the people were given that which was to open their hearts to the knowledge of the Christ of God. It is written that if the soul of an Israelite "sin through ignorance,"[759] "and if he have erred, and not observed all these commandments, which the LORD hath spoken unto Moses,"[760] "if his sin, which he hath sinned, come to his knowledge: then he shall bring his offering";[761] "the priest shall make an atonement for him, and it shall be forgiven him."[762] Again, if a soul trespass through ignorance, "The priest shall make an atonement for him concerning his ignorance wherein he erred and wist it not, and it shall be forgiven him."[763]

9. The apostle confessed a pure spirit before God because he knew, "I obtained mercy, because I did it in ignorance."[764] Paul was well educated in the law of Moses, for he was "taught according to the perfect manner of the law of the fathers,"[765] that is, he "profited in the Jews' religion."[766] Such a conversation contained "the form of knowledge and of the truth in the law,"[767] that is, in "the book of the law."[768] It is this law that, when heard and correctly obeyed, reveals from without the believer "the work of the law written in their hearts."[769] The work of the law "that is of the heart, in the spirit,"[770] is "the righteousness of the law."[771] Such

---

756 Ephesians 3:2
757 Ephesians 3:19
758 Ephesians 5:18
759 Leviticus 4:27
760 Numbers 15:22
761 Leviticus 4:28
762 Leviticus 4:26
763 Leviticus 5:18
764 1 Timothy 1:13
765 Acts 22:3
766 Galatians 1:14
767 Romans 2:20
768 Galatians 3:10
769 Romans 2:15
770 Romans 2:29
771 Romans 2:26

righteousness admits, "God hath sent forth the Spirit of his Son into your hearts,"[772] therefore the keeping of the glory of the law of Christ is fulfilled in the saying, "We through the Spirit wait for the hope of righteousness by faith."[773] This is why it is said, "The law was our schoolmaster to bring us unto Christ, that we might be justified by faith."[774]

10. Paul confessed a good conscience by faith and joined such a doctrine to the law because it was known, "After that faith is come, we are no longer under a schoolmaster."[775] That which was to point the people to righteousness by faith on the Spirit's law became "a stone of stumbling, and a rock of offence."[776] Because "the law is not of faith,"[777] but was rather accomplished through "carnal ordinances, imposed on them,"[778] it was that every operation of priest and convicted sinner was to point the people to that "more perfect tabernacle, not made with hands."[779] This allows us to know that "we have such an high priest, who is set on the right hand of the Majesty in the heavens"[780] who "became us, who is holy, harmless, undefiled, separate from sinners, and made higher than the heavens";[781] "who also maketh intercession for us";[782] and He says, "The Spirit and the bride say, Come."[783]

11. Who is the Bride of Christ but "the Lamb's wife,"[784] "that great city, the holy Jerusalem,"[785] even "the city of the living God"[786] wherein rests "the general assembly and church of the firstborn,"[787] which church

---

772 Galatians 4:6
773 Galatians 5:5
774 Galatians 3:24
775 Galatians 3:25
776 1 Peter 2:8
777 Galatians 3:12
778 Hebrews 9:10
779 Hebrews 9:11
780 Hebrews 8:1
781 Hebrews 7:27
782 Romans 8:34
783 Revelation 22:17
784 Revelation 21:9
785 Revelation 21:10
786 Hebrews 12:22
787 Hebrews 12:23

is upheld by "Jesus the mediator of the new covenant."[788] This Christ is in the midst of the Spirit's City within the Spirit's Church in "heaven itself, now to appear in the presence of God for us."[789] That of old was given to supply the mind with hope for the heart. It is for the believer to remain "looking unto Jesus the author and finisher of our faith,"[790] for by faith in His name, and from obeying to the counsel of His authority, we may claim righteousness by faithfully trusting on the operation of that High Priest over the LORD's living House for every woe, perplexity, and besetment. "We have an advocate with the Father,"[791] and "if we confess our sins, he is faithful and just to forgive us our sins, and to cleanse us."[792]

12. What is it that cleanses from all unrighteousness? It is said, "The blood of Jesus Christ his Son cleanseth us from all sin."[793] Will His blood physically pour out over our flesh? The literal ministration has come and gone, and it's work proved a failure among ministers who desired to give life to that which gave life by faith. Therefore "if the blood of bulls and of goats, and the ashes of an heifer sprinkling the unclean, snactifieth to the purifying of the flesh: how much more shall the blood of Christ, who through the eternal Spirit offered himself without spot to God, purge your conscience from dead works to serve the living God?"[794] As it once existed that the sinner brought an offering to make the flesh clean, so now it is that the believer, after personally accepting the weight and purpose of the Spirit's offering, is to enter into the presence of God with the words, "Draw nigh unto my soul, and redeem it,"[795] for it is written, "He shall redeem their soul from deceit and violence."[796] Recovery of the soul and spirit has always been the LORD's mission, and by actively accepting His sacrifice for our personal and devotional errors, it is that

---

788 Hebrews 12:24
789 Hebrews 9:24
790 Hebrews 12:2
791 1 John 2:1
792 1 John 1:9
793 1 John 1:7
794 Hebrews 9:13,14
795 Psalms 69:18
796 Psalms 72:14

by our faith He can now work for man what man has so pitifully been trying to work for himself – righteousness.

13. As the soul accepts the will of the Spirit and Priest of God, and joins by faith into His arms through the course of His mediation under the dominion of grace, that soul will confess, "We also joy in God through our Lord Jesus Christ, by whom we have now received the atonement."[797] For the saying is fulfilled in His Christ, "The priest shall make an atonement for his sin that he hath committed, and it shall be forgiven him."[798] Now, it is not that Christ "should offer himself often... for then must he often have suffered since the foundation of the world";[799] but rather once He "his own self bare our sins in his own body on the tree, that we, being dead to sins, should live unto righteousness."[800] It is the Father who for us "made peace through the blood of his cross, by him to reconcile all things unto himself...in the body of his flesh through death, to present you holy and unblameable and unreprovable in his sight."[801] Thus, "by one Spirit unto the Father,"[802] "Christ may dwell in your hearts by faith."[803]

14. Our sacrifice for sin is accomplished. Our atonement and reconciliation to the LORD is a living fact through Christ Jesus. By faith on His Man's understanding, the believer is "circumcised with the circumcision made without hands"[804] as soon as they willfully turn to that "more perfect tabernacle, not made with hands."[805] The eye of faith is to be found on God's Priest and His movements within His LORD's heavenly House, "for therein is the righteousness of God revealed from faith to faith."[806] It is because the Faith of Jesus rests in the heavenly Temple of God that the believer does not lose sight of the LORD and Father of

---

797   Romans 5:11
798   Leviticus 4:35
799   Hebrews 9:25,26
800   1 Peter 2:24
801   Colossians 1:20-22
802   Ephesians 2:18
803   Ephesians 3:17
804   Colossians 2:11
805   Hebrews 9:11
806   Romans 1:17

that Temple. Them that love His Son confess, "I bow my knees unto the Father of our Lord Jesus Christ, of whom the whole family in heaven and earth is named,"[807] for it is written, "Let us worship and bow down: let us kneel before the LORD our maker."[808] The reformer will know the Father, and in knowing the Father they will know the Son, which is why His Son says, "He that believeth on me, believeth not on me, but on him that sent me. And he that seeth me seeth him that sent me."[809]

15. Who is a liar, but them without the Spirit of God? "Hereby know we that we dwell in him, and he in us, because he hath given us of his Spirit."[810] God has given us His Spirit to teach and to convict, to pronounce and to dress, to direct and to subdue, and it is His instruction of soul regeneration that is to be obeyed for the purpose of mental and moral liberty. Our Father has spoken and ordained the process concerning soul redemption; who will hear Him? God has fulfilled the reconciliation of the penitent and heartbroken to God, their sins covered the moment their spirit accepts the invitation, yet who will hear, "Let him that is athirst come"?[811] The blood of God atones for every soul who would honestly let their heart intelligently feel after His Christ, yet the work of soul maintenance for the Spirit's righteousness is our work to accomplish. Therefore let the conscience find comfort in the Spirit's doctrine. Let the heart and mind embrace the doctrine of the Spirit that it may freely live in His name, ever progressing in a living experience by faith on His righteousness. There is no need to overthink the simplicity of faith, for "because he believed in his God,"[812] Daniel was saved from the mouth of lions, and will it not be our victory in Christ to say, "Thou hast delivered my soul from death: wilt not thou deliver my feet from falling, that I may walk before God in the light of the living?"[813]

---

807 Ephesians 3:14,15
808 Psalms 95:6
809 John 12:44,45
810 1 John 4:13
811 Revelation 22:17
812 Daniel 6:23
813 Psalms 56:13

9

By The River Jordan

1. "John did baptize in the wilderness, and preach the baptism of repentance for the remission of sins. And there went out unto him all the land of Judae'a, and they of Jerusalem, and were all baptized of him in the river of Jordan, confessing their sins."[814]

2. John preached purification by repentance for the cessation of sin in the inward parts, and he did this by bringing the attention of his hearers to Jordan. Many came from him pure in heart and mind, reconciled to the living God by faith, most desirous of that understanding concerning "the fellowship of the mystery."[815] And he revealed this doctrine of his LORD by the way of Jordan, but how and why?

3. Traveling back to Jordan, we read: "When ye see the ark of the covenant of the LORD your God, and the priests the Levites bearing it, then ye shall remove from your place, and go after it."[816] "It shall come to pass, as soon as the soles of the feet of the priests that bear the ark of the LORD, the Lord of all the earth, shall rest in the waters of Jordan, that the waters of Jordan shall be cut off from the waters that

---

814   Mark 1:4,5
815   Ephesians 3:9
816   Joshua 3:3

come down from above; and they shall stand upon an heap."[817] "Hereby ye shall know that the living God is among you."[818]

4. The LORD once told Moses, "Make thee an ark of wood";[819] "overlay it with pure gold, within and without shalt thou overlay it."[820] The ark was to be of wood, for it is written, "The tree of the field is man's life,"[821] and since it is that "all have sinned, and come short of the glory of God,"[822] the wood was to be overlaid with gold, or as it says concerning gold, "Take the spoil of gold...the store and glory,"[823] for it was in figure overlaid with glory or with righteousness. Within that chest of wood covered with gold were to rest the tables of the covenant, as it is written, "Put into the ark the testimony which I shall give thee,"[824] and, "There was nothing in the ark save the two tables which Moses put there."[825] As John did preach and edify many of his hearers in Jordan, he spoke on the work of One through flesh wearing the righteousness of His God and being filled with the testimony of His character, even as it is written, "He will magnify the law,"[826] and, "I bring near my righteousness."[827]

5. "The priests that bare the ark of the LORD's covenant stood firm on dry ground in the midst of Jordan,"[828] for it was that "when it passed over Jordan, the waters of Jordan were cut off."[829]

6. He who should appear before men, who beforehand bore the heart of the LORD's divine similitude, was to be "found in fashion as a man."[830] Christ labored on His Father's earth as His LORD's

---

817 Joshua 3:13
818 Joshua 3:10
819 Deuteronomy 10:1
820 Exodus 25:11
821 Deuteronomy 20:19
822 Romans 3:23
823 Nahum 2:9
824 Exodus 25:16
825 2 Chronicles 5:10
826 Isaiah 42:21
827 Isaiah 46:13
828 Joshua 3:17
829 Joshua 4:7
830 Philippians 2:8

representative, "being the brightness of his glory, and the express image of his person."[831] This Christ wore the righteousness of His Father by faith on His Spirit's will while in fully sinful human flesh. While covering humanity's organs with divinity's wisdom and power, this Man housed within His inward parts "that eternal life, which was with the Father,"[832] for it is written, "God anointed Jesus of Nazareth with the Holy Ghost and with power."[833] Herein it is fulfilled, "God was in Christ."[834] Christ, as that revelation of the Father's manner of love, bore the testimony of His LORD's name within His spirit, which is why He teaches, "That which is born of the Spirit is spirit."[835]

7. John pointed his hearers to that terrible wonder of God from their past history. "'The LORD is great and very terrible,'[836] said John, "'he shall baptize you with the Holy Ghost, and with fire';[837] therefore remember how it is said, 'I will give to Jerusalem one that bringeth good tidings.'"[838] Christ "came and preached peace,"[839] that is, "Preached the gospel,"[840] and John called the attention of those looking for the Christ to remember Jordan, confessing, "This is the word which by the gospel is preached unto you."[841]

8. The Ark of the Covenant was to create a way for the Israelites to pass through the waters. As "the feet of the priests that bare the ark were dipped in the brim of the water,"[842] the waters "stood and rose up upon an heap";[843] "all the Israelites passed over on dry ground."[844] God's Man; whose learning came from that Building above the earth;

---

831 Hebrews 1:3
832 1 John 1:2
833 Acts 10:38
834 2 Corinthians 5:10
835 John 3:6
836 Joel 2:11
837 Matthew 3:11
838 Isaiah 41:27
839 Ephesians 2:17
840 Luke 20:1
841 1 Peter 1:2
842 Joshua 3:15
843 Joshua 3:16
844 Joshua 3:17

conquered the constitution of human flesh and the sickness within it by that wisdom contained within His spirit; as it says, "Let the word of Christ dwell in you richly in all wisdom";[845] that His experience should be shared with whoever would care to overcome their own self even as He Himself overcame. Through the righteousness which is only by faith on His approach to godliness, they who would take hold on this Man's name will pass through waters onto dry ground, for the Spirit has promised, "When thou passest through the waters, I will be with thee."[846] But what do the waters represent for us? It is written, "Terrors take hold on him as waters,"[847] and, "Snares are found about thee, and sudden fear troubleth thee; or darkness, that thou canst not see; and abundance of waters cover thee."[848] Therefore it was fulfilled in Him, "The people which sat in darkness saw great light; and to them which sat in the region and shadow of death light is sprung up."[849]

9. Again it is known, "Dead things are formed under the waters,"[850] therefore it is written, "Jesus went unto them, walking on the sea."[851] It was ordained that Christ, "by the grace of God should taste death for every man,"[852] "that through death he might destroy him that had the power of death"[853] "and deliver them who through fear of death were all their lifetime subject to bondage."[854] Our High Priest desires to liberate every willing and humble spirit from self's "bondage of corruption"[855] and from "the spirit of bondage again to fear"[856] the religious world, therefore it is written, "He shall redeem their soul from deceit and violence."[857]

---

845   Colossians 3:16
846   Isaiah 43:2
847   Job 27:20
848   Job 22:10,11
849   Matthew 4:16
850   Job 26:5
851   Matthew 14:25
852   Hebrews 2:9
853   Hebrews 2:14
854   Hebrews 2:15
855   Romans 8:21
856   Romans 8:15
857   Psalms 72:14

10. This Christ conquered mental and spiritual death for us, and He let us know that He would by walking on water. They who would believe on the virtue of His name "are made nigh by the blood of Christ,"[858] that is, are brought to God through faith in the assurance of "the blood of his cross."[859] If death exists within and under the waters, and if His Man is above the waters that keep confusion, then the counsel is true, "Seek those things which are above, where Christ sitteth on the right hand of God."[860] Truly "our conversation is in heaven"[861] "where neither moth nor rust doth corrupt, and where thieves do not break through nor steal."[862] Therefore, "Look upon Zion...not one of the stakes thereof shall ever be removed,"[863] says the LORD, "neither shall any of the cords thereof be broken."[864] "Look unto me, and be ye saved."[865] If the believer should exercise a living faith on their salvation's Captain, they too will walk on the same water as their Lord of this transformation, for what is written? "When Peter was come down out of the ship, he walked on the water, to go to Jesus."[866]

11. The eye of faith allowed Peter to walk on water, "but when he saw the wind boisterous, he was afraid; and beginning to sink, he cried, saying, Lord, save me."[867] What then was the counsel given to Peter? "O thou of little faith,"[868] He said. It took faith to believe that an ark of wood and covered with gold should produce any effect on nature when carried by men. It was present faith that caused God to do "that which is against nature,"[869] for the waters did "stand upon an heap,"[870] and

---

858   Ephesians 2:13
859   Colossians 1:20
860   Colossians 3:1
861   Philippians 3:20
862   Matthew 6:20
863   Isaiah 33:20
864   Isaiah 33:20
865   Isaiah 45:22
866   Matthew 14:29
867   Matthew 14:30
868   Matthew 14:31
869   Romans 1:26
870   Joshua 3:13

"every thing was finished that the LORD commanded."[871] As soon as Joshua had finished rehearsing the Spirit's words, "the people removed from their tents, to pass over Jordan"[872] "not faithless, but believing."[873]

12. The LORD reports of His host, "Ye have not kept my ways, but have been partial in the law,"[874] therefore John said, "Make straight the way of the Lord."[875] The way of God is accomplished when one continues on "as seeing him who is invisible."[876] The one who rests in His every word by faith on the end to appear by that saying, to them will be given power to advance in what seems utterly far from accomplishment. Due to their faithfulness, the Israelites were told upon passing over Jordan, "Circumcise <u>again</u> the children of Israel the second time."[877] As these placed faith into the hand of God and were again recognized as His, so too when faith is placed on Him that will also conquer the waters of the soul and the terrors of the mind, the believer will then be "circumcised with the circumcision made without hands."[878] At this, John counseled his hearers, "Behold the Lamb of God."[879] In Jordan there was to be a second circumcision more perfect than the first. This is why John counseled, "God is able of these stones to raise up children unto Abraham."[880]

13. Why did John not say of their God, "And raise up children unto Himself?" It is because Christ "took on him the seed of Abraham,"[881] which seed is that seed "made like unto his brethren,"[882] for of His own brethren He said, "Whosoever shall do the will of God, the same is my brother."[883] It is for this reason that the Spirit says, "Thou, Israel,

---

871   Joshua 4:10
872   Joshua 3:14
873   John 20:27
874   Malachi 2:9
875   John 1:23
876   Hebrews 11:27
877   Joshua 5:2
878   Colossians 2:11
879   John 1:29
880   Matthew 3:9
881   Hebrews 2:16
882   Hebrews 2:16,17
883   Mark 3:35

art my servant, Jacob whom I have chosen, the seed of Abraham my friend."[884] The Israel of God are formed after the name and character of Abraham, which virtue Christ also took on, wherefore the Spirit says, "Look unto Abraham your father,"[885] for He meant that all should "walk in the steps of that faith,"[886] for "faith was reckoned to Abraham for righteousness,"[887] and after that faith was exercised, "he received the sign of circumcision."[888] The Israelites at Jordan commanded the attention of God by their faith in His counsel, as did Abraham please God from believing His promise, for Christ declared, "O faithless and perverse generation,"[889] to the end it would be known, "Thy faith hath saved thee."[890]

14. John pointed his hearers to a second circumcision as it was depicted of old. He said, "If the blood of bulls and of goats, and the ashes of an heifer sprinkling the unclean, sanctifieth to the purifying of the flesh: how much more shall the blood of Christ...purge your conscience from dead works to serve the living God?"[891] John took the people to the way of Jordan and taught how faith on the Spirit's course would pronounce justification, and from that sanctification a circumcision by "the Spirit of the living God; not on tables of stone, but in fleshly tables of the heart."[892] From yielding implicit faith on the fact that the LORD "hath reconciled us to himself by Jesus Christ,"[893] taking hold of every precious promise of hope given for the stability of the spirit and preservation of the will, the believer will know the LORD of this kindness, fulfilling the saying, "I will dwell in them, and walk in them."[894]

884　Isaiah 41:8
885　Isaiah 51:2
886　Romans 4:12
887　Romans 4:9
888　Romans 4:11
889　Matthew 17:17
890　Luke 7:50
891　Hebrews 9:13,14
892　2 Corinthians 3:3
893　2 Corinthians 5:18
894　2 Corinthians 6:16

15. Them of old who were again circumcised heard the word, "This day have I rolled away the reproach of Egypt from off you."[895] After that angel "descended from heaven, and came and rolled back the stone from the door,"[896] it was that a new hope entered into the atmosphere of the religious world for every spirit therein, and it was then reinforced, "I will not leave you comfortless."[897] It was said of old, "He will comfort all her waste places,"[898] and now it is fulfilled, "In Christ Jesus ye who sometimes were far off are made nigh by the blood of Christ."[899] Christ takes those ordinances that are "against us, which were contrary to us"[900] "after the commandments and doctrines of men,"[901] and in their place has permitted faith as the means to have us "quickened together with him."[902] Thus, it is said, "Whosoever believeth that Jesus is the Christ is born of God,"[903] for it is by faith on the doctrine of God that the spirit will achieve His righteousness by the gift of righteousness, to the end the soul would be purified by His Spirit, as it says, "Ye have purified your souls in obeying the truth through the Spirit."[904]

16. In both instances; that of Abraham and that of Israel led by Joshua; trust in the word of God provided circumcision through a faith that pronounced once righteous. John had carried his audiences to this pillar of their history to announce that faith would birth an experience apart from that commonly known, which is why to those who heard John, Christ said, "Except your righteousness shall exceed the righteousness of the scribes and Pharisees, ye shall in no case enter into the kingdom of heaven."[905] Thus, faith "on him that justifieth

---

895   Joshua 5:9
896   Matthew 28:2
897   John 14:18
898   Isaiah 51:3
899   Ephesians 2:13
900   Colossians 2:14
901   Colossians 2:22
902   Colossians 2:13
903   1 John 5:1
904   1 Peter 1:22
905   Matthew 5:20

the ungodly"[906] educates on this point: "God imputeth righteousness without works."[907]

17. John was pointing hearts to an instance of faith exercised by their own people, which faith they had forgotten through "Jewish fables, and commandments of men, that turn from the truth."[908] John announced: "Behold the Lamb of God who is to bear away our errors against our LORD and Father that we may more perfectly serve Him, even that Spirit who will operate through the members of the flesh while covered and filled with a divine law that we cannot perceive but by faith. 'What he hath seen and heard that he testifieth.'[909] 'He that hath received his testimony hath set to his seal that God is true.'"[910]

18. The Ark in the midst of the waters caused the waters to part, allowing the people to safely pass through. Christ appeared as the living oracle of the Spirit "who gave himself for our sins,"[911] to the end we might, "by the faith of him,"[912] safely pass into that heavenly Place of recovery "according to the will of God."[913]

19. Our Priest would have every believer keep His name at the center of their terrors as that Captain over the ship of their liberty from the island of personal and religious bondage. He has gained our victory over this death in His own soul and body for us, but who will believe the fact? An unstable heart is no more felt by personal and ignorant fear when in Christ's law, but who will experience this fact to obtain this testimony? John purified in the way of Jordan to call all to re-establish the LORD's benevolence within their spirit by an experimental religion on heaven's pure will. Christ said, "If ye were Abraham's children, ye would do the works of Abraham,"[914] for the work of Abraham is to be accomplished now. The seed of Abraham know, "Believe on

---

906   Romans 4:5
907   Romans 4:6
908   Titus 1:14
909   John 3:32
910   John 3:33
911   Galatians 1:4
912   Ephesians 3:12
913   Galatians 1:4
914   John 8:39

him whom he hath sent";[915] "believe on the name of his Son Jesus Christ";[916] for "he that believeth on the Son of God hath the witness in himself."[917] Having His witness for the Father's good kindness towards man's inward person, the believer has life, and that life is blessed of His Spirit, therefore "through the Spirit wait for the hope of righteousness by faith,"[918] because "the Spirit is life."[919]

20. John desired all to know that the faith of Abraham would reign in the priesthood of the Spirit's Christ. No longer would the weak order of men prevail among God's host, for the religious experience was to enter into the direct presence of the LORD and His Son by faith alone. In Jordan we find ourselves confronted with a testing judgment, which when obeyed resulted in blessing, and the lesson is for us. If the heart would obey the Spirit's counsel for the ransom and regeneration of the soul and spirit; a saying that confronts the carnal human sensibilities and challenge the perverse human rationale; our Father will finish the work. Obedience will engrave the promise within the conscience, "It is God which worketh,"[920] for experience from obedience will move the heart to confess, "I also labour, striving according to his working, which worketh in me mightily."[921]

21. The Christian becomes a co-worker with God, cooperating with His Spirit to perfect His name in them, and that perfecting "to the praise of the glory of his grace."[922] God has secured "a new and living way, which he hath consecrated for us"[923] to draw nearer to His throne "by the blood of Jesus"[924] "with a true heart in full assurance of faith."[925] Thus, for every inquiry, and for the accomplishment of His benevolent will, "ye are come unto mount Si'on, and unto the city of

---

915   John 6:29
916   1 John 3:23
917   1 John 5:10
918   Galatians 5:5
919   Romans 8:10
920   Philippians 2:13
921   Colossians 1:29
922   Ephesians 1:6
923   Hebrews 10:20
924   Hebrews 10:19
925   Hebrews 10:22

the living God"[926] which holds "the general assembly and church of the firstborn."[927] In this heavenly Building, Christ is "the mediator of the new covenant"[928] bearing "an unchangeable priesthood"[929] as that King of the LORD's righteousness upon grace's throne. Thus, when the sorrowful soul cries, "Rid me, and deliver me out of great waters,"[930] the Lord of this science will hear and say, "'I will,'[931] but what about you?"

22. "Peace, be still,"[932] says our Priest, for "the wind and the sea obey him."[933] Christ demolished spiritual confusion and then gave life for those errors that were "against us, which was contrary to us,"[934] for He and His Father said in council, "The wind was contrary unto them,"[935] that is, the "wind of doctrine, by the slight of men."[936] John knew that "where the Spirit of the Lord is, there is liberty,"[937] therefore he "bare witness unto the truth"[938] of the Spirit's intention and said, "Behold the Lamb of God!"[939]

23. Says this Lamb, "John came unto you in the way of righteousness,"[940] for all were taught by him in the manner of righteousness through faith by the way of Jordan. The end of faithfulness is a spirit that actuated our Priest to be "made in the likeness of men,"[941] to the end that His character would be reproduced not simply within us, but by revelation of His name through us, that those within our sphere would be touched and benefitted from observing His work in

---

926 Hebrews 12:22
927 Hebrews 12:23
928 Hebrews 12:24
929 Hebrews 7:24
930 Psalms 144:7
931 Mark 1:41
932 Mark 4:39
933 Mark 4:41
934 Colossians 2:14
935 Mark 6:42
936 Ephesians 4:14
937 2 Corinthians 3:17
938 John 5:32
939 John 1:36
940 Matthew 21:33
941 Philippians 2:8

our person, "that now at this time your abundance may be a supply for their want."[942] John came in the way of righteousness, that is, he taught many to cultivate faith by diligently exercising the members of the heart and mind through "the righteousness of faith,"[943] for there would be a doctrine from God's Spirit to obey, and that word preached being "the gospel of the kingdom of God."[944] It is this law of God's Spirit that, when accepted and acted out by faith, and when diligently divided in the presence of the Godhead, will bring the soul into complete harmony with His will and laws of government.

---

942   2 Corinthians 2:8
943   Romans 4:13
944   Romans 4:13

10

The Inward Voice Of The Gospel

1. "As much as in me is, I am not ashamed of the gospel of Christ: for it is the power of God unto salvation to every one that believeth."[945] "Therein is the righteousness of God revealed from faith to faith: as it is written, The just shall live by faith."[946]

2. What is the gospel of Christ? Says the apostle, "It is the power of God."[947] What is the power of God? It is written, "Thy power and thy glory."[948] The power of God is the glory of God, and wherein do we find the glory of God but in the gospel of Christ. Wherein does the glory of Christ originate, which glory is contained in His doctrine? It is said, "We beheld his glory, the glory as of the only begotten of the Father."[949] That which is of the gospel of Christ is the glory of the LORD His Father. Thus, if the glory of God is the power of God, then

---

945 Romans 1:16
946 Romans 1:17
947 Romans 1:16
948 Psalms 63:2
949 John 1:14

that within the voice of Christ should be "the righteousness of God revealed."[950]

3. The gospel of Christ is the righteousness of God ordained for soul redemption by faith to every one who would believe on this promise: "To give his life a ransom for many"[951] "to save them to the uttermost that come unto God by him."[952] God's Priest desires to bring the believer where? It is said, "Christ also hath once suffered for sins... that he might bring us to God."[953] The believer is to be gathered in Christ for perfection to be delivered unto God, as it says, "Having predestinated us unto the adoption of children by Jesus Christ to himself, according to the good pleasure of his will."[954] It is unto God Himself; "the LORD, the most high God, the possessor of heaven and earth";[955] that we are to be brought by our faith on His Spirit's will, and should the heart consent to "the word of the Lord Jesus,"[956] which is "the word of reconciliation,"[957] it is that we "might be made the righteousness of God in him."[958] But how is it that we are to be redeemed? The believer is recovered through faith, but faith in what? It is recorded, "Save me, O God, by thy name."[959] It is by faith on the virtue of the name of Christ that the believer will be made "holy and unblameable and unreprovable in his sight."[960]

4. Our High Priest longs "to present you faultless before the presence of his glory with exceeding joy,"[961] for it is Him whom "God hath set forth to be a propitiation through faith in his blood, to declare his righteousness for the remission of sins."[962] Before one may encounter

---

950   Romans 1:17
951   Mark 10:45
952   Hebrews 7:25
953   1 Peter 3:18
954   Ephesians 1:5
955   Genesis 14:22
956   Acts 19:10
957   2 Corinthians 5:19
958   2 Corinthians 5:21
959   Psalms 54:1
960   Colossians 1:22
961   Jude 1:24
962   Romans 3:24

the revealed glory of God, to hallow and admire and rest in that goodness, it is that the believer must take hold of the glory of His Son, which is the praise and righteousness of His Son's name.

5. Why does the believer need the righteousness of Christ? It is written, "Wherein he hath made us accepted in the beloved"[963] "for the remission of sins."[964] Without accepting the righteousness of Christ, one exudes "a zeal of God, but not according to knowledge."[965] "There is none other name under heaven given among men, whereby we must be saved,"[966] for only through the righteousness of His Christ's voice may it be said, "Leaving the principles of the doctrine of Christ, let us go on unto perfection."[967] Where is one to find themselves when once belief is secured in the doctrine of Christ's mediation? To excellence or to perfection; for this reason it says, "His name alone is excellent,"[968] and for this cause it says of His Priest, "Bringing many sons unto glory."[969]

6. The gospel is the revealed glory of God to place that glory of God in the one in whom that glory is revealed. The law of the doctrine of Christ is the road to acceptably keep the commandments of God, and this keeping "through the faith of Christ, the righteousness which is of God by faith."[970] This is the gospel, for it is "the light of the knowledge of the glory of God in the face of Jesus Christ."[971] It is the light of what in Christ? The knowledge of His God's glory, for it says, "The earth shall be filled with the knowledge of the glory of the LORD."[972] This is why the Father says of His Son, "I have put my spirit upon him"[973] "and the isles shall wait for his law."[974] For whose law should

---

963 Ephesians 1:6
964 Romans 3:25
965 Romans 10:2
966 Acts 4:12
967 Hebrews 6:1
968 Psalms 148:13
969 Hebrews 2:10
970 Philippians 3:9
971 2 Corinthians 4:6
972 Habakkuk 2:14
973 Isaiah 42:1
974 Isaiah 42:4

the Gentile denominations wait for? For the law of His Son, which is why the Father then says, "A law shall proceed from me,"[975] and His Son confirms, "I proceeded forth and came from God."[976]

7. We know that "whatsoever is born of God overcometh the world,"[977] and we know of "the city of the living God,"[978] and of the Son who has confessed that only He "is in the bosom of the Father,"[979] and that "the LORD came from Si'nai...with ten thousands of saints: from his right hand went a fiery law."[980]

8. The city of God with all that is therein, the ten laws of God, and the doctrine of God, are all given us personally from the LORD our God. The religious world was to wait on the law of Christ because only through this Faith could anyone come to the LORD His God; that is, come to perfectly love and do the acceptable righteousness of His God's Spirit. "According to his good pleasure which he"; He God the Father; "hath purposed in himself";[981] it is that by obeying the voice of the commandment of His Christ's Faith we may know the living God to further our recovery from mental and moral sin against Him. "The law of Christ"[982] is that which points the believer "unto the city of the living God, the heavenly Jerusalem...and to Jesus the mediator of the new covenant,"[983] allowing the believer to personally know "God the Judge of all."[984]

9. The righteousness of God; the glory of God as found in the power and wisdom of His Spirit; is revealed in the tidings of Christ for the believer to know and keep, for such "righteousness of God which is by faith of Jesus Christ"[985] is the end of the gospel that we may

---

975 Isaiah 51:4
976 John 8:42
977 1 John 5:4
978 Hebrews 12:22
979 John 1:18
980 Deuteronomy 33:2
981 Ephesians 1:9
982 Galatians 6:2
983 Hebrews 12:22-24
984 Hebrews 12:23
985 Romans 3:22

"be conformed to the image of his Son."[986] Therefore, by "the excellency of the knowledge of Christ Jesus,"[987] the Christian will declare, "I may know him."[988] And if it is that God would have us conformed, or reconciled to the character of His Son, this is doubtless a work of a second creation, which is why it is said, "The new man, which after God is created."[989]

10. Christ, "who is before all things, and by whom all things consist";[990] for in the beginning it was "God, who created all things by Jesus Christ";[991] plainly desires to purify the soul temple that His character may rest in it, and that His works may come forth from it. "The new man, which is renewed in knowledge after the image of him that created him,"[992] is the second creation of a being within the first, therefore to the second man there must also be a rest for the soul, even as there was to the first, wherefore it is confirmed, "We which have believed do enter into rest."[993]

11. He who said, "Come unto me...and I will give you rest,"[994] in the beginning said, "Six days shall work be done: but the seventh day is the Sabbath of rest, an holy convocation."[995] Now, "God blessed the seventh day,"[996] and "I know that, whatsoever God doeth, it shall be for ever: nothing can be put to it, nor any thing taken from it: and God doeth it, that men should fear before him."[997] This is why it says, "Thou blessest, O LORD, and it shall be blessed for ever."[998] Our entrance into the rest of this LORD on His seventh day is a sign witnessing to our devotion to His law of creation, wherefore if His Man, who is over

---

986 Romans 8:29
987 Philippians 3:8
988 Philippians 3:9
989 Ephesians 4:24
990 Colossians 1:9
991 Ephesians 3:9
992 Colossians 3:10
993 Hebrews 4:3
994 Matthew 11:28
995 Leviticus 23:3
996 Genesis 2:3
997 Ecclesiastes 3:14
998 1 Chronicles 17:27

this creation blesses our conversation, then the science of righteousness is a labor that will not be shunned or put off, which is why we are counseled, "Awake to righteousness."[999]

12. "Do we provoke the Lord to jealousy? are we stronger than he?"[1000] One of old confessed, "God is not a man, that he should lie; neither the son of man, that he should repent: hath he said, and shall he not do it? or hath he spoken, and shall he not make it good? Behold, I have received commandment to bless: and he hath blessed; and I cannot reverse it."[1001] The LORD has commanded His name's Memorial; can that commandment be reversed? Never can it be reversed, not by any one other than Him, and His faithful understand this fact, saying within themselves, "He hath blessed; and I cannot reverse it."[1002] God blessed the seventh day, but what does that mean? He sanctified this day and set it apart from every other day with His own seal and blessing, for which cause, when the new dispensation of Christ began, His Man confirmed His ministry's allegiance to His LORD's Sabbath by saying, "The Son of man is Lord even of the Sabbath day."[1003]

13. But to whom does the Sabbath law rest or belong? Notice that if Christ spoke of those sabbaths of the Jews, He would have said sabbaths, plural, but He plainly says, Sabbath, singular. The Spirit says, "The children of Israel shall keep the Sabbath,"[1004] for the Sabbath is for the Israel of God; but who are they? It is written of His host, "The people shall dwell alone, and shall not be reckoned among the nations."[1005]

14. "They are not all Israel, which are of Israel,"[1006] counsels the apostle; for there is a difference in keeping the seventh day and partaking of the seventh day's Sabbath rest, in that one bears the character of Israel while the other is nominally after the form. The Israel of

---

999   1 Corinthians 15:34
1000 1 Corinthians 10:22
1001 Numbers 23:19,20
1002 Numbers 23:20
1003 Matthew 12:8
1004 Exodus 31:16
1005 Numbers 23:9
1006 Romans 9:6

God are not reckoned among any earthy group, nor are they denominated, for these are of God and created by His Spirit and are known of Him in heaven while they are on earth, therefore being the creation of God they know the rest of their LORD and Father, for their experience matches the father of their heritage, as it says, "As a prince hast thou power with God and with men, and hast prevailed."[1007] "Every one that is called by my name," says the Spirit, "I have created him for my glory, I have formed him; yea, I have made him,"[1008] which is why only these can say, "I cannot go beyond the commandment of the LORD, to do either good or bad of mine own mind."[1009]

15. One cannot have the creative power of the gospel to conquer sin, and applied by the same God of creation, without the character of that God present in the experience. How the Spirit of God turns the spirit of the mind against self for the recuperation of self is "the mystery of godliness."[1010] Thus, "As thou knowest not what is the way of the spirit, nor how the bones do grow in the womb of her that is with child: even so thou knowest not the works of God who maketh all,"[1011] it is written. We do not know His methods, but it means nothing to the one who is of faith, for the work is supernatural and extremely incredible, and "if thou canst believe, all things are possible to him that believeth."[1012] What thing is possible for the one who would believe on the name of His Christ? It is that "we might be made the righteousness of God in him,"[1013] and, that "the righteousness of the law might be fulfilled in us,"[1014] and, that "the body of sin might be destroyed, that henceforth we should not serve sin,"[1015] and, that "by the obedience of one shall many be made righteous"[1016] through "abundance of

---

1007   Genesis 32:28
1008   Isaiah 43:7
1009   Numbers 24:13
1010   1 Timothy 3:16
1011   Ecclesiastes 11:5
1012   Mark 9:23
1013   2 Corinthians 5:21
1014   Romans 8:4
1015   Romans 6:6
1016   Romans 5:19

grace and of the gift of righteousness,"[1017] and, that "we might receive the promise of the Spirit."[1018] "Thanks be to God, which giveth us the victory through our Lord Jesus Christ."[1019]

16. All of these things, and more, are done by faith in Christ's name that we may know the living God to fall in awe of His character, and to have restored in us the image of disinterested love wrapped within the comfort of His Sabbath's rest and refreshing. All things are for the believer, "and if ye be Christ's,"[1020] "Christ is God's,"[1021] for "then are ye Abraham's seed,"[1022] "or rather are known of God."[1023] Being known of God, it is that we "joy in God through our Lord";[1024] our "fellowship in the gospel"[1025] awakens us to the "fellowship of the Spirit";[1026] for the entire purpose of the Spirit's Faith is to cause every believing soul to remain "alive unto God through Jesus Christ."[1027]

17. Who do believers become alive to? The believer is risen by Christ's name "through the faith of the operation of God"[1028] to know the benefit of His intercession, therefore it is said, "Our fellowship is with the Father, and with his Son Jesus Christ,"[1029] or rather, is of "fellowship of the Spirit"[1030] "to speak the mystery of Christ."[1031] It is "that God sent his only begotten Son into the world, that we might live through him,"[1032] therefore "being reconciled we shall be saved by his

---

1017 Romans 5:17
1018 Galatians 3:14
1019 1 Corinthians 15:57
1020 Galatians 3:29
1021 1 Corinthians 3:23
1022 Galatians 3:29
1023 Galatians 4:9
1024 Romans 5:11
1025 Philippians 1:5
1026 Philippians 2:1
1027 Romans 6:11
1028 Colossians 2:12
1029 1 John 1:3
1030 Philippians 2:1
1031 Colossians 4:3
1032 1 John 4:9

life."[1033] "We were reconciled to God by the death of his Son,"[1034] and our reconciliation does not remove the precepts of His God from us, but greatly magnifies them for our conversation, for we by faith rest in that "glory that excelleth."[1035]

18. This is the Faith of God, and to the believer belongs "the fulness of the blessing of the gospel of Christ"[1036] to advance in it. It is this gospel that is the announcement and pronunciation of the Spirit's righteousness and the duty of the Christian, for the religion of heaven's throne is the revelation of the Spirit in the mind of sinful flesh, even as "God was in Christ."[1037] This is the mystery that the believer is to speak, and it is all by faith in the blessed merits of His Man's voice, for "without faith it is impossible to please him."[1038]

19. It is by faith that the same creative power that called all things to be; which power still upholds all that was spoken into existence; will enter into the spirit of the believer, delivering health to the soul when once it does "receive with meekness the engrafted word."[1039] The doctrine of Christ is the Spirit's glory leading to deliverance from inherited and cultivated religious negligence, and the redemption of His Israel is "through sanctification of the Spirit and belief of the truth"[1040] to the end that these may receive "the sign of circumcision, a seal of the righteousness of the faith."[1041] "For he spake in a certain place of the seventh day on this wise,"[1042] seeing as how "there remaineth therefore a rest to the people of God."[1043]

20. The gospel of Christ is the power of God unto salvation, and it is an ever-living fact that by this law, all who would mentally and physically believe on it would find harmony with the image of the One

---

1033   Romans 5:10
1034   Romans 5:10
1035   2 Corinthians 3:10
1036   Romans 15:29
1037   2 Corinthians 5:19
1038   Hebrews 11:6
1039   James 1:21
1040   2 Thessalonians 2:14
1041   Romans 4:11
1042   Hebrews 4:4
1043   Hebrews 4:9

who spoke it. This image is revealed by His fourth commandment of His seventh day, and our compliance with that Faith, transforming our mind into the likeness of our Creator, will lead us to care for the Memorial of that Faith's song, moving us to say, "The desire of our soul is to thy name, and to the remembrance of thee."[1044] This Faith, because it is the LORD's Product; as His Son says, "The words that I speak unto you I speak not of myself,"[1045] and, "I have not spoken of myself; but the Father which sent me, he gave me a commandment, what I should say, and what I should speak";[1046] it is the means we love Him, "and this is love, that we walk after his commandments."[1047]

21. Again, who is the Author of this doctrine? Hear the witness of it: "He whom God hath sent speaketh the words of God."[1048] Yet on whom should the faith of the believer rest? It is said, "The Father loveth the Son, and hath given all things into his hand,"[1049] and again, "Looking unto Jesus the author and finisher of our faith."[1050] By faith, the believer is to look to the wisdom of God's Man for the end that His Father purposed in Him, that is, "like as Christ was raised up from the dead by the glory of the Father, even so we also should walk in newness of life."[1051] Like symbolizes like, and like as "death hath no more dominion over him,"[1052] "he that raised up Christ from the dead shall also quicken your mortal bodies by his Spirit"[1053] to fulfill the saying, "I will put my spirit within you, and cause you to walk in my statutes, and ye shall keep my judgments, and do them."[1054]

22. The Spirit of God is that which is to repair our inward parts so that we may sincerely confess, "I delight in the law of God after

---

1044 Isaiah 26:8
1045 John 14:10
1046 John 12:49
1047 2 John 1:6
1048 John 3:34
1049 John 3:35
1050 Hebrews 12:2
1051 Romans 6:4
1052 Romans 6:9
1053 Romans 8:11
1054 Ezekiel 36:27

the inward man."[1055] The work of redemption is the labor of His Spirit in bringing man back to full allegiance with Him through the means wrought in His Son's name, yet the believer must know, "It is given in the behalf of Christ, not only to believe on him, but also to suffer for his sake."[1056] For this cause, the spirit of the mind is to confess, "For peace I had great bitterness,"[1057] to the end it may hear, "Come unto me, all ye that labour and are heavy laden, and I will give you rest."[1058] The work of righteousness is a vocation most grievous against the inward impaired nature of the person, therefore to the Israel of God a season of refreshing is allotted for their toil with self. To the believer of Christ belongs the perpetual covenant of the Sabbath given at none other time than creation. The gospel is of washing, of rest and regeneration, and so too is the seventh day's Sabbath law ordained by the same LORD of the gospel. That spoken of by the Father, unless retracted or redacted by Him personally, "it is that which shall be."[1059]

1055   Romans 7:22
1056   Philippians 1:29
1057   Isaiah 38:17
1058   Matthew 11:28
1059   Ecclesiastes 1:9

11

His Pledge For Our Faithfulness

1. "Of him are ye in Christ Jesus, who of God is made unto us wisdom, and righteousness, and sanctification, and redemption: that, according as it is written, He that glorieth, let him glory in the Lord."[1060] "For if, when we were enemies, we were reconciled to God by the death of his Son, much more, being reconciled, we shall be saved by his life. And not only so, but we also joy in God through our Lord Jesus Christ, by whom we have now received the atonement."[1061]

2. Our love and gratitude towards the LORD's Priest is expressed by the fact that we believe by faith that He came out from the LORD His God, and in so believing, we trust that we are reconciled and secured to God His Father to intimately know both the Father and His Son. The pledge of God, His word and bond, which is our earnest and security, is that by actively believing on the virtue of the blood of this Christ for our regenerative course, we immediately have the virtue of Christ imputed to us that we may patiently come up higher in our reformatory experience. Nothing that we can do of our own selves may secure this manner of righteousness, for the gift of heaven's glory is already complete and awaiting human acceptance. From the moment our hearts plague us,

---

1060   1 Corinthians 1:30,31
1061   Romans 5:10,11

and we fall on our face at the knowledge of our shameful condition, repenting towards God for ignorantly breaking His laws and denying His name, and taking hold of the blood of His Son by faith on the end that His blood may procure, we are blessed to know that righteousness born of His Son's name, being justified by faith in His atoning blood to not only satisfy our error, but to also purge our conscience from that deviation. Truly Christ is to us wisdom, and righteousness, and sanctification, and redemption for our inward parts, seeing as how it is His Spirit's desire to "purge your conscience from dead works to serve the living God."[1062]

3. "The LORD giveth wisdom: out of his mouth cometh knowledge and understanding."[1063] Every word that comes out of God's mouth is to be for our personal and religious diet, and after digestion, it is to give new strength to the mind to carry out purer and still purer habits of devotion. Thus, "If ye love me,"[1064] says our Priest, "because ye have loved me, and have believed that I came out from God,"[1065] "keep my commandments."[1066] Should we, in childlike simplicity first believe, and actively follow after that belief in whatsoever the Lord of this course declares, "The Father himself loveth you, because ye have loved me," we will hear, "and have believed."[1067] Every word of God is given for examination and reproduction within the mind for the limbs of the body to carry out, thereby causing us to cease our own glory to stay on that righteousness freely given from God; this is the role and result of belief. Because we have believed the Spirit's counsel and have sought to apply it, that word is made unto us as wisdom, and our labor to place that wisdom personally into the conversation becomes our righteousness upheld by the righteousness of Christ to cover our shameful understanding as a lovely and impenetrable garment of light.

1062 Hebrews 9:14
1063 Proverbs 2:6
1064 John 8:42
1065 John 16:27
1066 John 8:42
1067 John 16:27

4. Wherefore "grace be with all them that love our Lord Jesus Christ in sincerity."[1068] Should we love the doctrine of the Spirit's High Priest, which love is first demonstrated in confidence towards His voice despite thought and inclination, the grace of God will be poured out into our soul. We are blessed "with all spiritual blessings in heavenly places in Christ"[1069] by faith on the hope of heaven's will, and the showers of grace administered by the Spirit of this ministry are what convicts the soul of sin, and of righteousness, and of judgment.[1070] After we have searched the scriptures for wisdom and revelation, after we have diligently applied that instruction to know the meaning behind the charge of the LORD, after we determine to learn the will our Father by experiencing His Son and Spirit's power and understanding, the law of His intention will lead the experience, bringing us into council with Him over His broken Law in our lives, compelling us to take hold of the blood of His Christ by faith when brought to the knowledge of our condition, beginning the process of sanctification, which is for complete obedience to His ten immutable laws by faith on the praise of His Son's intercession.

5. Sanctification of the soul's temple is not without obedience to the Law and Faith of heaven's LORD. The knowledge of sin comes only by the revelation of His character; "by the law is the knowledge of sin";[1071] for "until the law sin was in the world: but sin is not imputed when there is no law."[1072] Without knowledge of error against the LORD, man is yet dead while he lives. When man should be guilty of sin before God, there is hope, for if any "sin through ignorance,"[1073] and that ignorance become known to the conscience through the conviction of His Spirit, it will be forgiven them because it was done "ignorantly in unbelief."[1074] When seen and known of God to be diligent in understanding His ways, no matter how far off we are or how ignorant we

---

1068 Ephesians 6:24
1069 Ephesians 1:3
1070 John 16:8
1071 Romans 3:20
1072 Romans 5:13
1073 Leviticus 4:27
1074 1 Timothy 1:13

may perceive ourselves to be, the LORD God will take the perseveringly sincere spirit and bring them to the light of His glory, desiring that mind to know that not only is it dead and in need of a Savior, but that there is a course in the light of that Savior for its recovery, and "the law is light."[1075]

6. "Christ Jesus came into the world to save sinners,"[1076] "therefore will he teach sinners in the way."[1077] For, "All souls are mine,"[1078] "I have no pleasure in the death of him that dieth, saith the Lord GOD,"[1079] therefore "God so loved the world, that he gave his only begotten Son, that whosoever believeth in him should not perish, but have everlasting life."[1080] The ten laws of God cannot, of their own self, make one soul holy, but they are the means by which man may know that they are far from perfection's Standard. The Law of heaven's throne serves to build up a disgusting taste for religious error against sensual spiritual delights, yet it cannot heal the sinner of their cultivated or inherited error, but rather only inform the individual that they are indeed wrong in the sight of God. The Law serves to draw the sinner to see no exit from condemnation other than through His Son. Our plea for the cleansing and atoning blood of His Christ renders us pardoned and now forgiven of error to pursue a mental and moral course to recover our understanding. By faith on the name of heaven's mediation, the sinner may slowly assimilate the praise of Christ's law to their misunderstanding for strength from all temptation or inward agitation, for in being brought before His Spirit, it is that now His word and truth are hidden in the heart, never to be warred against because it is given life by the virtue of His Christ's name.

7. From first believing on the promise and pledge of God to impute the righteousness of His Son to their stained account, the sinner is justified, or sanctified, by experimental faith on the hope and will of the

---

1075 Proverbs 6:23
1076 1 Timothy 1:15
1077 Psalms 25:8
1078 Ezekiel 18:4
1079 Ezekiel 18:32
1080 John 3:16

Father. Men and women may live before the LORD as if they had never erred in judgment if they can receive and act out the word of revival and reform, and continue as diligent subjects of grace's kingdom. In truth, the mercy of God is a mystery wrapped within an endless chain of love. There is no soul forgotten of God, there is no heart that the living God will not console, for all souls, being purchased of His Son, belong to Him and are yet hoped for and longed after. Studying after and accepting the wisdom of God's Spirit will lead the believer to pick up and claim the righteousness of that wisdom, which wisdom and righteousness purifies the soul through the conviction of His Spirit over the heart. This order of reconciliation is to teach us that in Christ we are not only atoned for and reconciled to God, but that we are ransomed from personal and devotional death for deliverance from the oppression of our flesh through a love that is undeserved, yet freely given. The knowledge of His Christ's mediation is to us wisdom, righteousness, sanctification, and redemption, and this is the pledge and oath of the LORD to every penitent doer of redemption's law.

12

The Law Of His Faith

1. "Whosoever transgresseth, and abideth not in the doctrine of Christ, hath not God. He that abideth in the doctrine of Christ, he hath both the Father and the Son. If there come any unto you, and bring not this doctrine, receive him not into your house."[1081]

2. Transgression is accomplished against the foundation of the Spirit's doctrine so that the heart and the flesh may coexist within the body. As the heart does not care to believe any embracing of conflict is proof of purification, it is that the heart will accept self-violation at the expense of surrendering to self-development by faith. "Sin is the transgression of the law,"[1082] and all sin is the result of man breaking from the character of God's will "to transgress against our God in marrying strange wives."[1083] Because we violate self with foreign wives and strange creatures; with "graven images, and with strange vanities";[1084] the children within us cannot "speak in the Jews' language,"[1085] that is,

---

1081   2 John 1:9,10
1082   1 John 3:4
1083   Nehemiah 13:27
1084   Jeremiah 8:19
1085   Nehemiah 13:24

cannot speak "the Hebrew tongue,"[1086] but rather it is as it is written, "Ye have forsaken me, and served strange gods in your land."[1087]

3. "If I build again the things which I destroyed, I make myself a transgressor."[1088] The re-organization of sin after conviction of error occurs due to a higher regard for heart idols than that of God's voice. The tongues that work within our diminished frame produce children of "diverse and strange doctrines"[1089] "so that ye cannot do the things that ye would."[1090] Thus, the perplexed confess, "The good that I would I do not,"[1091] for the heart of the true believer is after doing good, for the mind of he or she after Christ desires to prove "the law that it is good."[1092] "We know that the law is good,"[1093] and that "a good understanding have all they that do his commandments,"[1094] yet to re-structure the error of the heart is to display an unstable "schism in the body,"[1095] even one that acknowledges the rebuke, "They did not like to retain God in their knowledge."[1096]

4. To cease building back the error of our conscience, to "lay aside every weight, and the sin which doth so easily beset,"[1097] it is that the doctrine of Christ needs to be accepted and established within the experience, for then the believer may confidently have "both the Father and the Son"[1098] to overcome self's irrational thoughts and feelings. It is said, "He loveth transgression that loveth strife,"[1099] yet the reformer longs "to pass over a transgression."[1100] It is true that by Christ "we have redemption through his blood, the forgiveness of

---

1086   Nehemiah 13:24
1087   Jeremiah 5:19
1088   Galatians 2:18
1089   Hebrews 13:9
1090   Galatians 5:17
1091   Romans 7:19
1092   Romans 7:16
1093   1 Timothy 1:8
1094   Psalms 111:10
1095   1 Corinthians 12:25
1096   Romans 1:28
1097   Hebrews 12:1
1098   2 John 1:9
1099   Proverbs 17:19
1100   Proverbs 19:11

sins,"[1101] but the mind must first accept the fact of comprehending the blessing through seeking to retain a personal knowing, "unless ye have believed in vain."[1102] "Your faith is vain; ye are yet in your sins";[1103] if there is a refusal to experimentally "believe on the name of the Son of God"[1104] "for remission of sins that are past, through the forbearance of God."[1105]

5. The message concerning "wisdom, and righteousness, and sanctification, and redemption,"[1106] is so crucial to our reception of the Spirit's fullness, and if none "bring this doctrine";[1107] in its fullness and entirety; "Receive him not,"[1108] we are counseled. Concerning doctrine, we read, "I give you good doctrine, forsake ye not my law,"[1109] and, "Words of faith and of good doctrine."[1110] The doctrine of Christ is of the law and faith of Christ, for we see also how it says, "Of the faith, and of the knowledge of the Son of God,"[1111] and, "The faith of the gospel."[1112] The doctrine of Christ is a law of faith that is the knowledge of the Father's Spirit, for the doctrine of Christ is doubtless "the mystery of the faith,"[1113] "the mystery of his will,"[1114] even that law "of the light of the knowledge of the glory of God in the face of Jesus Christ."[1115] Such knowledge is of "the law of faith"[1116] by "the

---

1101 Ephesians 1:7
1102 1 Corinthians 15:2
1103 1 Corinthians 15:17
1104 1 John 5:13
1105 Romans 3:25
1106 1 Corinthians 1:30
1107 2 John 1:10
1108 2 John 1:10
1109 Proverbs 4:2
1110 1 Timothy 4:6
1111 Ephesians 4:13
1112 Philippians 1:27
1113 1 Timothy 3:9
1114 Ephesians 1:9
1115 2 Corinthians 4:6
1116 Romans 3:27

law of Christ,"[1117] which speaks to advance "the gospel of the grace of God"[1118] through "the law of the Spirit."[1119]

6. "If there come any unto you, and bring not this doctrine, receive him not into your house."[1120] "Ye are the temple of God";[1121] "your body is the temple of the Holy Ghost";[1122] for in the believer rests His "house, that is, the temple"[1123] to be "built up a spiritual house."[1124] The spirit of the mind is to dwell within the law of "the kindness and love of God our Saviour toward man,"[1125] and "there is none good but one, that is, God,"[1126] therefore His science is that good to be established within the soul temple that the human being may "know that the law is good."[1127] The Ten Commandments and the doctrine of God are to rest in our inward parts by the work of the Holy Ghost, who in turn is to fashion us after His Son's character "in the likeness of His resurrection."[1128] The law that is of Christ is that Faith of "the fellowship of the mystery,"[1129] for "our fellowship is with the Father, and with his Son."[1130] This law is surely "the acknowledging of the mystery of God, and of the Father, and of Christ,"[1131] engraving within the flesh's mind "the acknowledging of the truth which is after godliness,"[1132] "for I know that in me (that is, in my flesh,) dwelleth no good thing."[1133]

1117 Galatians 6:2
1118 Acts 20:24
1119 Romans 8:2
1120 2 John 1:10
1121 1 Corinthians 3:16
1122 1 Corinthians 6:19
1123 1 Kings 6:17
1124 1 Peter 2:5
1125 Titus 3:4
1126 Mark 10:18
1127 1 Timothy 1:8
1128 Romans 6:5
1129 Ephesians 3:9
1130 1 John 1:3
1131 Colossians 2:2
1132 Titus 1:1
1133 Romans 7:18

7. This is "the faith of God's elect,"[1134] they who of the Father's knowledge "are called, and chosen, and faithful."[1135] The truth that is after godliness is doubtless "the doctrine which is according to godliness,"[1136] and "that the name of God and his doctrine be not blasphemed,"[1137] it is that through the Holy Ghost the believer is "to speak the mystery of Christ." [1138] For this cause, Scripture says, "Thy law is the truth,"[1139] and the Christian reformer is to "be sanctified through the truth";[1140] that is, "through sanctification of the Spirit and belief of the truth";[1141] that by the "renewing of the Holy Ghost,"[1142] "through the grace of the Lord Jesus Christ we shall be saved."[1143] We are washed by the saying of the Spirit and perfected by the grace of that commandment; "by grace are ye saved through faith";[1144] for which cause we carry "repentance toward God, and faith toward our Lord Jesus."[1145] "Christ liveth in me,"[1146] is the confidence gained by the Faith of His name, for His law in man through faith in His blood to recover the spirit is the doctrine of health. For "through faith in his blood,"[1147] the believer is to receive "the righteousness of God which is by faith of Jesus."[1148] It is then that "after that ye believed"[1149] "in the word of the truth of the gospel,"[1150] that "the Holy Ghost was given"[1151]

1134 Titus 1:1
1135 Revelation 17:14
1136 1 Timothy 6:3
1137 1 Timothy 6:1
1138 Colossians 4:3
1139 Psalms 119:142
1140 John 17:19
1141 2 Thessalonians 2:13
1142 Titus 3:5
1143 Acts 15:11
1144 Ephesians 2:8
1145 Acts 20:21
1146 Galatians 2:20
1147 Romans 3:25
1148 Romans 3:22,25
1149 Ephesians 1:13
1150 Colossians 1:5
1151 Acts 8:18

as "the earnest of our inheritance."[1152] "By the righteousness of One"[1153] "we shall be saved,"[1154] for through "the righteousness which is of God by faith,"[1155] we are to be handled by His Spirit, "that the righteousness of the law might be fulfilled in us."[1156] Our High Priest is ever working to bring us to the Spirit of His mediation, for He died and revived that we, as unjust creatures, may become creations of His name's praise. Therefore "that we might be made the righteousness of God in him,"[1157] this is the foundation of His doctrine.

8. Transgression comes to an end when learning, retaining, and assimilating the doctrine of Christ in the life. That which is pleasing to the LORD our Father is that all would be edified by the knowledge of His Son for "repentance unto life."[1158] The LORD would "have all men to be saved, and to come unto the knowledge of the truth,"[1159] and it is pure edification relating to the character of God in man through His will that is to bring life to the conscience. The transgressor is not a doer of the Spirit's law, for "every one that loveth him that begat loveth him also that is begotten of him."[1160] To step outside of God is to reject the testimony of His Son, and to forsake the commandments of God is to reject the blood and Spirit of God, for then it is believed perfection is of man. "Every one that loveth is born of God";[1161] "whosoever believeth that Jesus is the Christ is born of God";[1162] for "every one that doeth righteousness is born of him,"[1163] and it is our responsibility to acquaint self with the Father's manner of love to obtain the promised regeneration. It is our assignment to learn of and do the Spirit's

---

1152 Ephesians 1:14
1153 Romans 5:18
1154 Romans 5:10
1155 Philippians 3:9
1156 Romans 8:4
1157 2 Corinthians 5:21
1158 Acts 11:18
1159 1 Timothy 2:4
1160 1 John 5:1
1161 1 John 4:7
1162 1 John 5:1
1163 1 John 2:29

will, for "of his own will begat he us with the word of truth, that we should be a kind of firstfruits of his creatures."[1164]

9. It is for this reason that Christ and the LORD His Father cannot be separated, for He has said, "I ascend unto my Father, and your Father; and to my God, and your God."[1165] The God of Christ becomes the God of the believer; therefore the character of the Christ of God becomes that which is to rest in the believer through faith on the power of the word of His blood. The Christian is to be renewed in knowledge after the image of their Creator,[1166] and seeing as how Christ "is the image of the invisible God"[1167] and that "all things were made by him,"[1168] it is that from honoring the Spirit's Faith, we might "be conformed to the image of his Son."[1169]

10. Pure faith and love in the name of God is accomplished through the name of His Christ. The soul temple must be washed, and this "washing of water by the word."[1170] To not have this commandment of the Spirit is to have no opportunity to receive the refreshing benefit of His Christ's heavenly ministry. Concerning this Spirit, Christ says, "Whom the Father will send in my name,"[1171] because the Spirit "proceedeth from the Father."[1172] "It is the Spirit that beareth witness"[1173] to our acceptance of the LORD's gospel, for this benevolence is of life by the name of His Man, and it is of His Spirit because His blood is for the purpose of reconciling us to His Father. Christ's voice is ordained by God to cleanse all "to the uttermost that come unto God by him,"[1174] because Christ is now that Minister of righteousness, as it says, "All thy commandments are righteousness,"[1175] and, "A

1164 James 1:18
1165 John 20:17
1166 Colossians 3:10
1167 Colossians 1:15
1168 Colossians 1:16
1169 Romans 8:29
1170 Ephesians 5:26
1171 John 14:26
1172 John 15:26
1173 1 John 5:6
1174 Hebrews 7:25
1175 Psalms 119:172

sceptre of righteousness is the sceptre of thy kingdom."[1176] The believer is to be conformed to the present image of the LORD's Christ; which image is that of God His Father; through faith on His blood and by labors of edifying love through the knowledge His Spirit, and this is the fulfilling of the charge, "Walk in truth."[1177]

1176   Hebrews 8:8
1177   3 John 1:4

13

The Word Of His Patience

1. "Here is the patience of the saints: here are they that keep the commandments of God, and the faith of Jesus."[1178]

2. The patience of the saints of God, the determination of them "who through faith and patience inherit the promises"[1179] of God, is based upon that word advancing the immutability of the commandments of God. The patience of the living assembly is that of their faith and hope; for it is said, "Your patience and faith";[1180] therefore the Faith of patience must revolve around the saying, "The word of my patience."[1181] The Spirit says, "Hast kept my word, and hast not denied my name,"[1182] expressing that His word revolves around His name. Christ did say, "I have manifested thy name...and they have kept thy word";[1183] "thy word is truth."[1184] The word of His patience is the truth of His patience, for when once the ten laws of God are fused to the

---

1178 Revelation 14:12
1179 Hebrews 6:12
1180 2 Thessalonians 1:4
1181 Revelation 3:10
1182 Revelation 3:8
1183 John 17:6
1184 John 17:17

love of God, the believer will confess, "I will worship toward thy holy temple, and praise thy name."[1185]

3. Says Scripture, "Thou hast magnified thy word above all thy name,"[1186] and in another place it is written, "He will magnify the law, and make it honourable."[1187] It is said, "Thy way, O God, is in the sanctuary,"[1188] therefore "blessed are the undefiled in the way, who walk in the law of the LORD."[1189] The name of God shines forth from His Sanctuary, for the word of patience exalts the LORD's name as displayed by His ten precepts. It is for this cause that "the ministration of righteousness exceed in glory"[1190] that which had "a shadow of good things to come."[1191] That which was magnified carried no glory within itself until it met the blood of Christ. "That which remaineth is glorious"[1192] due to its birth from "that which is abolished,"[1193] fulfilling that which is "contrary to nature,"[1194] for He has said, "I will make darkness light before them,"[1195] and, "Ye shall be free."[1196]

4. Christ confessed, "The LORD hath anointed me to preach good tidings,"[1197] or rather, "To preach the gospel to the poor,"[1198] for tidings are nothing but news or doctrine, therefore He said, "I give you good doctrine, forsake ye not my law."[1199] "The law of the Spirit of life in Christ Jesus hath made me free from the law of sin and death,"[1200] says the reformer, for the word of His patience announces "liberty to the

---

1185 Psalms 138:2
1186 Psalms 138:2
1187 Isaiah 42:21
1188 Psalms 77:13
1189 Psalms 119:1
1190 2 Corinthians 3:9
1191 Hebrews 10:1
1192 2 Corinthians 3:11
1193 2 Corinthians 3:13
1194 Romans 11:24
1195 Isaiah 42:16
1196 John 8:36
1197 Isaiah 61:1
1198 Luke 4:18
1199 Proverbs 4:2
1200 Romans 8:2

captives, and the opening of the prison,"[1201] or rather "deliverance to the captives, and recovery of sight."[1202] "None saith, Restore,"[1203] says the Spirit, yet He has promised, "I will restore health unto thee, and I will heal thee of thy wounds."[1204] Therefore as it is said, "We are saved by hope,"[1205] so it is known, "Thy faith hath saved thee."[1206] "For by grace are ye saved through faith,"[1207] and seeing as how it is "the grace of God that bringeth salvation,"[1208] the "renewing of the Holy Ghost"[1209] is "through faith in his blood"[1210] for the purpose of inward liberty to joy in His ten immutable precepts of liberty.

5. The word of patience becomes the law of patience, and as patience is longsuffering, and "the longsuffering of our Lord is salvation,"[1211] it is that, "The word of my patience,"[1212] becomes, "The law of My salvation." As it is said, "The grace of God that bringeth salvation";[1213] "of which salvation the prophets...prophesied of the grace that should come";[1214] the word of salvation now becomes the word and law of grace. When Scripture says, "The faithful word,"[1215] such a saying is synonymous with the phrase, "Sound doctrine,"[1216] for both equate to the saying, "In the word and doctrine."[1217] And as it was seen how it is said, "I give you good doctrine, forsake ye not my law,"[1218] the Scripture records, "They were astonished at his doctrine: for his

---

1201 Isaiah 61:1
1202 Luke 4:18
1203 Isaiah 42:22
1204 Jeremiah 30:17
1205 Romans 8:24
1206 Luke 7:50
1207 Ephesians 2:8
1208 Titus 2:11
1209 Titus 3:5
1210 Romans 3:25
1211 2 Peter 3:15
1212 Revelation 3:10
1213 Titus 2:11
1214 1 Peter 1:10
1215 Titus 1:9
1216 2 Timothy 4:3
1217 1 Timothy 5:17
1218 Proverbs 4:2

word was with power."[1219] As the Spirit said, "Hast kept the word of my patience,"[1220] and as His law and word is synonymous with His doctrine, it is that the believer is to keep the blessed doctrine of His grace, even that "doctrine of Christ."[1221]

6. It is for this cause that the believer is counseled, "He that hath the Son hath life,"[1222] even "the grace of life"[1223] administered by "the Spirit of life"[1224] by faith on His voice. "They which receive abundance of grace and of the gift of righteousness shall reign in life,"[1225] and without grace, or "abundance of peace"[1226] given through the law of the LORD's Spirit, there can be no life within the soul, because "the Spirit is life."[1227] "The Spirit is life because of righteousness,"[1228] for the breath of life is in the light of His righteousness, and "the law is light,"[1229] and that "righteousness is an everlasting righteousness."[1230] "My righteousness shall not be abolished,"[1231] says the LORD, for it is even magnified and established by "that which is abolished."[1232] Thus, the doctrine of Christ is that commandment confessing, "We establish the law,"[1233] for it is through faith in His name "that the righteousness of the law might be fulfilled in us."[1234]

7. Indeed the word of Christ's patience is after "the word of the truth of the gospel,"[1235] and that word "of the truth which is after

---

1219 Luke 4:32
1220 Revelation 3:10
1221 2 John 1:9
1222 1 John 5:12
1223 1 Peter 3:7
1224 Romans 8:10
1225 Romans 5:17
1226 Psalms 72:7
1227 Romans 8:10
1228 Romans 8:10
1229 Proverbs 6:23
1230 Psalms 119:142
1231 Isaiah 51:6
1232 2 Corinthians 3:13
1233 Romans 3:31
1234 Romans 8:4
1235 Colossians 1:5

godliness."[1236] That doctrine of "the elect of God, holy and beloved,"[1237] revolves around holiness, or godliness through inward sanctification by the science of the Spirit's law, and this doctrine is "according to the faith of God's elect."[1238] The doctrine of Christ is "the gospel of the grace of God,"[1239] for the apostle writes, "I obtained mercy,"[1240] therefore he counsels, "We may obtain mercy, and find grace."[1241]

8. The testimony of Christ is herein understood as the doctrine of grace and mercy, for by "his mercy he saved us,"[1242] and through "his abundant mercy hath begotten us."[1243] Yet it is said, "Grace be unto you, and peace,"[1244] and, "Grace to you, and peace,"[1245] because "abundance of peace"[1246] and "abundant mercy"[1247] and "abundance of grace"[1248] are all one and the same, which is why Scripture says, "Abundance of peace and truth,"[1249] because "grace and truth came by Jesus Christ."[1250]

9. The patience of the saints is that doctrine of mental and moral recovery through the Spirit's grace, mercy, and peace, which is His power and wisdom. As patience is known as longsuffering, we see how suffering long is "of suffering affliction, and of patience."[1251] Those born to a moral recovery of their inward faculties through showers of grace not only hold fast to that doctrine of His suffering affliction, but also to the benefit of that doctrine upon their inward person. Herein

---

1236 Titus 1:1
1237 Colossians 3:12
1238 Titus 1:1
1239 Acts 20:24
1240 1 Timothy 1:16
1241 Hebrews 4:16
1242 Titus 3:5
1243 1 Peter 1:3
1244 Revelation 1:4
1245 Philemon 1:3
1246 Psalms 37:11
1247 1 Peter 1:3
1248 Romans 5:17
1249 Jeremiah 33:6
1250 John 1:17
1251 James 5:10

His believers find strength in "the law of Christ,"[1252] for therein "we see Jesus, who was made a little lower than the angels for the suffering of death, crowned with glory and honour; that he by the grace of God should taste death"[1253] "that he might bring us to God."[1254] It was Christ "who his own self bare our sins in his own body on the tree,"[1255] that we "should live unto righteousness"[1256] according "to the will of God."[1257] To have kept the word of His patience means to "have obeyed from the heart"[1258] heaven's doctrine, therefore it is said, "Live according to God in the spirit."[1259]

10. To His faithful, God's Man says, "You have hidden and concealed away in your heart the doctrine of grace and life expressed in My suffering affliction. 'Thou hast kept the word of my patience.'"[1260] Here are they that keep the commandments of God, for their conversation is "as it becometh the gospel of Christ,"[1261] "the faith of the gospel."[1262] Thus, "Let your conversation be as it becometh the gospel of Christ,"[1263] counsels the Spirit, for such a saying appropriates "behaviour as becometh holiness"[1264] to the heart of the conscience. It is heaven's desire "that we might be partakers of his holiness,"[1265] therefore it is said, "Glory ye in his holy name,"[1266] and, "Bless his holy name for ever and ever."[1267] The name of God is within His counsel, and His instruction is His truth, and "the word spoken"[1268] "was the

---

1252 Galatians 6:2
1253 Hebrews 2:9
1254 1 Peter 3:18
1255 1 Peter 2:24
1256 1 Peter 2:24
1257 1 Peter 4:2
1258 Romans 6:17
1259 1 Peter 4:6
1260 Revelation 3:10
1261 Philippians 1:27
1262 Philippians 1:27
1263 Colossians 1:27
1264 Titus 2:3
1265 Hebrews 12:10
1266 Psalms 105:3
1267 Psalms 145:21
1268 Hebrews 2:2

gospel preached,"[1269] "the word preached"[1270] of "great salvation."[1271] He that came to magnify the Father is seated on the right hand of God at "the throne of grace"[1272] for the purpose of creating a people after His manner of righteousness.

11. The believer is to uphold their personal religion through the law of Christ's heavenly ministry for the accomplishment of His Father's will. As sanctification of soul and spirit is the will of the Father for the one confessing His Son, it is that His grace and mercy is to wash "and renew a right spirit"[1273] in man to correctly "renew their strength"[1274] of mind and purpose. Without that ornament of holiness, that gift of righteousness, we are yet within our broken constitution and governed "through the deceitfulness of sin."[1275] Therefore if the Christian faithfully receives and follows after the name of His Christ; that is, the law of His patience; "Know that ye have eternal life,"[1276] says our "brother, and companion in tribulation, and in the kingdom and patience of Jesus Christ."[1277] The believer is to be brought under complete subjection to the commandments of God through sanctification wrought by the Spirit. For this cause, the confidence of the Christian is this: "Ye are complete in him, which is the head of all principality and power."[1278]

12. "God hath given to us eternal life, and this life is in his Son."[1279] The life that is in the knowledge of His Son is "all the fulness of the Godhead bodily,"[1280] therefore through active faith in His conversation we will be regenerated by the life of His name, and that restoration from "obeying the truth through the Spirit."[1281] His Spirit is our faith's

---

1269 Hebrews 4:2
1270 Hebrews 4:2
1271 Hebrews 2:3
1272 Hebrews 4:16
1273 Psalms 51:10
1274 Isaiah 40:31
1275 Hebrews 3:13
1276 1 John 5:13
1277 Revelation 1:9
1278 Colossians 2:10
1279 1 John 5:11
1280 Colossians 2:9
1281 1 Peter 1:22

life, for through the Spirit of God comes the LORD's fulness by the law of His Spirit to the penitent, making the saying true that says, "As many as received him, to them gave he power to become the sons of God."[1282] "To them that believe on his name,"[1283] the Spirit is given to advance their reconciliation to heaven's throne to become servants of His God's name, "that believing ye might have life through his name."[1284] So then Scripture does not lie when saying, "Whosoever believeth that Jesus is the Christ is born of God,"[1285] for through faith "we establish the law"[1286] to love His ten immutable precepts.

13. The believer receives power of the Spirit through faith on the merits of Christ to retain the moral image of God. The power given to the believer is through the name of His Christ for perfecting His manner of godliness, for even Christ was "declared to be the Son of God with power, according to the spirit of holiness, by the resurrection from the dead."[1287] As Christ was "quickened by the Spirit"[1288] and "made a quickening spirit,"[1289] the believer must know that God "shall also quicken your mortal bodies by his Spirit,"[1290] "that we should serve in newness of spirit."[1291] The mind is to house the name of God through active faith on the doctrine of His Christ. The mind is to be renewed through showers of grace to house the ten laws of God, and such a work is accomplished "through the faith of Christ, the righteousness which is of God by faith."[1292] The heaven's will is to have the reformer blessed with righteousness and filled fulness, to the end their character may match His Son's for accomplishing the work of His Son, thus fulfilling the saying, "Bringing many sons unto glory."[1293]

1282 John 1:12
1283 John 20:31
1284 John 20:31
1285 1 John 5:1
1286 Romans 3:31
1287 Romans 1:4
1288 1 Peter 3:18
1289 1 Corinthians 15:45
1290 Romans 8:11
1291 Romans 7:6
1292 Philippians 3:9
1293 Hebrews 2:10

14

Believest Thou This?

1. Says our High Priest, "I am the resurrection, and the life: he that believeth in me, though he were dead, yet shall he live: and whosoever liveth and believeth in me shall never die. Believest thou this?"[1294]

2. Do I believe what? What is it that our salvation's Governor would have us believe?

3. First, that within His voice is the word of the resurrection of the spirit of the heart and mind, and the life or health of that newness of mind. Second, that should we honestly confess every member within our inward parts to be dead and passed away from self's natural mind and the persuasion of the religious world, if we should surrender to the fact and remedy of our inherited and cultivated sickness, if we should believe on the virtue of His name; that by believing on His ministry of atonement we might receive knowledge to become sons and daughters of God; although dead in sins and trespasses, we; our person; should be "risen with him through the faith of the operation of God."[1295] And third, that should we remain faithful to the doctrine and medicine of God's Spirit, if we continue therein and advance by faith in the power

---

1294 John 11:25,26
1295 Colossians 2:12

of that instruction by the One who authorizes it, we will never die, or suffer the reproach of our heart, as He says, "If a man keep my saying, he shall never see death."[1296] When one may actively believe on the precepts of life contained within His voice; mentally and physically examining that voice to do the will of that voice; then it will be confessed, "I believe that thou art the Christ, the Son of God."[1297]

4. Christ has, in very short words, given us the living doctrine of God. The works that Christ should do at the time He spoke these things were to testify to "the glory of God, that the Son of God might be glorified thereby."[1298] Thus, "Said I not unto thee, that, if thou wouldest believe, thou shouldest see the glory of God?"[1299] He said before evincing the science of His intercession.

5. The events that took place when Christ raised Laz'arus from the dead represent the end of the Father's commandment for the sorrowful soul. Christ said that in this moment the Spirit's glory was to be revealed, even as one after Him should confess, "I am not ashamed of the gospel of Christ: for it is the power of God unto salvation to every one that believeth."[1300] The glory and power of God is here put on display, and such glory represented the joy of salvation for the believer, in that at last the heart may hear the voice of Christ say, "Loose him, and let him go."[1301] If the heart would humbly accept the law of His Faith saying, "Come forth,"[1302] then "like as Christ was raised up from the dead by the glory of the Father, even so we also should walk in newness of life. For if we have been planted together in the likeness of his death, we shall be also in the likeness of his resurrection."[1303]

6. It is by the glory of creation's decree that the believer is to be raised into newness of thought and feeling, and if raised according to

---

1296 John 8:51
1297 John 11:27
1298 John 11:4
1299 John 11:40
1300 Romans 1:16
1301 John 11:44
1302 John 11:43
1303 Romans 6:4,5

the same manner like as He was brought up by His Father, then what was the glory of the Father that raised up Christ from the grave?

7. Says Scripture, "If the Spirit of him that raised up Jesus from the dead dwell in you, he that raised up Christ from the dead shall also quicken your mortal bodies by his Spirit."[1304] The Spirit of God is the glory of God that raised His Man from the dead, for Christ was "put to death in the flesh, but quickened by the Spirit."[1305] Christ said that He is the life because He "through the eternal Spirit offered himself without spot to God"[1306] and was raised "after the power of an endless life,"[1307] therefore "he became the author of eternal salvation unto all them that obey him."[1308] "To them gave he power to become the sons of God,"[1309] and "this spake he of the Spirit, which they that believe on him should receive."[1310] Therefore it is a fact that "if any man have not the Spirit of Christ, he is none of his,"[1311] and this is true because "the Spirit is life."[1312]

8. Our Minister says, "He that believes in My voice, though he were dead, he will live," for "if ye through the Spirit do mortify the deeds of the body, ye shall live."[1313] The health of the Christian depends on a living and experimental faith on the LORD's doctrine so that the remedy for personal sin may flow from His Spirit into the soul's temple. It is a fact that the spirit of man may find recovery only "through sanctification of the Spirit and belief of the truth."[1314] After the heart has set itself to believe on the word of spiritual revival and reform, then that heart will be given into the hands of the Spirit for inward purification. As the Spirit works within the spirit of the mind the precepts of the Father's wisdom, it is for the believer to work out what is worked

---

1304   Romans 8:9-11
1305   1 Peter 3:18
1306   Hebrews 9:14
1307   Hebrews 7:16
1308   Hebrews 5:9
1309   John 1:12
1310   John 7:39
1311   Romans 8:9
1312   Romans 8:10
1313   Romans 8:13
1314   2 Thessalonians 2:13

in, thereby reforming the members of the body to fall subject to right reason and religion over impulse and passion. For this cause it is said, "He that hath the Son hath life,"[1315] for after Christ died and then revived, "God hath given to us eternal life, and this life is in his Son."[1316]

9. The life is the resurrection. It is therefore fair to say that He who honors the doctrine of Christ is in possession of the material for the resurrection of their spirit. The doctrine of Christ is the only counsel whereby it may be that "the very God of peace sanctify you wholly."[1317] The glory and power of God is in raising up the soul by faith on His voice to be "sanctified by the Holy Ghost."[1318] This is the glory of God's Spirit and Son, which is why it is said, "Truly our fellowship is with the Father, and with his Son."[1319] Fellowship with the Father is "fellowship of the Spirit,"[1320] and such communion is to leave the reformer "sanctified by God the Father, and preserved in Jesus Christ,"[1321] that is, preserved in "the law of Christ."[1322] The law and doctrine of His Christ is not without the Father and His Spirit, and the Spirit cannot be given without obedience to the words of His Christ, for it says, "Obeying the truth through the Spirit."[1323] The reality behind heaven's will is "that we might be justified by the faith of Christ,"[1324] and from believing on His Faith we will know "the power of his resurrection."[1325] Thus, it is well to understand that there is a difference in believing on the Faith of the Man and believing on the Man Himself, for our conversation is to be with the Faith of God's Man through confidence in His name, which is why it says, "Receive, I pray thee, the law from his mouth, and lay up his words in thine heart."[1326]

1315   1 John 5:12
1316   1 John 5:11
1317   1 Thessalonians 5:23
1318   Romans 15:16
1319   1 John 1:3
1320   Philippians 2:1
1321   Jude 1:1
1322   Galatians 6:2
1323   1 Peter 1:22
1324   Galatians 2:16
1325   Philippians 3:10
1326   Job 22:22

10. This is exactly what the Faith of Jesus is; it is the Spirit's glory emphasizing the power of the resurrection wrought by the knowledge of Christ to the praise of the LORD His Father. Christ will not be raising anyone willingly dead in personal and devotional error at the resurrection of the just; Laz'arus' resurrection cannot represent any thing but the glory and purpose of the Spirit fulfilled in sinful flesh. The resurrection of the just is for them that have been cleansed by faith on heaven's will, and in order to be justified by faith on the Spirit's will, one must endure an experience whereby they may not only be justified, but also from justification; justification is another term signifying sanctification, which is the cleansing of the inward parts "with the washing of water by the word";[1327] glorified by that same faith. Christ didn't just speak the Spirit's Faith through Laz'arus, but He also demonstrated it. Herein the promise was fulfilled, "I will put a new spirit within you; and I will take the stony heart out of their flesh, and will give them an heart of flesh,"[1328] for we are to be raised up in heart and mind to the know and love the LORD by the counsel of His Spirit, and "that which is born of the Spirit is spirit."[1329]

11. We are all born "bound hand and foot with graveclothes";[1330] "we are all as an unclean thing, and all our righteousnesses are as filthy rags";[1331] yet there exists "an high priest over the house of God"[1332] for our mental and moral refreshing. "We have an advocate with the Father"[1333] "who is even at the right hand of God, who also maketh intercession for us."[1334] It should be observed how it is said, "Thou art the Christ, the Son of God,"[1335] for Christ is both Messiah or King of God, and is also Son or Priest or Minister of God; these appellations equal one and the same thing. For the Majesty of heaven, "the power

---

1327 Ephesians 5:26
1328 Ezekiel 11:19
1329 John 3:6
1330 John 11:44
1331 Isaiah 64:6
1332 Hebrews 10:21
1333 1 John 2:1
1334 Romans 8:34
1335 John 11:27

of his Christ"[1336] is found in that He is "first being by interpretation King of righteousness,"[1337] and second, that He also "abideth a priest continually."[1338] The doctrine of God does not stop at Christ crucified, but it begins at Christ crucified and extends in to the fact that "when he had by himself purged our sins, sat down on the right hand of the Majesty on high,"[1339] for He is of God "the Son, who is consecrated for evermore."[1340] Therefore like as how "Aaron was separated...to burn incense before the LORD...and to bless in his name for ever,"[1341] "no man taketh this honour unto himself, but he that is called of God, as was Aaron. So also Christ glorified not himself to be made an high priest."[1342]

12. Consider how it is written, "Jesus lifted up his eyes, and said, Father, I thank thee that thou hast heard me."[1343] Christ here fulfills the counsel, "There is one God, and one mediator between God and men, the man Christ Jesus."[1344] In order for Laz'arus to be raised from the dead, Christ needed to intercede on his behalf to receive power to raise him up, for Christ said, "I do nothing of myself,"[1345] and, "It is my Father that honoureth me."[1346] We need our Prince and King if we should ever experience the benevolence of His and our God and Father, and the LORD's "king" is the chief priest of the LORD's religion, which is why He says, "Yet have I set my king upon my holy hill of Zion."[1347] Herein the saying is fulfilled, "He shall be a priest upon his throne."[1348]

1336 Revelation 12:10
1337 Hebrews 7:2
1338 Hebrews 7:3
1339 Hebrews 1:3
1340 Hebrews 7:28
1341 1 Chronicles 23:13
1342 Hebrews 5:4,5
1343 John 11:41
1344 1 Timothy 2:5
1345 John 8:28
1346 John 8:54
1347 Psalm 2:6
1348 Zechariah 6:13

13. Every thing that Christ did, He did not do it of Himself, for Himself, or within Himself, but rather He faithfully exercised the living power of His God to explain the relationship between Him and them who should believe on His doctrine. Christ is not just Christ to the believer; He is the Spirit's Christ and High Priest for the finishing of the LORD's benevolent will. It is this complete word of God that translates the spirit of the mind from earth to heaven for the full reception of health from the LORD our Father and His Son. This is why the believer must know that "we have such an high priest, who is set on the right hand of the throne of the Majesty in the heavens,"[1349] to the end they may honestly confess with all sincerity, "I delight in the law of God after the inward man."[1350] So then hear again the word of righteousness' Physician: "I am the resurrection, and the life: he that believeth in me, though he were dead, yet shall he live: and whosoever liveth and believeth in me shall never die. Believest thou this?"[1351]

1349 Hebrews 8:1
1350 Romans 7:22
1351 John 11:25,26

15

Behold The Lamb

1. "Behold the Lamb of God, which taketh away the sin of the world."[1352]

2. Christ takes, or bears away what sin of the religious world? The Lamb of God takes away what sin from the active believer? What exactly is one counseled to behold? When beholding the Lamb, what is it exactly that is to be observed?

3. What purpose did a lamb serve to the ancient priesthood? It is written, "A lamb for a sin offering."[1353] A sacrificed lamb is a figurative illustration of an offering for sin, which is why it is written of Christ, "Hath given himself for us an offering and a sacrifice to God for a sweetsmelling savour,"[1354] and, "Who through the eternal Spirit offered himself without spot to God,"[1355] and, "Who gave himself for our sins."[1356] To say, "Behold the Lamb," it is to say, "Behold, what manner of love the Father hath bestowed upon us."[1357] The offering

---

1352   John 1:29
1353   Leviticus 4:32
1354   Ephesians 5:2
1355   Hebrews 9:14
1356   Galatians 1:4
1357   1 John 3:1

for peace, sin, consecration, trespass, and thanksgiving for every one willing to serve the LORD His God, is settled. "Every one which seeth the Son, and believeth on him,"[1358] "whosoever believeth in him shall receive remission of sins."[1359] There are no ifs, no ands, and no buts or howsoever, "for by one offering he hath perfected for ever them that are sanctified."[1360] The issue, then, is who will take knowledge of His name to be "sanctified by God the Father";[1361] both mentally and morally; for there is no such thing as a literal vision of the Man, nor can any imagination of the Man suffice for what should appear by "rightly dividing the word of truth."[1362]

4. The state of every heart is naturally of the condition, "What I would, that do I not; but what I hate, that do I."[1363] What mind is this? It is not a mind converted to the Spirit's Faith. The mind will kill itself due to the natural allowance it gives to the heart, and as the individual abuses themselves; believing that such actions will quiet the void from within the soul; it will be exclaimed, "Who shall deliver me from the body of this death?"[1364]

5. What is the individual delivered from? It says, "The body of death."[1365] This same man wrote, "The Lord shall deliver me from every evil work,"[1366] for Paul knew how it was said of God's Christ, "To deliver their soul from death,"[1367] and this work aforementioned in the saying, "He shall redeem their soul from deceit and violence."[1368] The diagnosis that made the sacrifice of Christ a necessity fulfilled the sentiment, "Alienated and enemies in your mind by wicked works,"[1369] for the doctrine of the Lamb is after, and only after, liberty of the spirit of

---

1358 John 6:40
1359 Acts 10:43
1360 Hebrews 10:14
1361 Jude 1:1
1362 2 Timothy 2:15
1363 Romans 7:15
1364 Romans 7:24
1365 Romans 7:24
1366 2 Timothy 4:18
1367 Psalms 33:19
1368 Psalms 72:14
1369 Colossians 1:21

the mind that the believer may be perfect in thought and feeling by the Spirit to maintain themselves first on this earth before the LORD, and then on the earth to come. Such redemption reveals that the Spirit's will is mentally discerned and not rationalized or accomplished by fleshly traditional or political means, leaving us to understand that "through knowledge shall the just be delivered."[1370]

6. To behold the Lamb is to observe the fact that "unto GOD the Lord belong the issues from death"[1371] that we might excel in "the knowledge of the Son of God."[1372] The Spirit is calling for a reform in worship and service by them that would know Him. Religious tradition is garbage; "ye were not redeemed with corruptible things, as silver and gold, from your vain conversation received by tradition."[1373] Self cannot be trusted; "the natural man receiveth not the things of the Spirit of God."[1374] Look not to brother or sister, pastor, mother or father; "trust ye not in a friend, put ye not confidence in a guide."[1375] Today our High Priest gives the charge, "Give me thine heart, and let thine eyes observe my ways,"[1376] and, "Be wise, and guide thine heart in the way."[1377] It does not say to observe and keep the ways of another or of self, for only terrible spiritual agony awaits the one born of tradition and superstition. The believer is to personally ask their Priest, "What are these wounds in thine hands?"[1378] And when His voice is honestly sought, "he shall answer, Those with which I was wounded in the house of my friends."[1379] "Behold my hands and my feet, that it is I myself: handle me, and see."[1380]

7. "The church of my colleagues tortured the body of my Father's kindness," He will say when inquiring of His mediation's mission.

1370 Proverbs 11:9
1371 Psalms 68:20
1372 Ephesians 4:13
1373 1 Peter 1:18
1374 1 Corinthians 2:14
1375 Micah 7:5
1376 Proverbs 23:26
1377 Proverbs 23:19
1378 Zechariah 13:6
1379 Zechariah 13:6
1380 Luke 24:39

"Handle my name and see for yourselves, observe my office and take knowledge of my operation, that my ministry contains the only hope for the error within your heart and person, that it is the health of the sickness you have innocently inherited and naturally cultivated. 'Reach hither thy finger, and behold my hands; and reach hither thy hand, and thrust it into my side: and be not faithless, but believing.'"[1381]

8. To behold isn't simply to look, for the Spirit says, "Be wise,"[1382] and we do know how it is written, "The wise man's eyes are in his head."[1383] The eyes of the believer do not protrude out of his head, but they are rather turned inward, which is why it is counseled, "Examine yourselves."[1384] Your eyes are "the eyes of your understanding,"[1385] and to look is not in reality to lethargically look, but to rather pick up and handle according to saying, "I applied mine heart to know, and to search, and to seek out wisdom, and the reason of things."[1386] This is why the apostle begins his epistle by saying, "We have heard...we have seen with our eyes...we have looked upon, and our hands have handled."[1387] It was because the apostles willingly gave themselves over to studying the precepts of the Spirit's law that they could confidently confess, "We have seen and do testify that the Father sent the Son to be the Saviour of the world."[1388]

9. Our High Priest would not have an ignorant assembly; He would not have policy-loving hypocrites who despise the originality derived only from obedience to principle. To behold the Lamb is to "know him, and the power of his resurrection, and the fellowship of his sufferings, being made conformable unto his death."[1389] The doctrine of Christ, when actively experimented with, secures to the believer fellowship within the heavenly Building of the living God. Thus, to behold the

---

1381   John 20:27
1382   Proverbs 23:19
1383   Ecclesiastes 2:11
1384   2 Corinthians 13:5
1385   Ephesians 1:18
1386   Ecclesiastes 7:25
1387   1 John 1:1
1388   1 John 4:14
1389   Philippians 3:10

Lamb of God is to pursue the fulfillment of the character, "In his law doth he meditate day and night."[1390] It is not a strange thing to converse with our Priest's voice, or to expect such communication with His understanding to corral an experience with Him. Love that is sanctioned by reason will do all that is possible to never be separated from the One that the heart of the spirit has heard of and accepted.

10. It is said of one man anciently, "He sought to see Jesus who he was,"[1391] and for his efforts, the Spirit's Messenger reported of him, "He also is a son of Abraham."[1392] Herein is a fact: that "we should be called the sons of God"[1393] only through "the faith of Abraham."[1394] This man sought Christ by faith, and while never, up until that point, fully encountering Him, he did all that he did "in the fear of the LORD, faithfully, and with a perfect heart,"[1395] and was eventually blessed to have Christ even in his own home. For who was this man? It says, "A man that is a sinner."[1396] And this is documented for the believing reformer to know that whosoever "believeth on him that justifieth the ungodly, his faith is counted for righteousness."[1397] What does this mean? Have you believed from the heart on the doctrine of God? Do you know that doctrine to believe on it? Well, faith comes from hearing, and hearing is born from independently examining God's voice, and if one has heard in innocence, and has believed what they have heard is fact, and if from that fact are doers of what they have come to trust, then from taking courage on the Spirit's instruction, it is that now "your love may abound yet more and more in knowledge and in all judgment; that ye may approve things that are excellent; that ye may be sincere and without offence till the day of Christ."[1398]

1390   Psalms 1:2
1391   Luke 19:3
1392   Luke 19:9
1393   1 John 3:1
1394   Romans 4:16
1395   2 Chronicles 19:9
1396   Luke 19:7
1397   Romans 4:5
1398   Philippians 1:9,10

11. To behold the Lamb means to accept the fact of the sacrifice of God, and by faith in the merits of that offering, to allow the Spirit of that oblation access into the chambers of the heart that He may supply health to the spirit and soul temple. This work of health cannot begin until the heart should consent to look and live after His doctrine, and that observation is obtained only by faith on the end of His Man's name. Without personally grappling with the counsels of God, without wrestling with His and with self's mind, the original nature of man will consume the being. The heart of man "is corrupt according to the deceitful lusts,"[1399] and is framed to endorse violence against self due to its inherited trait of accepting violence against the character of God. Of the priesthood contained within the heart, it is said, "Her priests have polluted the sanctuary, they have done violence to the law."[1400] The sanctuary of the soul is made thin by the priests of the mind of the body exerting their influence over the members of the heart and mind, but by obeying the vision received of the Lamb, in the believer it will be fulfilled, "That takes away the sin of the world."[1401]

12. What is the sin of the world? What is "the spirit of error"[1402] that fulfills the counsel, "The whole world lieth in wickedness"?[1403] It is written, "All that is in the world, the lust of the flesh, and the lust of the eyes, and the pride of life, is not of the Father, but is of the world."[1404] The mind of the world is a mind refusing to diligently learn of and do the Faith of Christ, for this is a heart "that hath no rule over his own spirit,"[1405] and to bear no rule over the members of the flesh expresses the observation, "They hated knowledge, and did not choose the fear of the LORD: they would none of my counsel."[1406] Again, the Spirit

---

1399   Ephesians 4:22
1400   Zechariah 3:4
1401   John 1:29
1402   1 John 4:6
1403   1 John 5:19
1404   1 John 2:16
1405   Proverbs 25:28
1406   Proverbs 1:29,30

further explains this type of character by saying, "All they that hate me love death."[1407]

13. The call to behold Christ crucified is a call to reform the heart away from self and on to His course of learning. When once the soul has been brought to observe its Chief Physician, it will be fulfilled, "They shall look upon me whom they have pierced, and they shall mourn for him, as one mourneth for his only son, and shall be in bitterness for him, as one that is in bitterness for his firstborn."[1408] "After that ye heard the word of truth, the gospel of your salvation,"[1409] it is a fact that the sincere soul will have "sorrowed after a godly sort,"[1410] but where then must the eye turn after it has been made to feel sorry for its waywardness in the sight of God? Does Scripture only say, "Behold"? Behold what? Behold He who bears away the sin and error of the spirit of the world, but behold Him where? If the Lamb is sacrificed and dead, how then is He to be some place to bear away some thing? Our Priest says, "Observe My ways,"[1411] therefore the counsel must be heard, "Thy way, O God, is in the sanctuary."[1412]

14. The doctrine of the Lamb does not stop at the cross, but it is there ratified for a beginning. "When he had by himself purged our sins,"[1413] He afterward "sat down on the right hand of the Majesty on high";[1414] "wherefore he is able also to save them to the uttermost that come unto God by him, seeing he ever liveth to make intercession for them."[1415] Salvation, redemption, deliverance, recovery, and regeneration of the spirit of man, does not begin until the eye is found observing Christ in His office as High Priest; this is why it is counseled, "Our conversation is in heaven,"[1416] and, "If ye then be risen with Christ, seek

---

1407 Proverbs 8:36
1408 Zechariah 12:10
1409 Ephesians 1:13
1410 2 Corinthians 7:11
1411 Proverbs 23:26
1412 Psalms 77:13
1413 Hebrews 1:3
1414 Hebrews 1:3
1415 Hebrews 7:25
1416 Philippians 3:20

those things which are above, where Christ sitteth on the right hand of God."[1417] For "we have such an high priest, who is set on the right hand of the throne of the Majesty in the heavens; a minister of the sanctuary, and of the true tabernacle, which the Lord pitched, and not man."[1418] "He was made priest"[1419] "after the power of an endless life,"[1420] for He who "continueth ever, hath an unchangeablepriesthood."[1421]

15. Who is it that was ordained to put away and to pardon sin from the person? It is written, "The priest shall offer the sin offering, and make an atonement for him that is to be cleansed from his uncleanness."[1422] This is why it says, "We also joy in God through our Lord Jesus Christ, by whom we have now received the atonement."[1423] It was God who, "having made peace through the blood of his cross, by him to reconcile all things unto himself...in the body of his flesh through death,"[1424] purposed through His Christ to present us "holy and unblameable and unreproveable in his sight."[1425] None were made clean unless sanctified and blessed by the priest, for it says, "The priest shall make an atonement for him as concerning his sin, and it shall be forgiven him."[1426] This is why it is written of our heavenly Priest, "Who is even at the right hand of God, who also maketh intercession for us."[1427]

16. At this hour, humanity rests under "the time of reformation,"[1428] even the reformation of the inward parts by the Spirit's fullness. The eye of faith, when once beholding Christ on the cross, will not be left to view Him there, for He is not there, therefore by faith the word is fulfilled, "Who hath delivered us from the power of darkness, and hath

---

1417 Colossians 3:1
1418 Hebrews 8:1,2
1419 Hebrews 7:20
1420 Hebrews 7:16
1421 Hebrews 7:24
1422 Leviticus 14:19
1423 Romans 5:11
1424 Colossians 1:20-22
1425 Colossians 1:22
1426 Leviticus 4:26
1427 Romans 8:34
1428 Hebrews 9:10

translated us into the kingdom of his dear Son."[1429] This Christ, that the risen Savior and High Priest of every erroneous human being within the House of God in heaven, says, "I am he that liveth, and was dead; and, behold, I am alive for evermore, Amen."[1430] To behold the Lamb is not only to observe the Man pierced and beaten on a tree, and full of wounds pouring out with blood from His head to His feet for the tremendous violation of natural hardheartedness, but it is to see Him and to know Him in His full and present state, that He is "the Son of man, clothed with a garment down to the foot, and girt about the paps with a golden girdle."[1431] Thus, the revelation of the Lamb is our observing the order of His doctrine to confess, "The life which I now live in the flesh I live by the faith of the Son of God, who loved me, and gave himself for me,"[1432] and, "The law of the Spirit of life in Christ Jesus hath made me free from the law of sin and death."[1433]

17. From out of the Temple of God, blessings fall on the spirit of our faith to continue in the will of the Father and the Son. Christ offered Himself to give the trembling heart of any man or woman a second chance to continue in the probation that Adam failed to uphold. Man was created to honor the mental, moral, and physical laws of their health, by way of openly communing with the Spirit of God to keep His ten immutable laws of life, liberty, and benevolence. If the mind should only behold the cross, that mind will only find itself confronted with *God* being dead, leaving the heart to die within itself. And if only beholding *God* as a dead man, then that means as He is like us, and as He is subject to the death of man, as man cannot resurrect himself, then "if the dead rise not, then is not Christ raised: and if Christ be not raised, your faith is vain; ye are yet in your sins."[1434] But what does Scripture say? We are told that He is the Lamb that takes away. Christ is here presented as active after death, for He is "whom God hath

---

1429 Colossians 1:13
1430 Revelation 1:18
1431 Revelation 1:13
1432 Galatians 2:20
1433 Romans 8:2
1434 1 Corinthians 15:16,17

raised up, having loosed the pains of death: because it was not possible that he should be holden of it."[1435]

18. To behold the Spirit's Christ is to embrace the fact that He is not only a crucified and risen Savior, but it is to also concern the conversation with His new name and position after He was raised from the dead, for He is today life's Forerunner. "Christ glorified not himself to be made an high priest; but he that said unto him, Thou art my Son, to day have I begotten thee. As he saith also in another place, Thou art a priest for ever after the order of Melchis'edec." This Man is the LORD's true Priest over the Spirit's House in heaven, for He "is called of God, as was Aaron."[1436] Therefore "bless the LORD, O house of Aaron."[1437] "O house of Aaron, trust in the LORD,"[1438] for it is an ever present fact that "there is one God, and one mediator between God and men, the man Christ Jesus"[1439] who "God exalted with his right hand to be a Prince and a Saviour, for to give repentance to Israel, and forgiveness of sins."[1440]

1435 Acts 2:24
1436 Hebrews 5:4-6
1437 Psalms 135:19
1438 Psalms 115:10
1439 1 Timothy 2:5
1440 Acts 5:31

16

I Come To Do Thy Will

1. "Lo, I come: in the volume of the book it is written of me, I delight to do thy will, O my God: yea, thy law is within my heart."[1441]

2. What is the will that God designed for His Christ's accomplishment? And in the volume of what book is this will found?

3. "The words of the book of the covenant";[1442] that is, "the book of the law";[1443] contain the full will of the Spirit and the appointment of His Christ. Concerning His ancient nation, the LORD "commandedst them precepts, statutes, and laws, by the hand of Moses"[1444] which did "serve unto the example and shadow of heavenly things."[1445] As the earthly example of what should come after their dispensation maintained "ordinances of divine service, and a worldly sanctuary,"[1446] so "in the dispensation of the fullness of times,"[1447] after Christ should be

---

1441   Psalms 50:7,8
1442   2 chronicles 34:30
1443   Galatians 3:10
1444   Nehemiah 9:14
1445   Hebrews 8:5
1446   Hebrews 9:1
1447   Ephesians 1:10

raised from "the heart of the earth,"[1448] it was that He should become "an high priest of good things to come, by a greater and more perfect tabernacle,"[1449] "which the Lord pitched, and not man."[1450] Herein is the will of the LORD our Father, therefore it is said, "Now the righteousness of God without the law is manifested."[1451]

4. The praise of God is that which came out from the law; the law and the prophets; or rather that which "Moses in the law, and the prophets, did write."[1452] Paul once wrote, concerning them who claimed to be Jews, "Knowest his will...being instructed out of the law,"[1453] for it was that law entrusted to the seed of Moses and Aaron that did serve to instruct one on how to "keep the righteousness of the law,"[1454] which righteousness exemplified "the work of the law written in their hearts,"[1455] as it says, "The doers of the law shall be justified."[1456] There is only one law given that man may observe in order to obtain justification, and it is found in none other place than that given to Aaron, for it says, "Perfection were by the Levit'ical priesthood."[1457] That of old "sanctifieth to the purifying of the flesh,"[1458] and being an example of what should come after for believers "to offer up spiritual sacrifices, acceptable to God,"[1459] it would be that "the blood of Christ"[1460] should "purge your conscience from dead works to serve the living God."[1461]

5. That which Christ came to fulfill contained the means by which the righteousness of God could be made free for all to receive. For that entrusted to man by the hand of Moses "could not make him that

---

1448 Matthew 12:40
1449 Hebrews 9:11
1450 Hebrews 8:2
1451 Romans 3:21
1452 John 1:45
1453 Romans 2:18
1454 Romans 2:26
1455 Romans 2:15
1456 Romans 2:13
1457 Hebrews 7:11
1458 Hebrews 9:13
1459 1 Peter 2:5
1460 Hebrews 9:14
1461 Hebrews 9:14

did the service perfect, as pertaining to the conscience."[1462] God's Man appeared to verify and magnify the character of His Father, to the end that all who should see Him, and were willing to obey His speech, could maintain themselves in that same character by the divine aid His sacrifice should provide. Christ upheld every commandment of His LORD in sinful flesh for our example to follow, for He Himself says, "I have kept my Father's commandments."[1463] This is why the LORD said of old, "A law shall proceed from me,"[1464] and why Christ confirmed, "I proceeded forth and came from God,"[1465] which is why Christ said to His LORD and God, "Your law is in my heart,"[1466] for wrapped within the mind of the gospel of Christ is the ten precepts of His Father, and from that gospel also shines the brightness of His righteousness for mankind as found in His unchangeable Priesthood for them.

6. The doctrine of Christ is not without obedience to the Ten Commandments of God, nor is it without the principles of the Priesthood of His Faith. This is why Christ said, "I come to do thy will,"[1467] for the will of God does not end at the cross, but rather it was a precursor to satisfy the distaste of error that men may again know the LORD by the law of His Christ's voice, that men may translate the times and seasons of old to fit the current eye of faith for sincere and right devotion. It is for this reason that the Spirit says, "The doers of the law are justified,"[1468] and that law of types and shadows fits none other word than what is written and says, "The just shall live by his faith."[1469] That which should pronounce the Faith of God says, "Draw out and take you a lamb according to your families, and kill the passover,"[1470] and, "The priest shall make an atonement for them, and it shall be forgiven

---

1462 Hebrews 9:9
1463 John 15:10
1464 Isaiah 51:4
1465 John 8:42
1466 Psalms 40:8
1467 Psalms 40:7,8
1468 Romans 2:13
1469 Habakkuk 2:4
1470 Exodus 12:21

them."[1471] This is why it says, "Who through the eternal Spirit offered himself without spot to God,"[1472] and, "Christ our passover is sacrificed for us,"[1473] and, "By whom we have now received the atonement,"[1474] and, "Thou art a priest for ever."[1475]

7. Says Scripture, "No man taketh this honour unto himself, but he that is called of God, as was Aaron. So also Christ glorified not himself to be made an high priest; but he that said unto him, Thou art my Son, to day have I begotten thee. As he saith also in another place, Thou art a priest for ever after the order of Melchis'edec."[1476] And this is why our High Priest says, "I will declare the decree: the LORD hath said unto me, Thou art my Son; this day have I begotten thee. Ask of me, and I shall give thee the heathen for thine inheritance,"[1477] and, "Thou hast made me the head of the heathen: a people whom I have not known shall serve me,"[1478] for it is written, "It is Christ that died, yea rather, that is risen again, who is even at the right hand of God, who also maketh intercession for us."[1479] This is why the LORD said of the law of the Faith that should come from His name, "The isles shall wait for his law,"[1480] for it was purposed of God "that the Gentiles should be fellowheirs, and of the same body, and partakers of his promise in Christ by the gospel."[1481]

8. After He had passed away from the religious world and took His final breath, it was not long that before God there "stood a Lamb as it had been slain."[1482] This Lamb of God was not constrained to a cross, He was not bound by death, which is why it says, "Neither wilt thou

---

1471 Leviticus 4:20
1472 Hebrews 9:14
1473 1 Corinthians 5:7
1474 Romans 5:11
1475 Psalms 110:4
1476 Hebrews 5:4-6
1477 Psalms 2:7
1478 Psalms 18:43
1479 Romans 8:34
1480 Isaiah 42:4
1481 Ephesians 3:6
1482 Revelation 5:6

suffer thine Holy One to see corruption."[1483] It was Christ "God hath raised up, having loosed the pains of death: because it was not possible that he should be holden of it."[1484] So is this it? Is the work for salvation done? Is Christ raised from the dead all that must be heard and observed? Is the lot of every human now eternally secured?

9. Christ said on the cross, "It is finished,"[1485] yet in context, the will of God was not finished, but only that sacrifice which should satisfy the destruction of that wall between man and His LORD's Spirit. A sacrifice for sin, for peace, for trespass, was all that the lamb anciently symbolized, yet what is the point of a sacrifice without reaping the benefits of that sacrifice? What is the point of a sacrifice without an education on its necessity? And if Christ should be sacrificed, should it not be a concern as to who the priest of the sacrifice is? A lamb cannot sacrifice itself and offer its blood on behalf of the congregation. Is a sacrificed Lamb all that the will of God entails?

10. Christ was not a priest when He was on earth, and this is so "for Moses truly said unto the fathers, A prophet shall the Lord your God raise up unto you of your brethren, like unto me."[1486] If indeed statutes, judgments, ordinances, testimonies and commandments came from Moses to Israel, then it is a fact that Moses is a figurative representation of Christ and His doctrine for them that should believe on His name. The LORD Himself said of His Christ, "Whosoever will not hearken unto my words which he shall speak in my name, I will require it of him,"[1487] therefore it is fair to note these words of Christ: "The Son of man hath power upon earth to forgive sins."[1488] On earth Christ was a prophet, but there would come a time when that work and title should conclude to open up the true branch of His purpose, as it says, "He shall bear the glory, and shall sit and rule upon his throne; and he shall be a priest upon his throne."[1489]

1483 Psalms 16:10
1484 Acts 2:24
1485 John 19:30
1486 Acts 3:22
1487 Deuteronomy 18:19
1488 Luke 5:24
1489 Zechariah 6:13

11. Says our Priest, "This is the will of him that sent me, that every one which seeth the Son, and believeth on him, may have everlasting life."[1490] Does Christ say, "Which sees the cross?" Does He say, "Which sees Moses?" Does He say, "Which sees the Prophet?" This Man says, "Which sees the Son," and this meaning that as a "son" represents the title of a minister or priest, Christ is in fact counseling individuals who take confidence on the sacrifice of God for their recovery from error, who hear of His doctrine and the law of His Spirit, to consider the LORD's saying, "I will be to him a Father, and he shall be to me a Son."[1491] Christ would have every believer know that instruction magnifying the victory of the cross first conceived in Eden, which victory leads into His high priestly ministration for the fulfillment of that victory in the spirit of the believer.

12. When the heart has willingly and personally embraced the sight of Christ on the cross, it will cry out for a Savior. The heart only begins to feel its condition because "God hath sent forth the Spirit of his Son into your hearts, crying, Ab'ba, Father."[1492] As the heart turns to acknowledge God as Father, it is that a comforting warmth is added to the spirit, for now the heart knows that His Son "is able also to save them to the uttermost that come unto God by him, seeing he ever liveth to make intercession for them."[1493] Therefore "follow the Lamb whithersoever he goeth,"[1494] for He who is risen to stand by God within the House of God says, "Come and see."[1495]

13. It is the will of God that "after that the kindness and love of God our Saviour toward man appeared,"[1496] "that we, being dead to sins, should live unto righteousness."[1497] Christ did not lie when He said, "If I be lifted up from the earth, will draw all men unto me,"[1498] for

---

1490 John 6:40
1491 Hebrews 1:5
1492 Galatians 4:6
1493 Hebrews 7:25
1494 Revelation 14:4
1495 John 1:39
1496 Titus 3:4
1497 1 Peter 2:24
1498 John 12:32

from the confidence of the cross comes a true surrendering of self to Christ's law. Yet He says that He will draw all to Him, and as He is not dead, none are to be drawn to the mind of a dead *Christ*, and none are to have their hope cut off from hearing that *Christ* is only resurrected and that is all, but rather it should be heard, "Our conversation is in heaven,"[1499] which is why His Christ said, "Whither I go ye know, and the way ye know."[1500] Christ has died and resurrected for a reason, and that reason is to bring sinful men to His God by faith on His current counsel. What counsel is this? That law says, "The Son of man came... to give his life a ransom for many,"[1501] and the Place of this Faith of the Son and High Priest of God is as it is said, "I have seen thee in the sanctuary."[1502]

14. Notice that Christ says, "Which sees the Son and believes,"[1503] for the Faith of Jesus doesn't just contain the sight of Christ on a cross, it holds the vision of Him in the Temple above working on behalf of fallen humanity. A religion confessing Christ without acknowledging the Place of God's doctrine will struggle to maintain itself by traditions and superstitions. Therefore, this counsel must be allowed entrance into the heart, "Seek those things which are above, where Christ sitteth on the right hand of God,"[1504] for every one who has heard and believed the doctrine of Christ must observe the Son of man and of God in His office, for then may the spirit reap the full benefit of His ministration for inward renovation. When the believer studies after the Christ and Son of the Father, then may they hear the second part of His will and purpose: "This is the will of God, even your sanctification,"[1505] and, "Seeing ye have purified your souls in obeying the truth through the Spirit unto unfeigned love of the brethren, see that ye love one another."[1506]

1499 Philippians 3:20
1500 John 14:4
1501 Mark 10:45
1502 Psalms 63:2
1503 John 6:40
1504 Colossians 3:1
1505 1 Thessalonians 4:3
1506 1 Peter 1:22

15. It is here in the heavenly House of the LORD God that self-sacrificing love and godly affection is made plain to the soul. At the sight of Christ alive and fully clothed as God's Priest, John writes, "When I saw him, I fell at his feet as dead."[1507] At the sight of this Christ, the heart should declare, "My cogitations much troubled me, and my countenance changed in me."[1508] As the doctrine of heaven's Priest is observed both on earth and in heaven, the spirit will announce, "Lord, to whom shall we go? thou hast the words of eternal life. And we believe and are sure that thou art that Christ, the Son of the living God."[1509]

16. God would have every believer of His in an independent faith that is intellectually and spiritually sure, for as it is seen how God could surrender His name to suffer for man within the corrupt parts of man, only to die and then rise from the death of man to labor after the health of man; being now joined to God while also "being in the form of God"[1510] as "equal with God" in name;[1511] the heart will confess, "He laid down his life for us: and we ought to lay down our lives for the brethren."[1512] There is a charge given by God's Priest to His reformers, for, "By this shall all men know that ye are my disciples, if ye have love one to another,"[1513] He says, and the true fulfillment of this stewardship is expressed by a personal knowing of His love's root. As the soul beholds Christ officiating before God in the LORD's Apartments, the Spirit of Christ will bring the observer to declare to the world, "Being affectionately desirous of you, we were willing to have imparted unto you, not the gospel of God only, but also our own souls, because ye were dear unto us."[1514]

17. The will of heaven is that all who would feel after Christ should allow themselves time to rightly know Him in every aspect of knowing.

1507 Revelation 1:17
1508 Daniel 7:28
1509 John 6:68,69
1510 Philippians 2:6
1511 Philippians 2:6
1512 1 John 3:16
1513 John 13:35
1514 1 Thessalonians 2:8

This is why today Christ says, "Reach hither thy finger, and behold my hands; and reach hither thy hand, and thrust it into my side: and be not faithless, but believing."[1515] This is a most personal command, and He has said this so that mental taxation may be added to a physical exercise for recovery of the personal and spiritual diet for the uplifting of others. Christ says, "The Son can do nothing of himself, but what he seeth the Father do,"[1516] and as He saw and did, so too He counsels, "If ye keep my commandments, ye shall abide in my love; even as I have kept my Father's commandments, and abide in his love."[1517] As Christ existed under the shadow of His Father, so too the will of God declares that every believer should "be conformed to the image of his Son."[1518] When the doctrine of Christ is observed, when once the law of the Spirit is rightly divided through an experimental faith, the spirit will confess, "I delight in the law of God after the inward man."[1519] Herein the heart may hear and keep the charge, "Bear ye one another's burdens, and so fulfill the law of Christ."[1520]

18. After the Father had raised His Man from the grave, after "he was taken up; and a cloud received him out of their sight";[1521] He then made His way to God Himself and "into heaven itself, now to appear in the presence of God for us."[1522] "Then said he, Lo, I come to do thy will...By the which will we are sanctified through the offering of the body of Jesus Christ once for all. And every priest standeth daily ministering and offering oftentimes the same sacrifices, which can never take away sins: but this man, after he had offered one sacrifice for sins for ever, sat down on the right hand of God; from henceforth expecting till his enemies be made his footstool."[1523] For of old, and even today, "they truly were many priests, because they were not suffered to continue

---

1515   John 20:27
1516   John 5:19
1517   John 15:10
1518   Romans 8:29
1519   Romans 7:22
1520   Galatians 6:22
1521   Acts 1:9
1522   Hebrews 9:24
1523   Hebrews 10:9-13

by reason of death: but this man, because he continueth ever, hath an unchangeable priesthood."[1524]

19. The economy of ancient Israel only served one purpose, and that being to announce Christ's priestly office. This word of the law of man's recovery for inward immortality is the law of the Father's benevolence, and as that of old served as a vehicle to educate on the righteousness achieved by faith, it is a fact that "the law was our schoolmaster to bring us unto Christ, that we might be justified by faith."[1525] Being justified by faith in the doctrine of His Christ, the human being may now joy in the LORD His God, for their experience will draw the finger of His Spirit into their soul's temple for purification. By faith in the full purpose of this Spirit, the believer will know His voice to fulfill the charge, "Write them upon the table of thine heart,"[1526] for these are the ones that keep every immutable precept of the LORD, and uphold the Faith of His Son.

[1524] Hebrews 7:23,24
[1525] Galatians 3:24
[1526] Proverbs 3:3

17

He Whose Right It Is

1. "The burden of the word of the LORD to Israel":[1527] "O ye priests, this commandment is for you. If ye will not hear, and if ye will not lay it to heart, to give glory unto my name, saith the LORD of hosts, I will even send a curse upon you, and I will curse your blessings: yea, I have cursed them already, because ye do not lay it to heart. Behold, I will corrupt your seed, and spread dung upon your faces, even the dung of your solemn feasts; and one shall take you away with it."[1528]

2. The LORD declared that one should take away the priests with their devout religious feasts, and at the same time corrupt their seed. In one aspect, the seed of the priests were their many rituals and customs comprising a "law of commandments contained in ordinances,"[1529] which is why Christ said of them, "For laying aside the commandment of God, ye hold the tradition of men."[1530] "Full well ye reject the commandment of God, that ye may keep your own tradition."[1531] The

---

1527 Malachi 1:1
1528 Malachi 2:1-3
1529 Ephesians 2:15
1530 Mark 7:8
1531 Mark 7:9

seed of the priests would be them that issue from their sensual philosophical understanding, which is why Christ took "the handwriting of ordinances that was against us, which was contrary to us, and took it out of the way, nailing it to his cross; and having spoiled principalities and powers, he made a shew of them openly, triumphing over them in it."[1532]

3. Said the LORD of Israel, "I hate, I despise your feast days."[1533] Again, "I will also cause all her mirth to cease, her feast days, her new moons, and her sabbaths, and all her solemn feasts. And I will destroy her vines and her fig trees."[1534] This was said because it was observed by the LORD, "Ye have borne the tabernacle of your Mo'loch and Chi'un your images, the star of your god, which ye made to yourselves."[1535] "They have set up kings, but not by me: they have made princes, and I knew it not: of their silver and their gold have they made them idols, that they may be cut off. Thy calf, O Sama'ria, hath cast thee off; mine anger is kindled against them: how long will it be ere they attain to innocency?"[1536] "I will overturn, overturn, overturn, it: and it shall be no more, until he come whose right it is; and I will give it him."[1537]

4. Says the LORD of this host, "I scattered them with a whirlwind among all the nations whom they knew not,"[1538] yet there would come a point in time when within that scattering the saying would be fulfilled, "I will shake all nations, and the desire of all nations shall come."[1539] Although the seed of the priests contained the "precepts, statutes, and laws, by the hand of Moses,"[1540] and mingled "with divers and strange doctrines,"[1541] it is of a truth "that our Lord sprang out of Juda; of which tribe Moses spake nothing concerning priesthood."[1542] Thus it

---

1532   Colossians 2:14,15
1533   Amos 5:21
1534   Hosea 2:11,12
1535   Amos 5:26
1536   Hosea 8:4,5
1537   Ezekiel 21:27
1538   Zechariah 7:14
1539   Haggai 2:7
1540   Nehemiah 9:14
1541   Hebrews 13:9
1542   Hebrews 7:14

was known, "None ought to carry the ark of God but the Levites: for them hath the LORD chosen to carry the ark of God, and to minister unto him for ever,"[1543] yet with "the priesthood being changed, there is made of necessity a change also of the law (the law of the priesthood). For he of whom these things are spoken pertaineth to another tribe, of which no man gave attendance at the altar."[1544]

5. Thus, the LORD said, "I will corrupt your seed, and will do away you and with your law and tradition, and one will take your name away."[1545] This is why it is recorded, "When he had cried again with a loud voice, yielded up the ghost. And, behold, the veil of the temple was rent in twain from the top to the bottom,"[1546] for at this time the living God was no longer joined to the priesthood of the literal nation of Israel, the lot of priesthood now falling to His Son, as it says, "The Lord sware and will not repent, Thou art a priest for ever after the order of Melchis'edec."[1547] "Christ being come an high priest of good things to come, by a greater and more perfect tabernacle, not made with hands";[1548] the priesthood and "the law having a shadow of good things to come, and not the very image of the things";[1549] after "he had by himself purged our sins, sat down on the right hand of the Majesty on high"[1550] having fled "into heaven itself, now to appear in the presence of God for us."[1551]

6. The LORD warned the leadership of Israel by His servants to set themselves in right relation to His throne's religion. It was inevitable that that they would be taken away, for the Spirit prophesied of these things to come, and that both the rule and priesthood of His Son should be one most spiritual as opposed to that of the flesh. Thus, the LORD said, "I might break my covenant which I had made with all the people.

1543 1 Chronicles 15:2
1544 Hebrews 7:12.13
1545 Malachi 2:3
1546 Matthew 27:51
1547 Hebrews 7:21
1548 Hebrews 9:11
1549 Hebrews 10:1
1550 Hebrews 1:3
1551 Hebrews 9:24

And it was broken in that day: and so the poor of the flock that waited upon me knew that it was the word of the LORD,"[1552] wherefore it was fulfilled, "They that gladly received his word were baptized: and the same day there were added unto them about three thousand souls."[1553] Them that waited on the doctrine of God's Man with all of their heart, them that had heard and believed on His Faith while He was alive and with them, whether they were far or near, and bearing the testimony after He had been crucified, "They have taken away my Lord, and I know not where they have laid him,"[1554] rejoiced when they heard of His new priestly position. It was preached, "By his own blood he entered in once into the holy place, having obtained eternal redemption for us,[1555]" for "the Lord added to the church daily such as should be saved."[1556] Thus, the word was fulfilled, "He taketh away the first, that he may establish the second."[1557]

7. The LORD said, "My name shall be great among the Gentiles,"[1558] and by the death, resurrection, and high priestly ordination of His Christ, we "who sometimes were far off are made nigh by the blood of Christ"[1559] to the throne and Spirit of His LORD and Father. Thus it is fulfilled, "Having abolished in his flesh the enmity, even the law of commandments contained in ordinances; for to make in himself of twain, one new man, so making peace; and that he might reconcile both unto God in one body by the cross, having slain the enmity thereby."[1560] This Man is the One who replaced and magnified the priesthood of old, being now "the head over all things to the church,"[1561] "an high priest over the house of God."[1562] For this cause it is said, "Behold, a king shall reign in righteousness...a man shall be as an hiding place...The

---

1552 Zechariah 11:10,11
1553 Acts 2:41,47
1554 John 20:13
1555 Hebrews 9:12
1556 Hebrews 10:9
1557 Hebrews 10:9
1558 Malachi 1:11
1559 Ephesians 2:13
1560 Ephesians 2:13-16
1561 Ephesians 1:22
1562 Hebrews 10:21

eyes of them that see shall not be dim, and the ears of them that hear shall hearken,"[1563] which is why it is said, "Say unto the cities of Judah, Behold your God!"[1564] "Look upon Zion, the city of our solemnities... There the glorious LORD will be unto us a place of broad rivers and streams."[1565]

8. The doctrine of God encompasses the line of judgment that begins where it says, "A man of sorrows, and acquainted with grief,"[1566] and extends to announce, "He was wounded for our transgressions... and with his stripes we are healed,"[1567] and concludes with, "He shall see of the travail of his soul, and shall be satisfied: by his knowledge shall my righteous servant justify many."[1568] Christ fulfilled the word, "Thou shalt make his soul an offering for sin,"[1569] therefore to behold the Lamb is to observe the science of the true and full sin offering for spiritual error, and to also embrace the fact that He is now Governor over humanity being joined to it in life, death, and resurrection; "to this end Christ both died, and rose, and revived, that he might be Lord both of the dead and living."[1570] For "in all things it behoved him to be made like unto his brethren, that he might be a merciful and faithful high priest in things pertaining to God, to make reconciliation for the sins of the people."[1571]

9. We are living under "the time of reformation."[1572] How much longer must it be until professed believers observe Him as He is? Says the living House of heaven's Christ, "We shall be satisfied with the goodness of thy house, even of thy holy temple,"[1573] therefore how long should it be until there is unadulterated intercourse with the living God from out of this Building? No blessing falls into the soul's temple

---

1563 Isaiah 32:1-3
1564 Isaiah 40:9
1565 Isaiah 33:20,21
1566 Isaiah 53:3
1567 Isaiah 53:5
1568 Isaiah 53:11
1569 Isaiah 53:10
1570 Romans 14:9
1571 Hebrews 2:17
1572 Hebrews 9:10
1573 Psalms 65:4

unless the spirit should be translated from earth to heaven, for it is revealed, "Who hath blessed us with all spiritual blessings in heavenly places in Christ."[1574] The doctrine of Christ is not without the counsel of the Places of Christ and of God, for again the LORD God says, "My people shall dwell in a peaceable habitation, and in sure dwellings, and in quiet resting places."[1575] That peaceable habitation is in "the city of the living God, the heavenly Jerusalem."[1576] These sure plural dwellings and resting places are even the heavenly places, the two Apartments within the Temple of God; the Holy and the Most Holy Place; wherein Christ is High Priest, and wherein we see "Jesus the mediator of the new covenant."[1577]

10. By our active faith in His counsel of soul recovery, the Father will have "translated us into the kingdom of his dear Son,"[1578] wherein is "the general assembly and church of the firstborn, which are written in heaven."[1579] It is to this assembly that the believer should ultimately care to hold faithful membership. Wherefore "let God be true, but every man a liar,"[1580] for it is time to observe the charge, "Behold and study the Lamb," because the time is not afar off when the Jews who are not Jews should again say, "Crucify him, crucify him."[1581] Then it is "that they should make an image to the beast, which had the wound by a sword, and did live,"[1582] and the counsel should again become relevant, "Whosoever transgresseth, and abideth not in the doctrine of Christ, hath not God."[1583]

11. There will soon come a time when the doctrine of Christ will be crucified; when the body of the LORD knowledge will again be openly disrespected. For a failed attempt to know Him, due to a fear linked

---

1574 Ephesians 1:3
1575 Isaiah 32:18
1576 Hebrews 12:22
1577 Hebrews 12:24
1578 Colossians 1:13
1579 Hebrews 12:23
1580 Romans 3:4
1581 Luke 23:21
1582 Revelation 13:14
1583 2 John 1:9

with some stubborn imagination developed by the heart, them that should have known Him during this blessed and quiet period of stillness will reject Him at that time, along with the others "which say they are Jews, and are not, but are the synagogue of Satan."[1584] Now is the time to know the LORD and His Lord. Before "the land of Egypt shall not escape,"[1585] before the king of the north "shall enter also into the glorious land"[1586] by way of an image; and this image test being that test for the Spirit's converts to heaven's will; it is now that every professing believer should soberly know the reason for their faith intellectually, that spiritually they may discern the living God and His living Christ by the living Spirit, as opposed to that which is not God and "sensual, having not the Spirit."[1587]

12. The eye of faith should independently dwell on the full Faith of the Spirit, for before national apostasy should plague the earth, there must first come an open transgression of the doctrine of Christ. The soul temple needs to know that it has an Advocate before the LORD God's infinite throne, and the heart and spirit need to know that there is health for personal error, and not just health, but a resting Place for all who would accept the fact of their cancer for treatment. Christ "is gone into heaven, and is on the right hand of God; angels and authorities and powers being made subject unto him,"[1588] and it is time to hear, "Christ hath redeemed us from the curse of the law, being made a curse for us."[1589]

13. That written of Aaron has ceased and expanded that we may pick up ourselves in the blessed promises and divine power of God to regulate and to re-educate our conversation. Says our Priest, "All power is given unto me in heaven and in earth,"[1590] for the Father "hath in these last days spoken unto us by his Son";[1591] that is, by the Faith of

---

1584 Revelation 2:9
1585 Daniel 11:42
1586 Daniel 11:41
1587 Jude 1:19
1588 1 Peter 3:22
1589 Galatians 3:13
1590 Matthew 28:18
1591 Hebrews 1:2

Jesus; which is why it says of the present reformer, "The law of truth was in his mouth."[1592] This law of truth is of "peace and equity,"[1593] even liberty and rest with justice and righteousness, for this law is without doubt "the law of Christ"[1594] grounded in "the law of faith"[1595] maintained by a "spirit of faith,"[1596] bearing witness to "the law of the Spirit of life in Christ"[1597] to bring every believer to the same confession: "I delight in the law of God after the inward man."[1598] Thus, at this time the counsel is, "The mystery of God should be finished,"[1599] and, "Here are they that keep the commandments of God, and the faith of Jesus."[1600]

1592 Malachi 2:6
1593 Malachi 2:6
1594 Galatians 6:2
1595 Romans 3:27
1596 2 Corinthians 4:13
1597 Romans 8:2
1598 Romans 7:22
1599 Revelation 10:7
1600 Revelation 14:12

18

Your Most Holy Faith

1. "But ye, beloved, building up yourselves on your most holy faith, praying in the Holy Ghost, keep yourselves in the love of God, looking for the mercy of our Lord Jesus Christ unto eternal life."[1601]

2. The counsel of the apostle is for the believer is to build up their most holy faith, and if indeed our faith is to be most holy, it is that it must take on the sentiment, "Them that have obtained like precious faith with us through the righteousness of God and our Saviour Jesus Christ."[1602] To observe this instruction is to hear the counsel, "Earnestly contend for the faith which was once delivered to the saints,"[1603] for the faith "spoken before by the holy prophets, and of the commandment"[1604] "by the Lord, and was confirmed unto us by them that heard him,"[1605] was a most holy or benevolent law and doctrine, leaving it that the only way to obtain a knowledge of this Faith would be to observe the foundation of this Faith, as it says, "Most holy." This Faith secures to the believer both the righteousness of God and the virtue of Christ being

---

1601   Jude 1:20,21
1602   2 Peter 1:1
1603   Jude 1:3
1604   2 Peter 3:2
1605   Hebrews 2:3

found in the love of God, wherein rests the mercy of the LORD within His Holy Ghost.

3. It is apparent that the apostle would mention a most holy faith for the purpose of sending the believer to the Place that is most holy to the LORD, "for therein is the righteousness of God revealed from faith to faith."[1606] It is for this reason that we read how it was written of old, "Thou shalt make a vail of blue, and purple, and scarlet, and fine twined linen of cunning work: with cher'ubims shall it be made: and thou shalt hang it upon four pillars of shit'tim wood overlaid with gold: their hooks shall be of gold, upon the four sockets of silver. And thou shalt hang up the vail under the taches, that thou mayest bring in thither within the vail the ark of the testimony: and the vail shall divide unto you between the holy place and the most holy. And thou shalt put the mercy seat upon the ark of the testimony in the most holy place."[1607]

4. Again, "The priests brought in the ark of the covenant of the LORD unto his place, to the oracle of the house, into the most holy place, even under the wings of the cher'ubims: for the cher'ubims spread forth their wings over the place of the ark, and the cher'ubims covered the ark and the staves thereof above...There was nothing in the ark save the two tables which Moses put therein at Ho'reb, when the LORD made a covenant with the children of Israel, when they came out of Egypt."[1608]

5. The Most Holy Place "had the golden censer, and the ark of the covenant overlaid round about with gold, wherein was the golden pot that had man'na, and Aaron's rod that budded, and the tables of the covenant; and over it the cheru'bims of glory shadowing the mercyseat,"[1609] for herein we find ourselves confronted with that Faith delivered to them "of whom the world was not worthy."[1610]

6. John of old declared, "Study the Lamb," for he taught his hearers, "Seventy weeks are determined upon thy people and upon thy

---

1606 Romans 1:17
1607 Exodus 26:32-34
1608 2 Chronicles 5:7-10
1609 Hebrews 9:4,5
1610 Hebrews 11:38

holy city, to finish the transgression, and to make an end of sins, and to make reconciliation for iniquity, and to bring in everlasting righteousness, and to seal up the vision and prophecy, and to anoint the most Holy."[1611]

7. Now, John said, "I knew him not: but he that sent me to baptize with water, the same said unto me, Upon whom thou shalt see the Spirit descending, and remaining on him, the same is he which baptizeth with the Holy Ghost. And I saw, and bare record that this is the Son of God."[1612]

8. It was because of this vision, and because of this confirmation from the voice of God, that John knew that the saying was presently true, "Know therefore and understand, that from the going forth of the commandment to restore and to build Jerusalem unto the Messi'ah the Prince shall be seven weeks, and threescore and two weeks... After threescore and two weeks shall Messi'ah be cut off, but not for himself,"[1613] for which cause it is written, "He was wounded for our transgressions."[1614] As John calculated the prophetic time given to Daniel, he announced, "Take knowledge the Lamb's movements," and his calculations were made certain by this same Lamb and Son of God, who confirmed, "The time is fulfilled, and the kingdom of God is at hand."[1615]

9. The space of time given to Israel from the full restoration of Jerusalem until Christ should begin His mission was fulfilled at His baptism, yet it is written, "He was cut off out of the land of the living,"[1616] fulfilling the prophecy, "He shall confirm the covenant with many for one week: and in the midst of the week he shall cause the sacrifice and the oblation to cease."[1617] As a week is seven days, and as days are a symbol of years in prophecy,[1618] so Christ's ministry lasted seven years,

---

1611 Daniel 9:24
1612 John 1:33,34
1613 Daniel 9:25,26
1614 Isaiah 53:5
1615 Mark 1:15
1616 Isaiah 53:8
1617 Daniel 9:27
1618 Numbers 14:34

"which at the first began to be spoken by the Lord, and was confirmed unto us by them that heard him."[1619] Christ spent three and a half years physically doing the work of His Father, and then for another three and a half years afterwards, after He had passed from the earth and into heaven to assume His new office, His apostles finished the work among the Jews until it was told them, "It was necessary that the word of God should first have been spoken to you: but seeing ye put it from you, and judge yourselves unworthy of everlasting life, lo, we turn to the Gentiles."[1620]

10. From this point forward, Christ was to be a minister of the first Apartment of the Temple in heaven, the Holy Place. This is why when John is taken in vision to receive the revelation of the earth's ecclesiastical history, he writes, "I turned to see the voice that spake with me. And being turned, I saw seven golden candlesticks; and in the midst of the seven candlesticks one like unto the Son of man."[1621] At this time of John's vision, Christ is a minister of the first heavenly Apartment, "the first, wherein was the candlestick, and the table, and the shewbread; which is called the sanctuary."[1622] This is the Place where Christ was to be found for a long period of time, but there would come a time when those longs days would be ended, and then it would be fulfilled, "Blessed is he that waiteth, and cometh to the thousand three hundred and five and thirty days."[1623]

11. The full time containing the restoration of Jerusalem, the appearing and death of Christ, and the time that should progress to the blessed ending of the long days, the complete essence of this prophecy is found in the saying, "Unto two thousand three hundred days; then shall the sanctuary be cleansed."[1624] As days are a symbol for years,[1625] the full length of the prophecy was 2300 years, for at the end of these years a change would occur in the House of God, which change neither

---

1619 Hebrews 2:3
1620 Acts 13:46
1621 Revelation 1:12,13
1622 Hebrews 9:2
1623 Daniel 12:12
1624 Daniel 8:14
1625 Ezekiel 4:6

John nor Paul knew of, for even Paul confesses, "And after the second veil, the tabernacle which is called the Holiest of all";[1626] "of which we cannot now speak particularly."[1627] Nevertheless, "into the second went the high priest alone once every year, not without blood, which he offered for himself, and for the errors of the people: the Holy Ghost this signifying, that the way into the holiest of all was not yet made manifest, while as the first tabernacle was yet standing."[1628]

12. Because Christ ascended to be that Son and Priest over the true House of God in heaven, it is that He too maintains the same form of the priesthood that was anciently on earth. The LORD instructed Moses concerning the tabernacle in the wilderness, "According to all that I shew thee, after the pattern of the tabernacle, and the pattern of all the instruments thereof, even so shall ye make it."[1629] All these things did "serve unto the example and shadow of heavenly things, as Moses was admonished of God when he was about to make the tabernacle,"[1630] for they truly were "a shadow of things to come; but the body is of Christ."[1631] The economy of old, being a shadow of things to come, did stand "until the time of reformation,"[1632] until service to God should no more be temporal and literal but rather ultimately spiritual and eternal, "for Christ is not entered into the holy places made with hands, which are the figures of the true; but into heaven itself, now to appear in the presence of God for us."[1633]

13. Now when Christ ascended into heaven from the first disciples, it was told them, "Why stand ye gazing up into heaven? this same Jesus, which is taken up from you into heaven, shall so come in like manner as ye have seen him go into heaven."[1634] Christ "was taken up; and a

---

1626 Hebrews 9:3
1627 Hebrews 9:5
1628 Hebrews 9:7,8
1629 Exodus 25:9
1630 Hebrews 8:5
1631 Colossians 2:17
1632 Hebrews 9:10
1633 Hebrews 9:24
1634 Acts 1:11

cloud received him out of their sight";[1635] and it was told them, "He will return in like manner,"[1636] for at the end of the twenty-three hundred years the word was fulfilled, "The Son of man came with the clouds of heaven, and came to the Ancient of days."[1637] As He went up, so He would come again, and this word being misinterpreted for His second descent to the earth in violent royal glory, when in reality it would be fulfilled, "The Lord, whom ye seek, shall suddenly come to his temple, even the messenger of the covenant, whom ye delight in: behold, he shall come."[1638]

14. Christ did not come to the physical earth at the end of the days, and He could not have done such a thing. The true image must follow the figure as much as the figure follows the true. That of old was a shadow of heavenly things to come, and "Christ being come an high priest of good things to come"[1639] means that He is the true fulfillment of the old representative pattern of perfection. Christ must have a space of time allotted to Him for the purpose of executing those things pertaining to God in both Apartments of the House of God. Scripture plainly confesses that Christ will come to His Temple at the end of the days, but the question is, which Temple? Within the Temple were two rooms of labor, therefore one office should close and another should open, which is why at the end of the days, just as He had before said on earth, "The time is fulfilled," from heaven He said to His then disciples on earth, "There should be time no longer."[1640] "I have set before thee an open door, and no man can shut it."[1641]

15. It was at this time that Christ's office in the Holy Place ended, yet a new door of hope was opened to the one born of faith, as it says, "The temple of God was opened in heaven, and there was seen in his temple the ark of his testament."[1642] From this point forward, from the

---

1635   Acts 1:9
1636   Acts 1:11
1637   Daniel 7:13
1638   Malachi 3:1
1639   Hebrews 9:11
1640   Revelation 10:6
1641   Revelation 3:8
1642   Revelation 11:19

time of the new and final ministration of Christ, which transpires within "the temple of the tabernacle of the testimony in heaven";[1643] the Most Holy Apartment; until the complete end of this earth, the true Faith of the Spirit's host is to come from out of this Place of His current ministration. Christ is not in the Holy Place anymore, but is currently fulfilling the saying, "Into the second went the high priest alone once every year,"[1644] for this ministration covers that period of time known as the Day of Atonement, of which it says, "On that day shall the priest make an atonement for you, to cleanse you, that ye may be clean from all your sins before the LORD."[1645]

16. The most holy faith of the seed of Christ will be built up on the foundation of His doctrine, for "here are they that keep the commandments of God, and the faith of Jesus."[1646] What is observed in the second Apartment is most crucial for the health of the soul temple of every reformer, for the apostle wrote concerning the strengthening of personal faith: "Keep yourselves in the love of God, looking for the mercy of our Lord Jesus Christ unto eternal life."[1647] The love of God is in reality the law of Christ. Diligently studying and applying to the precepts of this doctrine provokes showers of mercy onto the spirit of the mind, as it says, "Hope to the end for the grace that is to be brought unto you at the revelation of Jesus Christ."[1648] This revelation of Christ is "the mystery of God, and of the Father, and of Christ; in whom are hid all treasures of wisdom and knowledge";[1649] made plain to the mental and moral faculties of our being, and obedience to this law of the Father's wisdom will procure mercy, or grace, which is to perfect in us a heart and mind for the LORD's eternal Country, even as the same sentiment is said in another way, "So might grace reign through righteousness unto eternal life."[1650]

1643   Revelation 15:5
1644   Hebrews 9:7
1645   Leviticus 16:30
1646   Revelation 14:12
1647   Jude 1:21
1648   1 Peter 1:13
1649   Colossians 2:2,3
1650   Romans 5:21

17. Obedience to the precepts of the doctrine of Christ will confer to the account of the believer the medicine of grace for the defects of the character, and for unlimited strength concerning the reconstruction of our mental and moral powers. The grace of God is "the gift of righteousness,"[1651] encouraging "justification of life,"[1652] which is why this substance is called, "The grace of life,"[1653] and why concerning grace the apostle wrote, "According to his mercy he saved us, by the washing of regeneration, and renewing of the Holy Ghost."[1654] This formula for the recovery of man we find in the second Apartment, for it says, "Wherein was the golden pot that had man'na, and Aaron's rod that budded"[1655] with also "the mercyseat"[1656] above "the tables of the covenant."[1657] In order for any thing to bud it needs rain, and this is why Paul confessed, "He did good, and gave us rain from heaven, and fruitful seasons, filling our hearts with food,"[1658] and, "Who hath blessed us with all spiritual blessings in heavenly places."[1659] Herein it is understood that our recovery cannot escape the science of heaven's second room.

18. The gospel of God is a law of mercy, for Christ declared, "He hath anointed me to preach the gospel to the poor; he hath sent me to heal the brokenhearted, to preach deliverance to the captives, and recovering of sight to the blind, to set at liberty them that are bruised, to preach the acceptable year of the Lord."[1660] We are living in the acceptable year of the LORD's Faith, and this year will not end until He should say so. In this year, the Father would "have all men to be saved, and to come unto the knowledge of the truth,"[1661] "that we may lead a quiet and peaceable life in all godliness and honesty. For this

---

1651 Romans 5:17
1652 Romans 5:18
1653 1 Peter 3:7
1654 Titus 3:5
1655 Hebrews 9:4
1656 Hebrews 8:5
1657 Hebrews 9:4
1658 Acts 14:17
1659 Ephesians 1:3
1660 Luke 4:18,19
1661 1 Timothy 2:4

is good and acceptable in the sight of God."[1662] It is for this cause that the believer should turn his or her mind "to the faith of God's elect, and the acknowledging of the truth which is after godliness,"[1663] for the law of Christ is after "the doctrine which is according to godliness,"[1664] that is, "Christ in you, the hope of glory."[1665] This is why at the end of the prophetic years, as He began the final phase of His ministry, Christ also said, "The mystery of God should be finished,"[1666] for the materials in the Most Holy are ordained to finalize the image of God in the believing soul temple of the spirit.

19. This most holy law of Jesus cannot exist without that in the Most Holy Room that both He and the LORD His Father occupy. The sight of the ark of God is a representation of what the faithful now behold, and as what is in the ark is to be written in the soul temple, the One before the ark and clothed in High Priestly garments has sprinkled His blood on the mercy seat, letting the observer know that if they would benefit from Him in this Place, His blood with the Spirit of His grace must be accepted. His purpose is "in bringing many sons unto glory,"[1667] for He suffered Himself to death "that he might bring us to God."[1668] By the Faith of Christ, the believer will be brought into close relations with both Christ and God, which is why Christ says, "If a man love me, he will keep my words: and my Father will love him, and we will come unto him, and make our abode with him."[1669]

20. Such honest communion with God's Lord will allow the saying to be fulfilled in the believer, "Sanctified by God the Father, and preserved in Jesus Christ."[1670] The believer is to be hidden in Christ from consistently applying His words to their heart, and this consistency upheld by the power of the human will joined to the creative

---

1662 1 Timothy 2:3
1663 Titus 1:2
1664 1 Timothy 6:3
1665 Colossians 1:27
1666 Revelation 10:7
1667 Hebrews 2:10
1668 1 Peter 3:18
1669 John 14:23
1670 Jude 1:1

power of God's grace by faith, as it says, "I laboured more abundantly than they all: yet not I, but the grace of God which was with me."[1671] The believer is to be sanctified by the Father while kept alive in and by the law of His Son, and the reality of the fact is as it says, "Sanctified by the Holy Ghost,"[1672] that is, "By the power of the Spirit of God."[1673] It is because the Spirit houses the grace of God that it is called, "The Spirit of grace,"[1674] thus the counsel is, "Be filled with the Spirit,"[1675] or rather, "Be filled with all the fullness of God."[1676] Therefore by "the fullness of the blessing of the gospel of Christ"[1677] the believer is to confess, "I delight in the law of God after the inward man."[1678]

21. Every instrument surrounding the ark of God is at this time an instructor to the reformer, saying, "Speak the mystery of Christ."[1679] The only way that one may speak the mystery of Christ; that is, "the mystery of godliness"[1680] emphasizing how that "God was manifest in the flesh";[1681] is to allow the mind to masticate the commandment that flows from out of the Spirit's second Room, counseling, "Ye shall afflict your souls, and offer an offering made by fire unto the LORD. And ye shall do no work in that same day."[1682] The fact that no work should be done should send the mind to the counsel, "To him that worketh not, but believeth on him that justifieth the ungodly, his faith is counted for righteousness,"[1683] for herein is the science behind the law of Christ concerning justification by faith in the merits of His blood, and as He with His own blood did sprinkle the mercy seat which is above the

---

1671   1 Corinthians 15:10
1672   Romans 15:16
1673   Romans 15:19
1674   Hebrews 10:29
1675   Ephesians 5:18
1676   Ephesians 3:19
1677   Romans 15:29
1678   Romans 7:22
1679   Colossians 4:3
1680   1 Timothy 3:16
1681   1 Timothy 3:16
1682   Leviticus 23:27,28
1683   Romans 4:5

immutable commandments of God,[1684] the counsel has become true without any doubt, "God hath from the beginning chosen you to salvation through sanctification of the Spirit and belief of the truth."[1685]

22. "Through sanctification of the Spirit, unto obedience and sprinkling of the blood of Jesus Christ,"[1686] the believer is to have every precept of God written in the temple of the spirit of the mind by "the Spirit of the living God; not in tables of stone, but in fleshly tables of the heart."[1687] The most holy faith of the believer is found in observing both the commandments of God and the Faith of His Son, and that observation had from obeying the doctrine of Christ through the power of His Spirit. This is why it says, "He that hath the Son hath life,"[1688] because it is known, "The Spirit is life,"[1689] for within the Spirit is the grace of life that every faithful believer may know, "Unto you it is given in the behalf of Christ, not only to believe on him, but also to suffer for his sake,"[1690] which is why our LORD today says, "Offer an offering made by fire."[1691] At this lot for the believer, our Priest counsels, "Every one shall be with salted fire,"[1692] for it is written, "He shall baptize with the Holy Ghost, and with fire."[1693]

23. Not one soul confessing Christ will, at this time, pass by Him without willingly suffering inward fire, for He says, "Behold, I will melt them, and try them."[1694] The great joy of the religion of Christ is in knowing that "even Christ pleased not himself,"[1695] "but made himself of no reputation...and being found in fashion as a man, he humbled himself, and became obedient unto death."[1696] As "the love of Christ

---

1684 Leviticus 16:14
1685 2 Thessalonians 2:13
1686 1 Peter 1:2
1687 2 Corinthians 3:3
1688 1 John 5:12
1689 Romans 8:10
1690 Philippians 1:29
1691 Leviticus 23:27
1692 Mark 9:49
1693 Matthew 3:10
1694 Jeremiah 9:7
1695 Romans 15:3
1696 Philippians 2:7,8

constraineth us,"[1697] it is that the religion's philosophy will become, "He died for all, that they which live should not henceforth live unto themselves, but unto him which died for them, and rose again."[1698] From experiencing the joy of humility, the spirit will willingly announce to the heart, "Die daily,"[1699] even because it longs to fulfill the charge, "If any man will come after me, let him deny himself, and take up his cross daily, and follow me."[1700] From consistently dividing and applying self to the Spirit's law, the spirit will confess to the members of the heart, "We would see Jesus,"[1701] and, "I may know him."[1702]

24. It is this mind of devotion that will receive full health only in the Room of Christ's present administration. The Faith of the believer can only be that most holy Faith ordained by God Himself, and that Faith is found in the Apartment announcing the revelation of the fact "of the light of the knowledge of the glory of God in the face of Jesus."[1703] Herein we are made to understand that the immutable precepts of God cannot be separated from the Faith of Christ, nor can the Faith of Christ achieve its purpose in Adam's soul without fully embracing the Ten Commandments of God. This is the most holy Faith that every believer is to be kept in by the Holy Ghost, as it says, "Who are kept by the power of God through faith unto salvation."[1704]

25. That "promise of life which is in Christ"[1705] is "the grace that is in Christ,"[1706] and this grace is "the salvation which is in Christ,"[1707] for it says, "The grace of God bringeth salvation."[1708] This salvation is for the recovery of the mental and moral faculties to sustain an eternal setting in a sinless atmosphere to continue this very work in the sight of God

---

1697 2 Corinthians 5:14
1698 2 Corinthians 5:15
1699 1 Corinthians 15:31
1700 Luke 9:23
1701 John 12:21
1702 Philippians 3:10
1703 2 Corinthians 4:6
1704 1 Peter 1:5
1705 2 Timothy 1:2
1706 2 Timothy 2:1
1707 2 Timothy 2:10
1708 Titus 2:11

and of angels, yet the work of recovery begins only by a diligent faith in that law explaining the full will and intention of the Son of God. For this cause, the counsel for our day is, "Do no work,"[1709] or rather, "Quit self-righteousness and break off the religious errors of your heart, with their traditional superstitions, by the wisdom and power of His Son's Spirit." The counsel is, "Worship God in the spirit, and have no confidence in the flesh";[1710] "put ye on the Lord Jesus Christ, and make not provision for the flesh";[1711] for through "the righteousness which is by faith,"[1712] it is to be fulfilled, "Great peace have they which love thy law,"[1713] which is why it says, "Grace and peace be multiplied unto you through the knowledge of God, and of Jesus our Lord, according as his divine power hath given unto us all things that pertain to life and godliness."[1714] Again, let us "grow in grace, and in the knowledge of our Lord and Saviour Jesus Christ."[1715]

1709 Leviticus 23:28
1710 Philippians 3:3
1711 Romans 13:14
1712 Hebrews 11:7
1713 Psalms 129:165
1714 2 Peter 1:2,3
1715 1 Peter 3:18

19

The Current Cleansing

1. "And he said unto me, Unto two thousand and three hundred days; then shall the sanctuary be cleansed."[1716] "And there was given me a reed like unto a rod: and the angel stood, saying, Rise, and measure the temple of God, and the altar, and them that worship therein. But the court which is without the temple leave out, and measure it not; for it is given unto the Gentiles."[1717]

2. The visions of Daniel and John harmoniously follow one another to bear fruit of the fact of the current heavenly position of God's Man. That which the Father "wrought in Christ, when he raised him from the dead, and set him at his own right hand,"[1718] became for us the "more excellent ministry"[1719] of "the Son, who is consecrated for evermore."[1720] Christ is the LORD's Priest "in the heavenly places,"[1721] not of "the holy places made with hands, which are the figures of the true; but

---

1716 Daniel 8:13
1717 Revelation 11:1,2
1718 Ephesians 1:20
1719 Hebrews 8:6
1720 Hebrews 7:28
1721 Ephesians 1:20

into heaven itself."[1722] Because the law of Aaron maintained a shadow of "good things to come, and not the very image of the things,"[1723] "in the dispensation of the fulness of times"[1724] it would be that Christ should become "a minister of the sanctuary, and of the true tabernacle, which the Lord pitched, and not man."[1725] It is for this reason that "our conversation is in heaven,"[1726] for it is in the Spirit's Building that every believer shares "such an high priest, who is set on the right hand of the throne of the Majesty in the heavens."[1727]

3. Now this word, "Until twenty three hundred days, and then will the temple be cleansed,"[1728] exposes the fact that a new vocation should arise in the Temple of heaven at the end of those days, or rather, at the end of those years. At the time of the first apostles, after "he was parted from them, and carried into heaven,"[1729] Christ was He who "entereth into that within the veil."[1730] This veil Paul mentions was not that veil as stated of old, as it says, "The vail shall divide unto you between the holy place and the most holy,"[1731] and, "The vail before the mercy seat, which is upon the ark,"[1732] but was rather "the hanging for the tabernacle door,"[1733] the first Apartment "which is called the sanctuary."[1734] From His ascension, until the times and season should warrant a fulfillment of the twenty three hundred prophesied years, which prophecy began at the word, "Seventy weeks are determined,"[1735] Christ would spend His entire time in "the first tabernacle, accomplishing the service of God."[1736]

1722 Hebrews 9:24
1723 Hebrews 10:1
1724 Ephesians 1:10
1725 Hebrews 8:2
1726 Philippians 3:20
1727 Hebrews 8:1
1728 Daniel 8:14
1729 Luke 24:51
1730 Hebrews 6:19
1731 Exodus 26:33
1732 Leviticus 16:2
1733 Exodus 39:38
1734 Hebrews 9:2
1735 Daniel 9:24
1736 Hebrews 9:6

4. As the ancient priesthood of Israel displayed that which was of a better hope and substance to come, so Christ should not remain in the first tabernacle for ever. It was told Moses, "Speak unto Aaron thy brother, that he come not at all times into the holy place within the vail before the mercy seat,"[1737] for "into the second went the high priest alone once every year, not without blood, which he offered for himself, and for the errors of the people."[1738] On the day that the priest should enter into the second Place, it was said, "On that day shall the priest make an atonement for you, to cleanse you."[1739] "It is a day of atonement, to make an atonement for you before the LORD your God."[1740] At the end of the twenty three hundred years, a new day would commence with a new labor and ministration for the LORD of heaven, and for them on earth in communion with the heavenly House of God. That work for Christ's congregation is defined by the saying, "Measure the temple of God,"[1741] for to measure is to scrutinize, which is why at this time of chastening the word is fulfilled, "The hour of his judgment is come."[1742]

5. The moment that Christ ceased His work in the Holy Place, He said to His followers, "I have set before thee an open door."[1743] When John had at first said, "I saw seven golden candlesticks,"[1744] he was taken into the first Apartment when first entered into vision; for Christ's office in John's day was within the first Place of the Temple; yet there would come a time when John should declare, "The temple of God was opened in heaven, and there was seen in his temple the ark of his testament,"[1745] John representing them that should be alive at the time of Christ's new position before His LORD. This change of ministration is defined by the saying, "The Son of man came...to the Ancient

---

1737 Leviticus 16:2
1738 Hebrews 9:7
1739 Leviticus 16:30
1740 Leviticus 23:28
1741 Revelation 11:1
1742 Revelation 14:7
1743 Revelation 3:8
1744 Revelation 1:12
1745 Revelation 11:19

of days,"[1746] and, "The Lord, whom ye seek, shall suddenly come to his temple,"[1747] for at this time "the judgment was set, and the books were open,"[1748] thus the word was fulfilled, "The hour of his judgment is come."[1749]

6. The coming of Christ to His Temple is the coming of Christ as High Priest to "the temple of the tabernacle of the testimony in heaven,"[1750] "the tabernacle which is called the Holiest of all."[1751] For over eighteen hundred years, Christ would serve His believers from out of the first tabernacle of the Temple, yet this ministration comes with an expiration date, and at the end of this date, one phase of His mediation would decay and another would blossom to bear the saying, "The mystery of God should be finished."[1752] The Sanctuary would be cleansed by Christ our High Priest, the books of the faithful believers would be revised to conclude who should be worthy of the kingdom of glory, and this revision of character and faith is defined by as investigative judgment against the righteous dead until it should be time to judge the righteous that are alive.

7. Only the righteous are judged in the investigative judgment, and this is known from how it is said, "God judgeth the righteous."[1753] It is the LORD who is currently "justifying the righteous, to give him according to his righteousness,"[1754] which is why this fact of the Faith of Jesus must be heard and observed: "We might be justified by the faith of Christ."[1755] Wherefore "according to the truth of the gospel,"[1756] "through the Spirit wait for the hope of righteousness by faith."[1757] This is why the Spirit told John to measure the Temple. Within heaven's

---

1746 Daniel 7:13
1747 Malachi 3:1
1748 Daniel 7:10
1749 Revelation 7:14
1750 Revelation 15:5
1751 Hebrews 9:3
1752 Revelation 10:7
1753 Psalms 7:11
1754 1 Kings 8:32
1755 Galatians 2:16
1756 Galatians 2:14
1757 Galatians 5:5

assembly are "the spirits of just men made perfect"[1758] along with them holding "the spirit that now worketh in the children of disobedient."[1759] There must be an investigation between the wheat and the tare, between them made perfect through faith in the law and creative power of God's Priest by a living experience in the joys and sufferings of His voice, and "them which glory in appearance, and not in heart,"[1760] who confess, "Ye now made perfect by the flesh."[1761]

8. The work of the investigative judgment is the fulfillment of the parable, "The king came in to see the guests."[1762] "He that hath the bride is the bridegroom,"[1763] and when Christ commenced the second phase of His work, the saying was fulfilled, "Behold, the bridegroom cometh."[1764] The final appearing of Christ to this earth, to receive the citizens of His kingdom for the new earth under new heavens, will be "when he will return from the wedding,"[1765] yet Christ coming to the second Apartment was Him receiving "dominion, and glory, and a kingdom,"[1766] even "the bride, the Lamb's wife," "that great city, the holy Jerusalem."[1767]

9. The guests of a wedding are neither the bridegroom nor the bride. The people of God who by faith enter into the second Room with Christ are as guests at a spiritual wedding within the spiritual kingdom of God and of Christ. The only way that Christ will ever have a people to claim at His appearing is if they remain joined to Him at His wedding while wearing "the wedding garment"[1768] given them, even the righteousness of His name. Hence the cleansing of the Sanctuary should not only be an official removing or pardoning of sin from the righteous, but of also a separation between the sinners and unbelievers

---

1758   Hebrews 12:23
1759   Ephesians 2:2
1760   2 Corinthians 5:12
1761   Galatians 3:3
1762   Matthew 22:11
1763   John 3:29
1764   Matthew 25:6
1765   Luke 12:36
1766   Daniel 7:14
1767   Revelation 21:10
1768   Matthew 22:11

of the House of God, as He says, "I judge between cattle and cattle, between the rams and the goats,"[1769] and, "I will judge between the fat cattle and between the lean cattle."[1770]

10. It is said, "Oxen might plow,"[1771] for "cattle" are a symbol of a servants or stewards. Upon leaving Egypt, Moses said, "Our cattle also shall go with us...for thereof must we take to serve the LORD our God,"[1772] for the judgment of cattle is as the Spirit's Faith judging His servants, and as rams and goats are a symbol of pride; as it says, "I saw the ram pushing,"[1773] and, "The he goat waxed very great";[1774] so His commandment is separating "the unjust unto the day of judgment."[1775] The fat cattle are not they outside of the LORD's Church, for "judgment must begin at the house of God."[1776] These are them "that walk after the flesh in the lust of uncleanness, and despise government,"[1777] or as our Priest says, "Those mine enemies, which would not that I should reign over them."[1778] Such "are murmurers, complainers,"[1779] "giving themselves over to fornication, and going after strange flesh"[1780] while "they profess that they know God."[1781] These will not surrender to the Spirit's righteousness "to retain God in their knowledge,"[1782] for because of fear and a failure to exercise faith by a spirit of unbelief, "being led away with the error of the wicked,"[1783] they "will not endure sound doctrine."[1784]

1769   Ezekiel 34:17
1770   Ezekiel 34:20
1771   1 Samuel 14:14
1772   Exodus 10:26
1773   Daniel 8:4
1774   Daniel 8:8
1775   2 Peter 2:9
1776   1 Peter 4:17
1777   2 Peter 2:10
1778   Luke 19:27
1779   Jude 1:16
1780   Jude 1:7
1781   Titus 1:16
1782   Romans 1:28
1783   2 Peter 3:17
1784   2 Timothy 4:3

11. "Because they received not the love of the truth, that they might be saved,"[1785] that they might endure the process of a moral recovery through "the knowledge of his will in all wisdom and spiritual understanding,"[1786] the fat cattle who are the rams and the goats fulfill the word, "The full soul."[1787] "They that are such serve not our Lord Jesus Christ, but their own belly."[1788] "They are the enemies of the cross (the experience) of Christ (the law of Christ's name): whose end is destruction, whose God is their belly, and whose glory is in their shame."[1789] Yet of that other class, it is said, "The righteous, and the wise, and their works, are in the hand of God."[1790]

12. "To the hungry soul every bitter thing is sweet,"[1791] for these have accepted the counsel, "Buy of me...and anoint thine eyes,"[1792] therefore concerning them that confess, "To die is gain,"[1793] it is promised, "Blessed are they which do hunger and thirst after righteousness: for they shall be filled."[1794] These are them that confess, "I count all things but loss for the excellency of the knowledge of Christ"[1795] "that I may know him."[1796] These are them "that have hazarded their lives for the name of our Lord,"[1797] for they have accepted this fact concerning a right character and personal religion: "It was perfect through my comeliness, which I had put upon thee, saith the Lord GOD."[1798]

13. Thus, a cleansing of the Spirit's House is ordained for the LORD to understand who is truly loyal to His Faith and to His ten immutable laws, which Faith and Law will be the ground that fills the atmosphere

---

1785   2 Thessalonians 2:10
1786   Colossians 1:9
1787   Proverbs 27:7
1788   Romans 16:18
1789   Philippians 3:18,19
1790   Ecclesiastes 9:1
1791   Proverbs 27:7
1792   Revelation 3:18
1793   Philippians 1:21
1794   Matthew 5:6
1795   Philippians 3:8
1796   Philippians 3:10
1797   Acts 15:26
1798   Ezekiel 16:14

of His new earth and heaven. There is a call at this time to observe the current Place of Christ's mediation, for as He is in the second Place with the Father and before that ark holding His Ten Commandments, it serves the one professing Christ to examine themselves according to the vision given John of the second Room in heaven. This is why it says, "Fear God, and give glory to him."[1799] "Worship him that made heaven, and earth, and the sea, and the fountains of waters";[1800] "for the hour of his judgment is come."[1801]

14. The vision of the Most Holy Apartment in heaven is a call for the believer to honor "the great God that formed all things."[1802] In order for one to acknowledge God as Creator, one must "commit the keeping of their souls to him in well doing, as unto a faithful Creator."[1803] In order to know God as Creator, one must surrender to His voice and power, which voice holds the same authority that brought all things to be, and which power is that same power that upholds all that was originally spoken. When it is known and accepted that it was "God, who created all things by Jesus Christ,"[1804] who is "the beginning of the creation of God,"[1805] whether it be the beginning of all things or "the beginning of the gospel,"[1806] the mind "renewed in knowledge"[1807] and "created in righteousness and true holiness"[1808] will receive "the sign of circumcision, a seal of the righteousness of the faith,"[1809] which declares, "In six days the LORD made heaven and earth, the sea, and all that in them is, and rested the seventh day: wherefore the LORD blessed the Sabbath day, and hallowed it."[1810]

1799　Revelation 14:7
1800　Revelation 14:7
1801　Revelation 14:7
1802　Proverbs 25:10
1803　1 Peter 4:19
1804　Ephesians 3:9
1805　Revelation 3:14
1806　Philippians 4:15
1807　Colossians 3:10
1808　Ephesians 4:24
1809　Romans 4:11
1810　Exodus 20:11

15. The current Place of God is not without the seal or sign of the living God's Faith flourishing within the person. The sight of the ark sends the mind to that contained within the ark, and "there was nothing in the ark save the two tables of stone, which Moses put there."[1811] Those tables given to Moses are there in heaven's ark, for all things on earth and sanctioned by the Father were "patterns of things in the heavens."[1812] What John saw in vision was the literal establishment of the LORD God, with the literal glory of God shadowing the mercyseat that sat on top of the literal ark of God holding the true copy of the Ten Commandments. "Christ is not entered into the holy places made with hands, which are the figures of the true,"[1813] for when the time should come for Him to declare, "There should be time no longer,"[1814] announcing that the twenty three hundred days, or years, are expired, the true High Priest of God moved from the first Apartment and into the second, in order to make perfect the spirits of men and women justified by faith in His sacrifice to honor one another from honoring the immutable precepts that He died for. It is here in this second Place of God that creation is to begin and finish; that is, the birth of "the new man, which after God is created";[1815] and if this new mind; as it says, "Transformed by the renewing of your mind"[1816] "are changed into the same image";[1817] is to undergo a creation by faith in the Spirit's doctrine, it must now at this time be heard, "We which have believed do enter into rest...For he spake in a certain place of the seventh day on this wise."[1818]

16. Christ is not alone while officiating on behalf of penitent Adam, but now, at this time, Christ stands before the LORD His Father who is examining every one that professes to be servants of His and keepers of His Son's Faith, "counting one by one, to find out

---

1811 1 Kings 8:9
1812 Hebrews 9:23
1813 Hebrews 9:24
1814 Revelation 10:6
1815 Ephesians 4:24
1816 Romans 12:2
1817 2 Corinthians 3:18
1818 Hebrews 4:3,4

the account"[1819] of their faithfulness. As Christ stands before the ark and communicating with His Father, the vision is purposed to send the mind to consider the fact that the doctrine of Christ ministers to the aid of the keeping of every commandment of God, and that one commandment which shines the brightest, illuminating all of the others, being the Sabbath of His seventh day, the Memorial of His power to create the world and the inward parts away from the error they were born in to. For it should be noted, that as of old the priest was counseled, "Take a censer full of burning coals...and put the incense upon the fire before the LORD, that the cloud may cover the mercy seat,"[1820] we see that it is Christ's righteousness "upon the testimony"[1821] that is necessary to acquire in the soul temple that which is contained within the ark.

17. The present cleansing of the Sanctuary is indeed an investigative judgment to cleanse that Temple of the fat ram-like and goat-like cattle from the thin and the lean cattle, for while His obedient servant endures a purification "through sanctification of the Spirit and belief of the truth,"[1822] it is that they must bear the experience recorded: "I have surely heard E'phraim bemoaning himself thus; Thou hast chastised me, and I was chastised, as a bullock unaccustomed to the yoke: turn thou me, and I shall be turned; for thou art the LORD my God. Surely after that I was turned, I repented; and after that I was instructed, I smote upon my thigh: I was ashamed, yea, even confounded, because I did bear the reproach of my youth."[1823] It is for this reason that the charge must be heard at this time, "Ye shall afflict your souls,"[1824] and, "Put ye on the Lord Jesus Christ, and make not provision for the flesh,"[1825] and this instruction defined by the counsel, "Examine yourselves, whether ye be in the faith."[1826] At this time does

---

1819 Ecclesiastes 7:27
1820 Leviticus 16:12,13
1821 Leviticus 16:13
1822 2 Thessalonians 2:13
1823 Jeremiah 31:18,19
1824 Leviticus 23:27
1825 Romans 13:14
1826 2 Corinthians 13:5

"the Lord GOD of hosts call to weeping, and to mourning, and to baldness, and to girding with sackcloth."[1827] For anciently, on the Day of Atonement, the congregation of Israel and Aaron were quiet while gathered about the Temple, checking their hearts and analyzing their manners of worship and service, quitting themselves of that which the then priest was purifying on their behalf.

18. Without self-examination and the examination done by the Godhead, there will be none to fulfill the word, "They may possess the remnant of E'dom, and of all the heathen, which are called by my name, saith the LORD that doeth this."[1828] There is a work to be done for every soul in this world, and the events revolving around the final "harvest of the earth"[1829] cannot begin until God's Priest has husbandmen loyal and faithful to His name, for it is written of our present day, "He is like a refiners fire, and like fullers' soap: and he shall sit as a refiner and purifier of silver: and he shall purify the sons of Levi."[1830] "They that are of the sons of Levi...receive the office of priesthood,"[1831] and it should be fulfilled in them, "My covenant might be with Levi,"[1832] and, "The law of truth was in his mouth."[1833] These are them that are born of the Spirit's creative science, who at the establishment of an openly apostate government will cry out, "Whosoever transgresseth, and abideth not in the doctrine of Christ hath not God."[1834]

19. Christ is purifying unto Himself men and women of His own likeness, and in order for them "to give the light of the knowledge of the glory of God in the face of Jesus"[1835] during a time when established *falsehood* is magnifying gross perdition, it is that today the counsel must be accepted and observed: "We are his workmanship, created in

---

1827 Isaiah 22:12
1828 Amos 9:12
1829 Revelation 14:15
1830 Malachi 3:3
1831 Hebrews 7:5
1832 Malachi 2:4
1833 Malachi 2:6
1834 2 John 1:9
1835 2 Corinthians 4:6

Christ Jesus unto good works, which God hath before ordained that we should walk in them."[1836] If we are, as says Scripture, "Created in Christ,"[1837] then we must have a Creator. Seeing as how if we confess, "It is he that hath made us, and not we ourselves,"[1838] it serves that there is a Memorial[1839] for us that we may observe the charge, "Know ye that the LORD he is God."[1840] How are we to know that the LORD is God? Says His Spirit, "Incline thine ear unto wisdom, and apply thine heart to understanding,"[1841] and, "Seekest...and searchest...and find the knowledge of God."[1842] For this cause we know, "The Son of God is come, and hath given us an understanding,"[1843] that we may know Him as He knew His Father, even as He says, "I was not rebellious, neither turned away back."[1844] "As the Father gave me commandment, even so I do."[1845] This is why our Priest says, "If a man love me, he will keep my words,"[1846] for in order to know the LORD's Son and to receive the seal of His Father, one must first examine the doctrine of His Prince and surrender self to the education of His Spirit.

20. This is the Faith of God's Priest, even the keeping of the commandments of God and the science of Jesus for a recovery of the mental and moral faculties for entrance into God's eternal Building through His Spirit. In this second Room, no one who enters will fail of reaching the commandment, "Speak the mystery of Christ."[1847] There is an investigative judgment of God currently in progress that He may have a House purified to carry out the thoughts of His heart for the religious world at the appointed time; these will fulfill the word, "There shall be a tabernacle for a shadow in the daytime from

---

1836 Ephesians 2:10
1837 Ephesians 2:10
1838 Psalms 100:3
1839 Genesis 2:3
1840 Psalms 100:3
1841 Proverbs 2:2
1842 Proverbs 2:4
1843 1 John 5:20
1844 Isaiah 50:5
1845 John 14:31
1846 John 14:23
1847 Colossians 4:3

the heat, and for a place of refuge, and for a covert from storm and from rain."[1848] It is now, in this our present day, when "the mystery of God should be finished, as he hath declared to his servants the prophets."[1849]

1848 Isaiah 4:6
1849 Revelation 10:7

20

O House Of Aaron

1. "But while he thought on these things, behold, the angel of the Lord appeared unto him in a dream, saying, Joseph, thou son of David, fear not to take unto thee Mary thy wife: for that which is conceived in her is of the Holy Ghost. And she shall bring forth a son, and thou shalt call his name JESUS: for he shall save his people from their sins."[1850]

2. The thoughtful mind must think, "Jesus has a people?" How is this possible? Is it not that Scripture says, "Who shall declare his generation?"[1851] "He was cut off out of the land of the living";[1852] this Christ was removed from the earth without wife or child; and yet He maintains a seed? Concerning this Jesus, it was said, "They shall call his name Emman'uel, which being interpreted is, God with us,"[1853] therefore this "us" is "His people," and to them, or us, belong a house of praise for health and for deliverance, "whose house are we, if we hold fast the confidence and the rejoicing of the hope firm unto the

---

1850 Matthew 1:20,21
1851 Isaiah 53:8
1852 Isaiah 53:8
1853 Matthew 1:23

end."[1854] From joining self to His house, from organizing the heart and mind after the religion of His intercession, this is how He will save, ransom, or recover, His people.

3. Salvation did not finalize at His crucifixion, but there it was rather ratified to the human race by the LORD God Himself. If Christ's name is to be a doctrine conveying the message that God is with us, then there must be a way for every believer to acknowledge His God as with them. If this Faith is to be the Spirit of His LORD with us, then there must be some thing given to every believer to set his or her affections intelligently on this fact. It is for this reason that the LORD anciently said, "Let them make me a sanctuary; that I may dwell among them."[1855] God with us is God's voice among us, and the way that God may be with and among us is if we are within and obedient to His counsel and instruction. The sincere believer will confess, "In thy fear will I worship toward thy holy temple,"[1856] for within the heavenly House of the Majesty rests His fear, which is why it is said, "The fear of the Lord, that is wisdom."[1857] The fear of God is that counsel found within the law and commandment that His Spirit has instructed, for God "hath in these last days spoken unto us by his Son."[1858]

4. The Father has concealed within "the doctrine of Christ"[1859] "the spirit of wisdom and revelation in the knowledge of him."[1860] "The LORD is in his holy temple,"[1861] and that is where He has always been, and by the Godhead's sacrifice, every believer is to be joined to the current ministry of His Church within this Temple. It was purposed of God, that by faith in the virtue of His Son, every believer would be joined "to the general assembly and church of the firstborn, which are written in heaven."[1862] This is why the Spirit directed Moses' thoughts

---

1854   Hebrews 3:6
1855   Exodus 25:8
1856   Psalms 5:7
1857   Job 28:28
1858   Hebrews 1:2
1859   2 John 1:9
1860   Ephesians 1:17
1861   Psalms 11:4
1862   Hebrews 12:23

when organizing Aaron's priesthood. He who came in the image of God was to offer up a perfect sin offering to God for every penitent human being that should walk the earth, and that ministration of old was but a representation of what currently is in heaven, therefore to His people it is counseled, "Bless the LORD, O house of Israel: bless the LORD, O house of Aaron."[1863]

5. Now, Aaron is passed away, along with the law of Moses and the honor bestowed on the literal nation of Israel. The LORD has cut off Himself from that literal nation, for He Himself has said, "For your transgressions is your mother put away."[1864] The LORD God counseled this people, "Plead with your mother, plead: for she is not my wife, neither am I her husband: let her therefore put away her whoredoms out of her sight, and her adulteries from between her breasts; lest I strip her naked, and set her as in the day that she was born, and make her as a wilderness."[1865] But because they refused to turn themselves to Him, confessing, "Abraham was one, and he inherited the land: but we are many; the land is given us for inheritance,"[1866] He promised, "I will overturn, overturn, overturn, it: and it shall be no more, until he come whose right it is; and I will give it him."[1867]

6. Christ has no generation on the face of the earth and yet He has a people, and the house of Aaron has been terminated since Christ ascended to take up the position as the LORD's High Priest, and yet the house lives on, and so the thoughtful mind must ask, "What saith the scripture?"[1868]

7. The new house of Aaron is that located in the heavenly Temple of the LORD's throne and headed by God's Christ; who Aaron of old foreshadowed; "a minister of the sanctuary, and of the true tabernacle, which the Lord pitched, and not man."[1869] The LORD pitched this Tabernacle in heaven and not any man or minister. This Temple existed

---

1863 Psalms 135:19
1864 Isaiah 50:1
1865 Hosea 2:2,3
1866 Ezekiel 33:24
1867 Ezekiel 21:27
1868 Romans 4:3
1869 Hebrews 8:2

before man, and its system was that relayed to Moses as a figure "till the seed should come to whom the promise was made."[1870] That seed was His Christ. He to whom the economy of Israel belongs is the Christ of God, and this economy no longer earthly and temporal, but Christ says, "My kingdom is not of this world,"[1871] for His authority rests within a spiritual kingdom "filled with the knowledge of his (the LORD God the Father's) will in all wisdom and spiritual understanding."[1872]

8. Those found in the heavenly Church of Christ; the true Aaron of the Spirit's faithful; are His people, for it is written, "I will worship toward thy holy temple, and praise thy name for thy lovingkindness and for thy truth."[1873] Again, within the Spirit's Building rests His fear which is the understanding of His wisdom, and this wisdom and knowledge is defined as His truth and loving-kindness. This truth of God is the doctrine and "law of Christ"[1874] after "the kindness and love of God our Saviour toward man."[1875] It is only by this law of the Faith of Jesus that the soul and spirit will be recovered to the will of the LORD's throne, for the Father, "who hath delivered us from the power of darkness, and hath translated us into the kingdom of his dear Son,"[1876] has ordained for every believer, through the law of His Faith, "to be conformed to the image of his Son."[1877] This is why it is said, "How excellent is thy lovingkindness, O God! therefore the children of men put their trust under the shadow of thy wings,"[1878] and, "O house of Aaron, trust in the LORD."[1879]

9. The saying is well known, "We shall not all sleep, but we shall all be changed,"[1880] and this change being when "this mortal must put on

---

1870 Galatians 3:19
1871 John 18:36
1872 Colossians 1:9
1873 Psalms 138:2
1874 Galatians 6:2
1875 Titus 3:4
1876 Colossians 1:13
1877 Romans 8:29
1878 Psalms 36:7
1879 Psalms 115:10
1880 1 Corinthians 15:51

immortality."[1881] Yet how can any one think on such a privilege without realizing that there is to be in this flesh a translation before this estate? Scripture, not the author, has said that every believer is first translated into the reign and kingdom of the LORD's Son for treatment and for education, and this translation on earth in sinful flesh. "Flesh and blood cannot inherit the kingdom of God,"[1882] for only "the spirit may be saved in the day of the Lord Jesus."[1883] What form is God of? Christ says of His Father, "God is a Spirit."[1884] From the foundation of the world it has always been "that the law is spiritual";[1885] for God is a Spirit; and should not the believer join themselves to God by His Spirit from their own spirit? This is why it is says, "I serve with my spirit in the gospel of his Son,"[1886] and, "Worship God in the spirit."[1887]

10. This is relevant because Scripture tells us that the Christ of God is to save the inward person; to recover the mental and moral constitutions; of His people. If we are "looking unto Jesus the author and finisher of our faith,"[1888] it is that we are looking not only at Him as crucified, nor simply at Him as resurrected, but also as Him alive and operating as One who "abideth a priest continually."[1889] The priesthood of Christ is crucial to our understanding because He is Head over the living Church of God in heaven, wherein rests "the spirits of just men made perfect."[1890] That of old confessed one who did the service as "made perfect by the flesh,"[1891] yet now it is not the flesh that is to find health by ritual or custom or policy. The conscience is where true perfection is to rest. The Father and the Son have promised

---

1881 1 Corinthians 15:53
1882 1 Corinthians 15:50
1883 1 Corinthians 5:5
1884 John 4:24
1885 Romans 7:14
1886 Romans 1:9
1887 Philippians 3:3
1888 Hebrews 12:2
1889 Hebrews 7:3
1890 Hebrews 12:23
1891 Galatians 3:3

to resurrect the spirit of the mind, for the power of Christ's Faith will "purge your conscience from dead works to serve the living God."[1892]

11. There is a reason why Christ says, "That which is born of the Spirit is spirit,"[1893] for it is known, "The spirit giveth life,"[1894] and, "Wisdom giveth life."[1895] Again, this is why the apostle says, "He that hath the Son hath life,"[1896] for it is known, "The Spirit is life."[1897] That which is of the Spirit is a mind "renewed in knowledge after the image of him that created him."[1898] Every sincere believer will be edified within the Church of Christ in heaven; there are no ifs or questions on the matter, for this is the knowledge of the Faith of God's Lord. Christ can only save His congregation if their spirits rest where He is, for as it is says, "He shall redeem their soul from deceit and violence,"[1899] so the spirit of man under the divine influence of His Spirit is to be regenerated with a new breath of existence to labor as He labored, to love and comfort as He edified, "that we may be able to comfort them which are in any trouble, by the comfort wherewith we ourselves are comforted of God."[1900]

12. The House of God is that Place for moral and spiritual regeneration, for within it rests the substance for the personal reformation that the human agent is to carry out once there is faith in the doctrine of the Godhead's love. Christ saving His people is nothing but the fulfillment of the saying, "He saved us, by the washing of regeneration, and renewing of the Holy Ghost."[1901] It is the Holy Ghost that is to revive the inward faculties of the believer through their exercised faith on the mediation of His Son. This is why "we might receive the promise of the Spirit through faith."[1902] The promises of God contained within

---

1892   Hebrews 9:14
1893   John 3:6
1894   2 Corinthians 3:6
1895   Ecclesiastes 7:12
1896   1 John 5:12
1897   Romans 8:10
1898   Colossians 3:10
1899   Psalms 72:14
1900   2 Corinthians 1:4
1901   Titus 3:5
1902   Galatians 3:14

His Spirit sum up "the blessing of Abraham,"[1903] that is, the gift of the name and character of Abraham working in the faithful hearer and doer of the Spirit's understanding. The name of Abraham is translated as, "The righteousness which is by faith,"[1904] and this is why the health of God is no longer understood from a religion born of the flesh, "for we through the Spirit wait for the hope of righteousness by faith."[1905] This is what it means to say, "God is with us."[1906] The truth of the Spirit's science is "that we might be justified by the faith of Christ, and not by the works"[1907] of religious policies, "for by grace are ye saved through faith."[1908]

13. This is why it is written, "Which were born, not of blood, nor of the will of the flesh, nor of the will of man, but of God."[1909] The blood, the flesh, the will, and the purpose of sinful man, these all work to uplift "the Circumcision in the flesh made by hands."[1910] This is why our Minister would have every believer hear the counsel, "Labour not to be rich: cease from thine own wisdom,"[1911] for by such actions we will receive that "circumcision made without hands, in putting off the body of the sins of the flesh by the circumcision of Christ."[1912] Where else may the Spirit's circumcision, made without hands, take place, but within that "greater and more perfect tabernacle, not made with hands"?[1913] It is here in this Tabernacle that when once the knowledge of God is observed, studied and then diligently applied to, the spirit will compel the will to put forth greater power against the body of the flesh's irrational constitution, for concerning the properly masticated

---

1903 Galatians 4:14
1904 Hebrews 11:7
1905 Galatians 5:5
1906 Isaiah 8:10
1907 Galatians 2:16
1908 Ephesians 2:8
1909 John 1:13
1910 Ephesians 2:11
1911 Proverbs 23:4
1912 Colossians 2:11
1913 Hebrews 9:11

and digested words of God, it is written, "They are life unto those that find them, and health to all their flesh."[1914]

14. It is clear that the purpose of the LORD's gospel is to recover the mind of mankind from their base passions and vain ambitions, and the only way to do this is through inward surgery by the doctrine of the master Surgeon and Physician. The spirit of the mind is to find health only through a reform on temperance; spiritually and physically; and it is only from communing with that Priest in the Room of the Spirit's ministration that the benefits of the gospel will take effect. "For this is the will of God, even your sanctification,"[1915] but what marks the beginning of sanctification? It says, "Ye should abstain."[1916] Abstain from what? "Abstain from pollutions of idols, and from fornication, and from things strangled, and from blood,"[1917] we are counseled. "Abstain from fleshly lusts, which war against the soul,"[1918] we are advised. So what is the counsel for the one who would quit their inward cultivated and inherited tendencies? "Put ye on the Lord Jesus Christ, and make not provision for the flesh,"[1919] it says, for the reformer is to hear, and in clear tones, "Live according to God in the spirit."[1920]

15. The spirit is to be joined to God Himself as a faithful doer and keeper of His commandments, and this faithfulness by communing with His Spirit when obeying the precepts of His doctrine, even as it says, "Ye have purified your souls in obeying the truth through the Spirit."[1921] Seeing as how the doctrine of Christ encompasses God's Man as crucified to Him as positioned as the LORD's Priest, it is that the words are today most applicable, "If any man serve me, let him follow me; and where I am, there shall also my servant be."[1922]

1914 Proverbs 4:22
1915 1 Thessalonians 4:3
1916 1 Thessalonians 4:3
1917 Acts 15:20
1918 1 Peter 2:11
1919 Romans 13:14
1920 1 Peter 4:6
1921 1 Peter 1:22
1922 John 12:26

16. Part of the Faith of the Son is found in the fact that His ministration moves and changes, even as it did of old. The two rooms of the Temple of God; the Holy and the Most Holy Place; on earth had their times and seasons of operation. "To make an atonement for the children of Israel for all their sins once a year,"[1923] "into the second went the high priest alone,"[1924] for "the way into the holiest of all was not yet made manifest, while as the first tabernacle was yet standing."[1925] While Christ ministered in the Holy Place, He could not enter the second phase of His work until the first should close. Therefore when the word was given, "Seventy weeks are determined upon thy people";[1926] which word began "from the going forth of the commandment to restore and to build Jerusalem,"[1927] 457B.C.; this date marking the beginning of the word, "Unto two thousand and three hundred days,"[1928] for these 2300 years extend to the end of "the thousand three hundred and five and thirty days"[1929] prophesied, which days began 508A.D. and ended 1843A.D., which ending marked the near transition of Christ's position in the Temple of God.

17. Proper calculation places the date Christ entered the second phase of His work at 1844A.D. At this time the word was fulfilled, "The Lord, whom ye seek, shall suddenly come to his temple."[1930] This is why, to those disciples who were alive when He entered into the second Apartment, the Spirit said, "Blessed is he that waiteth."[1931] Speaking of this future time of anticipation, the prophet wrote, "The vision is yet for an appointed time, but at the end it shall speak, and not lie: though it tarry, wait for it; because it will surely come, it will not tarry."[1932] Because of many doctrinal errors, the people of this age

---

1923 Leviticus 16:32
1924 Hebrews 9:7
1925 Hebrews 9:8
1926 Daniel 9:24
1927 Daniel 9:25
1928 Daniel 8:14
1929 Daniel 12:12
1930 Malachi 3:1
1931 Daniel 12:12
1932 Habakkuk 2:3

of expectation fell asleep to God's Faith, wherefore the Spirit counseled them, "Be watchful, and strengthen the things which remain."[1933] These disciples believed Christ was coming to destroy them that knew Him not, but He told them, "That which ye have already hold fast till I come,"[1934] for He was not coming to the earth, but rather "to the Ancient of days."[1935]

18. Humanity has existed under the second term of the Son and Christ of God since the above-mentioned date. This Christ says, "Where I am, there will I also be joined by My servant,"[1936] for His ministry has moved, therefore health and commandment is located in a new Place within heaven's Sanctuary. It is in the House of God where His people will be recovered in heart and mind to heaven's throne religion, and more specifically, respect given to His current Room and position will procure showers of grace into the soul for re-creating the inward person into His own very likeness. Upon entering into the Most Holy, wherein Christ is in direct fellowship with His Father for us, we see Him ministering before the ark of God sprinkled with the blood of His own sacrifice. This is the vision given the believer that it may be heard, "Speak the mystery of Christ,"[1937] for it is now to be fulfilled, "The mystery of God should be finished."[1938] This mystery is that "mystery of godliness"[1939] wherein "the name of our Lord Jesus Christ may be glorified in you, and ye in him, according to the grace of our God and the Lord Jesus Christ."[1940]

19. This is the salvation of His congregation, and it is "the grace of God that bringeth salvation."[1941] The recovery of man, "through sanctification of the Spirit and belief of the truth,"[1942] is ordained to bring

---

1933 Revelation 3:2
1934 Revelation 2:25
1935 Daniel 7:13
1936 John 12:26
1937 Colossians 4:3
1938 Revelation 10:7
1939 1 Timothy 3:16
1940 2 Thessalonians 1:12
1941 Titus 2:11
1942 2 Thessalonians 2:13

within the soul temple of every reformer the commandments of God and the knowledge of Jesus. In the Most Holy, wherein communion is now held for His assembly, the eye beholds the Son before the Father as the only means to reach the Father for conversion to keep what is inside of His ark, for it says, "The law of the LORD is perfect, converting the soul."[1943] Herein is the reason why the spirits of men sanctified by faith are made perfect, and it is that they may abide by that perfect Law of the Church and Government of the LORD, encountering it so that they may be converted to faithfully honor Him and His Son, yet this conversion only occurring when once the heart decides to obey and apply itself to the law of His benevolence, which is why it says, "The goodness of God leadeth thee to repentance."[1944]

20. The Spirit's Faith is the only means whereby the heart may begin to feel life's pangs. The sight of Christ on the cross will break the soul into a fever that can only be reduced when it should exercise faith on the fact that Christ is not dead, but is rather the minister of the soul and of the errors of the flesh's body. He is the High Priest over the soul temple and over the Church of God in heaven, and when the soul realizes the spiritual error of his or her humanity, they will eventually come to know how far off they are from the character that should have in them, and taking the hand of Christ by faith, His voice will lead them to a Building wherein will be engraved within them the immutable precepts that He died for. He will supply the person with the precepts of His Faith filled with all of the fullness of the His mediation's blessing, to the end that they may maintain their relationship with Him and with His Father while regulating themselves. Herein rests a present and eternal fact: "Our fellowship is with the Father, and with his Son Jesus Christ."[1945]

21. Never in the history of humanity is it truer that our conversation is to rest in heaven with the Father and with His Son as at this time. The promise is, "He will save His people,"[1946] and the counsel is,

---

1943 Psalms 19:7
1944 Romans 2:4
1945 1 John 1:3
1946 Matthew 1:21

"The word of our God shall stand for ever."[1947] The LORD has spoken the word, and as sure as "he commanded, and it stood fast,"[1948] even so it still stands as spoken by Him, "So shall my word be that goeth forth out of my mouth...it shall accomplish that which I please, and it shall prosper in the thing whereto I sent it."[1949] Where then has God sent His word for the one who should feel after His name? It says, "God, who commanded the light to shine out of darkness, hath shined in our hearts."[1950] The law of the Spirit is a message for the inward person within the hidden parts of the heart, for it should be recorded of every believer, "Ye have obeyed from the heart."[1951] Should the guard of the heart be allowed to fall, should inward error with doubts and all suppositions find silence, the law of God's voice will enter into the soul temple to incline the mind after the life of true health. It is therefore a fact that He will save His people. Wherefore, "according to your faith be it unto you."[1952]

1947   Isaiah 40:8
1948   Psalms 33:9
1949   Isaiah 55:11
1950   2 Corinthians 4:6
1951   Romans 6:17
1952   Matthew 9:29

21

To Escape The Seat Of Lies

1. It is now not long before the word should be fulfilled, "He doeth great wonders."[1953] Who is this "he" that is mentioned, and what are these wonders? It says, "There appeared a great wonder in heaven; a woman clothed,"[1954] and, "There appeared another wonder in heaven; and behold a great red dragon."[1955] A woman is figurative language denoting a church, as it says, "As the church is subject unto Christ, so let the wives be to their own husbands";[1956] a dragon, as we will see, is an illustration of a pagan State. These wonders are a woman; a church; and a state; a dragon; coming together under one banner. The doing or working of wonders is the fulfillment of the word, "That defileth";[1957] that is, "Defiled with women";[1958] and this defilement produces the saying, "Worketh abomination, or maketh a lie."[1959] The doing of, that is the working of, and there is here mentioned an open expression of an

---

1953 Revelation 13:13
1954 Revelation 12:1
1955 Revelation 12:3
1956 Ephesians 5:24
1957 Revelation 21:27
1958 Revelation 14:4
1959 Revelation 21:27

amalgamation between a woman and a beast, or a church and a state. When Jerusalem was to be destroyed by Rome, "Ye shall see the abomination of desolation, spoken of by Daniel the prophet, standing where it ought not,"[1960] counseled Christ on this subject. When it should be fulfilled, "He shall also enter into the glorious land,"[1961] when at this time a certain culture of Rome has infected modern-day Jerusalem, terrible distress against His Household is soon to commence.

2. He that should enter into the glorious land is that image of "the king of the north,"[1962] or is, "The robbers of thy people,"[1963] says the angel. Even of old it was said of this entity, "He shall stand in the glorious land, which by his hand shall be consumed,"[1964] which land was "a pleasant land, a goodly heritage of the hosts of nations."[1965] Concerning this land, the LORD said, "This is Jerusalem: I have set it in the midst of the nations and countries that are round about her,"[1966] and when again the second Jerusalem that *God* has created; as He says of her, "I create new heavens and a new earth";[1967] shall find herself spiritually consumed by the idolatrous and strange standards of Rome, it will be due to the fact that the word is fulfilled, "Saying to them that dwell on the earth, that they should make an image to the beast."[1968] The current glorious land of the earth will inevitably divide, for she will be conquered by force. When a new form of this nation's structure is joined to some woman of "the earth in the sight of men,"[1969] then the image of the first beast before it will be established.

3. The beast, or the kingdom, that came before the earth beast, was Papal Rome. This earth beast, when its place is set and the working of its order has begun, "exerciseth all the power of the first beast before

---

1960 Mark 13:14
1961 Daniel 11:41
1962 Daniel 11:40
1963 Daniel 11:14
1964 Daniel 11:16
1965 Jeremiah 3:19
1966 Ezekiel 5:5
1967 Isaiah 65:17
1968 Revelation 13:14
1969 Revelation 13:13

him,"[1970] and that power is as it is said, "Power was given him over all kindreds, and tongues, and nations."[1971] Herein we see civil authority bestowed upon an institution that desires worship, as it says, "All that dwell upon the earth shall worship him."[1972] Civil and religious power will be upheld "on the earth in the sight of men,"[1973] for again, "Satan's seat"[1974] will meet "them that hold the doctrine of Ba'laam, who taught Ba'lac,"[1975] or rather, a second Constantine will be led away by another ecclesiastical "false prophet that wrought miracles before him."[1976] Hence, the word will for a second time be fulfilled, "Power was given him that sat thereon to take peace from the earth, and that they should kill one another: and there was given unto him a great sword"[1977] along with "a pair of balances."[1978]

4. These things are important to consider, for the nation whose Constitution is founded on liberty and justice will be terribly defiled "after the error of Ba'laam for reward."[1979] The fact that such an error of an abomination; as it says, "Neither shall any woman stand before a beast to lie down thereto: it is confusion";[1980] takes place before it should be fulfilled, "He causeth all...to receive a mark...or the name of the beast,"[1981] is enough proof to understand that he who enters into the glorious land does not enter in physically, but rather by way of an erected image to tamper with the right hand and the forehead, the livelihood and the conscience, of the lands citizen. Such an image prepares the way for "the hour of temptation, which shall come upon all the world."[1982]

1970 Revelation 13:12
1971 Revelation 13:7
1972 Revelation 13:8
1973 Revelation 13:13
1974 Revelation 2:13
1975 Revelation 2:14
1976 Revelation 19:20
1977 Revelation 6:4
1978 Revelation 6:5
1979 Jude 1:11
1980 Leviticus 18:23
1981 Revelation 13:16,17
1982 Revelation 3:10

5. The first and most important decree against the House of God will appear at this time of established *abomination*, and their test is not the test of the religious world, but rather they will be proved according to how "in the province of Babylon"[1983] it is was once said, "Thou O king, has made a decree, that every man...shall fall down and worship the golden image."[1984] The test of image worship is the lot that will be conferred to the future Sha'drach, Me'shach, and Abed'-nego. These are them who maintain their conversation with the God of heaven; "his servants that trusted in him";[1985] therefore we know who these men represent, and it says, "O house of Aaron, trust in the LORD."[1986] A province is a country belonging to a kingdom or state either by conquest or colonization, and is usually situated at a distance from the kingdom or state, therefore this image consecrated in the Sate of the earth's new republic has happened due to an apostasy from within it in reference to a kingdom that it longs to honor in spirit and in error. When the earth beast should pick up the *falsehood* of the first beast before it, then the test to serve the appointed religion of the king by law will take place.

6. Consider how that when these of God "yielded their bodies, that they might not serve nor worship any god, except their own God," how Nebuchadnez'zar was "full of fury, and the form of his visage was changed."[1987] "Therefore he spake, and commanded that they should heat the furnace one seven times more than it was wont to be heated. And he commanded the most mighty men that were in his army to... cast them into the burning fiery furnace."[1988]

7. This scene will be reproduced. The actions of the king fulfill the saying, "And the nations were angry."[1989] Nations are better understood to mean religious denominations, even "they of the people and kindreds and tongues and nations."[1990] As Nebuchadnez'zar spoke, and

---

1983 Daniel 3:1
1984 Daniel 3:10
1985 Daniel 3:28
1986 Psalms 115:10
1987 Daniel 3:19
1988 Daniel 3:19,20
1989 Revelation 11:18
1990 Revelation 11:9

as his speech was filled with indignation, so when the people of God do not succumb to the pressures of the new republic to honor the legislated religion of that republic, it will be fulfilled, "He spake as a dragon."[1991] For "he had power to give life unto the image of the beast, that the image of the beast should both speak, and cause that as many as would not worship the image of the beast should be killed."[1992] The image test is a trial on loyalty to the LORD of heaven and of earth on the part of His own sanctified seed. The entire religious world honored the god and the dominion of Nebuchadrez'zar; the world was unaffected by the decree of the king. All the rulers of the provinces came out to worship the image of Nebuchadnez'zar; which in reality was the worship of a deified State; yet there were three souls who endured such provocation for their devout faith and love, with knowledge and respect to the true God, built up in them from their experience with His name in the presence of His Spirit.

8. These things should be considered because in the Place where Christ now ministers, the commandment is, "Know that I am God."[1993] Reformers who should be alive during this terrible time of a church and state government, and should not know the living God apart from the lie put forth by men in the face and shadow of the first beast before it, will be shaken out of the Godhead's heritage and inheritance. The believer is entered, by faith on the name and doctrine of the Son of God, into the second Apartment of the House of God where He now stands "in the presence of God for us."[1994] Many will fall and worship the ecclesiastically framed political image to be established because they have not taken the time to hear the commandments of God, and more specifically, the first four which confess, "Thou shalt love the Lord thy God with all thy heart, and with all thy soul, and with all thy mind, and with all thy strength."[1995]

1991 Revelation 13:11
1992 Revelation 13:15
1993 Psalms 46:10
1994 Hebrews 9:24
1995 Mark 12:30

9. It is the right and privilege of every reforming believer to know the living God, for some will not live to see the events so emotionally mingled within the heart of their tradition. A knowledge of the LORD and His Son will free the heart of its superstitious creeds wrapped in ignorant policies of devotion, for a heart willingly espoused to His Christ's name will not fight any experience to know Him and to "be found of him in peace, without spot, and blameless."[1996] Without taking the time to examine self in the face of Christ, blame will be registered to the account when loyalty has passed to an authority that is not divinely appointed. Ba'laam, a symbol of a false church, is to rise up on the scene again to gain political favor that the king may act as the conscience for the land in regard to her worship, yet the believer must know what the Spirit says on the matter: "I would not hearken unto Ba'laam."[1997] Every thing to be constructed by them that deceive by lies is of "Satan, which decieveth the whole world."[1998] This is why these priests and elders rest "where Satan's seat is,"[1999] and why today we should be found "above, where Christ sitteth on the right hand of God."[2000]

10. It is in the Most Holy Apartment where the believer may "know the love of Christ, which passeth knowledge,"[2001] wherein it is fulfilled, "Let the peace of God rule in your hearts,"[2002] and, "Let the word of Christ dwell in you richly in all wisdom."[2003] The only way to know the living God is to handle the knowledge of His peace, which is the Faith of His wisdom, "the word of the truth of the gospel."[2004] On the day when the priest entered into the Most Holy, it was known that he took the blood of a sacrifice and did sprinkle it on the mercy seat, and Christ has done no different. With His own blood He has sprinkled the mercy

---

1996 2 Peter 3:14
1997 Joshua 24:10
1998 Revelation 12:9
1999 Revelation 2:13
2000 Colossians 3:1
2001 Ephesians 3:19
2002 Colossians 3:15
2003 Colossians 3:16
2004 Colossians 1:5

seat that stands before Him in heaven's Temple, and this symbolizing that faith in the power of His blood holds access to that experience symbolized by the ark, even as it says, "Thou hast magnified thy word above all thy name."[2005] Wherefore the Faith of Jesus is the only means of encountering the commandments of God "that we should be a kind of firstfruits of his creatures."[2006] "Of his own will begat he us by the word of truth,"[2007] therefore it should now be heard, "Every one that loveth him that begat loveth him also that is begotten of him."[2008]

11. Who begat Christ? It is said, "The Spirit of him that raised up Jesus,"[2009] and, "Quickened by the Spirit,"[2010] for the believer must first acknowledge Him that begat before they may know Him that is born of Him. To know God, one must know the law of the Spirit's doctrine, and to know the Spirit's Faith, one must submit self under the jurisdiction of the Spirit instuction, which is why it says, "Believe on him that raised up Jesus our Lord from the dead."[2011] What was one marked attribute of God's three faithful stewards? It says that these "yielded their bodies."[2012] Due to embracing the fact that self needed to be denied that they might properly serve their God, these men became "sober, just, holy, temperate."[2013] One cannot progress in heaven's will without any reform on spiritual and physical temperance, for the LORD reduced Himself to place His counsel above His name, and Christ humbled Himself to become a minister of no reputation before His God "that ye through his poverty might be rich."[2014] So then is it wrong for Christ to say, "Whosoever will come after me, let him deny himself"?[2015]

12. When Christ ministered in the first Room of heaven's House, every believer had to follow Him by faith only when once they reported

---

2005 Psalms 138:2
2006 James 1:18
2007 James 1:18
2008 1 John 5:1
2009 Romans 8:11
2010 1 Peter 3:18
2011 Romans 4:24
2012 Daniel 3:28
2013 Titus 1:8
2014 2 Corinthians 8:9
2015 Mark 8:34

within themselves, "He must increase, but I must decrease."[2016] The mind of the present servant of God's Lord is, "I 'will be base in mine own sight,'"[2017] for the counsel is, "When wisdom entereth into thine heart, and knowledge is pleasant unto thy soul; discretion shall preserve thee, understanding shall keep thee: to deliver thee from the way of the evil man."[2018] When the newly organized ecclesiastical institution of the earth should seek out the then king Ba'lac, gross spiritual errors will so fly from the heaven of their dominion "insomuch that, if it were possible, they shall deceive the very elect."[2019] To stay from accepting the soon to be established lie, one must know "the faith of God's elect,"[2020] which faith is "the acknowledging of the truth which is after godliness."[2021]

13. "The way of life is above to the wise,"[2022] even "those things which are above, where Christ sitteth on the right hand of God,"[2023] for the error to stir up the movements of the earth belong to them that "abideth not in the doctrine of Christ."[2024] Christ has moved from the Holy to the Most Holy, and it is crucial for the believer to personally familiarize self with the instruments found in this Room, for it is written, "In his temple doth every one speak of his glory."[2025] Every one of the items in both Places of His Temple confesses to His Father's Majesty. Because many stop short of the knowledge of the Son, omitting from the understating the details of His high priestly ministration, many will be led to take the image given them of *godliness* for the true revelation of the will and character of *God*.

14. Even now is it so, that many receive "men's persons in admiration because of advantage,"[2026] while it is not heard that the word is

---

2016   John 3:30
2017   2 Samuel 6:22
2018   Proverbs 2:10-12
2019   Matthew 24:24
2020   Titus 1:1
2021   Titus 1:1
2022   Proverbs 15:24
2023   Colossians 3:1
2024   2 John 1:9
2025   Psalms 29:9
2026   Jude 1:15

fulfilled against them, "Through covetousness shall they with feigned words make merchandise of you."[2027] Individuals are yet sold for the error of their spiritual understanding, and this cycle remains to fill the earth with a most distasteful void, yet real health awaits the one who would be so bold as to bring God Himself to say, "Who is this that engaged his heart to approach unto me?"[2028]

15. The believer is to hear the counsel, "Guide thine heart in the way,"[2029] for God Himself will bring no soul to Him without their willing consent. "Let not that man think that he shall receive any thing of the Lord"[2030] without considering the counsel, "To this man will I look, even to him that is poor and of a contrite spirit, and trembleth at my word."[2031] This is why the doctrine of the second Apartment is, "Fear God...and worship him,"[2032] and, "Babylon is fallen,"[2033] and, "If any many worship the beast and his image, and receive his mark."[2034] Independently studying the voice of God under the supervision of His Spirit will produce a people "that keep the commandments of God, and the faith of Jesus."[2035] This is the goal of Christ's second administration, even to cleanse the Sanctuary of the sinners among His faithful, and to remove the sins of them found faithful, that during the time of the most notable lie, and then when that lie should act its part in fulfilling the word, "His deadly wound was healed,"[2036] they may "speak the mystery of Christ."[2037]

16. Every believing eye of faith should turn to the Place wherein rest heaven's congregation. There is a reason why the faithful "follow the Lamb whithersoever he goeth,"[2038] and it is to have in them the

---

2027 2 Peter 2:3
2028 Jeremiah 30:21
2029 Proverbs 23:18
2030 James 1:7
2031 Isaiah 66:2
2032 Revelation 14:7
2033 Revelation 14:8
2034 Revelation 14:9
2035 Revelation 14:12
2036 Revelation 13:3
2037 Colossians 4:3
2038 Revelation 14:4

same sentiment as the apostle: "And be found in him, not having mine own righteousness, which is of the law, but that which is through the faith of Christ, the righteousness which is of God by faith: that I may know him, and the power of his resurrection, and the fellowship of his sufferings, being made conformable unto his death; if by any means I might attain unto the resurrection of the dead."[2039] For this cause, our High Priest encourages every believer to enter into the Place where His name is at by saying, "Come and see,"[2040] and, "The Spirit and the bride say, Come."[2041] Who says come? The voice of Christ, the Spirit of His Father, and the bride of Christ; or rather, the doctrine of Christ, the Spirit of God, and "the bride, the Lamb's wife,"[2042] "the holy city Jerusalem"[2043] wherein rests "the general assembly and church of the firstborn, which are written in heaven."[2044]

17. "Truly our fellowship is with the Father";[2045] that is, "Fellowship of the Spirit";[2046] "and with his Son Jesus Christ";[2047] that is, "The law of Christ,"[2048] "the doctrine which is according to godliness."[2049] This is why it says of the divine process of purification, "Sanctified by God the Father, and preserved in Jesus Christ,"[2050] or rather, "Through sanctification of the Spirit and belief of the truth."[2051] This work equates to the fulfillment of the word, "The mystery of God should be finished,"[2052] which experience is, "Christ in you,"[2053] that it may be ultimately confessed, "I delight in the law of God after the inward man."[2054]

2039 Philippians 3:9-11
2040 John 1:46
2041 Revelation 22:17
2042 Revelation 21:9
2043 Revelation 21:10
2044 Hebrews 12:23
2045 1 John 1:3
2046 Philippians 2:1
2047 1 John 1:3
2048 Galatians 6:2
2049 1 Timothy 6:3
2050 Jude 1:1
2051 2 Thessalonians 2:13
2052 Revelation 10:7
2053 Colossians 1:27
2054 Romans 7:22

18. The hope of the LORD is to bring mankind to the will of His throne, and the Room where His Christ today mediates is that Place where this work is completed. The believer must know where they belong in order to keep self now and during the strange times that are ahead. At this time, accepting the righteousness of Christ's law will raise up His faithful "in the likeness of his resurrection,"[2055] yet one must join self by faith to the Place where this work is to commence, for the Spirit is raising up a generation to keep for Himself for ever.

2055 Romans 6:5

22

Purify Before The Time

1. "And I beheld another beast coming up out of the earth; and he had two horns like a lamb, and he spake as a dragon."[2056]

2. John saw, after the one "that killeth with the sword must be killed with the sword,"[2057] and after this one that destroyed had "one of his heads as it were wounded to death,"[2058] another beast coming up out of the earth. As the entire revelation is a figurative vision; as it says, "The book of this prophecy";[2059] the scene given us must be analyzed in a manner most crucial to purge from the symbolic representation a substance to fit a right frame. It should then be asked, "What is the earth?" We find our answer given by Scripture: "Shall the earth be made to bring forth in one day? or shall a nation be born at once?"[2060] And again, "What one nation in the earth is like thy people Israel."[2061]

3. The earth is a nation. John seeing another beast coming up out of the earth must mean another dominion coming up out of an already

---

2056 Revelation 13:11
2057 Revelation 3:10
2058 Revelation 3:3
2059 Revelation 22:19
2060 Isaiah 66:8
2061 1 Chronicles 17:21

formed nation. The earth is already present and existing when this other beast comes up out of it. This new beast comes up out of a nation separate from all other nations before it. This other beast coming up from a now old nation has two horns like a lamb and speaks with the tongue of a dragon. This other beast is not the same beast from which it comes, but is a gross distortion of it. As we do know the earth from which this beast springs is the United States; for it is said of her, "I have set it in the midst of the nations";[2062] due to the manner of its viewed environment, from out of the United States another beast will be drawn up, and one that is separate from its current fundamental belief of government.

4. That the other beast is organized under a perversion of the principles of its mother is seen in how it is written, "He doeth great wonders...in the sight of men."[2063] "In the sight of men," this means in the vision or in the light of men. It is written, "That which is highly esteemed among men is abomination in the sight of God,"[2064] for that done in the sight of men is that greatly revered by the heart and spirit of man. Again it is written, "To give the light of the knowledge of the glory of God in the face of Jesus,"[2065] for to be in the face of, that is the same as in the sight of, and to do any thing in the sight of men would mean to do all things according to the counsel and knowledge of men. Herein we find the two-horned beast governed by an apparently estranged government and dominated by a senate that would have their religious intentions civilly enacted, for there are no men that care for *heavenly wonders* but priests and elders of religion.

5. That done in the sight of men is abomination, so what, then, could be done by these men to be counted as an abomination? And again, what is meant by the word, "men"?

6. It is written, "Whereas there is among you envying, and strife, and divisions, are ye not carnal, and walk as men?"[2066] When John beholds

---

2062 Ezekiel 5:5
2063 Revelation 13:13
2064 Luke 16:15
2065 2 Corinthians 4:6
2066 1 Corinthians 3:3

this new beast, he sees this beast as it is in form when it ascends out of its father and mother. Already this new entity bears "two horns like a lamb,"[2067] and that word, "like," representing the fact that it does not have the actual horns, or character of a lamb, but has a name similar to a lamb. As the earth is a figurative representation of a nation, so the horns must stand for some thing also. It is written, "He had horns coming out of his hand: and there was the hiding of his power,"[2068] and, "My heart rejoiceth in the LORD, mine horn is exalted in the LORD."[2069] The horn is a symbol of the heart of power, and this new beast carries two forms of power within itself similar to a lamb, and as there is only one Lamb, this new nation "preacheth another Jesus"[2070] and "another gospel"[2071] at the expense of its heritage.

7. It is therefore evident that this new beast fulfills its duties in the sight of carnal individuals, riotous men, and so we must again asked, "What then could be done by these men to be counted as an abomination?"

8. We see changes in governmental principles because "false brethren unawares brought in"[2072] are leading the government of the earth beast. What are these men after? It is written, "Let us not be desirous of vain glory, provoking one another, envying one another,"[2073] for this perverse leadership desires glory for their counterfeit lamb-like institution, and in this it is seen why that done in their sight is abomination, even because it says, "He that turneth away his ear from hearing the law, even his prayer shall be abomination."[2074] These men have forsaken the commandments of God and the Faith of Jesus, and in its place do long to have erected "a false vision and divination, and a thing of nought, and the deceit of their heart."[2075] These are them

---

2067 Revelation 13:11
2068 Habakkuk 3:4
2069 1 Samuel 2:1
2070 2 Corinthians 11:4
2071 2 Corinthians 11:4
2072 Galatians 2:4
2073 Galatians 5:26
2074 Proverbs 28:9
2075 Jeremiah 14:14

that "would pervert the gospel of Christ...unto another gospel,"[2076] and it "is not another,"[2077] but is rather a distortion of the true to obtain political favor for their ambition.

9. These men may be likened to that "certain of the sect of the Pharisees which believed."[2078] As these anciently professed faith in the doctrine of Christ, even while confessing, "Command them to keep the law of Moses,"[2079] so these men who bear rule over the king of the earth beast confess loyalty to the law of their father, even "that man of sin...the son of perdition."[2080] These liars are become abominable to heaven because at this time, these men bear an ecclesiastical rule over the State that blatantly ignores counsel, "The woman shall not wear that which pertaineth unto a man, neither shall a man put on a woman's garment: for all that do so are abomination unto the LORD thy God."[2081] As was mentioned at the beginning of the previous chapter, a woman is a symbol of a church, and the fact that a church is wearing the robe of a civil authority, and that a man; a symbol of their king or head of their State; is executing the religious precepts of a church, is a testament to the fact that this new republic stands in violation of the values that it once upheld, and is a curse to the eyes of the LORD.

10. This new beast has killed its old form, for of old it was reported of it, "The earth helped the woman."[2082] The United States was built to end "the flood which the dragon cast out of his mouth,"[2083] literal and spiritual. Such a flood was not of literal water, but was of a flood of religious persecution; mental, moral, and physical; during "a time, and times, and half a time,"[2084] for "power was given unto him to continue forty and two months...to make war with the saints, and to overcome

---

2076 Galatians 1:6
2077 Galatians 1:7
2078 Acts 15:5
2079 Acts 15:5
2080 2 Thessalonians 2:3
2081 Deuteronomy 22:5
2082 Revelation 12:16
2083 Revelation 12:16
2084 Revelation 12:14

them."[2085] This flood of persecution stalled with the Declaration of Independence; hence the earth would become the new home for the principles of the gospel for all people, no matter who they should be, and under a government without a pope directing an ecclesiastical economy, or a king to bear rule. Nevertheless, the sun will fall from the heart of this land at the appointed time. This nation that once declared all men created equal with unalienable rights by their Creator, and that upheld life, liberty, and the pursuit of happiness for every conscience without discrimination, will fulfill the word, "The earth mourneth and fadeth away...because they have transgressed the laws, changed the ordinance, broken the everlasting covenant."[2086]

11. The everlasting covenant, that is even the Faith of "the blood of the everlasting covenant,"[2087] which law confesses, "Justified by his blood,"[2088] that is, "A man is justified by faith without the deeds of the law."[2089] The earth will soon hear the rebuke, "Whosoever transgresseth, and abideth not in the doctrine of Christ, hath not God,"[2090] for the entire aim of the law and doctrine of Christ is "that he might bring us to God."[2091] This is why it says, "We also joy in God through our Lord Jesus Christ, by whom we have now received the atonement,"[2092] for the Faith of Jesus is not only a law of recovery, for as "God is a Spirit,"[2093] "the kingdom of God is not meat and drink; but righteousness, and peace, and joy in the Holy Ghost."[2094] This is why it says, "Our fellowship is with the Father, and with his Son,"[2095] for the

---

2085 Revelation 13:5,7
2086 Isaiah 24:4,5
2087 Hebrews 13:9
2088 Romans 5:9
2089 Romans 3:28
2090 2 John 1:9
2091 1 Peter 3:18
2092 Romans 5:11
2093 John 4:24
2094 Romans 14:17
2095 1 John 1:3

word of Christ is joined to "fellowship of the Spirit"[2096] that all may be, before the living God, "perfect, as pertaining to the conscience."[2097]

12. The word that comes from God is spiritual and should be firstly accomplished in the realm of the spirit of the mind, which is why it says, "Whom I serve with my spirit in the gospel of his Son,"[2098] and, "Worship God in the spirit."[2099] Thus, by the name of Christ, "every tongue should confess that Jesus Christ is Lord, to the glory of God the Father."[2100] Every believer is to be of the Father "strengthened with might by his Spirit in the inner man,"[2101] for the Spirit is only given so that the faithful would hate being "not subject to the law of God."[2102] "The law is spiritual,"[2103] but it is believed that "by works of righteousness which we have done,"[2104] as according to a scripted traditional law, that "righteousness come by the law."[2105] But what is written? "No man is justified by the law in the sight of God,"[2106] but in the sight of men, fire from man will give life to that which is of no profit to God, for "the law is not of faith."[2107]

13. Herein we find ourselves under a new Republic, even a nation of the earth under a church and state government, which is the image of the first beast before it. Because the inward work of the Faith of Jesus is rejected, because the precepts of the authority of the LORD's voice are rejected within institutions professing themselves to be servants of the God of the Bible, a new order has taken root "where Satan's seat is."[2108] If men had honored the gospel's required experience they would have known the LORD's Spirit, and in knowing the

---

2096 Philippians 2:1
2097 Hebrews 9:9
2098 Romans 1:9
2099 Philippians 3:3
2100 Philippians 2:11
2101 Ephesians 3:16
2102 Romans 8:7
2103 Romans 7:14
2104 Titus 3:5
2105 Galatians 2:21
2106 Galatians 3:11
2107 Galatians 3:12
2108 Revelation 2:13

Spirit would have been "sanctified by God the Father,"[2109] that is, "sanctified by the Holy Ghost."[2110] Thus, in the United States the word would have been fulfilled, "Then had the churches rest throughout all Judae'a and Galilee and Sama'ria, and were edified; and walking in the fear of the Lord, and in the comfort of the Holy Ghost, were multiplied,"[2111] but because of spiritual negligence the earth is divided, and a newly constructed dark age begins.

14. It cannot be ignored that connected to the Holy Spirit of the LORD God our Father is His rest, which rest is soul recovery and spiritual edification. This is why it says, "We which have believed do enter into rest";[2112] "for he spake in a certain place of the seventh day on this wise, And God did rest the seventh day."[2113] No one will hear the charge, "The very God of peace sanctify you wholly,"[2114] unless through "the fulness of the blessing of the gospel of Christ"[2115] it is heard, "Prosper and be in health, even as thy soul prospereth."[2116] The soul is to find health from God's Spirit; "He shall redeem their soul,"[2117] says Scripture; and if the soul is not advancing in health, it is because it lacks the Spirit of the seventh day's rest and regeneration. For this cause, it is well for us to know that the Spirit is "the earnest of our inheritance"[2118] when once "after that ye believed, ye were sealed with that holy Spirit of promise."[2119]

15. "We might receive the promise of the Spirit through faith,"[2120] for if any be without the benefit of the Spirit, it is proof that faith and acceptance of the voice of God is not sincerely had. This is why it says,

---

2109 Jude 1:1
2110 Romans 15:16
2111 Acts 9:31
2112 Hebrews 4:3
2113 Hebrews 4:4
2114 1 Thessalonians 5:23
2115 Romans 15:29
2116 3 John 1:2
2117 Psalms 72:14
2118 Ephesians 1:14
2119 Ephesians 1:13
2120 Galatians 3:14

"If any man have not the Spirit of Christ, he is none of his."[2121] If the soul be without the Spirit and yet confesses *Christ*, it is as to say, "I run," while having no legs. If there is one saying, "I know *Jesus*," and yet fails to maintain that "communion of the Holy Ghost,"[2122] it is as to say, "I am alive," when the body is in a coma. The Spirit brings rest to the soul and delivers knowledge and love for the spirit's duty towards not only righteousness' daily assignment, but also for the day of rest as ordained of God, for these two agents; the LORD's Spirit and seventh-day Sabbath; empower love for the law of the Spirit, which love is the fuel stimulating godly fear for the commandments of God. Because that which comes up out of the earth will openly cast the Faith of the LORD and His commandments aside, apostasy will cause the history of the second and third church of the Revelation to repeat in one age, which will lead into the second and final rising of the stature of the fourth.

16. This is why it is important at this present time to know the science of the Father and His Son, for "he that saith, I know him, and keepeth not his commandments, is a liar, and the truth is not in him."[2123] It is written, "The Spirit is truth,"[2124] and, "The truth is in Jesus,"[2125] for the Spirit and Law of the Father, combined with the law of His Son's intercession, are an integral part of the believer's reformatory experience.

17. The eye of our faith should behold the Lamb where He currently stands, for in the "temple of the tabernacle of the testimony in heaven"[2126] is the LORD's High Priest over His congregation, wherein all are "to be conformed to the image of his Son."[2127] It is here where the faithful will hear, "God blessed the seventh day, and sanctified it,"[2128] for He who sanctifies by faith is the same that sanctified the seal of His Faith's Memorial. These things strange men will soon

---

2121 Romans 8:9
2122 2 Corinthians 13:14
2123 1 John 2:4
2124 1 John 5:6
2125 Ephesians 4:21
2126 Revelation 15:5
2127 Romans 8:29
2128 Genesis 2:3

openly defy, until at last the body of the law of Christ is again brazenly crucified, and then will the war rage against His commandments.

18. It is imperative at this time, above all things, that every believer know their responsibility toward God and toward one another, for most will not see these things come to pass; the length of the long-suffering of God now being without a timetable. On the record of every name for the ones who hope to see Christ in right glory, or who hope to see good events foretold, and yet fall short due to their passing; which is most certainly possible; there must be an opportunity to have it said of them, "Blessed are the dead which die in the Lord from henceforth: Yea, saith the Spirit, that they may rest from their labours; and their works do follow them."[2129] At this time, let the word be, "Every man that hath this hope in him purifieth himself, even as he is pure."[2130]

2129 Revelation 14:13
2130 1 John 3:3

23

They Should Make An Image

1. "There was lifted up a talent of lead: and this is a woman that sitteth in the midst of the e'phah. And he said, This is wickedness. And he cast it into the midst of the e'phah; and he cast the weight of lead upon the mouth thereof."[2131]

2. Zechariah beholds a most interesting vision. An e'phah is a system of measuring grain. In vision, it is here a figurative representation of some legitimate rule and order of weights and balances.

3. A woman is figurative language denoting a church. The angel speaking with the prophet cast a talent of lead; symbolized by a woman, or again, a church, according to the saying, "A talent of lead: and this is a woman";[2132] into the midst of the e'phah; which e'phah represents a system of justice; and here we have in vision a church in direct contact with the diverse measures of a judicial system, and such an institution is given the name, "Wickedness."[2133] It is written that the "treasures

---
2131 Zechariah 5:5-8
2132 Zechariah 5:7
2133 Zechariah 5:8

of wickedness"[2134] are "the scant measure that is abominable,"[2135] for we have before us an abominable institution, even an establishment "where Satan's seat is,"[2136] fulfilling the vision, "He that sat on him had a pair of balances in his hand."[2137]

4. Who or what is this that should deserve the name, "Wickedness"? It is written, "The words of a talebearer are as wounds,"[2138] for "he speaketh fair."[2139] His "hatred is covered by deceit, his wickedness shall be shewed."[2140] The king of the institution of wickedness is a talebearer whose intentions are covered, thus in him the word is fulfilled, "Of your own selves shall men arise, speaking perverse things, to draw away disciples after them."[2141] Who was Paul talking to? Who should fulfill the prophecy, "After my departing shall grievous wolves enter in among you, not sparing the flock"?[2142] It says, "He sent to Eph'esus, and called the elders of the church."[2143] Them that should work wickedness after the first apostles passed away, and even while some were still alive, were none other than the elder of the churches.

5. Zechariah is beholding an ecclesiastical institution placed "between the earth and the heaven,"[2144] representing the fact that it is acting as the conscience of men both religiously; as "the sun, and the moon, and the stars, even all the host of heaven...the LORD thy God hath divided unto all nations under the whole heaven";[2145] and civilly; to "them that dwell on the earth, and to every nation, and kindred, and tongue, and people."[2146] This talebearer is "the son of wickedness,"[2147]

2134 Micah 6:10
2135 Micah 6:10
2136 Revelation 2:13
2137 Revelation 6:5
2138 Proverbs 26:22
2139 Proverbs 26:25
2140 Proverbs 26:26
2141 Acts 20:30
2142 Acts 20:29
2143 Acts 20:17
2144 Zechariah 5:9
2145 Deuteronomy 4:19
2146 Revelation 14:6
2147 Psalms 89:22

even that "son of perdition"[2148] whose institution is called, "Wickedness," of which wickedness is an express image of, "That Wicked."[2149] This is that Abominable Wickedness who "withholdeth that he"; that Wicked; "might be revealed in his time"[2150] to fulfill the saying, "His deadly wound was healed: and all the world wondered after the beast."[2151]

6. It must then be asked, "What is this particular Wickedness?" It is written, "If a man take a wife and her mother, it is wickedness."[2152] Concerning the function of a mother we read, "Keep thy father's commandment, and forsake not the law of thy mother."[2153] Since Scripture depicts a woman as representing a church, and since a mother represents the full essence of her daughter, if a man; a king or the head of a government; should take a church and the law of her traditional upbringing to himself, it is wickedness. Now, as a kingdom or governmant is symbolized by a beast; as it says, "The fourth beast shall be the fourth kingdom";[2154] so in vision we have the fulfillment of the saying, "Neither shall any woman stand before a beast to lie down thereto: it is confusion."[2155]

7. Herein we have a nation in vision under a new order fulfilling the word, "I have seen violence and strife in the city...Mischief also and sorrow are in the midst of it. Wickedness is in the midst thereof: deceit and guile depart not from her streets."[2156] The Wickedness in the midst of the earth, both civilly and religiously, is spiritual violence and strife, religious deceit and guile, therefore the word is fulfilled, "Where envying and strife is, there is confusion and every evil work."[2157] This talebearer is none other than "the false prophet that wrought miracles,"[2158]

2148 2 Thessalonian 2:3
2149 2 Thessalonians 2:8
2150 2 Thessalonians 2:6
2151 Revelation 13:3
2152 Leviticus 20:14
2153 Proverbs 6:20
2154 Daniel 7:23
2155 Leviticus 18:23
2156 Psalms 55:9-11
2157 James 3:16
2158 Revelation 19:20

even the earth beast formed after the abominable image of the first beast before him, whose image magnified a government under a union between law and religion. Of this earth beast it can be said, "In heart ye work wickedness; ye weigh the violence of your hands in the earth,"[2159] for such an entity fulfills the character of how it is written, "O Joshua the high priest, thou, and thy fellows that sit before thee."[2160]

8. The fellows that sit before this high priest; who is called "Joshua" and "Ba'lac";[2161] are even them that have their religious ambitions executed civilly by him. By the power of the king who will tell them, "I will promote thee unto very great honour, and I will do whatsoever thou sayest unto me,"[2162] "they are men wondered at,"[2163] men who have seduced the king "so that he maketh fire come down from heaven"[2164] to honor their charge, "Come therefore, I pray thee, curse me this people"[2165] "which covereth the face of the earth."[2166] This is that one who "deceiveth them that dwell on the earth by the means of those miracles which he had power to do in the sight of the beast,"[2167] that is, in the sight or light of an economy under an ecclesiastical government ran by a religious constitution. This is why it is called, "Wickedness," for this new republic bears the character of Satan who declares, "I will ascend into heaven, I will exalt my throne...I will sit also upon the mount of the congregation...I will be like the most High."[2168]

9. This is where Satan's seat is; a government whose rule over religion is enforced by civil laws; which is why the third church is linked to the third seal, for the history of the church at that time revealed her to be one of compromise against the principles of the Christ's mediation and of the commandments of God. This history will be repeated, as the

---

2159 Psalms 58:2
2160 Zechariah 3:8
2161 Revelation 2:14
2162 Numbers 22:17
2163 Zechariah 3:8
2164 Revelation 13:13
2165 Numbers 22:17
2166 Numbers 22:11
2167 Revelation 13:14
2168 Isaiah 14:13,14

thirteenth division of the Revelation explains, and it is for this reason that ones professing the name of Christ not only know the law of the Son, but also that of the Father. The church elders who should work this wickedness at the time appointed will long to have the State church as governor over the affairs of both the secular and religious world. An erroneous schism in the Constitution of the earth, along with false and strangled doctrines, will work to press the heart of its citizens to render obedience to the image, or government, that they are establishing.

10. This is why every believer should know, for himself or herself, "the light of the knowledge of the glory of God in the face of Jesus Christ."[2169] It is not just the face of Jesus that we need, for the blatant act to exalt self above God, in whatever manner, is proof that there is an inward lacking of an intelligent morality. The present Faith of God does not just contain food for the mental and spiritual portions of the being, but most importantly, it emphasizes the fact of a moral change in the character of the doer of the religion of God's throne. Thus, for every doer of His Spirit's law, the confession is made, "Our fellowship is with the Father, and with his Son,"[2170] for from beholding and experiencing the Godhead's science, "we all, with open face beholding as in a glass the glory of the Lord, are changed into the same image from glory to glory, even as by the Spirit of the Lord."[2171] This is why the Spirit's creation says, "The law of the Spirit of life in Christ Jesus hath made me free from the law of sin and death."[2172]

11. What is the ultimate factor that heals our character? Is it belief upon a perception of *God* and a supposition of what *His* truth and doctrine is? It says, "Are changed as by the Spirit of the Lord."[2173] Now, this Spirit is that "Spirit of truth, which proceedeth from the Father."[2174] This Spirit is that same Spirit concerning the "fellowship of the Spirit,"[2175] which fellowship, if rejected, warrants the counsel,

---

2169 2 Corinthians 4:6
2170 1 John 1:3
2171 2 Corinthians 3:18
2172 Romans 8:2
2173 2 Corinthians 3:18
2174 John 15:26
2175 Philippians 2:1

"Except a man be born of water and of the Spirit, he cannot enter into the kingdom of God."[2176] Who ushers the believer in to the benefits of the mediation of Christ? What is it that actually gives birth to the new person in the sight of God? One may profess *Christ*, but it is the Spirit of His intercession that bears witness to our acceptance of the Spirit's sacrifice, which is why it says, "The Spirit is life because of righteousness,"[2177] and, "The Spirit itself beareth witness with our spirit, that we are the children of God."[2178]

12. Therefore through the doctrine Christ; which educates on all points concerning "the ordinances of justice,"[2179] which are the principles of "the knowledge of his will in all wisdom and spiritual understanding";[2180] the sincere and diligent heart of the Spirit's reformer will conclude, "Thy law do I love."[2181] It is well to know that it is a natural disposition to hide the mind from the things connected to the LORD God; Eden's first pair evince this fact. For this innate nature in us, the Godhead took pity on us and offered Themselves an everlasting sacrifice for our thoughts and feelings. It is the role of the Spirit to reverse the base constitution of man that he or she may grasp a higher and more mindful nature when once the saying of God is obeyed through that same Spirit. Thus, having a better mind inclined to stay on heavenly things, we may hear the counsel, "Ye have purified your souls in obeying the truth through the Spirit,"[2182] for it is the Spirit that is to sanctify the soul found reverencing the throne of His LORD and the mediation of His Son. And when bowed before this throne, who is it that we see is joined to Him that sits on the throne? It says, "The Lamb which is in the midst of the throne."[2183]

13. The LORD's throne is a symbol of His ten laws, and the doctrine of the Lamb is at the center of the Ten Commandments of

---

2176   John 3:5
2177   Romans 8:10
2178   Romans 8:16
2179   Isaiah 58:2
2180   Colossians 1:9
2181   Psalms 119:163
2182   1 Peter 1:22
2183   Revelation 7:17

God; the image of the throne and government of God is the LORD's Faith. The institution that works abominable wickedness will only do so for their rejection of the Spirit's authority over the work of His Son, "for they being ignorant of God's righteousness, and going about to establish their own righteousness, have not submitted themselves unto the righteousness of God."[2184]

 14. One may ask, "How is one is brought to surrender to the righteousness of God?" It is written, "Through the Spirit wait for the hope of righteousness by faith."[2185] The issue at hand is loyalty to the commandments of God and faith towards Christ's name and ministration for the gifts of righteousness to know and obey the God of His voice. What then is given to them that obey His voice? It is written, "The Holy Ghost, whom God hath given to them that obey him."[2186] It is the Father who is to work regeneration in us as we act out the hope of the words of His Son, therefore it must be understood that he "that hath this hope in him purifieth himself, even as he is pure."[2187] There is a call to cease every preconceived notion attached to the mind of the stomach's appetite to relinquish the will, humbly and patiently, to Christ's regimen. Surrendering is achieved through diet. Without taking an effort to correctly place the gift offered by God through His Spirit to the feeble portions of the being by prayer, faith, and fasting from self, the conversation will not draw to itself those good precepts that maintain inward integrity to rightly direct outward ambitions.

 15. For an intemperate and impatient spirit, for a lack of knowledge and virtue; which is a testament to a lacking of heaven's spirit of love and godly benevolence; John saw a new kingdom of the earth that "spake as a dragon"[2188] "in the sight of the beast."[2189] It is the order of God that His Faith moves every obedient soul to learn how to cultivate within self a faith that will stand during this dreadful time. The

---

2184 Romans 10:3
2185 Galatians 5:5
2186 Acts 5:32
2187 1 John 3:3
2188 Revelation 13:11
2189 Revelation 13:14

most holy faith of His believer is formed from out of the Most Holy Place of His current mediation. The gospel is to add rest to the anxious and diseased mind as it studies the divine remedy for personal and presumptuous spiritual errors, and in doing so, it is to cause the eye to behold the character of God, that a moral awakening would fasten in the believer an impenetrable fear and love of God. Such a recovery of the moral faculties through spiritual truth is to lead to "a seal of the righteousness of the faith," [2190]"for he spake in a certain place of the seventh day on this wise."[2191]

16. Herein is the root of the error found within the new republic of the earth beast: her churches neglect the seal and the Spirit enjoined to the *gospel* that they profess to observe. It is the commandment of Jesus joined to obedience to the commandments of God; which obedience is had only "through sanctification of the Spirit and belief of the truth";[2192] that is to "make you perfect in every good work to do his will, working in you that which is wellpleasing in his sight."[2193] Yet, what is written? "Without faith it is impossible to please him."[2194] The heart must add trust to God in addition to faith in His name, for the events that will take place at the hand of the false State prophet occur due to an open distrust in the voice, purpose, and authority of God, thus a woman and the law of her mother will be nationally welcomed in to the seat of government, bearing the charge, "Righteousness come by the law."[2195] Herein the word is fulfilled, "To build it an house in the land of Shi'nar,"[2196] that is, "That they should make an image to the beast."[2197]

2190 Romans 4:11
2191 Hebrews 4:4
2192 2 Thessalonians 2:13
2193 Hebrews 13:21
2194 Hebrews 11:6
2195 Galatians 2:21
2196 Zechariah 5:11
2197 Revelation 13:14

24

The Law Of Truth And Peace

1. In vision, John beheld a leopard beast rise up from the sea, and then concerning this beast, reported, "I saw one of his heads as it were wounded to death."[2198] Herein the word is fulfilled, "I will break Pharaoh's arms, and he shall groan before him with the groanings of a deadly wounded man,"[2199] for the word was to be fulfilled, "Ty'rus did build herself a strong hold, and heaped up silver as the dust, and fine gold as the mire of the streets. Behold, the Lord will cast her out, and he will smite her power in the sea; and she shall be devoured with fire."[2200] "He that leadeth into captivity shall go into captivity: he that killeth with the sword must be killed with the sword."[2201]

2. One of the heads of the leopard beast was to suffer a wound, but which head, or which order of its government? The answer is found in the sayings, "Pharaoh's arms,"[2202] and, "Her power in the sea."[2203] The Spirit says, "I will take away his blood out of his mouth, and his

---

2198 Revelation 13:3
2199 Ezekiel 30:24
2200 Zechariah 9:3,4
2201 Revelation 3:10
2202 Ezekiel 30:24
2203 Zechariah 9:4

abominations from between his teeth,"[2204] for "there was given unto him"; the leopard beast; "a mouth speaking great things and blasphemies; and power was given unto him to continue forty and two months."[2205] That power which the Spirit smote to the ground was that which gave the beast strength to "speak great words against the most High,"[2206] and to "wear out the saints of the most High, and think to change times and laws,"[2207] even the civil and political dimension of Papal dominion. After this point of "her space to repent of her fornication";[2208] which was 42 months or 1260 days (years); it would be fulfilled, "Ash'kelon shall see it, and fear; Ga'za also shall see it, and be very sorrowful, and Ek'ron."[2209]

3. As it says, "Ash'kelon will see the LORD's hand and will fear,"[2210] the saying is at this time fulfilled, "Seal the book, even to the time of the end: many shall run to and fro, and knowledge shall be increased."[2211] The fall of the political head of the leopard beast equates to the fulfillment of the word, "I will cut off the pride of the Philis'tines,"[2212] for it was at the time appointed, the end of the 42 months, that the leopard beast suffered his wound. The people of God at this time, who were joined to His voice, knew the times and seasons of which they lived in, therefore they preached the counsel, "Fear God, and give glory to him,"[2213] hence Ash'kelon and Ga'za and Ek'ron; symbols of Gentile Christian or Catholic factions born out of the Protestant reformation; are reported by Zechariah as at this time fearing God and His doctrine.

4. Yet there is something interesting to note, for although these Gentiles should be brought to fear the Father and His Son in a most decent manner, there would be a time of sorrow allotted to them. What

---

2204 Zechariah 9:7
2205 Revelation 13:5
2206 Daniel 7:25
2207 Daniel 7:25
2208 Revelation 2:21
2209 Zechariah 9:5
2210 Zechariah 9:5
2211 Daniel 12:4
2212 Zechariah 9:6
2213 Revelation 14:7

should happen to them? It would be fulfilled, "Her expectation shall be ashamed."[2214] What expectation? At this time, God's Priest told them, "I will come on thee as a thief, and thou shalt not know what hour I will come upon thee."[2215] In this age, the flock of Christ spread the word, "Behold, the bridegroom cometh,"[2216] but for the falsehood that remained in them from their wounded mother, they believed the second coming of Christ in unimaginable glory to be imminent, when in reality God's Christ explained the nature of His appearing by saying to them examined Scripture, "I will not blot out his name out of the book of life, but I will confess his name."[2217]

5. The fact that Christ is yet confessing names before His Father is enough proof that His work in heaven was not finished and that His anticipated appearance was not to the earth. The saying was to be fulfilled, "The Lord, whom ye seek, shall suddenly come to his temple, even the messenger of the covenant, whom ye delight in,"[2218] for them that unlawfully sorrowed; proving that they did not actually delight in His name due to embracing an unhealthy state of disappointment; fulfilled the saying, "A bastard shall dwell in Ash'dod."[2219] Christ did not come to the earth, but rather to "the temple of the tabernacle of the testimony in heaven,"[2220] the second Room within the LORD's heavenly Sanctuary. Of old it was said, "This same Jesus, which is taken up from you into heaven, shall so come in like manner as ye have seen him go into heaven";[2221] for "a cloud received him out of their sight";[2222] and at this time the word was fulfilled as it was promised, for "one like the Son of man came with the clouds of heaven, and came to the Ancient of days."[2223]

2214 Zechariah 9:5
2215 Revelation 3:3
2216 Matthew 25:6
2217 Revelation 3:5
2218 Malachi 3:1
2219 Zechariah 9:6
2220 Revelation 15:5
2221 Acts 1:11
2222 Acts 1:9
2223 Daniel 7:13

6. These things are important to consider because the prophets testify to the fact that the Spirit's operation has set into place a new order of heavenly acceptance. Many at this former time of expectation fell to shame and sorrowed for their misunderstanding of the heavenly Sanctuary, returning into their homes and dying in the comfort of the tradition of their wounded mother, fulfilling the saying, "Babylon is fallen, is fallen."[2224] But to the blessed of the LORD who did follow His name by faith into the new Room of His Son's mediation, the saying was fulfilled, "Unto the rest in Thyati'ra,"[2225] "he that remaineth, even he, shall be for our God."[2226] These that remained with God and with Christ heard the word, "I have loved thee."[2227] "I have set before thee an open door, and no man can shut it: for thou hast a little strength, and hast kept my word, and hast not denied my name."[2228]

7. Now, the name of the living God is, "Merciful and gracious, longsuffering, and abundant in goodness and truth,"[2229] yet them that defied the name of God at this time said, "Would to God we had died by the hand of the LORD in the land of Egypt, when we sat by the flesh pots, and when we did eat bread to the full."[2230] Yet the LORD also says of Himself, "Keeping mercy for thousands, forgiving iniquity and transgression and sin, and that will by no means clear the guilty,"[2231] wherefore it is fulfilled, even at this day, "A bastard shall dwell in Ash'dod."[2232] The LORD's High Priest closed the first door of His heavenly ministry and began His work in the second. As much faith and obedience it took to remain faithful under His first work, so it is the same for believers under His second and final. But what is now observed in the new Room is not in the first, for by the vision of John, the Spirit has directed the

---

2224 Revelation 14:8
2225 Revelation 2:24
2226 Zechariah 9:7
2227 Revelation 3:9
2228 Revelation 3:8
2229 Exodus 34:6
2230 Exodus 16:3
2231 Exodus 34:7
2232 Zechariah 9:6

believer to observe within their current conversation the counsel, "There was seen in his temple the ark of his testament."[2233]

8. As the old testament had an assignment, or as the "first covenant had also ordinances of divine service, and a worldly sanctuary,"[2234] so the heavenly Sanctuary is regulated by the same, for "it was therefore necessary that the patterns of things in the heavens should be purified with these; but the heavenly things themselves with better sacrifices than these."[2235] Within the heavenly Temple of God we see "Jesus the mediator of the new covenant"[2236] as "an high priest over the house of God."[2237] The new testament, or the new covenant, also holds the true Temple of the Spirit's ark, seeing as how it holds the LORD's true Sanctuary, which Temple is not on earth but in heaven wherein rests "the general assembly and church of the firstborn."[2238] To them that should be alive when Christ's office is to be found in the second Room of the heavenly Sanctuary; which is yet us alive today; it is that what is held within the ark of the blood of the new covenant is to be honored just as much as the blood sprinkled on top of it.

9. The counsel for this year and season of atonement is, "Afflict your souls, and offer an offering made by fire unto the LORD."[2239] The counsel is, "Ye people, pour out your heart before him,"[2240] for at this time God's Priest calls His congregation "to weeping, and to mourning, and to baldness, and to girding with sackcloth."[2241] The word is, "Afflict your souls by handling yourselves before My face and by my name," for His Priest knows the end of this process of purification, saying, "The fast of the seventh...shall be to the house of Judah joy and gladness, and cheerful feasts; therefore love the truth and peace."[2242] At this time,

---

2233 Revelation 11:19
2234 Hebrews 9:1
2235 Hebrews 9:23
2236 Hebrews 12:24
2237 Hebrews 10:21
2238 Hebrews 12:23
2239 Leviticus 23:27
2240 Psalms 62:8
2241 Isaiah 22:12
2242 Zechariah 8:19

self-regulation and self-denial is to heal a certain people to fulfill the word, "The law of truth was in his mouth."[2243] Every active believer is to become aquatinted with the law of love and truth and peace, for obedience to this law is to create within the hearer and doer a spirit in harmony with the LORD's ten laws.

10. That within the ark of the second Room is secured by the doctrine of the blood and Spirit of His Christ. As John is a symbol of them who should on earth see these things for themselves, it is a fact that the current believer now has their attention moved to behold the Faith of Jesus as the means for allowing one to honor the precepts that regulate heaven's throne. There is a reason why the apostle counseled, "This is he that came by water and blood, even Jesus,"[2244] and why Christ says, "Except a man be born of water and of the Spirit, he cannot enter into the kingdom of God."[2245] The water is a symbol of baptism, and here it is not a literal baptism by literal water, but of "the washing of water by the word."[2246] Hence, one is purified by the fire of the Spirit upon their inward parts to offer up an offering by that fire that works in them, fulfilling the counsel, "Ye have purified your souls in obeying the truth through the Spirit."[2247]

11. The law of the Spirit's Faith demands a confession of "your love in the Spirit."[2248] The soul is to become aquatinted with the counsel and instruction of the Father from embracing the office of His Son and Spirit, for only by doing the Spirit's law may one have the chance to offer their "bodies a living sacrifice, holy, acceptable unto God."[2249] This is exactly the purpose of this season of atonement. Every believer is to become a living and not a dead sacrifice to God, which is why it says, "He shall sit as a refiner and purifier of silver."[2250] The fact that our bodies are to become living sacrifices is proof that the members

---

2243   Malachi 2:6
2244   1 John 5:6
2245   John 3:5
2246   Ephesians 5:26
2247   1 Peter 1:22
2248   Colossians 1:9
2249   Romans 12:1
2250   Malachi 3:3

of our inward parts are to be for good service to our LORD and High Priest. Paul said, "If I be offered upon the sacrifice and service of your faith,"[2251] for the commission of the faithful is a "work of faith, and labour of love."[2252] None may achieve this privilege unless they cooperate with Christ's Spirit for cleansing their mental, moral, and physical members.

12. Christ now works in the second Apartment of the Temple of God to make the hope of newness a living fact. The will of God for the one who believes on His Son's voice is sanctification, which is the process whereby every faculty of the human being finds harmony with the LORD's commandments. How is this purification made possible? It says, "Through sanctification of the Spirit and belief of the truth."[2253] This is the only way one may obtain His manner of salvation, and this salvation strictly defined as, "The grace of God that bringeth salvation."[2254] Herein it is a fact that the salvation of God is the fulfillment of the saying, "Renew a right spirit within me,"[2255] for the deliverance promised to us is for our spirit, which is why it is well to know that "through knowledge shall the just be delivered."[2256] It is the wisdom of His grace contained within His blood's active profession that is to recover our mind of understanding "by the washing of regeneration, and renewing of the Holy Ghost."[2257] The soul is to come by this health that it may hold a proper conversation before God's throne, and with the reception of grace's gift upon the spirit's conscience, it is to be heard, "Every man that hath this hope in him purifieth himself."[2258]

13. A self-relinquishing spirit is to know God to keep every word that falls out from Him. Out of the mouth of God Himself came the Ten Commandments and the Faith of His Son, and the Spirit of this ministry calls all who would feel after Him to enter by faith into the

---

2251 Philippians 2:17
2252 1 Thessalonians 1:3
2253 2 Thessalonians 2:13
2254 Titus 2:11
2255 Psalms 51:10
2256 Proverbs 11:9
2257 Titus 3:5
2258 1 John 3:5

Room where He is at, that they may more perfectly love self and other spirits from surrendering their will to "love the truth and peace."[2259]

14. These things are so examined as they are because she who suffered a deadly wound is to fulfill the word, "Him that passeth by,"[2260] and, "Him that returneth."[2261] The spirit of the leopard beast that was smitten is in fact set to return, and this time in a far more grand and complete way, for at the time appointed it will be fulfilled, "His deadly wound was healed,"[2262] for he "shall ascend out of the bottomless pit, and go into perdition."[2263] Its power is blessed by that nation formed after its image, and it is for this reason that it is crucial to personally know the LORD through His doctrine. It is certain that most will not see the day of perdition, nor will they see the day of wickedness; as there is no longer a table of prophetic time; therefore at this hour the word should be observed for all preparation; whether we should live or die; "Acquaint now thyself with him, and be at peace...Receive, I pray thee, the law from his mouth, and lay up his words in thine heart."[2264]

15. "Turn you to the strong hold, ye prisoners of hope,"[2265] you that are "a prisoner of Jesus Christ."[2266] For, says the Spirit, "For sin and for uncleanness,"[2267] "the eyes of man, as of all the tribes of Israel, shall be toward the LORD."[2268]

2259 Zechariah 8:19
2260 Zechariah 9:8
2261 Zechariah 9:8
2262 Revelation 13:3
2263 Revelation 17:8
2264 Job 22:21,22
2265 Zechariah 9:12
2266 Philemon 1:2
2267 Zechariah 13:1
2268 Zechariah 9:1

25

The Heart Of The Serpent

1. "Now the serpent was more subtil than any beast of the field which the LORD God had made."[2269]

2. The serpent was more subtil above every creature, but how? It is written, "There met him a woman with the attire of an harlot, and subtil of heart. She is loud and stubborn; her feet abide not in her house."[2270] Because of a deceitful heart, the feet of the serpent did not rest in his house, and it is evident that the serpent rejected the natural purpose given to him by the Creator. It rejected the fabric of its constitution, it rejected the inherited maxim of its species, it rejected the lot given to it by God, and in thus rejecting the estate conferred upon it, it also rejected God's authority over it.

3. Again, how then did the serpent cultivate its subtleness after God Himself "saw that it was good"?[2271] What was the good that God saw of it? What is that "good"? Says Scripture, "Let us not be weary in well doing...Let us do good unto all men."[2272] Again, "Let no corrupt communication proceed out of your mouth, but that which is good to

---

2269   Genesis 3:1
2270   Proverbs 7:19,11
2271   Genesis 1:25
2272   Galatians 6:9,10

the use of edifying, that it may minister grace unto the hearers."[2273] To do well is to minister for the purpose of edifying to the praise of the Creator's name. Of all that God created, He saw that it perfectly administered the peculiar health that He had ordained for it to give to the entire creation. But the serpent stepped out of the realm of its order. In its heart, it refused to consent to be useful to its environment. Its philosophy had constrained its heart to believe, "Am I my brother's keeper?"[2274]

4. There then must be a reason why the serpent came to the woman, and it is because she bore the same disposition as him. Eve observed the cursed tree as one "to make one wise,"[2275] and the serpent, observing Eve as born from the man of God, must have taken her to be one possessing the same mind as God, although seeing in her the same philosophical juncture to which he had himself arrived. To Eve, the tree possessed the full knowledge of the LORD's voice and the knowledge to go along with that understanding to worship Him, even as did Adam, and all without personal diligent study and faithful agitation of her heart and mind. To the serpent, it appears that Eve was its tree of knowledge, for if it could possibly lead Eve to know that a creation of God also bore the same contemplation as her, then the serpent would have a new hope and domain, a new lot assigned to him by one who should be equal with God on all points, and for his own personal advantage.

5. It is indeed possible that the serpent turned his attention to Eve not because she may have been the weaker creation, but because it plainly saw that in the woman rested the same ideology as it. As timid and as reverent as the woman may have appeared to be by her husband, the serpent watched them, and in watching, he observed the honesty of their devotion. He heard Adam confess, "I will set no wicked thing before mine eyes,"[2276] and although he saw that Adam

---

2273 Ephesians 4:29
2274 Genesis 4:9
2275 Genesis 3:6
2276 Psalms 101:3

obeyed the command, "Do, as thou hast said,"[2277] he saw Eve eating from the cursed tree through her eyes, and viewing her bodily language from such a diet, he knew that his lowly estate would be better off in the hands of one that, he believed, held his mind, but with the same power and persuasion of God.

6. The serpent bears a consciousness alike to Eve, letting the reader know that whatever creature God created, it was in fact as Scripture says, a "living creature."[2278] This also sheds light on the fact that the living creatures lacked one thing that Adam and Eve possessed, which lacking made them solely "living," and that is a thinking and feeling conscience. The fact that the serpent turned subtle in its heart, and appears to display no shame for defecting from its Creator, and from the domain from which by birth it was constrained, displays a separate mind from Eve, who confessed, "God hath said,"[2279] even though she carried within herself unbelief in what God had actually said. Hence Adam eventually said of Eve, "The mother of al living,"[2280] because although she carried the full capability of exercising her mental and moral faculties, she placed the living portion of her nature; the carnal "which is corrupt according to the deceitful lusts";[2281] above her higher mental and moral faculties. She willingly and consciously violated her own conscience and the spirit of His knowledge.

7. Eve's violation did not begin when she physically ate of the tree, for it began the moment she heard from Adam, "Thou shalt not eat of it."[2282] From this point forward she set her thoughts on that tree, and from her imagination, gave herself over to base thoughts concerning its fruit, and thus began Eve's consumption, and the idea of her Creator as a liar, for she observed no ill effect from her musing. In Eve we can understand that inward character is not transferable and that a hopeful faith is not inherited from birth. Faith needs both willing deprivation and honest cultivation of self. Eve being purged from Adam gave her

---

2277   Genesis 18:5
2278   Genes 2:19
2279   Genesis 3:3
2280   Genesis 3:20
2281   Ephesians 4:22
2282   Genesis 2:17

no more right, and contained no more honest power to honor God's voice, than did a creature born from the earth, which earth obeyed its LORD and was praised, for "God saw that it was good."[2283] The serpent and the woman share the same mind, but Eve being the one who contained "the breath of life,"[2284] and was not just a living creature but was also "a living soul,"[2285] should have taken the confrontation with the serpent as an opportunity to exercise the little faith that she had. From that exercising, she would have been blessed with the knowledge she hoped to gain apart from her coarse imaginations.

8. Herein it is understood why no thing of the ground was given to the first pair for their diet. All "wherein there is life"[2286] had a menu separated by God for them not to be eaten by them born of Adam. As it says, "Out of the ground the LORD God formed every beast,"[2287] and, "God said, Let the earth bring forth the living creatures,"[2288] if Eve, who mentally ate that which came out of the ground and enflamed her nature to encourage apostasy from obedience, how much more dreadful will the human nature ignorantly and blindly fall from the literal mastication and digestion of such that are from the ground? There is a blatant cruel and irreverent spirit in the animal formed out of the ground, and not just the ground, for Scripture says, "Every living creature that moveth, which the waters brought forth."[2289] These creatures are living, and being called, "Living," they are dangerous by their blood and nature to the disposition of the human being, which is why God said, "I have given you every herb bearing seed...to you it shall be for meat."[2290]

9. God knew the danger that rested in the consumption of the flesh of what He had made "living." These creature may have been constructed by God to serve for only one purpose, as He says, "Let

---

2283 Genesis 1:12
2284 Genesis 2:7
2285 Genesis 2:7
2286 Genesis 1:30
2287 Genesis 2:19
2288 Genesis 1:24
2289 Genesis 1:21
2290 Genesis 1:29

them"; man and woman; "have dominion over the fish of the sea, and over the fowl of the air, and over the cattle, and over all the earth, and over every creeping thing that creepeth upon the earth."[2291] The fact that there exists no functioning conscience in these creatures to know right and/or from wrong informs us that they need a higher source of intelligence to rule them. The privilege of this rule was given to man, and as the "living" was to fall subject to man, man in turn was to fall subject to God from the labor of his authority over unstable creatures. If man should eat the living, God must have known that the living portions of their being; which God did not create them without; should be magnified to overthrow the innocent laws of their mental, moral, and spiritual being. Thus, by consuming the flesh of creatures, the physical frame of man would quickly deteriorate without him knowing, just as the spiritual and moral should also evaporate without him perceiving.

10. The LORD gave Adam a plain diet because He knew that certain things taken into the stomach produce negative blood; for "the life of the flesh is in the blood";[2292] and achieve an overworked digestive system, which will inevitably cause brain power to be given to the organs of the body, causing mental fatigue and hurtful unnecessary agitation within the heart and mind. Without the powers of the brain able to properly function to strenuously rightly divide the LORD's voice, the heart would not honestly care to independently search after heaven's will, thus fulfilling the word, "After their own lusts shall they heap to themselves teachers, having itching ears."[2293] Heaven's plain diet is for the purpose of the son and daughter of God who want to know Him, and the diligence it takes to build up an intelligent manner of eating is also a test of faithfulness, for all personal application will add strength to the inward person, and blessing from His Spirit.

11. Because Eve, within her heart, ate from that cursed tree, every effect that takes place from eating meat, mentally and morally, took fast hold within her human being. This is how the serpent knew that he could manipulate her. Eve may have possessed the same unlimited

---

2291 Genesis 1:26
2292 Leviticus 17:11
2293 2 Timothy 4:3

capabilities of heaven's messengers, but as she fell to lust, she desired a teacher to give her what she did not physically care to give herself, and so believed the tree to be a good minister for her inward inclinations. This is how the woman could obey the creature above the Creator, and how the Israelites obeyed the creatures of their customs above the Creator, and it is how the woman of the earth beast will obey the meat of the philosophy of men above the truth of the Creator's heavenly tidings.

12. As it says of the dragon and the serpent, "The dragon persecuted the woman,"[2294] and, "The serpent cast a flood from its mouth after the woman,"[2295] we see that the two, the dragon and the serpent, are one and the same. The dragon is a symbol of Pagan Rome, it is a symbol of idolatrous Roman standards both religiously and politically, and when the strange values of Rome enter into a woman of the earth, Pagan Rome will have a new title and a new religion within a new fraudulent State. The philosophy of the serpent will cause a new species of invention to occur within a church of the earth, to cause a national union among like-factions. Continual disobedience to the Spirit's voice will eventually lead to the consumption of flesh meats, that is, "divers and strange doctrines."[2296] From these doctrines, because none within these houses know the living God, again the creature will be observed above the Creator, and the saying will be fulfilled, "He maketh fire come down from heaven on the earth in the sight of men."[2297]

13. That which comes out of this new republic will be drawn from certain priests, for the fire is brought down by their spirit and invention, seeing as how within them "are the spirits of devils, working miracles."[2298] From "giving heed to seducing spirits, and doctrines of devils,"[2299] it will be fulfilled, "Men, leaving the natural use of the woman, burned in their lust one toward another."[2300] New philosophies will distort the

---

2294 Revelation 12:13
2295 Revelation 12:15
2296 Hebrews 13:9
2297 Revelation 13:13
2298 Revelation 16:14
2299 1 Timothy 4:1
2300 Romans 1:27

knowledge of God's High Priest to bring an accepted religion into the courts of the State, and as the idolatrous and corrupt practices of the serpent are introduced into an already apostatized woman, due to her diet, she will take those creeds and so mingle them with her own, even removing or reinterpreting her own beliefs just to find harmony with the State for temporal and eternal supremacy. It is for this reason that all professing the name of Christ, and loyalty to the LORD God and Father, should at this time know the will of His mediation.

14. This woman is already deceived at heart, and the serpent looks for a most opportune time to approach her. As the serpent is a beast symbolized by the dragon, and as the dragon is a symbol of Satan, the dictates of his heart are, "I will ascend into heaven, I will exalt my throne above the stars of God: I will sit also upon the mount of the congregation."[2301] The desire for a church and state government is on Satan's heart, thus we have before us what is called, "Satan's seat."[2302] Philosophies seasoned with professed Christian values are waiting to seduce the already dead women of the earth. God had said to Adam, "If you eat then you die," and due to her mental consumption, Eve was already dead before she physically tasted the material grown on the tree. Then came the serpent preaching "great swelling words of vanity"[2303] to "allure through the lusts of the flesh."[2304] As it happened to Eve, and as it happened to the early Christian church, so too will it happen again.

15. The serpent represents a system of understanding without full use of the conscience and without the need for heaven's moral principles to regulate the heart's posture. If the serpent could be joined to the woman born of the man of God, the two would be a most devastating force. As the serpent exists without a conscience or without any moral law written within it, it should long to reign within a dominion free from the injunction of the conscience. And if the woman was joined to the serpent, which serpent has its power and authority in its

---

2301 Isaiah 14:12,13
2302 Revelation 2:13
2303 2 Peter 2:18
2304 2 Peter 2:18

voice, the woman could use the serpent to cement her laws, causing the serpent to act as the conscience for her environment. Thus the word is fulfilled through a terrible distortion, "Let every soul be subject unto the higher powers. For there is no power but of God: the powers that be are ordained of God. Whosoever therefore resisteth the power, resisteth the ordinance of God."[2305]

16. The dragon; who is a symbol of Pagan Rome; was built primarily on the notion that the State of Rome is essentially a "Supreme Being" alone. Whatever the State declared was as if spoken by a god, therefore to violate the State of Rome was to defy the god of the Roman State. When such an entity anciently joined forces with a "certain of the sect of the Pharisees which believed,"[2306] the early church combined both paganism and the Christian religion under Constantine's rule to create a most dreadful beast. At this time, Satan's seat was just that, a seat that needed to be filled, and eventually the saying would be fulfilled, "The dragon gave him his power, and his seat, and great authority."[2307] Whom did the dragon, Pagan Rome, give his seat to? It is written, "The mystery of iniquity doth already work: only he who now letteth will let, until he be taken out of the way."[2308]

17. He who was taken out of the way was the dragon; the pagan religion of Rome; fulfilling the word, "The daily sacrifice shall be taken away, and the abomination that maketh desolate set up."[2309] Paganism was at this time universally draped under a garment of Christianity, and its new head was not the Spirit Christ, but rather the spirit of "that man of sin...the son of perdition."[2310] These things happened because of "a falling away first,"[2311] and as it then happened, another falling away by the spirit of the dragon will happen again.

18. Apostasy will find itself in an already apostate church professing service to *the Father* and *His Son*, and she will fall even further away

---

2305 Romans 13:1,2
2306 Acts 15:5
2307 Revelation 13:2
2308 2 Thessalonians 2:7
2309 Daniel 12:11
2310 2 Thessalonians 2:3
2311 2 Thessalonians 2:3

from heaven's religion than she already now is. When once paganism is embraced within her, whatever that creed may be and however it is accomplished, she will join herself to the government of the earth, and through his voice will cement her reign under a pretended honor for her *Christ*. This is why a living and experimental faith in the Faith of Jesus to obtain knowledge of the Spirit's name is important. Today is our opportunity to know the science of the Spirit's benevolent will, and apart from inherited or self-cultivated traditional belief, for a faith that will keep and preserve our spirit.

19. Many believers who profess faith in *God's Christ* will at this later time honor the image set up against His name, and they will do so because they do not know the living God. The Faith of Jesus is ordained to regenerate the moral character of the hearer and doer of that Faith, and that alleviation to the conscience comes only by having the commandments of God written within the walls of the heart, and kept within the ark of the spirit in the soul's temple. Obedience to the precepts that are attached to the Spirit's sacrifice and to Christ's mediation are to bring us to reverence the ten laws of His God, for the controversy is in fact against the authority of the LORD's voice of commandments. If there is now a refusal to know the wisdom of His voice, whoever should be alive at the time of the amalgamation of a dark church and State economy in the earth will die within their self. Today is our opportunity to personally know the doctrine of the LORD's Son and Spirit.

26

A Fearful Disposition

1. "And I beheld another beast coming up out of the earth; and he had two horns like a lamb, and he spake as a dragon."[2312]

2. When it says, "Shall the earth be made to bring forth in one day? or shall a nation be born at once?"[2313] it is plain to see that the earth is a figurative illustration of a nation. Daniel says, "Four great beasts came up from the sea, diverse one from another,"[2314] and within the same chapter he records what the angel said to him: "These great beasts, which are four, are four kings, which shall arise out of the earth."[2315] The earth and the sea in Daniel's vision are one. The use of the word, "another," means fresh, new, distinct, diverse, individual. Another beast arose from the same earth and foundation as the other beasts, and as the others were diverse one from another, so this new two horned beast that John sees should be diverse from the ones before it.

3. As this beast came up from the earth, from a nation, it is evident that the earth from which it came has a living history before it surfaced

---

2312 Revelation 13:11
2313 Isaiah 66:8
2314 Daniel 7:3
2315 Daniel 7:17

from it. Herein the word is fulfilled, since at this day the empires of the world from Babylon to Papal Rome have fallen from universal authority, "One is, and the other is not yet come; and when he cometh, he must continue a short space,"[2316] for as five kingdoms are fallen, and the sixth is yet present, this two horned beast should indeed be that next power, which kingdom is to bless the healing of the fifth, for the fifth "is the eighth, and is of the seventh, and goeth into perdition."[2317] John observes this two horned nation as coming up from the sixth kingdom of the earth, and this nation is born with two horns like a lamb and with the voice of a dragon, and from the grammar with which it is described, it appears that John first observed the horns and body, and then a short time later heard his voice.

4. What does it mean to speak as a dragon? It says, "The dragon persecuted the woman,"[2318] and, "The dragon stood to devour."[2319] Thus, it should be asked, "Is persecution impulsive? Does anger have order? Why should the two-horned beast immediately draw the stereotype of an outwardly persecuting power after its professed innocence fades away? Does persecution begin outwardly? What is crueler than outward or physical persecution? And what sequence of events actually lead up to the type of unstable character that the dragon displays?"

5. The voice of the dragon may be one of violence, and, as the dragon is a symbol of the Sate of Rome in its Pagan phase, its voice of persecution is doubtless found in its power to enact and to execute laws, and especially for religion. To speak as a dragon means to possess the inward qualities of a dragon, for speech is only occasioned due to an inward response from external stimulus. This new beast wore two horns like a lamb; it bore two core powers of supposed innocent tenderness; yet inwardly it possessed the mind and practice of a dragon. It is for this reason that it must be considered, "What may be the intrinsic values of a dragon?"

2316 Revelation 17:10
2317 Revelation 17:11
2318 Revelation 12:13
2319 Revelation 12:4

6. It is written, "Levi'athan the piercing serpent...the dragon that is in the sea."[2320] The dragon is Levi'athan, and it is also the serpent. What are the inward qualities of the dragon and serpent Levi'athan? It is written, "His strength is in his loins, and his force is in the navel of his belly."[2321] "Will he make many supplications unto thee? will he speak soft words unto thee?"[2322] "Who can discover the face of his garment? or who can come to him with his double bridle?"[2323] "Out of his mouth go burning lamps, and sparks of fire leap out,"[2324] for the force of the dragon is indeed within its belly, which is why it is counseled, "Mark them which cause divisions and offences contrary to the doctrine which ye have learned; and avoid them. For they that are such serve not our Lord Jesus Christ, but their own belly; and by good words and fair speeches deceive the hearts of the simple."[2325] This is why we see the serpent counseling Eve, despite the fact that the counsel of God was given and yet stood, "Ye shall not surely die."[2326] The serpent promised, "Your eyes shall be opened, and ye shall be as gods,"[2327] wherefore it must then be asked, "How did the serpent know this?" To him was given to eat not that "fruit of a tree yielding seed,"[2328] but rather "every green herb for meat."[2329] The only way that the serpent could have known that she should not die, but rather have her eyes enlightened, was if it had itself ate from the tree and experienced either the promised curse, or the nothingness of the violation, attached to it.

7. It is evident that the serpent left off the natural use conferred to it by God and sought its own direction. God had said to Adam, "In the day that you eat of this tree, you will suffer the death that I have authorized its fruit to carry," and although Adam did not eat of it, the serpent

---

2320   Isaiah 27:1
2321   Job 40:16
2322   Job 41:3
2323   Job 41:13
2324   Job 41:19
2325   Romans 16:17,18
2326   Genesis 3:4
2327   Genesis 3:5
2328   Genesis 1:29
2329   Genesis 1:30

knew something more than what was being told them. The serpent left its natural diet and wandered from its God, and whether filled with disappointment or prideful ambition, it became more subtle in its heart than any beast that God had made, letting us know that not all of the creatures carried the same feverish spirit as the serpent, the serpent truly making itself of note in vision to Moses for its more openly vile character.

8. The serpent said, "You will know good and evil," for a creature being created without knowledge of good and evil cannot at once admit this fact to another. Adam and Eve were created without a mind desirous of good and evil, they were truly as innocent as we are today at birth and as children, therefore within their nature they should want either good or evil, they should care to only "make the tree good... or else make the tree corrupt."[2330] The creatures did not have a mind for choice in the matter, for they were created as "living," they were formed without a sober mental and moral law written within them, thus fulfilling the saying, "The spirit of the beast that goeth downward to the earth."[2331] "As is the earthy, such are they also that are earthy,"[2332] and that of the earth is naturally "foolish, disobedient, deceived, serving diverse lust and pleasures, living in malice and envy, hateful, and hating one another."[2333] The spirit of the earth embraces "excess of wine, revelings, banquetings, and abominable idolatries,"[2334] and this is the ground from whence all things, including man, are born.

9. Although such a spirit existed within the creatures of God, it was in man that God bestowed the pleasure of rising above such a mind, and that the creature born in this ignorance would find right use and guidance by ones entrusted with a moral compass, and with higher capabilities of perception and comprehension. It appears that the serpent rejected the lot of man and of God over it, and so chose its own way from out of the meditations of its own belly. It could not

---

2330 Matthew 12:33
2331 Ecclesiastes 3:21
2332 1 Corinthians 15:48
2333 Titus 3:3
2334 1 Peter 4:3

have known the end of the fruit of the tree unless it had indulged in it, for as it was born without a knowledge of good and evil, but of only an error that needed correction from man, it must be that Eve knew that the tree was *good* from observing the evidence of its supposed goodness in the serpent. The serpent ate and became more subtle, more deceived in its heart against the LORD, and after Eve ate, she became also more of the same, yet neither the other creatures nor Eeve appear to be converted to a new mind from their consumption. It was only after Adam had eaten that "the eyes of them both were opened,"[2335] and so also must have been the inward code of the creatures.

    10. That which gave the serpent its voice came from its own belly, which belly is of an appetite of soft and exciting imaginative words to compel the flesh to move the body. The serpent embraced the fact that it no longer only knew what had been etched into its familial inheritance, but that now in it the word was fulfilled, "Ye are gods; and all of you are children of the most High."[2336] Now, built up on a new constitution due to removing himself from his allotted diet, the word was fulfilled, "Thine heart was lifted up because of thy beauty, thou hast corrupted thy wisdom by reason of thy brightness."[2337] Therefore when the serpent saw Eve, after having studied her loyalty to *God*, it was fulfilled, "I will lay thee before kings, that they may behold thee,"[2338] for he saw that Eve embraced his mind, and knowing that she too wanted to be a king, approached her with a double bridle as burning lamps and sparks of fire.

    11. Out of the mouth of the serpent came a doctrine clothed in a spurious garment light. The serpent, full of "a mouth speaking great things and blasphemies...against God, to blasphemy his name, and his tabernacle, and them that dwell in heaven,"[2339] having removed himself from the Spirit's order, through his new artful speech, he sought to implant his seed within the heart of the woman. It is in this same

---

2335 Genesis 3:7
2336 Psalms 82:6
2337 Ezekiel 28:17
2338 Ezekiel 28:17
2339 Revelation 13:5,6

manner that the dragon will infect the two-horned beast, which dragon is this same serpent. Speech is not at first physical and audible; it begins in the spirit of the mind. That which will come from the two-horned beast will be, at first, an appearance of kindness and neutrality for the soul and spirit, but the philosophies that will come from it will bear a double heart executed through its judicial system.

12. The serpent is symbol of a strange philosophy invented through an idolatrous and self-exalting spirit. When such a spirit is joined to a woman professing to be of the *Son* of *God*, it will again be fulfilled, "His power shall be mighty, but not by his own power,"[2340] thus repeating the history, "Power was given to him that sat thereon to take peace from the earth."[2341] Again, it will be fulfilled, "Through his policy also he shall cause craft to prosper in his hand,"[2342] thus again fulfilling the word, "He that sat on him had a pair of balances in his hand."[2343]

13. Because there will be a few who will refuse that which comes from out of his mouth; both civilly and religiously; this beast will then speak as a dragon, as opposed to how it first spoke through its miraculous thoughts to convert many to its ideologies. Hence it should be heard at this hour of atonement to heaven's LORD and God, "Walk not as other Gentiles, in the vanity of their mind,"[2344] and, "Let them alone: they be blind leaders of the blind. And if the blind lead the blind, both shall fall into the ditch."[2345]

14. What is written of this ditch advertised by the serpent? It says, "He maketh a path to shine after him; one would think the deep to be hoary."[2346] The ditch is the deep, which shining path is a doctrine that embraces "the depths of Satan,"[2347] which depths are according to the saying, "He magnified himself even to the prince of the host,"[2348] and,

---

2340 Daniel 8:24
2341 Revelation 6:4
2342 Daniel 8:25
2343 Revelation 6:5
2344 Ephesians 4:17-19
2345 Matthew 15:14
2346 Job 41:32
2347 Revelation 2:24
2348 Daniel 8:11

"I will be like the most High."[2349] The house "without any order, and where the light is as darkness,"[2350] is where the mind of the serpent rests, and upon entrance to his living quarters he says, "I have decked my bed with coverings of tapestry, with carved works, with fine linen of Egypt,"[2351] that is, with "profane and vain babblings, and oppositions of science falsely so called."[2352] The new republic born from out of the nation before it, which nation is that current power who swiftly took the domain of the world after 1773A.D., and is yet still in power, will be a nation transformed by spiritual philosophical falsehood, which is why it is called, "The false prophet that wrought miracles."[2353]

15. A study of the Spirit's doctrine, which embraces the principles, "Fear God...and worship him that made,"[2354] and, "Babylon is fallen, is fallen,"[2355] and, "If any man worship the beast and his image, and receive his mark,"[2356] will draw the humble hearer and doer of the Spirit's law to correctly hear the charge, "Behold the Lamb."[2357] The power of this instruction is to cause a mental and moral regeneration within the obedient from their personal application of the spiritual truths given them by it. "The holy commandment delivered unto them"[2358] will lead to them "understanding what the will of the Lord is,"[2359] which will is the sanctification of the inward members to find harmony with the commandments of God, and not just with His Faith.

16. The doctrine of the serpent is a speech promoting intemperate and irrational liberty of self from the LORD's voice; it is a philosophy that surrenders the will to the reins of the heart's natural estate, leaving morality of thought and feeling without the dictates of a sympathetic conscience transformed by faith's learning and exercise. It is apparent

---

2349 Isaiah 14:14
2350 Job 10:22
2351 Proverbs 7:16
2352 1 Timothy 6:20
2353 Revelation 19:20
2354 Revelation 14:7
2355 Revelation 14:8
2356 Revelation 14:9
2357 John 1:29
2358 2 Peter 2:21
2359 Ephesians 5:17

that such strange things will pervert an already perverted woman of the earth, and when this perversion has reached a point of unity among her diverse factions, she will assume the form of the dragon and will seek to advance her cause from his mouth. This is why it is counseled, "Suffer not a woman to teach, nor to usurp authority over the man,"[2360] for at the time appointed, a woman will wear the robe of a man, and again it will be fulfilled, "She wrote letters in Ahab's name, and sealed them with his seal, and sent the letters unto the elders and to the nobles."[2361]

[2360] 1 Timothy 2:12
[2361] 1 Kings 21:8

27

Stedfast Unto The End

1. Says Scripture, "He, being full of the Holy Ghost, looked up stedfastly into heaven, and saw the glory of God, and Jesus standing on the right hand of God, and said, Behold, I see the heavens opened, and the Son of man standing on the right hand of God."[2362]

2. Again, at another time it is written, "As he journeyed, he came near Damascus: and suddenly there shined round about him a light from heaven: and he fell to the earth, and heard a voice saying unto him, Saul, Saul, why persecutest thou me? And he said, Who art thou, Lord? And the Lord said, I am Jesus whom thou persecutest."[2363]

3. Both Paul and Stephen, by vision, observed where Christ was after He had ascended to His LORD. Stephen amazingly testifies that he saw the heavens opened, and it was in the space of this opening that he saw God's Man, letting us know that the heavens are a structure having doors. For by the glory that he witnessed, Stephen must have fallen short of words, and so called what he saw

---

2362 Acts 7:55,56
2363 Acts 9:3-5

to be, "Heavens," yet in truth what he saw was what John saw and recorded: "I looked, and, behold, a door was opened in heaven."[2364]

4. What Stephen saw was what John saw, and they both saw that "a throne was set in heaven, and one sat on the throne...And he that sat was to look upon like a jasper and a sardine stone: and there was a rainbow round about the throne, in sight like unto an emerald. And round about the throne were four and twenty seats: and upon the seats...four and twenty elders sitting, clothed in white raiment; and they had on their heads crowns of gold...And before the throne there was a sea of glass like unto crystal: and in the midst of the throne, and round about the throne, were four beasts full of eyes before and behind."[2365]

5. The vision given to these men revealed the Father of Christ and the majesty of His heavenly Building, but it also revealed Christ "transfigured before them."[2366] Christ said, "Hereafter shall the Son of man sit on the right hand of the power of God,"[2367] for He "is set down at the right hand of the throne of God."[2368] When the Spirit's men saw the LORD's Man, they saw "in the midst of the seven candlesticks one like unto the Son of man, clothed with a garment down to the foot, and girt about the paps with a golden girdle."[2369] "His face did shine as the sun, and his raiment was white as the light."[2370] "His raiment became shining, exceeding white as snow; so as no fuller on earth can white them."[2371] Thus, Christ is observed as clothed in the high priestly garments of one who was head over the house of God, and was seen positioned by the throne of God in the doors of God's Temple, even as John records: "I saw...one like unto

---

2364   Revelation 4:1
2365   Revelation 4:2-6
2366   Mark 9:2
2367   Luke 22:69
2368   Hebrews 12:2
2369   Revelation 1:13
2370   Matthew 17:2
2371   Mark 9:3

the Son of Man, clothed with a garment down to the foot, and girt about the paps with a golden girdle."[2372]

6. It is clear that, from what the items of the room reveal, that this first door in heaven was the first place of labor for the ministers of the earthly sanctuary. We have revealed to us the candlestick, "for there was a tabernacle made; the first, wherein was the candlestick, and the table, and the shewbread; which is called the sanctuary. And after the second veil, the tabernacle which is called the Holiest of all."[2373] This is why Stephen said, "I saw the heavens opened," and did not say, "I saw heaven opened." John saw a door opened in heaven, denoting singularity of time and space. John saw God's Man, at first, as a minister within the Holy Place in heaven, for John would later again say, "The temple of God was opened in heaven."[2374] John observed two temples opened in heaven at two separate and distinct times, yet in vision, Stephen saw the full glory of the Faith of Jesus, for he saw both doors opened in heaven with Christ by the Throne and Government of His LORD and Father.

7. The magnitude of this vision suffered blindness on Paul for three days. "I could not see for the glory of that light,"[2375] he said. But when his sight did return to him, he was a man of a new tongue. Those that had only known Saul as that persecutor were warmed by the comfort of his new person, for he reports, "They glorified God in me."[2376] This is the true hope of any one willing to allow their heart to enter into the doors of heaven. After his vision, "Saul arose from the earth; and when his eyes were opened, he saw no man,"[2377] which is why he counsels, "Henceforth know we no man after the flesh...If any man be in Christ, he is a new creature: old things are passed away; behold, all things are become new."[2378] And again, when preaching on the new name of

---

2372 Revelation 1:13
2373 Hebrews 9:2,3
2374 Revelation 11:19
2375 Acts 22:11
2376 Galatians 1:24
2377 Acts 9:8
2378 2 Corinthians 5:16,17

God's Man, Paul taught, "We have an advocate with the Father"[2379] who "is able also to save them to the uttermost that come unto God by him, seeing he ever liveth to make intercession for them."[2380]

8. These things are so mentioned because it was told us, "This same Jesus, which is taken up from you into heaven, shall so come in like manner as ye have seen him go into heaven,"[2381] and, Christ says, "Hereafter shall ye see the Son of man sitting on the right hand of power, and coming in the clouds of heaven."[2382] Now, if Christ wanted us to think on His final descent by the words here mentioned, He would have said, "In the glory of His Father with his angels,"[2383] for at this appointment, "the Lord cometh with ten thousands of his saints...to execute judgment, and to convince."[2384] The fact that Christ connects His coming to His position at the right hand of God distinguishes an order within His position at the right hand of His LORD. It is written, "We have such an high priest, who is set on the right hand of the throne of the Majesty in the heavens,"[2385] and if at the right hand as Son and Minister over that which was "the example and shadow of heavenly things";[2386] which things concern "the Levit'ical priesthood";[2387] then as that of old had times and seasons for its office, so too Christ, who exists within "the figures of the true";[2388] that is, "of the true tabernacle, which the Lord pitched";[2389] His office should likewise have times and seasons. Man would observe Christ by the right hand of God at all times within the two doors of the heavens, yet what should mark His move into the second door to begin a new season of ministry would be His appearance solely in the clouds of heaven; as he ascended into the first Room of His LORD, so He would come into the second.

2379   1 John 2:1
2380   Hebrews 7:25
2381   Acts 1:11
2382   Matthew 26:64
2383   Matthew 16:27
2384   Jude 1:14,15
2385   Hebrews 8:1
2386   Hebrews 8:5
2387   Hebrews 7:11
2388   Hebrews 9:24
2389   Hebrews 8:2

9. Herein it is fulfilled, "One like the Son of man came with the clouds of heaven, and came to the Ancient of days, and they brought him near before him."[2390] At this time, the ministry of Christ changes from the Holy to the Most Holy Place, fulfilling the word, "The Lord, whom ye seek, shall suddenly come to his temple."[2391] Although this fact has been before stated and proven, it should be noted that in every point as He was taken up, so should He come again. Christ was indeed taken by clouds; that is, angels; into heaven from the earth at His ascension, but He was also not without visions of confirmation "by many infallible proofs."[2392] As those visions testified to the current place and position of His office, so when it should be time for Him to come again in like manner, we should not be left without a vision of His new place and position in the plan of redemption.

10. This is truly a remarkable thing. A vision plainly marked the doctrine of Christ in the beginning of the gospel, and again it would be most certain that the same events would surround the movements of His high priestly office at the end of that first movement, for at this time "the mystery of God should be finished."[2393] During the time when "the vision of the evening and the morning"[2394] should be finished, the counsel would be given to the disciples of Christ, "The vision is yet for an appointed time, but at the end it shall speak, and not lie: though it tarry, wait for it; because it will surely come, it will not tarry."[2395] What vision was to come? It was the vision that was to fulfill the saying, "The Lord, whom ye seek, shall suddenly come to his temple."[2396]

11. The disciples of this period anxiously awaited the coming of their salvation's Captain, and for not having an understanding on the Sanctuary erected by Moses, they misinterpreted the Spirit's sayings concerning a physical appearance in the clouds as His coming in unimaginable glory and vengeance, therefore an additional word was

---

2390 Daniel 7:13
2391 Malachi 3:1
2392 Acts 1:3
2393 Revelation 10:7
2394 Daniel 8:26
2395 Habakkuk 2:3
2396 Malachi 3:1

given to strengthen them: "Behold, his soul which is lifted up is not upright in him: but the just shall live by his faith."[2397] The fact that these hopeful individuals were to consider the foundation of their Protestant heritage; which was the law of justification by faith; that study was to send them to investigate the Place of justification. Yet the Spirit reports of them at this time, "I have not found thy works perfect before God,"[2398] for the word was fulfilled, "While the bridegroom tarried, they all slumbered and slept."[2399] This is why the Spirit said, "Tarry and wait,"[2400] for during this period, the word was fulfilled, "I will cause you to pass under the rod, and I will bring you into the bond of the covenant: and I will purge out from among you the rebels, and them that transgress against me."[2401]

12. By this purging it was to be fulfilled, "I will take away the names of Ba'alim out of her mouth, and they shall no more be remembered by their name."[2402] "I will bring them forth out of the country where they sojourn, and they shall not enter into the land of Israel: and ye shall know that I am the LORD,"[2403] for He said, "I will even betroth thee unto me in faithfulness: and thou shalt know the LORD."[2404] "I will betroth thee unto me for ever; yea, I will betroth thee unto me in righteousness, and in judgment, and in lovingkindness, and in mercies,"[2405] said the Spirit, hence He gave the word, "Blessed is he that waiteth, and cometh to the thousand three hundred and five and thirty days."[2406]

13. At the end of these days, a vision was to fill the hearts of the faithful few who waited on God's Lord and took confidence on the word, "The days are at hand, and the effect of every vision,"[2407] and, "Thus saith the Lord GOD; There shall none of my words be prolonged

---

2397 Habakkuk 2:4
2398 Revelation 3:2
2399 Matthew 25:5
2400 Habakkuk 2:3
2401 Ezekiel 20:37,38
2402 Hosea 2:17
2403 Ezekiel 20:38
2404 Hosea 2:20
2405 Hosea 2:19
2406 Daniel 12:12
2407 Ezekiel 12:23

any more, but the word which I have spoken shall be done."[2408] Hence, at the end of the full "two thousand and three hundred days,"[2409] the vision was given, "And the temple of God was opened in heaven, and there was seen in his temple the ark of his testament."[2410] At this time the disciples of the faith of Christ saw Him enter into the second door of heaven to complete the final portion of His ministry, and therein was seen shining before Him the ark of His Father, which ark held the ten laws of God, and one law shining most radiant in its appearance, reading, "Remember the Sabbath day, to keep it holy."[2411] "The seventh day is the Sabbath of the LORD."[2412]

14. The law of the seventh-day Sabbath is the foundation of the LORD's Faith. It is the mark of the authority of God's Spirit over creation's science and is a discourse on the love of God, therefore when one submits allegiance to this LORD, that loyalty cannot be without the seal of the confession of His authority over their inward parts. The Protestants at this time had come out of a house that achieved open "blasphemy against God, to blaspheme his name, and his tabernacle, and them that dwell in heaven."[2413] Under the reign of their mother, many "were slain for the word of God, and for the testimony which they held."[2414] Because they had failed to hear the counsel, "Strengthen the things which remain, that are ready to die,"[2415] at this time the Spirit sought to place into the mind of the faithful the end of the Faith of Jesus, confirming, "We might be made the righteousness of God in him."[2416]

15. For more than 2000 years, the Spirit's fame had been honored without respect to His name or character. After the passing of the first apostles, the philosophies and popular sophistries of ministers

---

2408   Ezekiel 12:28
2409   Daniel 8:14
2410   Revelation 11:19
2411   Exodus 20:8
2412   Exodus 20:10
2413   Revelation 13:6
2414   Revelation 6:9
2415   Revelation 3:2
2416   2 Corinthians 5:21

took hold of the simple science of the apostles' speech and perverted them. Paganism, with its rites and service to obscure mysteries, with its "days, and months, and times, and years,"[2417] took control of the Spirit's instruction by unconverted Christian men and women. This spirit led to the development of one "who opposeth and exalteth himself above all that is called God, or that is worshipped,"[2418] and it was him that fulfilled the prophecy, "He shall speak great words against the most High, and shall wear out the saints of the most High, and think to change times and laws."[2419] This enemy of all that concerns heaven's throne religion, this "throne of iniquity"[2420] magnifying "the mystery of iniquity,"[2421] "cast down the truth to the ground; and it practised, and prospered."[2422]

16. Protestants who had escaped the heritage of their former house did not know the character of the living God. Throughout their career, although the reformation had opened the mind to the falsehood of the Papacy and to the imaginary creed of Catholicism, Protestants spent much of their time bickering over doctrines and subscribing to the tenets of their leaders above learning of and doing the Spirit's Faith. When the vision of Christ in the second Apartment of heaven's Sanitarium should come, when the Protestant churches should have gone through a purging for faithfulness to that new revelation, they were to behold the key to the health of their ignorance to find unity among one another. But because the spirit of their mother rested within their heart, Christ said of them, after observing them, "I know thy works, that thou hast a name that thou livest, and art dead,"[2423] for the Faith which should give them life would be made manifest to them, and that Faith being of obedience to the name of the One by the right hand of God for the purpose of knowing and remembering His God's name.

2417   Galatians 4:10
2418   2 Thessalonians 2:4
2419   Daniel 7:25
2420   Psalm 94:20
2421   Psalms 94:20
2422   Daniel 8:12
2423   Revelation 3:1

17. The commandment that says, "Remember," is that precept concerning His Sabbath. The LORD counsels to remember this day because He knew that much would happen to cause *it* to be forgotten. Such a law did not originate on stone in the mountain, but after He had created all things, the LORD ordained His seventh-day Memorial for all of mankind. The early Christians; supposed converts from a pagan and Jewish religion; subscribed to a Sunday worship due to the fact that they repeated the history, "They feared the LORD, and made unto themselves of the lowest of them priests of the high places, which sacrificed for them in the houses of the high places. They feared the LORD, and served their own gods."[2424] As time went forward, through the work of strange self-imposing philosophies and the work of the Papacy, the Spirit's seventh day was forgotten, hence "unto this day they do after the former manners: they fear not the LORD, neither do they after... the law and commandment which the LORD commanded the children of Jacob, whom he named Israel."[2425]

18. After a long season of dominion under an ungodly institution, the time came for His worshippers to return to His throne. The centuries had stripped God from His gospel, for both Catholics and Protestants had supplanted the Spirit's purpose for the hopes of men, removing the Father from His Christ, wherefore now the appointed vision was given: Christ stood by the right hand of the throne of God, and with His own blood sprinkled over the ark, announced to every one professing His name, "Bind up the testimony, seal the law among my disciples."[2426] Now, at former "times of this ignorance God winked at; but now commandeth all men every where to repent,"[2427] for the vision is clear, and it is most certain, that every active believer will be examined of God for loyalty to His commandments by exercising faith on the power and wisdom of the blood of His Son.

19. It is now the duty of every believer to separate and move on from received tradition, for it indeed stems from them that fulfill the

---

[2424] 2 Kings 17:32,33
[2425] 2 Kings 17:34
[2426] Isaiah 8:16
[2427] Acts 17:30

saying, "These nations feared the LORD, and served their graven images, both their children, and their children's children: as did their fathers, so do they unto this day."[2428] There is a Faith of God, and it now rests within the Most Holy Apartment of the LORD's heavenly House. As it was in the beginning of the gospel, so too has it happened at the beginning of the end of this world's age, for the Faith of His Christ is no longer to be found in the first Room of heaven, but rather in "the temple of the tabernacle of the testimony in heaven."[2429] The times of ignorance are past, the order of God and of Christ is made manifest, for "it is said, To day if ye will hear his voice, harden not your hearts, as in the provocation."[2430] "For we are made partakers of Christ, if we hold the beginning of our confidence stedfast unto the end."[2431]

20. "Take heed, brethren, lest there be in any of you an evil heart of unbelief, in departing from the living God. But exhort one another daily, while it is called To day; lest any of you be hardened through the deceitfulness of sin."[2432] At this time, for the one who would see Christ as He stands before the LORD His God, it is yet even counseled, "Cast not away therefore your confidence, which hath great recompence of reward. For ye have need of patience, that, after ye have done the will of God, ye might receive the promise. For yet a little while, and he that shall come will come, and will not tarry. Now the just shall live by faith."[2433]

2428 2 Kings 17:41
2429 Revelation 15:5
2430 Hebrews 3:15
2431 Hebrews 3:14
2432 Hebrews 3:12,13
2433 Hebrews 10:35-38

28

Vash'ti The Queen

1. "He maketh fire come down from heaven on the earth in the sight of men."[2434]

2. The king of the earth beast will work many things in the sight of religious men, and this phrase, "In the sight of men," means that there will be a hierarchal reproduction of how it is written, "The power of Persia and Media, the nobles and princes of the provinces, being before him."[2435] The "him" spoken of, that is the king Ahasue'rus, and them before him were the men under whose sight, under whose instruction, he worked. As the Revelation given John is not a vision of civil happenings, but is rather a vision of church history, the nobles and princes mentioned should be viewed not as simply maintaining civil authority or intelligence, but rather legislative ecclesiastical governance. These men, in whom the king fulfills the petition of in the Revelation, should be likened to "the seven chamberlains that served in the presence of Ahasue'rus the king,"[2436] "the seven princes

---

2434 Revelation 13:13
2435 Esther 1:3
2436 Esther 1:10

of Persia and Media, which saw the king's face, and which sat the first in the kingdom."[2437]

3. The question then arises, "How is it that men, preferably leading church bishops, have, in the Revelation, come into such political favor with the throne of the government?" The answer is that something took place within the foundation of that government to place authority where it need not be. The fact that men are working miracles by the earth beast tells of the fact that, beforehand, there was some error that occurred within the earth. What may that error have been? It is written, "When the heart of the king was merry with wine, he commanded...to bring Vash'ti the queen before the king with the crown royal, to shew the people and the princes her beauty: for she was fair to look on. But the queen Vash'ti refused to come at the king's commandment by his chamberlains: therefore was the king very wroth, and his anger burned in him."[2438]

4. It must be understood that a queen is the consort of a king; she is a woman who is also the sovereign of a kingdom. Now, originally, "Vash'ti the queen made a feast for the women in the royal house which belonged to king Ahasue'rus,"[2439] and while her feast was going on, the king "made a feast unto all his princes and his servants."[2440] A woman, in the language of Scripture, is a figurative representation of a church, and we have here before us, within the same house and government of the king, the vision of a church and State dominion separate from one another; one feast obliging to the service of men, the other to that of women.

5. When the king of the government requested his queen, his consort, to join him in his feast, to the service of men, she refused, and the king became furious at this. When he fell to wrath due to embarrassment, what then did the king do? He sent to the men that stood in his presence for guidance about what should be done to the queen. What did they say? "Let there go a royal commandment from

---

2437 Esther 1:14
2438 Esther 1:10-12
2439 Esther 1:9
2440 Esther 2:18

him, and let it be written among the laws of the Persians and the Medes, that it be not altered, That Vash'ti come no more before king Ahasue'rus; and let the king give her royal estate unto another that is better than she,"[2441] they said. The idea was to erase the existence of the queen from the royal house and to give her royal estate to another more fitting. Then, "When the king's decree which he shall make," said his wise men, "shall be published throughout all his empire, (for it is great,) all the wives shall give to their husbands honour, both to great and small."[2442]

6. The violation that the queen committed was not apparently only against the king, for it was reported, "Vash'ti the queen hath not done wrong to the king only, but also to all the princes, and to all the people that are in all the provinces."[2443] With a new consort beside the throne, women may fall subject not just to men, but also to the order of the provinces of which they belong, and herein we have the controversy revealed to us. The consort and sovereign over the government of the then earth is its Constitution, and with the queen of the land gone; for she protects the rights over the feast of women; then may men act as they so please to obtain jurisdiction over all the women of the land.

7. As the land currently stands, there is a distinction between the order of the government and the order of any church. It should be observed that when the throne and government sought the queen, it was after his heart had been made drunk that he summoned her, that is, she who is the mind and beauty of the throne. Scripture says, "They also have erred through wine,"[2444] and this erring better defined by the counsel, "Avoiding profane and vain babblings, and oppositions of science falsely so called: which some professing have erred."[2445] Wine is figurative language denoting doctrine, for the error that will take place within the earth will be due to drunkenness by wine, that is,

---

2441 Esther 1:19
2442 Esther 1:20
2443 Esther 1:16
2444 Isaiah 28:7
2445 1 Timothy 6:20,21

by "foolish questions, and genealogies, and contentions, and strivings about the law."[2446] There will be bickering within the ecclesiastical institutions of the earth "through philosophy and vain deceit, after the tradition of men, after the rudiments of the world, and not after Christ."[2447] Herein a new religious philosophy will exist to compromise the earth's mind.

8. At this time "shall men arise, speaking perverse things, to draw away disciples after them."[2448] At this time, he who works in the presence of men will say, "Bring Vash'ti the queen before the king with the crown royal,"[2449] and when she will not consent to the orders of the king, when she cannot do any thing contrary to the mind established within her, when she begins to frustrate the power of the kingdom, then will it be said, "Let it be written among the laws of the Persians and the Medes, that it be not altered, That Vash'ti come no more before king."[2450]

9. The movements contained in every part of the vision given John are ecclesiastical, therefore we know that these men, before whom the earth beast acts, long to have a religious amendment formed within the queen that will subject every women in every province, great or small, to their jurisdiction through the king. And this language is not foreign, for it says, "He causeth all, both small and great."[2451] Thus, in the Revelation we see history being repeated from how it says, "The king did according to the word of Memu'can."[2452] The word of this man Memu'can, to the king, was "as if a man had enquired at the oracle of God."[2453] Error will enter into the mind of the throne of the earth, and it will give its ear and hands to do the work of ones "having a form of godliness, but denying the power thereof."[2454] Because these "false

---

2446 Titus 3:9
2447 Colossians 2:8
2448 Acts 20:30
2449 Esther 1:11
2450 Esther 1:19
2451 Revelation 13:16
2452 Esther 1:21
2453 2 Samuel 16:23
2454 2 Timothy 3:5

apostles, deceitful workers, transforming themselves into the apostles of Christ,"[2455] have no power of God to accomplish their mission, they must replicate "the doctrine of Ba'laam, who taught Ba'lac to cast a stumblingblock."[2456]

10. "Let the king give her royal estate unto another that is better than she,"[2457] say these men in order to act out their impure ambitions. And when the king has been persuaded by the appearance and words of their profession, "We will have 'the king's decree which he shall make,'[2458] saying, 'Every man should bear rule in his own house,'"[2459] they say. Herein is the ambition of them in the presence of the king, that a man "rule his own house,"[2460] for then "shall he take care of the church of God."[2461] If this is not done, "This deed of the queen shall come abroad unto all women, so that they shall despise their husbands in their eyes, when it shall be reported, The king Ahasue'rus commanded Vash'ti the queen to be brought in before him, but she came not. Likewise shall the ladies of Persia and Media say this day unto all the king's princes, which have heard of the deed of the queen. Thus shall there arise too much contempt and wrath,"[2462] they believe.

11. The Constitution is correct; she should not be joined to the feast of men; but when once "a royal commandment"[2463] is made to exchange sentiments within her for another disposition, or to completely remove laws form her tongue, when she will not violate her own conscience to disrupt the peace of the land, then she will be taken out of the way to have her estate adjusted. It says that the king "decreed against her,"[2464] and this is the decree that the house of God should be aware of. When the king decrees a woman should join him

---

2455 2 Corinthians 10:13
2456 Revelation 2:14
2457 Esther 1:19
2458 Esther 1:20
2459 Esther 1:22
2460 1 Timothy 3:5
2461 1 Timothy 3:5
2462 Esther 1:17,18
2463 Esther 1:19
2464 Esther 2:1

unlawfully in his throne's room, then the word will be fulfilled, "They should make an image to the beast."[2465] That which came before the earth beast was the Papacy, and the Papacy was an economy governed by a church and State dominion.

12. When the image and spirit of the Papacy should be reproduced, it will be published in every province, "To you it is commanded, O people, nations, and languages, That at what time ye hear the sound of the cornet, flute, harp, sackbut, psaltery, dulcimer, and all kinds of musick, ye fall down and worship the golden image."[2466] This is why it is important to hear and obey the counsel, "Fear God, and give glory to him; for the hour of his judgment is come: and worship him that made heaven, and earth, and the sea, and the fountains of waters,"[2467] for then we will be able to hear, "If any man worship the beast and his image, and receive his mark in his forehead, or in his hand, the same shall drink of the wine of the wrath of God."[2468]

13. An investigation of the Spirit's doctrine shows that the principles of government contained within Christ's Faith were the root of the quick and powerful ascendancy of the United States to power. This nation was blessed of God to have founding fathers who understood the controversy of their own fathers, and who even risked their own lives to ensure that a land free of a king or a pope would never find place among us. Every one professing the name of Christ must have a living experience with that name if they would be able to remain strong when the queen comes under attack. To know God is to do as it is said, "We have heard...we have seen with our eyes...we have looked upon, and our hands have handled."[2469] Every believer is to have had "begged the body of Jesus"[2470] "till we all come in the unity of the faith, and of the knowledge of the Son of God, unto a perfect man, unto the measure of the stature of the fulness of Christ."[2471]

2465 Revelation 13:14
2466 Daniel 3:4,5
2467 Revelation 14:7
2468 Revelation 14:9,10
2469 1 John 1:1
2470 Matthew 27:58
2471 Ephesians 4:13

14. The same error that will happen in the future is that which anciently took place and give birth to the Papacy, and this occurred because it was not heard, "Every one that loveth him that begat loveth him also that is begotten of him."[2472] It does not say, "Every one that loves the Begotten loves also Him that begat." The apostle constructed his words in this manner because he was there when Christ said, "Every man therefore that hath heard, and hath learned of the Father, cometh unto me."[2473] Unless one should consent to allow the LORD and Father of Christ; He who begat; into the heart and over the personal religion, none will hear the voice of His Christ's law. So then again, "Who begat Christ?" It says, "The Spirit of him that raised up Jesus from the dead."[2474] Christ was "put to death in the flesh, but quickened by the Spirit,"[2475] and this is why it says, "Believe on him that raised up Jesus our Lord from the dead."[2476]

15. If faith lacks in the Spirit of God to instruct and to regenerate the heart and mind, there will be no advancing mind to observe that law of Christ's priesthood. The words of Christ are nothing without the Father, for who gave Christ the gospel that we profess to know? With His own mouth God's Priest says, "The Father gave me commandment."[2477] The Faith of Jesus did not come from Him, but rather it was the LORD His Father that said, "A law shall proceed from me."[2478] "The law of Christ"[2479] is "the faith of God,"[2480] therefore our acceptance of the Spirit's Faith cannot be without the Spirit of God, which is why it says, "It is the Spirit that beareth witness,"[2481] and, "He that hath the Son hath life."[2482] What is life? "The Spirit

---

2472 1 John 5:1
2473 John 6:45
2474 Romans 8:11
2475 1 Peter 3:18
2476 Romans 4:24
2477 John 14:31
2478 Isaiah 51:4
2479 Galatians 6:2
2480 Romans 3:3
2481 1 John 5:6
2482 1 John 5:12

is life,"²⁴⁸³ and this is why it says, "If any man have not the Spirit of Christ, he is none of his,"²⁴⁸⁴ and, "Every one that loveth him that begat loveth him also that is begotten of him."²⁴⁸⁵

16. They who will take the name, "The false prophet that wrought miracles,"²⁴⁸⁶ are them that work contrary to the law of the Spirit's kindness. The end of obedience to the precepts and ordinances of justice is to fulfill the saying, "Ye have purified your souls in obeying the truth through the Spirit unto unfeigned love of the brethren."²⁴⁸⁷ Sanctification by the Spirit of God from obeying the law of the Faith of God leads to godly benevolence, to sanctified affection for all spirits to bring every heart to God's Church and State, even as Christ endured the same purification "that he might bring us to God."²⁴⁸⁸ Wherefore what right does one man have over the conscience of another man? If this should occur then man becomes the judge of man, and if the judge of man then he becomes the authority over the moral actions and principles of man, and if man elevates his level of morality over another man, then he becomes lord of that man, and in essence, the god and law of that man. Because man cannot compel man to obey his prescribed remedy for the moral sickness within him and around his environment, men will seek out a means to enact that which they cannot do, for they are not God, and for a failure to independently wait on the Spirit's religion, they do not have God on their side. Thus, men will resort to the king and queen of the earth's many provinces, and as this is so, and as it will in fact happen, what right does a civil entity have in unlawfully adjusting, or regulating, the level of morality of his citizen? "Why is my liberty judged of another man's conscience?"²⁴⁸⁹

17. The answer is given us from the men of God. Three faithful men of the Hebrews were compelled to honor the image of the king

---

2483   Romans 8:10
2484   Romans 8:9
2485   1 John 5:1
2486   Revelation 19:20
2487   1 Peter 1:22
2488   1 Peter 3:18
2489   1 Corinthians 10:29

of Babylon, but they did not. For remember the word that the Spirit had given at that time: "Now have I given all these lands into the hand of Nebuchadnez'zar the king of Babylon...all nations shall serve him, and his son, and his son's son, until the very time of his land come: and then many nations and great kings shall serve themselves of him. And it shall come to pass, that the nation and kingdom which will not serve the same Nebuchadnez'zar the king of Babylon, and that will not put their neck under the yoke of the king of Babylon, that nation will I punish, saith the LORD, with the sword, and with the famine, and with the pestilence, until I have consumed them by his hand."[2490]

18. Now, the LORD said to serve the king of Babylon, but the men of God did not serve him, so then the men of God must be slain by God, right? The account says, concerning the decreed consumption of God's men, "Nebuchadnez'zar the king was astonied, and rose up in haste, and spake, and said unto his counsellors, Did not we cast three men bound into the midst of the fire? They answered and said unto the king, True, O king. He answered and said, Lo, I see four men loose, walking in the midst of the fire, and they have no hurt; and the form of the fourth is like the Son of God."[2491]

19. The LORD gave the king power, but not in matters of religion or of worship. The lesson is that State power is only for a State's room, that church power is only for the church, and that the two should not be combined. If religion and government are joined together, the people of God have a right to avoid and protest its amalgamation, and it is known, by the record of God's men, that no saying formed against them will harm their spirit. This is the doctrine of God, and it is now, in fairly quiet times of civil and religious peace, that every believer should know the laws of the Spirit's Church and Government, even the laws and service of health for the soul's temple. Only them that have beforehand endured "the days of their purifications"[2492] will have

---

2490 Jeremiah 27:6-8
2491 Daniel 3:24,25
2492 Esther 2:12

it said of them in the books of heaven: "Here are they that keep the commandments of God, and the faith of Jesus."[2493]

20. The storm that the House of the LORD God must first pass through on earth is a period where the religious age is brought under a new and gross religious republic. Concerning the queen Vash'ti, soon it will be heard how certain ministers mistreated her, that "they knew her, and abused her all the night until the morning: and when the day began to spring, they let her go."[2494]

[2493] Revelation 14:12
[2494] Judges 19:25

29

That Beast Of The Earth

1. "I beheld another beast coming up out of the earth; and he had two horns like a lamb, and he spake as a dragon."[2495]

2. To better understand what the earth is a symbol of, we read: "What one nation in the earth is like thy people Israel."[2496] The earth is a symbol of a nation. As the Revelation is primarily a vision concerning church matters, it is fair to note that the earth here mentioned may not simply be a political nation, but should follow the pattern of how it says, "That dwell on the earth, and to every nation, and kindred, and tongue, and people."[2497] When the first angel's message was given, it was not given in legislative courts or to ones bearing civil authority, for it says, "He that overcometh, and keepeth my works unto the end, to him will I give power over the nations: and he shall rule them."[2498] The one who ruled the nations was one "famous according as he had lifted up axes upon the thick trees,"[2499] and he ruled no political entity, but rather religious denominations.

2495   Revelation 13:11
2496   1 Chronicles 17:21
2497   Revelation 14:6
2498   Revelation 2:26,27
2499   Psalms 74:5

3. As it says, "Every kindred, and tongue, and people, and nation,"[2500] and as the word, "nation," is mentioned last to sum up the fact that every preceding title fits into it, it is that we are looking at religious factions of different names and doctrines, we are seeing many "after their families, after their tongues, in their lands, after their nations."[2501] "The earth and them which dwell therein"[2502] are equivalent to "them that dwell on the earth"[2503] being "the inhabiters of the earth."[2504] At Christ's high priestly coronation, John wrote, "Every creature which is in heaven, and on the earth, and under the earth, and such as are in the sea, and all that are in them, heard I saying, Blessing,"[2505] for whether it is in heaven or on earth, or under the earth and in the sea, we have, recorded in the Revelation, religious institutions hallowing the name of God and of Christ.

4. In the beginning, the gospel "was preached to every creature which is under heaven."[2506] If under heaven then they are dwellers not in heaven; that is, they are not joined "to the general assembly and church of the firstborn, which are written in heaven";[2507] but are rather dwellers on earth, and this is why it says, "The most High divided to the nations their inheritance."[2508] What was their inheritance? It says, "The sun, and the moon, and the stars, even all the host of heaven... which the LORD thy God hath divided unto all nations under the whole heaven."[2509] Thus, them that dwell on the earth, and them under the earth and within the sea, are "Gentiles in the flesh...aliens from the commonwealth of Israel, and strangers from the covenants of promise, having no hope, and without God in the world."[2510]

2500 Revelation 5:9
2501 Genesis 10:31
2502 Revelation 13:12
2503 Revelation 13:14
2504 Revelation 8:13
2505 Revelation 5:13
2506 Colossians 1:23
2507 Hebrews 12:23
2508 Deuteronomy 32:8
2509 Deuteronomy 4:19
2510 Ephesians 2:11,12

5. Them being under heaven means that their inheritance is pulled from heaven; that is, from the sun, the moon, and the stars; and are not "them that dwell in heaven,"[2511] for the heaven of the LORD is as it is said, "Thou heaven, and ye holy apostles and prophets."[2512] "The whole family in heaven and earth"[2513] says, "I bow my knees unto the Father of our Lord Jesus Christ,"[2514] yet them that dwell only on the earth honor an "altar with this inscription, TO THE UNKNOWN GOD,"[2515] due to keeping the tradition of their mother "that selleth nations through her whoredoms, and families through her witchcrafts."[2516] When John observes a beast, a government, arising from the earth, it is that a new civil entity is arising from a previously constructed civil government, and it will most likely be a power constructed from the order of its previous earth or dominion. This earth beast is born from its supposed Protestant foundation, and John observes its apostate intangibles the moment that it springs up onto the scene of action.

6. John said that he saw another beast come up out of the earth. In addition to the previous beast, the Papacy, he saw a different beast arising on the scene of action. Another Gentile faction was to arise in addition to the faction before it, and did even spring from it to uphold many of its erroneous customs and manners of conversation. This new beast will have dominion over them that dwell on the earth, and again, as the vision given John does not ultimately explain a governmental outline of the events mentioned within it, it is fair to conclude that this beast, or government, will exercise itself over the religion of the land. Them that dwell on the earth are them under heaven and whose devotion is drawn from what is figuratively in the sky above, and herein we see a civil government exercising religious authority, but not before first being persuaded to the necessity of controlling the conscience of the people.

2511 Revelation 13:6
2512 Revelation 18:20
2513 Ephesians 3:15
2514 Ephesians 3:14
2515 Acts 17:23
2516 Nahum 3:4

7. The fact that there is a spirit to compel men to worship is proof that the religion imposed on the people by this new beast is different from the earth that it came from. The new republic will carry within it a new religion; a new religiously framed philosophical and political doctrine; and it will compel all within its jurisdiction to honor this tradition. It says, "He exerciseth all the power of the first beast before him, and causeth the earth and them which dwell therein to worship the first beast,"[2517] and this worship is nothing less than the fulfillment of the saying, "If any man worship the beast and his image, and receive his mark in his forehead, or in his hand."[2518] In this verse we have a summation of the work of the new republic, for a government alone does not care about religious worship, yet a government that has its conscience compromised will have his eyes fixed on things it would not have considered on his own. The mind of the land set towards protecting the earth will come under an abuse by "them which say they are Jews, and are not, but are the synagogue of Satan."[2519]

8. We next hear how this new republic works, for "he maketh fire come down from heaven on the earth in the sight of men,"[2520] that is, "deceiveth them that dwell on the earth by the means of those miracles which he had power to do in the sight of the beast."[2521] The new religion is administered by "the astrologers, the stargazers, the monthly prognosticators"[2522] of the empire; "the wise men, the astrologers, the magicians, the soothsayers."[2523] "The seven chamberlains that served in the presence of Ahasue'rus the king"[2524] will reproduce themselves at this time to bring all to their allegiance through the power of the State, for they bear within themselves "seducing spirits, and doctrines of devils."[2525] It should be considered that none should need to deceive

---

2517 Revelation 13:12
2518 Revelation 14:9
2519 Revelation 2:9
2520 Revelation 13:13
2521 Revelation 13:14
2522 Isaiah 47:13
2523 Daniel 2:27
2524 Esther 1:10
2525 1 Timothy 4:1

any that are in agreement, for the new government, under a pretended lamb-like business, will work by the coarse spirit within it to gain supporters for its cause.

9. Scripture tells of another two-horned beast that governed the earth, and it also had two horns symbolizing two national powers joined into one head or mind, the Medes and the Persians. A horn is a symbol of power, and although John observed two horns as a lamb on the head of the earth beast, those horns are centered upon the mind and personality of a dragon, therefore their root is not ultimately innocent, as the illustration of a lamb may depict, but is rather founded upon deception. This earth beast wears two coats, two cloaks, or two characters, and the appearance of the horns is to compel the mind to believe in its temporal and eternal innocence, yet his demeanor could not be hidden from John in vision.

10. The earth that the earth beast sprung up from was once fair, she was quiet and her mind was formed by the counsel, "Stand fast therefore in the liberty wherewith Christ hath made us free."[2526] Yet, it should happen that her spirit will be compromised to have the saying again repeated, "Ye were now turned, and had done right in my sight, in proclaiming liberty every man to his neighbour; and ye had made a covenant before me in the house which is called by my name: but ye turned and polluted my name, and caused every man his servant, and every man his handmaid, whom ye had set at liberty at their pleasure, to return, and brought them into subjection, to be unto you for servants and for handmaids."[2527]

11. The nation that the earth beast derives its original heritage from is not the first beast before it, but rather from the earth before it. The image that it retains is that of the first beast before it, but its heritage is founded upon the principles of the earth from which it springs, and its main religious principle was, "Nation shall not lift up a sword against nation, neither shall they learn war any more. But they shall sit every man under his vine and under his fig tree; and none shall make them afraid: for the mouth of the LORD of hosts hath spoken it. For

---

2526 Galatians 5:1
2527 Jeremiah 34:15,16

all people will walk every one in the name of his god, and we will walk in the name of the LORD our God for ever and ever."[2528] These are the principles of religion and conscience as stated in the First Amendment of the United States Constitution, and Scripture says that the Spirit spoke these things beforehand to come to pass, but where, of old, is this word to be found? He says: "Behold, I create new heavens and a new earth: and the former shall not be remembered, nor come into mind."[2529]

12. A new heavens and a new earth was to spring up, for a government formed under Protestant principles was to reign over the entire earth. But, according to the Revelation, the earth is inevitably comprised. An unlawful combination of religion and government will fall out of her womb. When a compromise occurs in the supreme law of the land, a new entity will arise from that molestation, and this new two-horned republic is that creature bearing the image of the first beast before it.

13. It is without a doubt that when John saw this new beast, its body and its head were of a similar likeness to that of the first beast before it. This beast, in vision, sprung up onto the scene already bearing the likeness of the leopard beast, yet it is an entirely different and independent species from it. It at first will speak innocently, yet being wrapped within a spirit of guile, them that dwell in heaven will be able to recognize the dragon's voice from that of the LORD's Christ, for He says, "My sheep hear my voice, and I know them, and they follow me";[2530] "these are they which follow the Lamb whithersoever he goeth."[2531] The image of Christ walking from one room into another room signifies that there is more than one room of worship for the believer in heaven. Them that dwell in heaven rest in that Place of God holding two Apartments, which is why it says, for them of the Spirit's family on earth whose faith

---

2528 Micah 4:3-5
2529 Isaiah 65:17
2530 John 10:27
2531 Revelation 14:4

reaches up into the heavenly Temple, "Seek those things which are above, where Christ sitteth on the right hand of God."[2532]

14. These things are important to consider because the wolves of the new republic will feign themselves as leaders of the *kingdom of God*. Them that will speak "flattering words"[2533] under "a cloke of covetousness"[2534] will by their appearance deceive many. Because there were none with knowledge, nor any that maintained a pure experimental conversation with God and with Christ before this established economy, them that dwell on the earth will be persuaded by the deeds done of these men by the hand of the king of the land, and so the king will be persuaded to counsel to the people, "saying to them that dwell on the earth, that they should make an image to the beast."[2535] The people will demand a change in their government and it will happen because they do not know the name of God or the character and priestly position of His Christ. The Spirit's Son stands by the throne of the LORD His Father; God's High Priest is joined to the LORD's heavenly Government; wherefore no church or government of man has any right to assume that which is perfectly upheld by God and forbidden to them by the appointment of His Son.

15. The men of Daniel's time once spoke against him. These men approached the king "to establish a royal statute, and to make a firm decree, that whosoever shall ask a petition of any God or man for thirty days...shall be cast into the den of lions."[2536] The king agreed and signed the decree. Daniel disobeyed the decree, praying to the LORD as was his usual norm, and being found by these men in prayer, he was at once sent to face the penalty for violation. Did Daniel perish? "The king arose very early in the morning, and went in haste unto the den of lions. And when he came to the den, he cried with a lamentable voice unto Daniel: and the king spake and said to Daniel, O Daniel, servant of the living God, is thy God, whom thou servest continually, able to deliver

---

2532 Colossians 3:1
2533 1 Thessalonians 2:5
2534 1 Thessalonians 2:5
2535 Revelation 13:14
2536 Daniel 6:7

thee from the lions? Then said Daniel unto the king, O king, live for ever."[2537]

16. Unlawful authority over religion does not rest within the scope of the government's power. Government is given no power to decree worship of any kind, and the servants of the living God are not given to serve that religion which is decreed by a secular force, even though it says, "Render therefore unto Caesar the things which are Caesar's; and unto God the things that are God's."[2538] We have a line drawn before us between law and religion: that which is to be ascribed to God, let it be for God, and that of Caesar; the government and law of the land; let it thus be for him. This is why Scripture says, "God is not the author of confusion."[2539] But what is confusion? It says, "Neither shall any woman stand before a beast to lie down thereto: it is confusion."[2540]

17. God is not the author of a woman unlawfully spreading herself for a beast, or a church unlawfully entertaining the authority of a State within and over her. The woman of the earth beast will full the word, "She increased her whoredoms: for when she saw men pourtrayed upon the wall, the images of the Chalde'ans pourtrayed with vermilion, girded with girdles upon their loins, exceeding in dyed attire upon their heads, all of them princes to look to, after the manner of the Babylonians of Chalde'a, the land of their nativity: and as soon as she saw them with her eyes, she doted upon them, and sent messengers unto them into Chalde'a. And the Babylonians came to her into the bed of love, and they defiled her with their whoredom, and she was polluted with them, and her mind was alienated from them."[2541]

18. Says the Spirit of this institution: "Ye have sent for men to come from far, unto whom a messenger was sent; and, lo, they came: for whom thou didst wash thyself, paintedst thy eyes, and deckedst thyself with ornaments, and satest upon a stately bed, and a table prepared before it, whereupon thou hast set mine incense and mine oil. And a

---

2537 Daniel 6:19-21
2538 Mathew 22:21
2539 1 Corinthians 14:33
2540 Leviticus 18:23
2541 Ezekiel 23:14-17

voice of a multitude being at ease was with her: and with the men of the common sort were brought...Then said I unto her that was old in adulteries, Will they now commit whoredoms with her, and she with them? Yet they went in unto her, as they go in unto a woman that playeth the harlot."[2542] "In all thine abominations and thy whoredoms thou hast not remembered the days of thy youth, when thou wast naked and bare, and wast polluted in thy blood."[2543]

19. The work to unfold within the Land of Liberty and Opportunity is one that will be the greatest test for the Spirit's men and women. It is now, at this time, that the professed of God's Christ should know the name and knowledge of His intercession. "The excellency of the knowledge of Christ"[2544] is, that "where the Spirit of the Lord is, there is liberty."[2545] Every believer has in them a government within his or her heart, and a place of worship in the spirit of their mind. Refusing to endure our personal religion's learning with God's Priest will not birth a person formed after His likeness, but rather one after the image of the beast, wherein the heart, and the mind of the members of the flesh, govern the spirit of the mind. For "he that hath no rule over his own spirit is like a city that is broken down, and without walls,"[2546] wherefore it is counseled, "Be renewed in the spirit of your mind."[2547] As much as a State has no unjust authority over a church, and likewise a church over a State, so too the heart has no right to unjustly rule the mind, and this natural error of the human being receives health from learning of and doing the doctrine of Christ.

20. The image of this Christ is contrary to that of the earth beast, for the new republic will seek honor from compromising not only its own conscience, but also that of his people, while God's Man gives and receives honor from free love tried and purified by faith on His name. Of Satan it is said, "That opened not the house of his prisoners,"[2548] yet

---

2542 Ezekiel 23:39-44
2543 Ezekiel 16:22
2544 Philippians 3:8
2545 2 Corinthians 3:17
2546 Proverbs 25:28
2547 Ephesians 4:23
2548 Isaiah 14:17

what is the foundation of the doctrine of Christ? It says, "To proclaim liberty to the captives, and the opening of the prison to them that are bound."[2549] This is why them that will push for the movement to have a new order to Liberty's Constitution are "them of the synagogue of Satan,"[2550] for in heart and purpose they dwell "even where Satan's seat is."[2551] Satan is that doctrine of confusion within the imaginations of priests and elders within the religious world, and for this cause, the believer should view the true order of Christ's form in the presence of God. Them that inwardly possess the structure of the earth beast will be drawn to worship him, but them that now escape the law of sin within the members of their heart will later on be as Daniel and his companions, even as individuals saved and rescued from both the fire and the lion.

2549 Isaiah 61:1
2550 Revelation 3:9
2551 Revelation 2:13

30

Ha'man

1. "And he doeth great wonders, so that he maketh fire come down from heaven on the earth in the sight of men."[2552]

2. The Revelation is a vision of church history. The "he" mentioned above cannot be solely a political figure, even though he is. How is it that such a claim may be justified? These same events recorded in the Revelation are rehearsed in the history of Esther, for Scripture says, "After these things did king Ahasue'rus promote Ha'man the son of Hammed'atha the A'gagite, and advanced him, and set his seat above all the princes that were with him. And all the king's servants, that were in the king's gate, bowed, and reverenced Ha'man: for the king had so commanded concerning him. But Mor'decai bowed not, nor did him reverence. Then the king's servants, which were in the king's gate, said unto Mor'decai, Why transgressest thou the king's commandment?"[2553]

3. Just as in the Revelation, in Esther we are not told of the events before power is conferred to specific individuals. It should be noted that there is a decree made of the king; that is, "According to the state

---

2552 Revelation 13:13
2553 Esther 3:1-3

of the king,"[2554] and, "According to the law";[2555] for the worship and honor of a man, letting us know that the king "sat on the throne of his kingdom"[2556] and that no other power existed beside him. It should also be noted how that the man promoted was not just any man, but that he was the son of a man, and this fulfilling the word, "He that delicately bringeth up his servant from a child shall have him become his son at the length."[2557] This son, Ha'man of Hammed'atha, was promoted to the position of his father, but who was his father? It says, "We have had fathers of our flesh which corrected us, and we gave them reverence,"[2558] and, "Ye fathers, provoke not your children to wrath: but bring them up in the nurture and admonition of the Lord. Servants, be obedient to them that are your masters according to the flesh."[2559] A "son" is a religious minister forwarding the faith of a religious institution, even as it says, "As a son with the father, he hath served with me in the gospel."[2560]

4. Thus, the man Ha'man fulfills the word, "Every high priest taken from among men is ordained for men in things pertaining to God, that he may offer both gifts and sacrifices for sins: who can have compassion on the ignorant, and on them that are out of the way; for that he himself also is compassed with infirmity. And by reason hereof he ought, as for the people, so also for himself, to offer for sins."[2561] At this time the king said to His new high priest, "Thou art my Son, this day have I begotten thee."[2562]

5. We are not told what occurred to have this man ascend the ranks of the priesthood to be above "the king's most noble princes,"[2563] nevertheless he was promoted, and soon after this promotion, "the king took his ring from his hand, and gave it unto Ha'man the son of

---

2554 Esther 1:7
2555 Esther 1:8
2556 Esther 1:2
2557 Proverbs 29:21
2558 Hebrews 12:9
2559 Ephesians 6:4,5
2560 Philippians 2:22
2561 Hebrews 5:1-3
2562 Hebrews 1:5
2563 Esther 6:9

Hammed'atha the A'gagite, the Jews' enemy. And the king said unto Ha'man, The silver is given to thee, the people also, to do with them as it seemeth good to thee."[2564] This is how it is fulfilled, "He had power to give life unto the image of the beast,"[2565] for this Ha'man was given the king's authority over legislative matters, which was something, it appears, not even given to them "which sat first in the kingdom."[2566] Of these wise men, the king physically did their counsel himself, but when it came to matters of religion, he did not ask the head priest any questions nor did he raise any dispute, but freely gave him his own reign.

6. Let it not be forgotten that this man Ha'man was only the highest of "the king's most noble princes."[2567] A "prince" is a chief elder of a religious denomination, for it says, "The renowed of the congregation, princes of the tribes of their fathers,"[2568] and, "The princes of Israel, heads of the house of their fathers."[2569] Again, a "prince" is the head of a house, and a "house" is illustrative language delineating a church, as it says, "The house of God, which is the church of the living God."[2570] We know that this chief position is given to Ha'man because Ha'man thought that the king had an occasion to further promote him, and "Ha'man thought in his heart, To whom would the king delight to do honour more than to myself?"[2571] How is it known that there exists a greater separation between the highest of the princes and the office of, "Delight"? It says, "Let the royal apparel be brought which the king useth to wear, and the horse that the king rideth upon, and the crown royal which is set upon his head: and let this apparel and horse be delivered to the hand of one of the king's most noble princes, that they may array the man withal whom the king delighteth to honour, and bring him on horseback through the street of the city, and proclaim before him, Thus shall it be done to the man whom the king delighteth to

---

2564 Esther 3:10,11
2565 Revelation 13:15
2566 Esther 1:14
2567 Esther 6:9
2568 Numbers 1:16
2569 Numbers 7:2
2570 1 Timothy 3:15
2571 Esther 6:6

honour."²⁵⁷² This man Ha'man longed for the light a royal throne to clothe his devotional body.

7. Ha'man may have had the king's ring, a symbol of executive and legislative authority, but he was not clothed "in royal apparel of blue and white, and with a great crown of gold, and with a garment of fine linen and purple."²⁵⁷³ Ha'man was simply the head bishop over the house, the church, of the king, and we know this from how it is said, "All the king's servants"; his sons; "that were in the king's gate."²⁵⁷⁴ What is this gate? An example is seen from how it is said, "Then he brought me to the door of the gate of the LORD's house which was toward the north; and, behold, there sat women weeping for Tam'muz."²⁵⁷⁵

8. Again it is written: "Thus saith the Lord GOD; The gate of the inner court that looketh toward the east shall be shut the six working days; but on the Sabbath it shall be opened, and in the day of the new moon it shall be opened. And the prince shall enter by the way of the porch of that gate without, and shall stand by the post of the gate, and the priests shall prepare his burnt offering and his peace offerings, and he shall worship at the threshold of the gate: then he shall go forth; but the gate shall not be shut until the evening. Likewise the people of the land shall worship at the door of this gate before the LORD in the sabbaths and in the new moons. And the burnt offering that the prince shall offer unto the LORD in the Sabbath day shall be six lambs without blemish, and a ram without blemish."²⁵⁷⁶

9. And again, it is said more definitively: "This is the service of the families of the Ger'shonites, to serve, and for burdens: and they shall bear the curtains of the tabernacle, and the tabernacle of the congregation, his covering, and the covering of the badgers' skins that is above upon it, and the hanging for the door of the tabernacle of the congregation, and the hangings of the court, and the hanging for the door of the gate of the court, which is by the tabernacle and by the altar round

---

2572 Esther 6:8,9
2573 Esther 8:15
2574 Esther 3:2
2575 Ezekiel 8:14
2576 Ezekiel 46:1-4

about, and their cords, and all the instruments of their service, and all that is made for them: so shall they serve. At the appointment of Aaron and his sons shall be all the service of the sons of the Ger'shonites, in all their burdens, and in all their service: and ye shall appoint unto them in charge all their burdens. This is the service of the families of the sons of Ger'shon in the tabernacle of the congregation: and their charge shall be under the hand of Ith'amar the son of Aaron the priest."[2577]

10. Herein is conclusive evidence to explain the position of the son of Hammed'atha; the one named Ha'man that is "Ba'laam, who taught Ba'lac to cast a stumblingblock."[2578] This is he who works in the sight of men by the ring of the king of the land. By him, all things fallen from heaven unto the earth were "written according to all that Ha'man had commanded unto the king's lieutenants, and to the governors that were over every province, and to the rulers of every people of every province according to the writing thereof, and to every people after their language; in the name of king Ahasue'rus was it written, and sealed with the king's ring."[2579] This is what the Spirit meant by the saying, "And deceiveth them that dwell on the earth by the means of those miracles which he had power to do in the sight of the beast."[2580]

11. Ha'man, who is in reality Ba'laam, joined to the throne or government of Ahasue'rus, or Ba'lac, will, by the State, or the government's Constitution, when he sees Mor'decai refuse to reverence him, the highest bishop over the gate of the kingdom's practice, seek to destroy him. This man Ha'man wants worship, and not really him, but rather the imagination formed out of the stomach of his appetite, and because there are "certain people scattered abroad and dispersed among the people in all the provinces,"[2581] whose "laws are diverse from all the people,"[2582] letters will be sent "by posts into all the king's provinces, to destroy, to kill, and to cause to perish, all Jews, both young

---

2577 Numbers 4:24-28
2578 Revelation 2:13
2579 Esther 3:12
2580 Revelation 13:14
2581 Esther 3:8
2582 Esther 3:8

and old, little children and women."[2583] Herein we have the quaking of the earth under the fulfillment, "The nations were angry,[2584]" for it says, "He spake as a dragon."[2585]

12. The nations mentioned are not political nations, but are rather ecclesiastical families. This bishop Ha'man is head over the religious factions of the earth's beast, and in his heart he says, "All this availeth me nothing, so long as I see Mor'decai the Jew sitting at the king's gate."[2586] "Mor'decai sat in the king's gate"[2587] as a rebel who would not unlawfully honor the State's practice. There were then no laws against Mor'decai and his people, and so as far as he could, he did abide by the king's charge. For this same Mor'decai "stood in the gate of the camp, and said, Who is on the LORD'S side?"[2588] and for his protest; as it says, "Mor'decai bowed not, nor did him reverence";[2589] "they hanged Ha'man on the gallows that he had prepared for Mor'decai."[2590] Thus it was fulfilled, "They brought those men which had accused Daniel, and they cast them into the den of lions, them, their children, and their wives."[2591]

13. Here is another lesson given us of the limited power entrusted to civil government. The Spirit says, "No weapon that is formed against thee shall prosper; and every tongue that shall rise against thee in judgment thou shalt condemn. This is the heritage of the servants of the LORD."[2592] The time of the established new republic will be a terrible time for the servant of the living God. The example that we have of Mor'decai shows that when a head prince and bishop is given power to enact laws and amendments in favor of worship and devotion, that as it is reported of Mor'decai, how "he stood not up, nor moved for him,"[2593]

2583 Esther 3:13
2584 Revelation 11:18
2585 Revelation 13:11
2586 Esther 5:13
2587 Esther 2:21
2588 Exodus 32:26
2589 Esther 3:2
2590 Esther 7:10
2591 Daniel 6:24
2592 Isaiah 54:17
2593 Esther 5:10

letters and writings of commandments sealed with the king's name by one of his head ecclesiastical officials will be delivered swiftly to the violator. What will be persecution to the Jews will be but an enforced adherence to the laws of the land by any means necessary for the ones administering them. Nevertheless, "the people that do know their God shall be strong, and do exploits."[2594]

14. It is inevitable that ecclesiastical powers will gravitate to occupy the seat of civil legislation to fulfill perverse spiritual ambitions, for the Spirit Himself has said so. Sensuous and carnal bishops will take a political seat by the throne of the land, and this particular principle of a bishop they will among themselves enforce and misconstrue: "One that ruleth well his own house, having his children in subjection with all gravity."[2595] The aim is to rule well the houses and the conscience of the majority by subtle force, for it will be fulfilled, "Will he force the queen also before me in the house?"[2596] Just as the king stepped aside, placing power into the hand of the man that he had promoted to execute justice on religious matters as he saw fit, so too the throne of the earth's beast will surrender its will to the will of ones that should be promoted as overseer to all things concerning religion within the empire – its foundation, its destiny, and its heresy.

15. The earth beast will execute the violence it deems necessary against them that would serve the living Father and His Son. Because the Revelation is a vision of church history, the decrees that are executed primarily for religious reasons cannot be ordained unless through the State. That put forth by head princes will be executed in the name and authority of the government in the person of the king, therefore by the voice of civil legislation will that fire of their heaven fall onto the earth under the guidance and administration of them bestowed to sacred offices. That "he" spoken of who deceives and works is indeed the State of the earth enflamed by ones under a pretended moral cause. Because

---

2594 Daniel 11:32
2595 1 Timothy 3:4
2596 Esther 6:8

of such individuals, it will be fulfilled against the Spirit's convert, "They spake daily unto him."[2597]

16. The beast of the earth at this time is a representative of that which fulfills the name, "The daily sacrifice,"[2598] while holding the image of "the abomination that maketh desolate."[2599] This same "daily" is represented by the great red dragon, "that old serpent, called the Devil, and Satan, which deceiveth the whole world,"[2600] and this is how we know Ha'man as "the false prophet that wrought miracles"[2601] "and deceiveth them that dwell on the earth by the means of those miracles."[2602] It is in this period of time that the prophets of confusion will speak the language of the daily to the seed of God and against all who fall under the description of heretic to the empire's religion, fulfilling the word, "He persecuted the woman."[2603] By the means of the power entrusted to him by the dragon; his State authority; these "men of corrupt minds, and destitute of the truth, supposing that gain is godliness,"[2604] will do all within their power to ascend into the courts of the throne to execute their will. Thus, at the time appointed, it will again be fulfilled, "There was war in heaven."[2605]

17. Today, we should become cognizant of the saying, "The king and Ha'man sat down to drink."[2606] This scene depicts the hour of darkness that will combine the horse that was red with the horse that was black to uphold the spirit and image of the pale horse.

2597 Esther 3:4
2598 Daniel 8:11
2599 Daniel 12:11
2600 Revelation 12:9
2601 Revelation 19:20
2602 Revelation 13:14
2603 Revelation 12:13
2604 1 Timothy 6:5
2605 Revelation 12:7
2606 Esther 3:15

31

The Will And Nature Of The Beast

1. "The Father loveth the Son, and sheweth him all things that himself doeth: and he will shew him greater works than these, that ye may marvel. For as the Father raiseth up the dead, and quickeneth them; even so the Son quickeneth whom he will. For the Father judgeth no man, but hath committed all judgment unto the Son: that all men should honour the Son, even as they honour the Father. He that honoureth not the Son honoureth not the Father which hath sent him."[2607]

2. We have before us a hierarchy of authority, wherein One of greater authority elevates the lesser to the same status. The Father has given His Son equal power of name with His name. "It pleased the Father that in him should all fulness dwell,"[2608] and this same image is reproduced in the saying, "The dragon gave him his power, and his seat, and great authority."[2609] The father of the earth beast, and of the beast before it, is the dragon, for in it rests the mind and character of its

---

2607 John 5:20-23
2608 Colossians 1:19
2609 Revelation 13:2

father. A characteristic of the LORD God the Father is that He is who raises the dead, and when we hear John say, "I beheld another beast coming up out of the earth,"[2610] it can only mean that we are viewing an entity being raised to life that the dead may have a form of *life* within itself.

3. Says Scripture, "Who knoweth the spirit of man that goeth upward, and the spirit of the beast that goeth downward to the earth?"[2611] Again, "The woman said unto Saul, I saw gods ascending out of the earth. And he said unto her, What form is he of? And she said, An old man cometh up; and he is covered with a mantle. And Saul perceived that it was Samuel."[2612] And again, "The scripture saith unto Pharaoh, Even for this same purpose have I raised thee up, that I might shew my power in thee, and that my name might be declared throughout all the earth."[2613] Thus, Christ says of Himself, "And I, if I be lifted up from the earth, will draw all men unto me."[2614]

4. It is interesting to note that, when the woman saw what she saw come up out of the earth, Saul said, "What is his form?"[2615] That which came up out of the earth had a mold and configuration of Samuel, but it was not Samuel. An image and an appearance came up from the earth in a certain likeness, for when that two-horned beast comes up out of the earth, as John sees it rising onto the scene of action, it is already bearing the configuration "of the beast, which had the wound by a sword, and did live."[2616] If the dragon once raised a church institution to prominence before, there is no reason to doubt that it will not again serve in the same manner.

5. The image of that first beast is of a woman set "upon a scarlet coloured beast, full of names of blasphemy, having seven heads and ten horns."[2617] The second picture of her is given to us by John: "And

---

2610 Revelation 13:11
2611 Ecclesiastes 3:21
2612 1 Samuel 28:13,14
2613 Romans 9:17
2614 John 12:32
2615 1 Samuel 28:14
2616 Revelation 13:14
2617 Revelation 17:3

I stood upon the sand of the sea, and saw a beast rise up out of the sea, having seven heads and ten horns, and upon his horns ten crowns, and upon his heads the name of blasphemy. And the beast which I saw was like unto a leopard, and his feet were as the feet of a bear, and his mouth as the mouth of a lion: and the dragon gave him his power, and his seat, and great authority."[2618] This is that power that fulfills the saying, "He magnified himself even to the prince of the host, and by him the daily sacrifice was taken away, and the place of his sanctuary was cast down. And an host was given him against the daily sacrifice by reason of transgression, and it cast down the truth to the ground."[2619] "His power shall be mighty, but not by his own power."[2620]

6. Who is it that magnified himself against the Prince of the host and thought to "stand up against the Prince of princes"?[2621] Scripture tells us of "a great red dragon, having seven heads and ten horns, and seven crowns upon his heads. And his tail drew the third part of the stars of heaven, and did cast them to the earth: and the dragon stood before the woman which was ready to be delivered, for to devour her child as soon as it was born."[2622]

7. This "man child"[2623] is God's Man, and if His Christ, then who does the dragon symbolize? We are told, "Herod, when he saw that he was mocked of the wise men, was exceeding wroth, and sent forth, and slew all the children that were in Beth'lehem, and in all the coasts thereof, from two years old and under, according to the time which he had diligently enquired of the wise men."[2624]

8. At the birth of Christ, it was the spirit of Rome that sought His demise, but the Spirit's child was kept safe by His parents. Again at the end of His life, Christ would be crucified according to the authority

---

2618 Revelation 13:1,2
2619 Daniel 8:11,12
2620 Daniel 8:24
2621 Daniel 8:25
2622 Revelation 12:3,4
2623 Revelation 12:5
2624 Matthew 2:16

of this same power, yet would He be "caught up unto God, and to his throne."[2625]

9. The dragon is a symbol of pagan Rome. Eventually, there would come a time when the daily; pagan Rome; would be replaced, as it says, "Only he who now letteth will let, until he be taken out of the way,"[2626] and, "From the time that the daily sacrifice shall be taken away, and the abomination that maketh desolate set up."[2627] That force called, "The abomination that makes desolate," is the fellowship of "the throne of iniquity"[2628] with "the mystery of iniquity."[2629] He who had power to restrain or to magnify was the dragon, but in time, he and all of his intangibles would magnify the place of "that man of sin,"[2630] creating what would become the Papacy. Hence, the place of the pagan sanctuary was cast down, and when once an apostate Christian church took allegiance with it, much of its polytheistic and idolatrous customs covered with a "cloak of maliciousness"[2631] an erroneous cult.

10. Herein the dragon gave the first beast his own power and seat in the judicial system over religious and legislative matters with great authority "over all kindreds, and tongues, and nations"[2632] "to change times and laws."[2633] The vision of a woman; a church; on top of a dragon; a pagan civil power and government; is the image of a throne of iniquity wherein the character is accomplished: "Thine heart is lifted up, and thou hast said, I am a God, I sit in the seat of God, in the midst of the seas."[2634] This is the image of "the son of perdition; who opposeth and exalteth himself above all that is called God, or that is worshipped; so that he as God sitteth in the temple of God, shewing himself that he is God."[2635] Thus, as it says, "They shall place the abomination that

---

2625 Revelation 12:5
2626 2 Thessalonians 2:7
2627 Daniel 12:11
2628 Psalms 94:20
2629 2 Thessalonians 2:7
2630 2 Thessalonians 2:3
2631 1 Peter 2:16
2632 Revelation 13:7
2633 Daniel 7:25
2634 Ezekiel 28:2
2635 2 Thessalonians 2:3,4

maketh desolate,"[2636] this that was placed of old; the State of Rome under legal dominion of an apostate Christian church; is the image and spirit of the two-horned beast that we observe coming up out of the earth.

11. The fact that another beast is coming up out the earth serves to announce the fact that it is dead, even as it says, "Thou hast a name that thou livest, and art dead."[2637] Again it is fulfilled, "His power shall be mighty, but not by his own power,"[2638] for this two-horned beast has received power from the State institution before it, to own life within its deadness. It is said of the LORD, "He raiseth up the poor out of the dust, and lifteth up the beggar from the dunghill, to set them among princes, and to make them inherit the throne of glory,"[2639] and so too will the dragon of the earth fulfill the word, "Power was given to him... and he that sat on him had a pair of balances in his hand...over the fourth part of the earth, to kill with sword, and with hunger, and with death."[2640] It is the Spirit of the Father that raises the dead, and it is the spirit of the dragon that will raise an apostate church to assume a new civil republic on the earth.

12. This same beast and false prophet that comes up from the earth fulfills the role of the dragon, in that he "causeth the earth and them which dwell therein to worship the first beast."[2641] By him the saying will be fulfilled, "The beast that thou sawest was, and is not; and shall ascend out of the bottomless pit, and go into perdition: and they that dwell on the earth shall wonder,"[2642] and, "His deadly wound was healed: and all the world wondered after the beast."[2643] This two-horned beast therefore fulfills the prophecy, "One is, and the other is not yet come; and when he cometh, he must continue a short space. And the beast that was, and is not, even he is the eighth, and is of the

---

2636 Daniel 11:31
2637 Revelation 3:1
2638 Daniel 8:24
2639 1 Samuel 2:8
2640 Revelation 6:3-8
2641 Revelation 13:12
2642 Revelation 17:8
2643 Revelation 13:3

seven, and goeth into perdition."[2644] The one who goes into perdition is even "the son of perdition,"[2645] and his perdition is furthered by the seventh kingdom; the two-horned beast; for the government before the seventh is the sixth, from whence this two-horned creature is born.

13. The order given us in relation to the uncomely union of the dragon, the beast, and the false church to come, it is but a counterfeit rendition of the Father, the Son, and the Holy Ghost. Even though the dragon is known to be pagan Rome, it cannot be forgotten who his author is, for it says, "The great dragon was cast out, that old serpent, called the Devil, and Satan."[2646] Satan longs to fulfill the saying, "I will be like the most High,"[2647] and because God is no author of confusion, it is the devil who will move men to ignore the counsel, "Neither shall any woman stand before a beast to lie down thereto: it is confusion."[2648] This confusion is what John saw rising from the earth, and as Satan is the father of this error, it is that his son must raise up and heal his own personal creation, the first beast before the two-horned one, even as it sees what it's father has done before him.

14. For this cause, "the scripture saith unto Pharaoh, Even for this same purpose have I raised thee up, that I might shew my power in thee, and that my name might be declared throughout all the earth."[2649] This is the purpose of the two-horned beast; that he would be the agent whereby it is prepared to declare the name of the Serpent throughout the earth. It is therefore fair to call this beast that "worketh abomination"[2650] spiritual Egypt, for it says, "Pharaoh king of Egypt, the great dragon that lieth in the midst of his rivers."[2651] As waters are a symbol of "peoples, and multitudes, and nations, and tongues,"[2652] and as this dragon of Egypt rests at the center of their religious beliefs, it

---

2644 Revelation 17:10,11
2645 2 Thessalonians 2:3
2646 Revelation 12:9
2647 Isaiah 14:14
2648 Leviticus 18:23
2649 Romans 9:17
2650 Revelation 21:27
2651 Ezekiel 29:3
2652 Revelation 17:15

is that this two-horned beast comes from, and is, a nation at the center of the earth. This is why the Spirit said of His ancient host, "This is Jerusalem: I have set it in the midst of the nations and countries that are round about her,"[2653] for this Egypt that is Jerusalem is "a pleasant land, a goodly heritage of the hosts of nations."[2654]

15. The two-horned beast springs from this pleasant land, and so the prophecy, at the appointed time, will be fulfilled, "He shall also enter into the glorious land,"[2655] and this entrance is accomplished when the power of the glorious land begins "saying to them that dwell on the earth, that they should make an image to the beast, which had the wound by a sword, and did live."[2656] The land that fulfills the saying, "I create new heavens and a new earth,"[2657] the land wherein it should be praised that "none did compel" the conscience, but that "they should do according to every man's pleasure,"[2658] this land that holds a Constitution authorized to limit civil authority for the purpose of raising up no tyranny, this nation will corrupt the mind that reasonably and respectably governs it. From out of this nation, which nation is diverse from any before it, will come up one diverse from it, but similar to the ones before it, bearing the likeness of the spirit that it originally sought liberty from.

16. The purpose for this Egyptian Jerusalem is to prepare the way for an institution of gross perdition. Then will it be announced, "Babylon the great is fallen, is fallen."[2659] Then will the ascension of this eight kingdom fulfill the word, "As it began to dawn toward the first day of the week...there was a great earthquake."[2660] It is now, during relatively peaceful civil and religious times, that a personal knowing of the Father and His Son should commence. Before any of these things come to pass, at this present time, the Spirit says, "Hurt not the earth,

---

2653 Ezekiel 5:5
2654 Jeremiah 3:19
2655 Daniel 11:41
2656 Revelation 13:14
2657 Isaiah 65:17
2658 Esther 1:8
2659 Revelation 18:2
2660 Matthew 28:1,2

neither the sea, nor the trees, till we have sealed the servants of our God in their foreheads."[2661]

17. We today exist under a sealing period and during a time of inward reform and regeneration, that whether we live or die, we might be preserved and recognized in the heavenly records as men and women "that have hazarded their lives for the name of our Lord Jesus Christ."[2662] For, the confession of Christ towards one that honored the LORD His God incorrectly was, "Ye worship ye know not what,"[2663] yet after she had encountered His voice and then shared that encounter, what then was the testimony of them that did not know the LORD? They said, "We believe, not because of thy saying: for we have heard him ourselves."[2664] These individuals do put us to shame. To hear the LORD's voice for self's own good is the end of the matter. The saying came from the woman to others, and these, being not satisfied with her saying, came to Christ personally, and from their personal interaction with His speech, "many more believed because of his own word."[2665] So then, do we have a mind to pick up the culture of Bere'a? "They received the word with all readiness of mind, and searched the scriptures daily, whether those things were so,"[2666] and this is the current lot for the one who will declare, "That I may know him, and the power of his resurrection."[2667]

18. If there is no experience in the resurrection and high priestly ordination of God's Christ, there will be an acceptance of the *resurrection* of that false *Christ* because the image of its counterfeit spirit rests within the heart. "We have such an high priest, who is set on the right hand of the throne of the Majesty in the heavens,"[2668] and we will never know this fact until self's throne is put down and that minister of our members is refreshed. The faith of the Lamb, extending from His cross

---

2661 Revelation 7:3
2662 Acts 15:26
2663 John 4:22
2664 John 4:42
2665 John 4:41
2666 Acts 17:11
2667 Philippians 3:10
2668 Hebrews 8:1

to every thing concerning His heavenly mediation, is the diet of the believer to have restored in them the moral image of God.

19. This two-horned beast longs to have power that it may enact prescriptions to alleviate the moral void that it observes. Its power and doctrine is not of the living God, but of the dragon, and it will enforce religious laws and amendments to honor the code of its heart. It is for this reason that the message for us today is, "Fear God, and honor Him who is the Creator of all things."[2669] The counsel is, "Bind up the testimony, seal the law among my disciples,"[2670] for the Spirit says, "I will put my laws into their mind, and write them in their hearts: and I will be to them a God, and they shall be to me a people: and they shall not teach every man his neighbour, and every man his brother, saying, Know the Lord: for all shall know me."[2671]

20. The time will come when we will hear the earth's new pagan creature say, "My meat is to do the will of him that sent me, and to finish his work."[2672] His work is to cause "the earth and them which dwell therein to worship the first beast,"[2673] and his will is of the devil's ancient creed that says, "I will exalt my throne above the stars of God: I will sit also upon the mount of the congregation."[2674] Must falsehood exhibit more faithful determination than ones hopeful to know the living God? It is time to personally know the LORD's voice and to hear the commandment, "Ye shall afflict your souls, and offer an offering made by fire unto the LORD. And ye shall do no work in that same day: for it is a day of atonement, to make an atonement for you before the LORD your God."[2675]

2669 Revelation 14:7
2670 Isaiah 8:16
2671 Hebrews 8:10,11
2672 John 4:34
2673 Revelation 13:12
2674 Isaiah 14:13
2675 Leviticus 23:27,28

32

The Gravity Of The Earth And The Agitation Awaiting It

1. "And I beheld another beast coming up out of the earth."[2676]

2. It appears that when viewing the vision of the two-horned beast, that the beast is all that is generally considered above the earth from which it springs. If John saw a beast coming up from the earth, then the earth is just as important as the beast, for within the earth is the story of the beast's conception. How is it that such a grotesque and perverted creature comes from, in vision, something as plain and as quiet as the earth? The answer is that within the earth rests a disturbance so magnificent that it gives birth to a new entity. We are not told the full and open history from the time of the earth's issues until the new republic should be born, but what is clearly evident is that the earth suffers an error; it suffers an attack against itself; and it appears that the attack against itself comes from within itself.

3. It is fair to note the sex of the earth, for we are told that it is a she. "The earth helped the woman, and the earth opened her

---

2676 Revelation 13:11

mouth, and swallowed up the flood,"[2677] says Scripture. If a beast is coming up out of the earth, then a new creature is being born from a woman. She that held in check the spirit of Papal persecution was the force behind the Conscience of North American Independence; she was the inspiration behind what would later find itself refined as the United States Constitution. For one woman; the spirit of the earth; helped to protect another woman; that woman of God; who fled into the wilderness and hid for twelve hundred sixty years from the serpent and dragon. We have before us the fulfillment of the word, "Vash'ti the queen made a feast for the women in the royal house which belonged to king,"[2678] for at her conception, the queen of the earth helped her that had suffered for so long a period, granting her liberty of conscience to serve *God* according to the dictates of her own heart.

4. John saw this earth swallow up the flood of the dragon, which means that her mouth was once opened and then it shut up that flood, but then John observed, at some point, another beast coming up from the earth. This that came from her was not a she, as she is, but is a he, as it says, "He had two horns like a lamb, and he spake as a dragon."[2679] The language of the dragon is persecution. He is known for "speaking oppression and revolt, conceiving and uttering from the heart words of falsehood."[2680] Such a character does not at once oppress in the language of legislative wrath, for the dragon is cunning, and will at first work by his lamb-like entities to gain hearts to himself, but then will, with that which was swallowed up, manifest himself against God's host. These two entities are different; the earth and the product from her womb; and although we are not directly told what leads to such a tragedy within the earth's core, it is not hard to consider how that the earth was most likely wrongfully abused.

5. What appears before John is the same power under different phases. The only way any thing can ever come up from the earth is if

---

[2677] Revelation 12:16
[2678] Esther 1:9
[2679] Revelation 13:11
[2680] Isaiah 59:13

there is a breaking in the surface of the earth. When the new republic is born from the old, it should fulfill the saying, "Jesus, when he had cried again with a loud voice, yielded up the ghost. And, behold, the veil of the temple was rent in twain from the top to the bottom; and the earth did quake, and the rocks rent; and the graves were opened; and many bodies of the saints which slept arose, and came out of the graves after his resurrection."[2681]

6. When the body of the law and doctrine of Christ is again openly violated on earth, an earthquake will occur, and the earth will give birth to a new form of government. The fact that the earth is mentioned with so little of a description proves that it is its own force. The earth is not like any of the other kingdoms because it stands by a Constitution that holds the hands of the government in check, allowing civil offices their own territory and religious offices their own room. Each of the beasts of prophecy have an image to them because they are perversely involved with a dominion that stands in the way of some kind of humane tolerance.

7. The earth; the spirit and conscience of the United States; is diverse from all other kingdoms of Bible prophecy. Scripture says, "The earth bringeth forth...as the garden causeth...to spring forth,"[2682] for this earth is a garden unlike any other vineyard, even "like Eden,"[2683] for "joy and gladness shall be found therein, thanksgiving, and the voice of melody."[2684] Concerning this pleasant land, the Spirit says, "Be ye glad and rejoice for ever in that which I create: for, behold, I create Jerusalem a rejoicing, and her people a joy. And I will rejoice in Jerusalem, and joy in my people: and the voice of weeping shall be no more heard in her, nor the voice of crying."[2685] What weeping and crying, of old, took place? It says, "The lords of the heathen have broken down the principal plants thereof, they are come even unto Ja'zer, they wandered through the wilderness: her

---

2681 Matthew 27:50-53
2682 Isaiah 61:11
2683 Isaiah 51:3
2684 Isaiah 51:3
2685 Isaiah 65:18,19

branches are stretched out, they are gone over the sea. Therefore I will bewail with the weeping of Ja'zer the vine of Sib'mah: I will water thee with my tears, O Hesh'bon, and Elea'leh: for the shouting for thy summer fruits and for thy harvest is fallen. And gladness is taken away, and joy out of the plentiful field; and in the vineyards there shall be no singing, neither shall there be shouting."[2686]

8. From this prophecy it is fulfilled: "And when he had opened the fifth seal, I saw under the altar the souls of them that were slain for the word of God, and for the testimony which they held."[2687]

9. The first beast that came up before the two-horned beast destroyed a terrible amount of God's people by such means as the Inquisition. Protestants were persecuted for rejecting the tremendous fallacies of the Papacy, and during this time the saying was being fulfilled, "The holy city shall they tread under foot forty and two months."[2688] The Protestant church is not that holy city, but there is only one "city of the living God,"[2689] even "that great city, the holy Jerusalem."[2690] Not only did the Papacy devour individuals contrary to her, she was bearing a false rule in direct conflict with the LORD's name and throne. "There was given unto him"; that Wicked of religious error; "a mouth speaking great things and blasphemies; and power was given unto him to continue forty and two months,"[2691] and it was during this time that heaven's woman "fled into the wilderness, where she hath a place prepared of God, that they should feed her there a thousand two hundred and threescore days."[2692]

10. The forty-two months are the same as the two hundred and threescore days, or years, and these are synonymous with the time, and times, and half a time that she did fly into the wilderness to fulfill. Yet the time came when the earth would help this precious daughter of God, and she would serve to protect that woman with

---

2686 Isaiah 16:8-10
2687 Revelation 6:9
2688 Revelation 11:2
2689 Hebrews 12:22
2690 Revelation 21:10
2691 Revelation 13:5
2692 Revelation 12:6

all of her power. At some future point in the history of this same earth, John observed, coming from out of her, a beast bearing the image of the beast before it. Her surface was cracked, a shaking of her fundamental principles gave rise to the defamation of the foundation that she made it a point to establish, and the word again came from heaven's throne, "The earth also was corrupt before God, and the earth was filled with violence."[2693] How did it become corrupt? It says, "Her priests have polluted the sanctuary, they have done violence to the law." [2694]

11. At this time in ecclesiastical history, there is a violation against "the law of Christ,"[2695] which is "the law of faith,"[2696] "the law of the Spirit of life,"[2697] "the ordinances of justice."[2698] Apostasy will creep into the woman that the earth longs to protect, and that woman will turn against her protector to fulfill the saying, "And shall make her desolate and naked, and shall eat her flesh, and burn her with fire."[2699] Unhappy with her obscure language, an unsatisfied and intemperate religious host will rise up against her to produce the end that they desire. A defamation of the doctrine of Christ, and a pretended sympathy for the welfare of the dwellers on the earth, will cause a new beast to arise on the scene. It is after the earth is shaken that she then quakes into an opening to give birth to the image of the first beast before it, yet the events surrounding the declining society of the earth to compel her to fall sick and shake and tremble, we are not fully told.

12. Nevertheless, when the values of the United States are exchanged for the idolatrous and covetous standards of Rome, then will the child of the earth work under the influence of religious ministers to advance philosophical notions for filling laws and lawmakers with their *Christ's* language. With what Scripture reveals

---

2693 Genesis 6:11
2694 Zephaniah 3:4
2695 Galatians 6:2
2696 Romans 3:27
2697 Romans 8:2
2698 Isaiah 58:2
2699 Revelation 17:6

of these turbulent times that are near ahead, "Take heed to yourselves, lest at any time your hearts be overcharged with surfeiting, and drunkenness, and cares of this life, and so that day come upon you unawares,"[2700] says the Spirit. John observed, in addition to the leopard beast, another beast ascending from the earth, which earth beforehand shut up the flood of Papal persecution, yet now has opened her mouth to release a beast with that same spirit. To them that dwell in heaven at this time; that is, in the Habitation and Sanctuary of the LORD their God, and that rest in the Courts of His holiness with His High Priest; this time will be the greatest test and purging for them while on earth.

13. It is for this reason that every one professing active belief on the name of the Spirit's Christ should pick up the demeanor, "We have heard him ourselves,"[2701] which is why the Spirit counsels, "Come now, and let us reason together,"[2702] and, "Ask me of things to come concerning my sons, and concerning the work of my hands command ye me. I have made the earth, and created man upon it."[2703] "The sons of the stranger shall not drink thy wine, for the which thou hast laboured: but they that have gathered it shall eat it, and praise the LORD; and they that have brought it together shall drink it in the courts of my holiness."[2704]

14. Therefore "give him"; our LORD's Priest; "no rest, till he establish."[2705] Do not quit yourselves because His speech is not easily understood. "As the heavens are higher than the earth, so are my ways higher than your ways, and my thoughts than your thoughts,"[2706] says the LORD our God, yet none of this stops Him from considering "our frame; he remembereth that we are dust."[2707] You cannot hear what the living God has to tell you will with noise surrounding

---

2700 Luke 21:34
2701 John 4:42
2702 Isaiah 1:18
2703 Isaiah 45:11,12
2704 Isaiah 62:8,9
2705 Isaiah 62:7
2706 Isaiah 55:9
2707 Psalms 103:14

you. The Spirit will announce to every faithful soul, "Take thou away from me the noise of thy songs; for I will not hear the melody of thy viols. But let judgment run down as waters, and righteousness as a mighty stream."[2708] What is this judgment that is righteousness? He says, "A law shall proceed from me, and I will make my judgment to rest for a light of the people."[2709]

15. It was Christ who came into the Spirit's religious world to "set judgment in the earth,"[2710] which is why God said, "The isles shall wait for his law."[2711] What law? "The doctrine of Christ";[2712] "the law of Christ."[2713] Diligently studying and applying the law and doctrine that is "of the faith, and of the knowledge of the Son of God,"[2714] will apprise the heart of its condition that it may take courage to chase after the medicine and ointment of the Spirit for sustenance. The Spirit says, "In righteousness shalt thou be established,"[2715] therefore "it shall be our righteousness, if we observe to do all these commandments before the LORD our God, as he hath commanded us."[2716] God's Priest says, "If ye love me, keep my commandments,"[2717] letting us know that the doctrine of Christ has precepts to be obeyed in addition to the LORD's. For this cause the ordinances of justification are those statutes and judgments necessary to leave off the condemnation, "Neither were they obedient unto his law."[2718]

16. As much mental agitation it takes to hear the voice of God's Chief Angel, it should be that the believer is equally agitating his or her LORD and Father personally. Scripture tells us to do so; the Spirit tells us to command Him of His own thoughts and works; His plea for our education should not be ignored. The storm that will

---

2708 Amos 5:23,24
2709 Isaiah 51:4
2710 Isaiah 42:4
2711 Isaiah 42:4
2712 2 John 1:9
2713 Galatians 6:2
2714 Ephesians 4:13
2715 Isaiah 54:13
2716 Deuteronomy 6:25
2717 John 14:15
2718 Isaiah 42:24

break out into the earth; in the form of an ecclesiastically functioning tyrannical government; will fulfill the word, "Thy destroyers and they that made thee waste shall go forth of thee."[2719] This will be a great time of purging for the Spirit's household. The foul seed will be separated from the good seed, for the perfect seed is to exit this period of church history "to keep seed alive upon the face of the earth"[2720] when it should be fulfilled, "His deadly wound was healed."[2721] Heaven's soldiers at that time will "turn many to righteousness as the stars for ever and ever,"[2722] and these will be them who today, during this present time of probation in heaven's mental and moral learning, are compassionately "understanding what the will of the Lord is."[2723]

2719 Isaiah 49:17
2720 Genesis 7:3
2721 Revelation 13:3
2722 Daniel 12:3
2723 Ephesians 5:17

33

The Earth And The Sea

1. "And I stood upon the sand of the sea, and saw a beast rise up out of the sea."[2724] "And I beheld another beast coming up out of the earth."[2725]

2. John records that he observed two entities arising from two distinct places. Why is not enough attention given to where these two kingdoms are formed? John saw a beast rising from the sea and another from the earth, therefore the sea and the earth are just as important as the beasts themselves. The visions of chapters twelve, thirteen, and fourteen of the Revelation, are one vision. Before an idea drawn of the imagery contained within them is drawn outside of them, it is fair to first look within the vision, which is but a symbolic representation of literal facts revealed out of order, yet in full order according to the portion of the revealed vision. For this cause, the student of prophecy is responsible for considering the proper definition of the sea and the earth.

3. To understand this sea we must begin at the place where it is first mentioned. Unlike in the prophecy of Daniel where many beasts

---

2724 Revelation 13:1
2725 Revelation 13:11

are the products of the sea, only one beast is formed out of what is contained within the sea in the Revelation, and this lets us know that the vision of John is specific to only one power at one point in time. The beasts of Daniel are political pagan entities, yet the last beast mentioned, the fourth beast, has a beast come up within it that is not seen as a beast, but rather as a little horn that serves as a fifth kingdom from the fourth's head, or mind. This horn is not like the other beasts, because not only should he have "magnified himself to the prince of the host,"[2726] but he also "cast down the truth to the ground,"[2727] and because he "opposeth and exalteth himself above all that is God, or that is worshipped,"[2728] it is fulfilled in this power, "He shall destroy wonderfully, and shall prosper, and practise, and shall destroy the mighty and the holy people."[2729]

4. Every thing in the Revelation is not real, but is rather a delineation of some real thing to tangibly appear in a reasonable manner. It should not be forgotten that the Revelation is completely told from the perspective of one who beforehand confesses, "I was in the Spirit."[2730] As Christ tells us, "God is a Spirit,"[2731] and as He again says, "A spirit hath not flesh and bones,"[2732] so no thing given to John should contain flesh and bones, but should be of the same substance as God, seeing as how it comes from Him. The vision of the Revelation is literally of the Spirit's mind and not of His Christ's, which is why John says of his state when receiving this discourse, "Immediately I was in the spirit."[2733]

5. The Revelation, besides being a visual and spiritual compilation of the Spirit's sayings, "the words of this prophecy"[2734] are important because God's Man sent to John "his angel to shew unto his servants

---

2726   Daniel 8:11
2727   Daniel 8:12
2728   2 Thessalonians 2:4
2729   Daniel 8:24
2730   Revelation 1:10
2731   John 4:24
2732   Luke 24:39
2733   Revelation 4:2
2734   Revelation 1:3

the things which must shortly be done."[2735] But where are the things of "the words of the book of this prophecy"[2736] to be completed? Says heaven's Priest, "I Jesus have sent mine angel to testify unto you these things in the churches."[2737]

6. As the visions given Daniel are constrained upon civil entities and events, the Revelation given John is but a vision of ecclesiastical entities and events. The little horn of Daniel; who is the first beast of the thirteenth division of the Revelation; did not directly come up out of the sea, but rather from a beast that came up out of the sea. The two beasts are in fact one; the fourth beast and the little horn forming two phases of the fourth beast; as the vision declares, but the beast from which the little horn derives its heritage was born from the same place as the others before it, but of the little horn it is said, "He shall be diverse."[2738] It is said of this little horn, "He shall speak great words against the most High, and shall wear out the saints of the most High, and think to change times and laws,"[2739] for in this horn we have a match with the beast that John saw, for to John's beast of the sea, "there was given unto him a mouth speaking great things and blasphemies... against God, to blaspheme his name, and his tabernacle, and them that dwell in heaven. And it was given unto him to make war with the saints, and to overcome them: and power was given him over all kindreds, and tongues, and nations."[2740]

7. The question, then, should arise, "Why did Daniel only see a horn while John saw the horn's structure?" The little horn of Daniel and the leopard beast of John are the same, yet it is as if, in Daniel, attention is diverted to only one arena of the horn, while the other is left off. Daniel's visions express kingdoms from their political actions and dispositions. The little horn is diverse from the rest because he is not simply political, but he is also ecclesiastical in a way that perverts the name of the living God. The power abused by the horn in Daniel's

---

2735 Revelation 1:1
2736 Revelation 22:19
2737 Revelation 22:16
2738 Daniel 7:24
2739 Daniel 7:25
2740 Revelation 13:5-7

vision is strictly civil, yet the reason for it's ambition is given to John, for it wants to be worshipped as the true *God* of gods and as God Himself. Because John's vision is a figurative sketch of church history, the beasts of the Revelation are not only viewed as political creatures, but are a mixture of an active civil and religious force, which is why Daniel could not fully expound on what the Spirit revealed to John.

8. The beasts that came up before John are a perverse mixture of church and State; an understanding of their origin is crucial to comprehend the fact behind their vision. Because the leopard beast is the little horn and because the little horn was not born from the sea of the other beasts before it, but from the mind of the grotesque beast before it, the sea and the sand of the Revelation given to John and Daniel are an aid to understanding the essence of the tribe that arises from it.

9. John saw a beast rising from the sea as he stood on the sand of that sea, so what could this mean? It says, "I will multiply thy seed as the stars of the heaven, and as the sand which is upon the sea shore."[2741] Stars compose the sand of the sea, and when John had earlier wondered of what the definition of stars were, he was told, "The seven stars are the angels of the seven churches."[2742] Stars are angels, and angels are men who are religious messengers. Before John was given this vision of the leopard beast, speaking of the work of the dragon, he says, "His tail drew the third part of the stars of heaven, and did cast them to the earth."[2743] The stars appear to form the ground that John stands upon in the thirteenth division of the Revelation, and as it says, "There was war in heaven,"[2744] and as the dragon is a symbol of "that old serpent, called the Devil, and Satan,"[2745] so a portion of God's supporters were gathered of the dragon from out of that religion within the LORD's heaven, as it says, "There appeared a woman in heaven."[2746]

10. It is known that Satan truly gathered a host about him in heaven. These are those "angels which kept not their first estate, but left their

---

2741 Genesis 22:17
2742 Revelation 1:20
2743 Revelation 12:4
2744 Revelation 12:7
2745 Revelation 12:9
2746 Revelation 12:1

own habitation,"[2747] and the language of the Revelation has relayed the same information concerning not celestial beings, but rather mortal men. There is a particular seed of men, who in the beginning of heaven's tidings, were once angels of the Spirit, but were cast down to earth and rejected of heaven for "having great wrath"[2748] against the LORD's Establishment. Thus, it says that no other portion of the dragon but the tail drew these stars, and it is well to know that "the prophet that teacheth lies, he is the tail."[2749]

11. The dragon; because it is evident that we are found under the spirit of Rome at the beginning of the vision within the twelfth division of the Revelation; is a symbol of the pagan heritage of Rome, and the history of the Catholic church tells how that the false philosophies of Roman paganism began to mingle with men convinced of the authenticity of the apostles' doctrine. The simplicity of the gospel began to lose its individual purity due to the fact that the supposed angels of the Roman Christian churches sought to amend their Jewish and heathen customs to please both parties within their tent, for the majority of the Christian church was composed of Jews and Gentile Jewish converts, which converts were from pagan roots, as it says, "Strangers of Rome, Jews and proselytes."[2750] "Through philosophy and vain deceit, after the tradition of men, after the rudiments of the world, and not after Christ,"[2751] the Christian church began to accept and preach "another Jesus"[2752] and "another gospel."[2753] Many of the heathen rites and doctrines were established under a Christian garb. Eventually Christian ministers adopted the Levit'ical hierarchy of the ancient Israelite priesthood, where the high priest became what was known as the head bishop, and the priests and Levites becoming known as deacons and presbyters.

2747   Jude 1:6
2748   Revelation 12:12
2749   Isaiah 9:15
2750   Acts 2:10
2751   Colossians 2:8
2752   2 Corinthians 11:4
2753   2 Corinthians 11:4

12. There was no other way for the dragon to accomplish his work other than by subtly polluting an institution of the Spirit. The moment was right and the established religion was perfect, and because past heritage and tradition is not so easily overcome, especially when appearing to the conscience to be forced onto the heart's mind, that coarse spirit of religious error knew that he could have his own host comprised of voluntarily uneducated and self-righteous superstitious ministers who would hear and accept the saying, "If thou therefore wilt worship me, all shall be thine."[2754] It is no surprise why this church chose the name Catholic; which name means universal; for even at their beginning the apostle confessed of them, "Your faith is spoken of throughout the whole world,"[2755] nevertheless these were most violent in their understanding, for it was necessary to tell them, "By the deeds of the law there shall no flesh be justified in his sight."[2756] These unsanctified ministers expressed their lack of conversion by announcing, "Righteousness come by the law,"[2757] and, "Ye now made perfect by the flesh."[2758]

13. The dragon succeeded in drawing away them that "profess that they know God; but in works they deny him, being abominable, and disobedient, and unto every good work reprobate."[2759] These being without the LORD and His High Priest, due to willingly removing themselves from His Spirit, were "them which say they are apostles, and are not,"[2760] and so it was necessary to tell them, "I have somewhat against thee, because thou hast left thy first love. Remember therefore from whence thou art fallen."[2761] These had fallen from the same place as Eve, in that they also "worshipped and served the creature more than the Creator."[2762] The creature in both instances was not

---

2754 Luke 4:7
2755 Romans 1:8
2756 Romans 3:20
2757 Galatians 2:21
2758 Galatians 3:3
2759 Titus 1:16
2760 Revelation 2:2
2761 Revelation 2:4,5
2762 Romans 1:25

necessarily the serpent, but rather the subtle doctrine of the serpent. Its "great swelling words of vanity"[2763] did "pervert the gospel of Christ"[2764] to move the apostle to write, "I fear, lest by any means, as the serpent beguiled Eve through his subtilty, so your minds should be corrupted from the simplicity that is in Christ."[2765]

14. Nevertheless, despite the plea of the apostles, it was fulfilled, "After my departing shall grievous wolves enter in among you, not sparing the flock,"[2766] and these terrible enemies of the Spirit's law were none other than "the elders of the church."[2767] Thus, we are brought to the vision of John, wherein on the sand of the sea John stood, and where on the same ground of the fallen elders of the Christian church John observed a beast rising. John becomes a partaker in the event from this position, for it was these men who fulfilled the word, "The mystery of iniquity doth already work: only he who now letteth will let, until he be taken out of the way."[2768] By the time we reach the thirteenth division of the Revelation, he who did let and restrained did quit his stance, fulfilling the word, "The dragon gave him his power, and his seat, and great authority."[2769]

15. For this reason we must now turn our attention to the sea of the vision, for this same little horn is that leopard beast born from out of some sea.

The Sea

16. Scripture says, that at some point in the history of the dragon, that "he was cast out into the earth, and his angels were cast out with him."[2770] For this reason it was said, "Woe to the inhabiters of the earth and of the sea! for the devil is come down unto you."[2771]

2763 2 Peter 2:18
2764 Galatians 1:7
2765 2 Corinthians 11:3
2766 Acts 20:29
2767 Acts 20:17
2768 2 Thessalonians 2:7
2769 Revelation 13:2
2770 Revelation 12:9
2771 Revelation 12:12

17. The dragon and his host were cast out of the presence of the LORD's Spirit and found a home in the sea and among them of His earth. What is in the sea? "Waters," in the language of prophecy, represent religious people, tribes, and multitudes, but what else holds the sea? Scripture says, "God created great whales, and every living creature that moveth, which the waters brought forth."[2772] What may a great whale represent? It says, "Pharaoh king of Egypt...Thou art like a young lion of the nations, and thou art as a whale in the seas,"[2773] and, "Pharaoh king of Egypt, the great dragon that lieth in the midst of his rivers."[2774] This is that "dragon that is in the sea,"[2775] where through him many bear the name of, "Pharaoh."

18. The dragon, his religion, and his host, comprise the sea, and in the sea should be one as a great whale, as a great priest like Pharaoh who holds the saying of Pharaoh, "Who is the LORD, that I should obey his voice to let Israel go?"[2776] This same philosophy is held by the religion of the Devil, for it is said of the spirit of this religion, "That opened not the house of his prisoners."[2777] Herein the sea is composed of ones who bear the character, "I am a God, I sit in the seat of God, in the midst of the seas,"[2778] and are ordained by one who says, "I will ascend into heaven, I will exalt my throne above the stars of God: I will sit also upon the mount of the congregation, in the sides of the north: I will ascend above the heights of the clouds; I will be like the most High."[2779]

19. The beasts of Daniel came by political winds of strife, yet it is quite different for the leopard beast of the Revelation, which beast is the little horn of Daniel's fourth beast. The dragon gave up itself to the leopard beast in another manner, for the whole purpose was to fulfill the saying, "They worshipped the dragon which gave power

---

2772 Genesis 1:21
2773 Ezekiel 32:2
2774 Ezekiel 29:3
2775 Isaiah 27:1
2776 Exodus 5:2
2777 Isaiah 14:17
2778 Ezekiel 28:2
2779 Isaiah 14:13,14

unto the beast."[2780] For this cause it says, "The daily sacrifice was taken away, and the place of his sanctuary cast down,"[2781] and again, "They shall take away the daily sacrifice, and they shall place the abomination that maketh desolate,"[2782] for it was to be fulfilled, "He shall magnify himself in his heart, and by peace shall destroy many."[2783]

20. The one magnified is "the daily," which is also the dragon, which is a symbol of paganism and its pagan State. Paganism was not literally taken away, and John sees this, for it was to be worshiped under the dominion of the little horn, which horn is the leopard beast. This that came from the sea in the sight of John was born in the sight of Christian priests who longed to exalt a pagan and idolatrous heritage under a pretended Christian name. For this cause it was fulfilled, "The sea arose by reason of a great wind that blew,"[2784] even the "the wind of doctrine, by the sleight of men, and cunning craftiness, whereby they lie in wait to deceive."[2785]

21. In the thirteenth division of the Revelation, we are introduced to the true form of the Papacy in its beginning. It is born from the traditional and philosophical heresies of pagans, it is conceived under the falsehood of a modern Levit'ical priesthood through carnal and apostate individuals; priests who knew neither God nor His Christ; who not only joined such an error to the doctrine of Christ, but also managed to coerce such a fraudulent institution into the State of Rome to become the State of Rome. It appears that before us in vision is the creation of "the throne of iniquity"[2786] by men not "found any more in heaven."[2787] If not in heaven then they are on earth, and if on earth they honor that given to the dwellers of earth by God, as it says, "The sun, and the moon, and the stars, even all the host of heaven...which the LORD thy

---

2780 Revelation 13:4
2781 Daniel 8:11
2782 Daniel 11:31
2783 Daniel 8:25
2784 John 6:18
2785 Ephesians 4:14
2786 Psalms 94:20
2787 Revelation 12:8

God hath divided unto all nations under the whole heaven."[2788] Seeing as how these have a mind philosophically engaged towards *Christ* and His *apostles*, their heaven should be clothed in superstitions forcefully justified by a Christian name.

22. Men of an impure religion born of a surface ascent to the fact behind the LORD's doctrine worked for the birth of the leopard institution. This is the sea from which the leopard beast is conceived, and in this sea are the dragon and his host, or Pagan and Papal Rome and their falsehood with the grotesque religion of Satan and his falsehood. Just as important as the beast is to the vision, so is the sea and sand for our understanding, for without "the blasphemy of them which say they are Jews, and are not, but are the synagogue of Satan,"[2789] there is no leopard beast.

23. Again, it should not be forgotten that the Revelation is a vision of ecclesiastical history. After this apostate church should rest under a white, and then a red, and then a black horse, it then rose up as a horn and power diverse from the kingdoms before it. This same leopard beast came up from the sea of its pollution as a pale horse bearing the emblem of its father and "having seven heads and ten horns, and upon his horns ten crowns, and upon his heads the name of blasphemy."[2790] The sea, then, and the earth of the Revelation, put forth important elements on their own that hold practical health for our understanding. The beasts are no more important than the places from whence they spring, for without a proper understanding of where they derive their particular ambitions and traits of character, we are left to misinterpret and misunderstand the instruction that the Spirit has left us.

24. Just as these beasts come from where they must, so the believer should hear, "Look unto me, and be ye saved, all the ends of the earth: for I am God, and there is none else."[2791] God Himself says that there is no other LORD or God but Him, yet there is an institution honored as *God's*, and one who exalts himself to be the chief vicar and high priest

---

2788 Deuteronomy 4:19
2789 Revelation 2:9
2790 Revelation 13:1
2791 Isaiah 45:22

of *Christ* and of *God*. Christ Himself says, "My kingdom is not of this world,"[2792] and "when Jesus therefore perceived that they would come and take him by force, to make him a king, he departed again into a mountain himself alone."[2793] There will never again be any earthly representation of the LORD God on earth; such as enjoy spiritual and moral error are "they who separate themselves, sensual, having not the Spirit."[2794]

25. Therefore "if any many have not the Spirit of Christ, he is none of his."[2795] The reign of God's High Priest is not on this earth. God Himself said concerning the throne of David, "It shall be no more, until he come whose right it is; and I will give it him."[2796] He who came; He whose right that throne is; that is His Christ, for it says, "He shall build the temple of the LORD; and he shall bear the glory, and shall sit and rule upon his throne; and he shall be a priest upon his throne."[2797] This Christ is "the man whose name is The BRANCH,"[2798] and His LORD says, "I cause the Branch of righteousness to grow up unto David; and he shall execute judgment and righteousness in the land. In those days shall Judah be saved, and Jerusalem shall dwell safely: and this is the name wherewith she shall be called, The LORD our righteousness. For thus saith the LORD; David shall never want a man to sit upon the throne of the house of Israel; neither shall the priests the Levites want a man before me."[2799]

26. For this cause, the LORD says, "I will set up one shepherd over them, and he shall feed them, even my servant David; he shall feed them, and he shall be their shepherd. And I the LORD will be their God, and my servant David a prince among them; I the LORD have spoken it."[2800] This is why it says, "The Lamb which is in the midst of

---

2792 John 18:36
2793 John 6:15
2794 Jude 1:19
2795 Romans 8:9
2796 Ezekiel 21:27
2797 Zechariah 6:13
2798 Zechariah 6:12
2799 Jeremiah 33:14-18
2800 Ezekiel 34:23,24

the throne shall feed them, and shall lead them unto living fountains of waters."[2801]

27. Christ's reign as the Spirit's Chief Priest is found at the center of His LORD's throne, "for when he saith all things are put under him, it is manifest that he is excepted, which did put all things under him."[2802] It is therefore time to behold our LORD and to cease observing the gods and the creatures of men. "We have such an high priest, who is set on the right hand of the throne of the Majesty in the heavens,"[2803] and there is an emphasis of these "heavens" for our learning, for "the heaven, even the heavens, are the LORD'S: but the earth hath he given to the children of men."[2804] That on earth is given to the disobedient hardened within themselves and in their traditions, for "all things that are done under heaven"[2805] are that "sore travail"[2806] which the LORD has "given to the sons of man to be exercised therewith."[2807] On earth is a feast of "adultery, fornication, uncleanness, lasciviousness, idolatry, witchcraft, hatred, variance, emulations, wrath, strife, seditions, heresies, envyings, murders, drunkenness, revellings."[2808] Such is accomplished for the sake of ones "desirous of vain glory"[2809] and are advanced by the preaching, "You are justified by the law."[2810]

28. This is why we should know that "we might be justified by the faith of Christ"[2811] to uphold the position, "That I may know him, and the power of his resurrection, and the fellowship of his sufferings, being made conformable unto his death; if by any means I might attain unto the resurrection of the dead."[2812] This is the only means whereby we may quench our inherited and self-cultivated spirit of error. It is not

---

2801 Revelation 7:17
2802 1 Corinthians 15:27
2803 Hebrews 8:1
2804 Psalms 115:16
2805 Ecclesiastes 1:13
2806 Ecclesiastes 1:13
2807 Ecclesiastes 1:13
2808 Galatians 5:19-21
2809 Galatians 5:26
2810 Galatians 5:4
2811 Galatians 2:16
2812 Philippians 3:10,11

know how long until the Spirit should see fit to release that creature born of the earth and bearing the image of the leopard beast, and for that reason it should be heard and confessed, "Take knowledge of the Lamb, for 'thy God reigneth.'[2813] 'Worship God in the spirit, and rejoice in Christ Jesus, and have no confidence in the flesh.'[2814] 'Set your affection on things above, not on things on the earth.'"[2815]

29. The forming of the leopard beast, as it happened before, will happen again. The believer should personally know the living God and His voice, that whether they live to see what is expected or die before what is pronounced should be established, strength may be added to their inward person to combat that same spirit of the institutions spoken of. The leopard beast has already risen and is yet wounded, and before she can reclaim her throne in full health as Mistress of the religious world, there should be a terrible falling away in the earth, which terror only a faith established by a tried love will be able to endure.

[2813] Isaiah 52:7
[2814] Philippians 3:3
[2815] Colossians 3:2

34

Dinah And She'chem

1. The saying will again be fulfilled, "In the latter times some shall depart from the faith, giving heed to seducing spirits, and doctrines of devils,"[2816] for it is written, "I saw three unclean spirits like frogs come out of the mouth of the dragon, and out of the mouth of the beast, and out of the mouth of the false prophet."[2817]

2. These spurious doctrines have a beginning, for by the counsel of these spirits, the two-horned beast "deceiveth them that dwell on the earth by the means of those miracles"[2818] which proceed from this instruction. Therefore it must be considered, "How does this entity even achieve the end that is spoken of for it? How does falsehood enter into the spirit of the mind of men to draw them away from religious simplicity? What causes one to vacate the premises of the Faith of God to subscribe to philosophically seducing thoughts and notions?" These questions have been mentioned and answered before, but now we add the figure of an illustration to beautify our discourse.

2816   1 Timothy 4:1
2817   Revelation 16:13
2818   Revelation 13:14

3. The seduction that will be performed to draw the earth into greater religious error against heaven will not be of any fancy happening, but the times will again recommend the saying, "These things I have written unto you concerning them that seduce you."[2819] This seduction is of ministers through "great swelling words of vanity"[2820] who "allure through the lusts of the flesh, through much wantonness."[2821] And herein is their doctrine: "Ye shall not surely die,"[2822] and, "Ye are gods,"[2823] and, "All the congregation are holy, every one of them, and the LORD is among them,"[2824] and, "You are justified by the law,"[2825] and, "Righteousness come by the law."[2826] Such falsehood will enter into the ones of rank within the churches of the earth from "giving themselves over to fornication, and going after strange flesh."[2827] These that "despise government"[2828] are them that will run "greedily after the error of Ba'laam"[2829] for some schism within their heart, but what deviation may cause them to nationally violate themselves and others through their imaginations?

4. In the manner that it happened of old between the Christian church of Rome and the State of Rome, it will happen again. The Apostle John lived in a time where heaven was regarded by its professors as being unsatisfactory. It was for this reason that he wrote, "Whosoever transgresseth, and abide the not in the doctrine of Christ, hath not God."[2830] John literally saw various Christian churches ignoring the counsel, "Have no fellowship with the unfruitful work of darkness,"[2831] for these works were the heathen customs and mysteries practiced and

---

2819 1 John 2:26
2820 2 Peter 2:18
2821 2 Peter 2:18
2822 Genesis 3:4
2823 Psalms 82:6
2824 Numbers 16:3
2825 Galatians 5:4
2826 Galatians 2:21
2827 Jude 1:7
2828 2 Peter 2:10
2829 Jude 1:11
2830 2 John 1:9
2831 Ephesians 5:11

upheld by "fornication, and all uncleanness, or covetousness,"[2832] which is why it was told them, "Let no man deceive you with vain words,"[2833] and, "It is a shame even to speak of those things which are done of them in secret."[2834] Heathen worship and service was making its way into the Christian camp, and such a devotional routine was even being replaced with Christian names, which is why Paul wrote to the churches, "There be some that trouble you, and would pervert the gospel of Christ."[2835]

5. This perversion of the gospel had its roots in men whose ideologies were not only estranged by Greek and Roman philosophical understandings on life and religion, but also whose interpretation of the apostles' speech ran through the religions of Egypt and of eastern foreign lands. Such tainted minds read Scripture as they did history or philosophy and desired a union among all philosophical thought and religions, most preferably that practice of Christians with all the world's religious practices. As the times moved forward, ministers of the Christian church had picked up so many pagan thoughts and doctrines that it compelled the apostle to write, "They went out from us, but they were not of us; for if they had been of us, they would no doubt have continued with us: but they went out, that they might be made manifest that they were not all of us."[2836] There was at this time an official division between them that feared God's Priest and honored the will of living God, and them that confessed service to "the image which fell down from Jupiter."[2837]

6. The spirit and simplicity of heaven's Faith was quenched by the doctrines "of false brethren unawares brought in";[2838] the same internal apostate subtleties that caused the early Christian church to fall will be repeated in the church of the nation in the earth to appear. These things are seen from the record given us of Dinah the daughter of Leah.

2832 Ephesians 5:3
2833 Ephesians 5:6
2834 Ephesians 5:12
2835 Galatians 1:7
2836 1 John 2:19
2837 Acts 19:35
2838 Galatians 2:4

7. Scripture says: "When She'chem the son of Ha'mor the Hi'vite, prince of the country, saw her, he took her, and lay with her, and defiled her."[2839]

8. Dinah went out to see the daughters of the land, but what daughters and what land? Scripture says, "Esau took his wives of the daughters of Canaan; A'dah the daughter of E'lon the Hit'tite, and Aholiba'mah the daughter of A'nah the daughter of Zib'eon the Hi'vite."[2840] As a woman or a daughter is prophetically a symbol of a church, we have a church of Jacob; and this Jacob being the beloved of God; wandering off among the churches of Canaan, to see and to observe them.

9. As a name in the Bible is synonymous with the inward character of the person that is mentioned, to understand the depth of the story, along with the foreshadowing of its events in the history of the church of Rome, the names of the key persons involved must be defined.

10. Dinah in the Hebrew tongue means justice or judgment. Ha'mor in Hebrew; compiling the most fitting definitions to draw a proper conclusion; means donkey, a male ass from its redness, and further, it means to boil up, to ferment with scum, to glow with redness, or to be red. And She'chem, in the Hebrew, this name is in reference, figuratively, to the neck as being the place of burdens. It means to load up on the back of man or beast, or to incline the shoulder to bear a burden. Canaan also means to bring down low to humiliation, to humble self under subjection.[2841]

11. Based upon a clearer understanding of the names involved, we find ourselves viewing a church, whose foundation is justice and judgment, going to observe the ways of other temples that rest under burdensome subjections, or under doctrines "having their conscience seared with a hot iron."[2842] Ha'mor is defined as an ass in his redness, and since an ass is a beast, his image unmistakably points to that "great red dragon"[2843] known as that "scarlet coloured beast,"[2844] a symbol, in

---

2839 Genesis 34:2
2840 Genesis 36:2
2841 The definition of these names are referenced by Strong's Concordance
2842 1 Timothy 4:2
2843 Revelation 12:3
2844 Revelation 17:3

the Revelation, of pagan Rome. The father and the son are one, for the praise derived from pagan religions attributes righteousness to its subscribers from "the works of their hands."[2845] It was purposed through the sacrifice of Christ "that through death he might destroy him that had the power of death, that is, the devil; and deliver them who through fear of death were all their lifetime subject to bondage."[2846] This bondage that many were; and oddly still are; subject to was that error of "bondage under the elements of the world."[2847] This is why John wrote, "The lust of the flesh, and the lust of the eyes, and the pride of life, is not of the Father, but is of the world."[2848]

12. Because the majority of the Christian church, in the beginning, was comprised of both Jews and pagan converts to Judaism, the ones in responsible positions at that time made, what they believed, to be proper adjustments to reach their congregations. Heathen rites and customs were combined with Jewish feasts and ordinances for a new order of Christian religion. These two classes of converts to heaven's religion; Jews and Gentile Jews; existed beforehand in useless ceremonies and rituals that did no good thing for the spirit and character of their inward person. This is why God's Christ, "having abolished in his flesh the enmity, even the law of commandments contained in ordinances"[2849] upholding "a shew of wisdom in will worship, and humility, and neglecting of the body,"[2850] says, "Be renewed in the spirit of your mind."[2851] This is why the Spirit counsels, "Worship God in the spirit, and rejoice in Christ Jesus, and have no confidence in the flesh."[2852] By God's Christ, religion to God was to move from the physical to the spiritual, for God's Priest is no longer on earth and His God is not flesh, neither is their Temple found in any thing of like manner as that of man, or in any thing crafted by man.

2845 Revelation 9:20
2846 Hebrews 2:14,15
2847 Galatians 4:3
2848 1 John 2:16
2849 Ephesians 2:15
2850 Colossians 2:23
2851 Ephesians 4:23
2852 Philippians 3:3

13. The church of "the ordinances of justice";[2853] who was born "in the beginning of the gospel"[2854] as "the house of God, which is the church of the living God, the pillar and ground of the truth";[2855] somehow finds herself among the polytheistic and superstitious churches of the land, and is defiled by the burdensome standards of the prince of the sects of that land. These standards took this church and negligently laid with this church, placing into this church that spirit revered by ones existing "in lasciviousness, lusts, excess of wine, revellings, banquetings, and abominable idolatries."[2856] This is why the apostles counseled, "For this ye know, that no whoremonger, nor unclean person, nor covetous man, who is an idolater, hath any inheritance in the kingdom of Christ and of God,"[2857] and, "Little children, keep yourselves from idols."[2858]

14. The apostle counseled Christian churches, "The darkness is past,"[2859] and observe his language, for he says, "Past," and not, "Passed." That old way of existing by "gifts and sacrifices, that could not make him that did the service perfect, as pertaining to the conscience,"[2860] and by that "which stood only in meats and drinks, and diverse washings, and carnal ordinances,"[2861] God's Man vanquished "through the eternal Spirit" to purge every willing "conscience from dead works to serve the living God."[2862] This is why the apostle wrote, "Every one that loveth him that begat loveth him also that is begotten of him."[2863] "The Spirit of him that raised up Jesus from the dead"[2864] was of the LORD His Father, and the only way to receive the full health and experience of His benevolent will is through His Spirit's law and judgment. If Christ by this Spirit was quickened in the flesh and also raised from the

---

2853 Isaiah 58:2
2854 Philippians 4:15
2855 1 Timothy 3:15
2856 1 Peter 1:3
2857 Ephesians 5:5
2858 1 John 5:21
2859 1 John 1:8
2860 Hebrews 9:9
2861 Hebrews 9:10
2862 Hebrews 9:14
2863 1 John 5:1
2864 Romans 8:11

dead, is anything less to be expected of any one believing on His name? "Days, and months, and times, and years,"[2865] along with images and rituals and policies, began to cloud the Christian church from God due to her admitting a pagan atmosphere into her conversation, altering the reality of the believer's necessary experience to obtain knowledge of heaven's revealed will and intention.

15. Throughout their season of early courting and affection, the order and doctrines of paganism "loved the damsel, and spake kindly unto the damsel."[2866] It is no surprise, for this dragon is also that serpent, and generations beforehand, another woman of God confessed, "The serpent beguiled me."[2867] This is why the apostle wrote, "Lest any man should beguile you with enticing words,"[2868] "I fear, lest by any means, as the serpent beguiled Eve through his subtilty, so your minds should be corrupted from the simplicity that is in Christ."[2869]

16. The apostle Paul expresses terrible pain and sorrow for the religious errors brought into the churches. His tone reveals one whose heart would not allow him to cover his inward thoughts, for he writes, "Out of much affliction and anguish of heart I wrote unto you with many tears; not that ye should be grieved, but that ye might know the love which I have more abundantly unto you."[2870] Paul wrote to the churches, "It is reported commonly that there is fornication among you, and such fornication as is not so much as named among the Gentiles,"[2871] for he began to see, and to take knowledge of the fact that others also saw, that there was no distinguishing feature between the Christian churches and the pagan houses. At this time the saying was fulfilled: "The time will come when they will not endure sound doctrine; but after their own lusts...shall turn away their ears from the truth, and shall be turned unto fables."[2872]

2865 Galatians 4:10
2866 Genesis 34:3
2867 Genesis 3:13
2868 Colossians 2:4
2869 2 Corinthians 11:3
2870 2 Corinthians 2:4
2871 1 Corinthians 5:5
2872 2 Timothy 4:3,4

17. A church of the LORD born of His pure doctrines found; Dinah; herself in a relationship that fulfilled the word, "And such as do wickedly against the covenant shall he corrupt by flatteries."[2873] Them that did "profess that they know God; but in works they deny him, being abominable, and disobedient, and unto every good work reprobate";[2874] are them that fulfilled the saying, "If they had been of us, they would no doubt have continued with us."[2875] What did these priests within the Christian church fail to continue in? Says the Spirit, "They continued not in my covenant."[2876] Now, the covenant is not the covenant of Christ, but in every dispensation that a covenant has existed, that covenant belongs to the living LORD God. Passing over the old covenant, it was the blood of His Christ that ratified the LORD's new covenant, which is why the apostle wrote, "We also joy in God through our Lord Jesus Christ, by whom we have now received the atonement."[2877]

18. Herein we find our conflict. Because only *Christ* is acknowledged as the *God* of the majority; due to the amalgamation of philosophical theories with the interpretations of various religious practices to comprise one universal faith; there is no need to consider that Christ became both sacrifice and sinner not only for Himself or for every sincere believer, but as He says, "The reproaches of them that reproached thee are fallen upon me."[2878] Christ appeared not only to provide mankind with a second probation to continue in the experience that Adam failed in, but He also came to "magnify the law, and make it honourable."[2879] The new religion established by the Jewish and Gentile Jewish churches; which called themselves Christians; idolized the man *Christ* as they did one of their ancient prophets or ancestral pagan deities. *Christ* was honored as the top pagan god, and his *apostles* as such also, and the plain faith of heaven's Christ delivered

---

2873 Daniel 11:32
2874 Titus 1:16
2875 1 John 2:19
2876 Hebrews 8:9
2877 Romans 5:11
2878 Psalms 69:9
2879 Isaiah 42:21

them by the first apostles was forgotten, that this Messenger of the new covenant is who "God exalted with his right hand to be a Prince and a Saviour, for to give repentance to Israel, and forgiveness of sins."[2880]

19. Why is repentance necessary? Is repentance due to a perception of falsehood living within the heart, or must that wrong find itself defined before I may know what to be sorry for? How can one know what to repent for? And how can one know why they need a Christ and a Priest for repentance?

20. Lost in the universal faith being established by them that did not continue in the Spirit's higher learning, even while the apostles were alive, was the Father and the role of His Spirit in educating and converting the soul. His Christ confessed, "The Father gave me commandment,"[2881] and this commandment spoken by Christ is "the word of the truth of the gospel."[2882] If the Father gave the gospel, should not all things regarding the Father be considered also? It is this counsel that is to land the faithful in the presence of the living God that they may encounter the image they naturally break, that from this confrontation it might be fulfilled, "I will put my law in their inward parts, and write it in their hearts; and will be their God, and they shall be my people."[2883] This is the object of the new covenant will; to sanctify the obedient hearer and doer of the doctrine of Christ to retain the moral image of God as depicted through His Ten Commandments; and because the early Christian church magnified *Christ* as an idol and not as a living Savior, their heart did not experience, and could not embrace, the fact of a necessary mediator for their natural illness.

21. This is why the apostle wrote to the churches, "Truly our fellowship is with the Father, and with his Son."[2884] Without considering the Spirit's law, without studying after the full doctrine of God within the old and the new testaments; or covenants; a singular devotion was given to *Christ* to maintain an unconverted service, and such

---

2880   Acts 5:31
2881   John 14:31
2882   Colossians 1:5
2883   Jeremiah 31:33
2884   1 John 1:3

a service was held at the expense of hearing the declaration, "Unto him"; "the Father of our Lord Jesus Christ";[2885] "be glory in the church by Christ Jesus throughout all ages, world without end. Amen."[2886] The Father and the Son cannot be separated; the commandments of God with the Spirit of God cannot be separated from the law of the religion of Christ's heavenly mediation; and because John saw this separation occurring, "Whosoever transgresseth, and abideth not in the doctrine of Christ, hath not God,"[2887] he counseled.

22. Because the foundation of the doctrine of Christ is justification by faith; which in reality is sanctification by faith; a violation or a transgression of God's doctrine is, "Ye now made perfect by the flesh."[2888] Righteousness by an exercised faith in heaven's knowledge was cast aside and new forms of old errors began to take the place of the work of the Spirit within the Christian church. Herein paganism lent its arm to the Christian religion, and she accepted it. To reach a people only accustomed to signs and times and images, instead of agitating themselves to understand the LORD's manner, the elders of the churches erected idols to make the teachings of the apostles plainer. It was to "the elders of the church"[2889] that Paul referenced when he said, "Of your own selves shall men arise, speaking perverse things, to draw away disciples after them."[2890] Even before his death, what the Spirit had revealed to Paul was taking place, for in secret places "She'chem spake unto his father Ha'mor, saying, Get me this damsel to wife."[2891]

23. As strange standards crept into the early church because she would not remain at home to investigate the LORD's doctrine, apostasy took fast hold of her. It will be no different for the church of the earth beast, for she is who gives counsel to form an image to the first beast before it. Says Scripture, "There was none like unto Ahab, which did sell himself to work wickedness in the sight of the LORD, whom

---

2885 Ephesians 3:14
2886 Ephesians 3:21
2887 2 John 2:9
2888 Galatians 3:3
2889 Acts 20:17
2890 Acts 20:29
2891 Genesis 34:3,4

Jez'ebel his wife stirred up,"[2892] and if indeed there is to be an image made to the first beast, then this new republic can be expected to be governed by a woman, a church, an ecclesiastical assembly. This is why it is important to cultivate an intelligent faith through a personal "love in the Spirit."[2893] It is not enough to simply believe in *Christ*; what is belief without personal understanding? The believer needs to embrace a mental and moral re-education at the hand of God's Spirit "by the washing of regeneration, and renewing of the Holy Ghost."[2894] Burdens and vain ceremonies of *righteousness* corrupted the church and took minds away from God and from His Christ, and without surrendering the will to the influence of the Spirit, that same spirit of error will encapsulate our being.

24. Thus the doctrine of the new religion of the empire of the earth beast will be one of liberty without morality, *righteousness* without self-effacing love, the idolatry of a perception of *Christ* and of *God* without the necessary fact or the experience, and the love of self above God Himself. In these quiet times of religious peace, it is well to know His Christ's law by the work and the effect of the Spirit's righteousness upon the soul and spirit. Whenever such apostasy should happen again, the servants of the Spirit should have heard beforehand, "Ye have purified your souls in obeying the truth through the Spirit,"[2895] "that they may recover themselves out of the snare of the devil."[2896] In order to keep from the religious error to come, the reforming Christian, according to Scripture, must today embrace obeying the counsels of Christ's heavenly ministry, diligently searching after those precepts in the LORD's Bible to know what they must apply self to by the counsel of the Spirit of God. Because idolatry infected the early church, both the Father and His Son were shut out from them, and it is now time to engage self to approach God Himself to know the precious promise concerning the recovery of our soul's temple.

2892 1 Kings 21:25
2893 Colossians 1:8
2894 Titus 3:5
2895 1 Peter 1:22
2896 2 Timothy 2:26

25. When She'chem; that "prince of the country"[2897] of bondage; should get his way with Dinah the daughter of Leah, this same Dinah who wandered from her estate will abuse her position. To stand for the LORD's laws and the Testimony of His Christ at this time of open spiritual debauchery will take a mind that cannot be cultivated at that time of distress, but at a season before. Today is that present season wherein "ye shall afflict your souls, and do no work at all"[2898] to unlawfully procure the effect of righteousness, applying the heart to the counsel, "Buy of me,"[2899] and, "Open the door,"[2900] and, "Hear the voice of the Son of God,"[2901] and, "Go and take,"[2902] and, "Command ye me,"[2903] and, "Break off thy sins by righteousness,"[2904] and, "If any man will come after me, let him deny himself, and take up his cross daily, and follow me. For whosoever will save his life shall lose it: but whosoever will lose his life for my sake, the same shall save it."[2905] Paganism anciently saved and honored its life by hiding under and within a professed Christian woman, and that apostate entity governed its State and that State's religion. This is the image of the beast, which image we will personally own, and inevitably succumb to at the time appointed, if not found as hearers and doers of every word of God in its proper context.

2897 Genesis 34:2
2898 Leviticus 16:29
2899 Revelation 3:18
2900 Revelation 3:20
2901 John 5:25
2902 Revelation 10:8
2903 Isaiah 45:11
2904 Daniel 4:27
2905 Luke 9:23,24

35

The Fall Of The Glory Of All Kingdoms

1. It is known that Babylon was "the glory of kingdoms."[2906] Such an empire was as "a tree in the midst of the earth, and the height thereof was great. The tree grew, and was strong, and the height thereof reached unto heaven, and the sight thereof to the end of all the earth: the leaves thereof were fair, and the fruit thereof much, and in it was meat for all: the beasts of the field had shadow under it, and the fowls of the heaven dwelt in the boughs thereof, and all flesh was fed of it."[2907]

2. Babylon carried impressive credentials. This kingdom was not just a dominion that filled the entire earth and reached up to heaven, but it was filled with diversity without discrimination. It maintained liberty for all and held materials that every individual on the earth could bless themselves in and with. It had a king who was not only militarily perfect, but in his heart displayed a soft and tender intelligence towards all cultures, even as it says concerning the LORD's elect Hebrews, "The king communed with them."[2908]

2906 Isaiah 13:19
2907 Daniel 4:10-12
2908 Daniel 1:19

3. No other empire within the old testament is noted by God Himself to have controlled the earth as this Babylon did under its particular king Nebuchadnez'zar. Of all of the Mesopotamian kings, of all of the rulers of the provinces of Babylon, the LORD God has given a fair history of this man, his person, his mind and his kingdom, because of all the kings that came before him; and then after him in the regions of the beginnings of the world who knew not God;this one pagan king honestly confessed, "I blessed the most High, and I praised and honoured him that liveth for ever."[2909] Such a confession was similar to Daniel, for he "blessed the God of heaven."[2910] After encountering such as God as was Daniel's, the king confessed, "How great are his signs! and how mighty are his wonders! his kingdom is an everlasting kingdom, and his dominion is from generation to generation,"[2911] for under this converted kingdom, Babylon greatly flourished as a powerhouse.

4. In Nebuchadrez'zar the saying is fulfilled, "The Gentiles should be fellowheirs, and of the same body, and partakers of his promise in Christ by the gospel."[2912] This man did not know the living God, yet after his personal encounters with Him impressed a certain reverence on the members of his mind, he confessed, "I Nebuchadnez'zar praise and extol and honour the King of heaven."[2913] So then, as this man again fulfills the word, "God would justify the heathen through faith,"[2914] it is that he should not simply be looked at as a man, but as a State or Empire under a new condition under God. This new Nebuchadrez'zar that held a living conscience to heaven's throne is a representation of the nation that would fulfill the word, "I create new heavens and a new earth."[2915] Such a nation would declare God as King over the heart and conscience, as did this man, and leave that which pertains to God to Him, and that which God has left to the king for the king, that he would accomplish much in respect of His name.

2909 Daniel 4:34
2910 Daniel 2:19
2911 Daniel 4:3
2912 Ephesians 3:6
2913 Daniel 4:37
2914 Galatians 3:8
2915 Isaiah 65:17

5. Nebuchadnez'zar learned his lesson: man is not above God, and no man is above the law of the land. The fact that he at last acknowledges God as both "the Lord of heaven"[2916] and "the King of heaven,"[2917] is proof that a natural division between church and state existed in Babylon after the king's conversion, and then until his death. For this cause there is no further error reported of this king of Babylon by God in Scripture. The greatness of this tree that filled the entire earth was true, even as it was said of old concerning Egypt and Assyria. For "his height was exalted above all the trees of the field, and his boughs were multiplied, and his branches became long because of the multitude of waters, when he shot forth. All the fowls of heaven made their nests in his boughs, and under his branches did all the beasts of the field bring forth their young, and under his shadow dwelt all great nations. Thus was he fair in his greatness, in the length of his branches: for his root was by great waters."[2918]

6. The same vision that Nebuchadnez'zar received was spoken against Pharaoh king of Egypt, for the two nations, in a higher context, are one. "Thou hast lifted up thyself in height, and he hath shot up his top among the thick boughs, and his heart is lifted up in his height,"[2919] it was said of Pharaoh, and the report of Nebuchadnez'zar is similar: "Then shall his mind change, and he shall pass over, and offend, imputing this his power unto his god."[2920]

7. This king of Babylon, after repeatedly beholding the fact that it is God "who is the blessed and only Potentate, the King of kings, and Lord of lords";[2921] "the king spake, and said, Is not this great Babylon, that I have built for the house of the kingdom by the might of my power, and for the honour of my majesty?"[2922] Notice his words, how he says, "The house of the kingdom," for the king sought to magnify "the house

---

2916 Daniel 5:23
2917 Daniel 4:37
2918 Ezekiel 31:3-7
2919 Ezekiel 31:10
2920 Habakkuk 1:11
2921 1 Timothy 6:15
2922 Daniel 4:30

of his god"[2923] within his heart and his kingdom, at which point, "when his heart was lifted up, and his mind hardened in pride, he was deposed from his kingly throne."[2924] It was the throne that the king possessed; "The God of heaven hath given thee a kingdom, power, and strength, and glory";[2925] it was told him, for a civil room was the limit of his power and jurisdiction. As he allowed his heart to be drawn to God, he oddly began to question the sovereignty given him over his heart and his empire, causing the king to offend the prescribed line of his dominion, moving him to subscribe to a rule that had no life or relevance outside of his imagination.

8. This king Nebuchadnez'zar of Babylon and Pharaoh king of Egypt are synonymous with that nation that would surpass them, and all other kingdoms, in glory. This same Egypt is noted "as a whale in the seas,"[2926] as one "situate at the entry of the sea, which art a merchant of the people for many isles,"[2927] as was Ty'rus. This nation that should come from God would fulfill the word, "This is Jerusalem: I have set it in the midst of the nations and countries that are round about her,"[2928] for he would be "a tree in the midst of the earth."[2929] Notice that it does not say, of that special nation to come, that it would be a beast in the midst of the earth, but rather it would be a bright and delicate entity, for "the leaves thereof were fair, and the fruit thereof much, and in it was meat for all."[2930] Yet at some point it would be told to him, "Let his heart be changed from man's, and let a beast's heart be given unto him,"[2931] for it should be fulfilled, "Thy kingdom is divided."[2932]

9. Concerning Egypt, the Spirit said, "Because thou hast lifted up thyself in height, and he hath shot up his top among the thick boughs, and his heart is lifted up in his height; I have therefore delivered

---

2923 Daniel 1:2
2924 Daniel 5:20
2925 Daniel 2:37
2926 Ezekiel 32:2
2927 Ezekiel 27:3
2928 Ezekiel 5:5
2929 Daniel 4:10
2930 Daniel 4:12
2931 Daniel 4:16
2932 Daniel 5:28

him,"²⁹³³ and because the king of Babylon forgot "that the most high God ruleth in the kingdom of men,"²⁹³⁴ the downfall of the most powerful kingdom on earth occurred because the king exalted himself against the LORD's estate on earth and in heaven. After the kingdom was placed under the accepted order of God, the Babylonian State would violate his order by serving vanity through stolen vessels of God, for "they drank wine, and praised the gods of gold, and of silver, of brass, of iron, of wood, and of stone"²⁹³⁵ out of "the golden and silver vessels which his father Nebuchadnez'zar had taken out of the temple which was in Jerusalem."²⁹³⁶ The line had been crossed; the instruments of God's religion had mingled with Babylon's State; and that night the kingdom was "given to the Medes and Persians."²⁹³⁷

10. This Babylon was given into the hand of a two-horned power, as it says, "A ram which had two horns."²⁹³⁸ Babylon was delivered into the hand of a two-horned beast, and that prophesied nation holding the glory, the military and economical might of Egypt and Babylon with Ty'rus and Jerusalem combined, upon committing similar offense against things relating to God and His vessels, will be given over to be governed by the heart of a beast, even as by the spirit of a "great dragon that lieth in the midst of his rivers."²⁹³⁹ Supreme authority wasn't just stripped from Babylon, it says, "Thy kingdom is divided,"²⁹⁴⁰ and this can only mean the fulfillment of the word, "After thee shall arise another kingdom inferior to thee."²⁹⁴¹ This is why it says, "At the noise of the taking of Babylon the earth is moved,"²⁹⁴² for the like events will fulfill the saying, "I beheld another beast coming up out of the earth."²⁹⁴³

2933 Ezekiel 31:10,11
2934 Daniel 4:17
2935 Daniel 5:4
2936 Daniel 5:2
2937 Daniel 5:28
2938 Daniel 7:3
2939 Ezekiel 29:3
2940 Daniel 5:28
2941 Daniel 2:39
2942 Jeremiah 50:46
2943 Revelation 13:11

11. The kingdom being divided is the nation of the earth being divided, and that which came up out of the earth is a beast bearing the image of the beast before it, and there is no justification in believing that that which ascends from the earth is as great as that from whence it came. Remember that inferior kingdoms were to proceed from Babylon, and this two-horned beast rises from out of the foundation of a modern State similar in military and industrial greatness to Babylon, therefore it should be inferior to its father and mother, existing like as that "bear" who "raised up itself on one side,"[2944] for this bear had two horns, "but one was higher than the other."[2945] Thus, when once the earth from which this two-horned entity springs is divided, because it will inevitably fulfill the saying, "The king...worshipped Daniel, and commanded that they should offer an oblation and sweet odours unto him,"[2946] then will the standards of the earth divide and be given into the hands of an ecclesiastical creature.

12. The inferiority that this new republic from out of the earth should possess may not be what typical inferiority may demand, for this is most certainly a world power that "exerciseth all the power of the first beast before him, and causeth the earth and them which dwell therein to worship the first beast."[2947] The imperfection of this beast will be the same imperfection of the beast before it, and that is a lack of mental and moral soundness within its government, it's temples and institutions, and within it's citizens. Concerning this two-horned beast, the living "God is not in all his thoughts,"[2948] and this is why "his mouth is full of cursing and deceit and fraud,"[2949] for it says, "He maketh fire come down from heaven on the earth in the sight of men."[2950] An error will occur within the religious heritage of the earth that will fulfill the

---

2944   Daniel 7:5
2945   Daniel 8:3
2946   Daniel 2:46
2947   Revelation 13:12
2948   Psalms 10:4
2949   Psalms 10:7
2950   Revelation 13:13

word, "Give her royal estate unto another,"²⁹⁵¹ for she is become "as water spilt on the ground, which cannot be gathered up again."²⁹⁵²

13. A new order of government will exist. A religious institution will be made "ruler over the whole province"²⁹⁵³ and "chief of the governors over all the wise men."²⁹⁵⁴ Such a reign will be as it says, "Daniel sat in the gate of the king,"²⁹⁵⁵ for this Daniel was "master of the magicians."²⁹⁵⁶ The magicians, and the astrologers, and the sorcerers, and the Chalde'ans, all exist under the name of religion within the kingdom, for the king came to these whose profession was, "Wot ye not that such a man as I can certainly divine?"²⁹⁵⁷ When it was seen that "an excellent spirit, and knowledge, and understanding, interpreting of dreams, and shewing of hard sentences, and dissolving of doubts, were found in the same Daniel,"²⁹⁵⁸ the king worshipped him and commanded all others to do the same, even as the same honor was given to Ha'man, for the two-horned beast will exalt the horn of its religious institution above its civil, even admitting its laws to find new expression by ones who are portrayed as having in them "the spirit of the gods."²⁹⁵⁹

14. Morality will then find its definition by ones whose main concern is, "Who is the greatest in the kingdom of heaven?"²⁹⁶⁰ Should men take it upon themselves to concern themselves with that which does not concern them? Hear the interesting instruction of the Spirit concerning an event to occur in the rise and fall of the empires of prophecy: "In the days of these kings shall the God of heaven set up a kingdom, which shall never be destroyed: and the kingdom shall not be left to other people."²⁹⁶¹ What does it say? It says, "A kingdom that

---

2951   Esther 1:19
2952   2 Samuel 14:14
2953   Daniel 2:48
2954   Daniel 2:48
2955   Daniel 2:49
2956   Daniel 5:11
2957   Genesis 44:15
2958   Daniel 5:12
2959   Daniel 5:14
2960   Matthew 18:1
2961   Daniel 2:44

God will establish will not be left to other people, neither will it be destroyed." This LORD confessed, "I will overturn, overturn, overturn, it: and it shall be no more, until he come whose right it is; and I will give it him."[2962] Babylon, Medo-Persia, and Greece all fell off of the scene and were replaced by Rome, at which time the Christ of God was born while it held sway over the entire earth. It was then fulfilled, "He shall reign over the house of Jacob for ever; and of his kingdom there shall be no end."[2963]

15. When Christ had offered Himself as a perfected sacrifice for the atonement of every human being to know the living name of the LORD His God, it was fulfilled, "The seed should come to whom the promise was made."[2964] The promise was, "Tell the stars, if thou be able to number them: and he said unto him, So shall thy seed be,"[2965] for "he saith not, And to seeds, as of many; but as of one, And to thy seed, which is Christ."[2966] Thus, the tribes of the religious world are to become Christ's inheritance at the end of their full run, which is why He is called, "The first begotten of the dead, and the prince of the kings of the earth."[2967] As He currently awaits the true reception of His own kingdom of glory, it is that first, after His death, "him hath God exalted with his right hand to be a Prince and a Saviour."[2968] This fulfills the word, "The Lamb which is in the midst of the throne,"[2969] for He yet holds a throne in the center of the LORD His God's throne as that "throne of grace";[2970] concerning this throne it is said, "The kingdom shall not be left to other people."[2971]

16. A great fabrication will arise by ones who will have a desire to place the kingdom of their *Christ* in the laws and lawmakers of that new Republic from whence the earth beast springs. This same fraudulent

---

2962 Ezekiel 21:27
2963 Luke 1:33
2964 Galatians 3:19
2965 Genesis 15:5
2966 Galatians 3:16
2967 Revelation 1:5
2968 Acts 5:31
2969 Revelation 7:17
2970 Hebrews 4:16
2971 Daniel 2:44

spirit, as advertised by the Papacy, will be reproduced, for the image of the Papacy is their desire. These individuals, who are gross idolaters of some image of some *Christ*, and who are not partakers of the experience and power with the joys and sufferings within Christ's law, will ignore the fact that the reign of God's Christ is constrained and willingly subject to the LORD's heavenly Government, and this they will omit for the advancement of their covetous imaginations. Therefore "having eyes full of adultery, and that cannot cease from sin,"[2972] new moral prescriptions will be recommended for every citizen and institution to follow. "Whoso falleth not down and worshippeth"[2973] "therefore resisteth the power, resisteth the ordinance of God,"[2974] it will be said, and "should be cast into the midst of a burning fiery furnace."[2975]

17. No kingdom or institution of heaven's LORD and God can or will ever again be on this earth, nor has it been commissioned of God by any fable or tradition, for it is said, "Her child was caught up unto God, and to his throne."[2976] At this present hour, and for more that 1800 years, it has always been, "The kingdom of Christ and of God."[2977] This is the dominion that the LORD "wrought in Christ, when he raised him from the dead, and set him at his own right hand in the heavenly places,"[2978] which is why, with His own mouth, His High Priest says, "And am set down with my Father in his throne."[2979] Concerning this kingdom, His Chris said, "My kingdom is not of this world,"[2980] therefore it is written, "Behold, a king shall reign in righteousness, and princes shall rule in judgment. And a man shall be as an hiding place,"[2981] and, "Look upon Zion, the city of our solemnities: thine eyes shall see Jerusalem a quiet habitation, a tabernacle that shall not be taken down; not one of the

---

2972 2 Peter 2:14
2973 Daniel 3:11
2974 Romans 13:2
2975 Daniel 3:11
2976 Revelation 12:5
2977 Ephesians 5:5
2978 Ephesians 1:20
2979 Revelation 3:21
2980 John 18:36
2981 Isaiah 32:1,2

stakes thereof shall ever be removed, neither shall any of the cords thereof be broken. But there the glorious LORD will be unto us a place of broad rivers and streams."[2982]

18. This is why Paul writes to the truly converted to heaven's throne religion, "Ye are come unto mount Si'on, and unto the city of the living God, the heavenly Jerusalem, and to an innumerable company of angels, to the general assembly and church of the firstborn, which are written in heaven, and to God the Judge of all, and to the spirits of just men made perfect, and to Jesus the mediator of the new covenant, and to the blood of sprinkling, that speaketh better things than that of Abel. See that ye refuse not him that speaketh."[2983] Who is He that we are to not refuse? The LORD God "hath in these last days spoken unto us by his Son,"[2984] that is, has communed with His faithful by "the law of Christ"[2985] and "the doctrine of Christ."[2986] Such communion announces, "Our fellowship is with the Father, and with his Son Jesus Christ,"[2987] and, "The LORD is our judge, the LORD is our lawgiver, the LORD is our king; he will save us."[2988]

19. The lawgiver of the prophesied apostate church is not God, for she stands in violation of her position in relation to Him, therefore she must violate His name and attribute her power unto her god, for her men will say, "We have no king but Caesar."[2989] The order of the crucifixion against the body of the Spirit's knowledge will be repeated, for "both Herod, and Pon'tius Pilate, with the Gentiles, and the people of Israel, were gathered together."[2990] "All the chief priests and elders of the people took counsel against Jesus to put him to death: and when they had bound him, they led him away, and delivered him to Pon'tius

---

2982 Isaiah 33:20,21
2983 Hebrews 12:22-25
2984 Hebrews 1:2
2985 Galatians 6:2
2986 2 John 1:9
2987 1 John 1:3
2988 Isaiah 33:22
2989 John 19:15
2990 Acts 4:27

Pilate the governor."[2991] The professed church of *God* and the State of Rome came together to violate the body of the LORD's knowledge, and it will again be fulfilled by the powers within the earth. The apostate two-horned entity of the Revelation bears the image of the Papacy who also "made war with the Lamb"[2992] by the body of His believers through the defilement of His voice and character, and that same spirit will be fully reproduced while the desecration of the body of His will advances.

20. It is now the time to hear and examine the saying, "He took on him the seed of Abraham,"[2993] for even the Spirit's Christ existed to His God "through the righteousness of faith."[2994] This Christ existed every single day of His life by faith on the voice of the living God, and His charge for every believer is, "If ye keep my commandments, ye shall abide in my love; even as I have kept my Father's commandments, and abide in his love."[2995] Obedience to the commandments of Christ will lead the hearer and doer of those ordinances to keep the commandments of His LORD and God, for the doctrine of Christ is at the center of His LORD's ten immutable precepts. Faith to this Christ means an encounter with God and His Spirit for purification of the mental and moral parts of the human being, to the end we may confess with His Christ, "I love the Father."[2996] The nation that will arise as a great spiritual deceiver will lack every principle of godly truth and sincerity, and the vision of such a nation is to awaken within the soul the present need for self-examination by the character of heaven's throne.

21. The heart should embrace self-restraint and self-development by learning of and doing heaven's will if it would ever see or hear any good thing from God's Priest. If there is no sanctification taking place within the conversation, quit that practice and policy and subscribe to a new beginning as a child in heart. The purpose of the doctrine of Christ is to place the obedient into the hand and presence of God for healing

---

2991 Matthew 27:1,2
2992 Revelation 17:14
2993 Hebrews 2:16
2994 Romans 4:13
2995 John 15:10
2996 John 14:31

"through sanctification of the Spirit and belief of the truth."[2997] "Unto you it is given in the behalf of Christ, not only to believe on him, but also to suffer for his sake,"[2998] for the liars that will operate this erroneous country to come will be them that "desire to make a fair shew in the flesh"[2999] to "constrain you to be circumcised; only lest they should suffer persecution for the cross of Christ."[3000] For fear of the pain of certain scars that will be received, these chief priests will abandon the Spirit's appointed baptism and will subscribe to another *Christ*, another *God*, another *baptism*, and for their error, they will violate themselves with the State of the earth to become a terror to its inhabitants.

22. "Ye that seek the LORD: look unto the rock whence ye are hewn, and to the hole of the pit whence ye are digged. Look unto Abraham your father, and unto Sarah that bare you: for I called him alone, and blessed him, and increased him,"[3001] says the Spirit. "Ye therefore, beloved, seeing ye know these things before, beware lest ye also, being led away with the error of the wicked, fall from your own stedfastness."[3002] For "many shall follow their pernicious ways; by reason of whom the way of truth shall be evil spoken of. And through covetousness shall they with feigned words make merchandise of you."[3003] "Wherefore, beloved, seeing that ye look for such things, be diligent that ye may be found of him in peace, without spot, and blameless. And account that the longsuffering of our Lord is salvation."[3004]

2997 2 Thessalonians 2:13
2998 Philippians 1:29
2999 Galatians 6:12
3000 Galatians 6:12
3001 Isaiah 51:1,2
3002 2 Peter 3:17
3003 2 Peter 2:2,3
3004 2 Peter 3:14,15

36

Mischievous Betrayers

1. It is no lie that the kingdom of the Medes and the Persians draws similarities to that two-horned beast that should arise from the earth. Concerning the fall and aftermath of the dominion of the kingdom of Babylon, the Watcher said to those who had charge, "Leave the stump of his roots in the earth,"[3005] for although Babylon should pass away from the scene of action, its spirit should rest in the earth, and in that which would inevitably spring from it. Although the Medes and the Persians did not pass Babylon for brilliance, the spirit of Babylon yet remained and continued in them, even until Rome, and in Rome she still exists. For this reason it is not hard to imagine that the apostate nation which rises from the earth should bear the same principles of its ancestry, for he will, and in a terribly vile and disrespectfully crude manner.

2. As the Medes and the Persians arose from an utterly brilliant and flawless empire, so too will the two-horned beast of the earth. And just as the government of the Medes and Persians eventually embarked on a cunning mission to abuse its power against a man of God, so too that which arises from the earth will do in like manner against the

---

3005 Daniel 4:15

LORD's then denomination. Because this same earth beast carries a form similar to that beast arising from Babylon, we may look at the first two-horned beast of Scripture to understand the hierarchical system of that other one to come. For Scripture says, "It pleased Dari'us to set over the kingdom an hundred and twenty princes, which should be over the whole kingdom; and over these three presidents; of whom Daniel was first: that the princes might give accounts unto them, and the king should have no damage."[3006]

3. The hierarchy of Daniel's two-horned beast is a government branch consisting of princes, presidents, and then a king. That the king should receive no damage, all things in the government pass from the princes to the presidents, and from the presidents all things are reviewed, and are then either executed or declined by the king. This is a similar order to that of the United States. Our current government has power divided between its three branches. The first Article of the Constitution creates and vests legislative power in Congress. The second Article places executive power in the President of the United States. The third Article of the Constitution confesses that the United States judicial power will be in the Supreme Court and other such inferior courts that Congress has created or should create. In order for any law to pass, at least two of the branches must agree upon it. Any law must be blessed by Congress and signed by the President. A law's enforcement demands the Executive to initiate the undertaking and the judiciary to pronounce it. Such a division of powers serves as a sort of check on government power. That the government might not encroach upon the private sphere of his citizens to begin a tyrannical rule similar to that which provoked its genesis, the Constitution was born. The Constitution both halts and strengthens the government's mind when protecting its citizens, and because such a work was constructed to serve the public, its frame is terribly hard to alter.

4. Herein we are brought back to Scripture, where in relation to the laws of the Medes and Persians we read, "The law of the Medes and Persians is, That no decree nor statute which the king establisheth may

---

[3006] Daniel 6:1,2

be changed."[3007] We find ourselves confronted with; when observing the second beast of Bible prophecy; a deformed version of the United States within the Medo-Persian Empire, for although the laws of this people "altereth not,"[3008] even as it is a terrible offense to unlawfully handle that contained within the United States Constitution, there appears to be no check on the branches of the Medo-Persian dominion, which kingdom is ultimately religious at heart. Herein we are introduced to the means by which certain men bring down fire from heaven upon them on earth. As the heavens are made up of "two great lights"[3009] and "the stars also,"[3010] the heaven from which these men derive their privilege cannot be from any thing but the sun, the moon, and the stars of their order, or "the presidents of the kingdom, the governors, and the princes, the counsellors, and the captains,"[3011] with the king their sun, for it says, "These presidents and princes assembled together to the king."[3012]

5. As the vision of the Revelation is a vision of ecclesiastical history, them that exist in the presence of the government of the earth beast; for the government spoken of acts on behalf of the ambitions of vain priests; have their heart and mind established towards a religious movement. These individuals have assembled together with the legislative branches of the earth "to establish their own righteousness,"[3013] abusing the Constitution of the land to advance their own imaginary religious cause. Now, as Scripture says, "When Solomon had made an end of praying, the fire came down from heaven,"[3014] it is clear that answered prayers and approved supplications on behalf of the king resulted in an act of God. So these men, who have joined themselves to their god; the corrupt government of the earth; will pray for specific devices to be enacted through the sun, the moon, and the stars, for this fire is nothing

---

3007 Daniel 6:15
3008 Daniel 6:12
3009 Genesis 1:16
3010 Genesis 1:16
3011 Daniel 6:7
3012 Daniel 6:6
3013 Romans 10:3
3014 2 Chronicles 7:1

but religious laws from deranged chief priests passed through their State "to find occasion against Daniel concerning the kingdom."[3015]

6. The images of the beasts given Daniel are not pure. Sick and strangely built animals are portrayed to the prophet because the nature and essence of their substance is not of God. When we hear of a ram with two horns, and that one horn was higher than the other, would this be a fit offering for sacrifice to God? Says the Spirit, "Ye brought that which was torn, and the lame, and the sick; thus ye brought an offering: should I accept this of your hand?"[3016] "Cursed be the deceiver, which hath in his flock a male, and voweth, and sacrificeth unto the Lord a corrupt thing."[3017] Again, the Spirit says, "If a soul sin, and commit any of these things which are forbidden to be done by the commandments of the LORD...he shall bring a ram without blemish,"[3018] for any other creature, such as one with horns uneven, is corrupt and unacceptable. When we see such a ram in vision, and a goat with multiple horns, the message relayed is that these are in fact impure creatures.

7. If God will not accept such creatures, who would? The angel told Daniel, "The prince of the kingdom of Persia withstood me."[3019] This prince is the same "prince of the power of the air,"[3020] the governor of "the spirit that now worketh in the children of disobedience,"[3021] even "that old serpent, called the Devil, and Satan, which deceiveth the whole world."[3022] We may now understand why the earth beast is called the false prophet that "deceived them that had received the mark of the beast, and them that worshipped his image,"[3023] for he bears the religious emblem of his father. It is therefore true that neither of the beasts revealed to Daniel or John are pure. As we see what events transpired against Daniel by this Medo-Persian government, we are brought to

---

3015   Daniel 6:4
3016   Malachi 1:13
3017   Malachi 1:14
3018   Leviticus 5:17,18
3019   Daniel 10:13
3020   Ephesians 2:2
3021   Ephesians 2:2
3022   Revelation 12:9
3023   Revelation 19:20

view the movement initiated against the living House of God at the time appointed by the corrupt Republic of the two-horned entity of the Revelation.

8. When a certain religious institution confesses, "The king hath brought me into his chambers,"[3024] we may know that the values advanced by the earth; both religious and civil; will come under gross manipulation. These individuals that sought an occasion against Daniel had no good thing in their heart, and by craft, they boxed in the government with greater chains than it already had in existence. "Establish the decree, and sign the writing, that it be not changed,"[3025] say they to the Executor, and trusting in the confederacy bound to an oath for justice, the king thought no thing of their request, for they played to the sound of his heart and to the pomp of his position when demanding, "Make a firm decree, that whosoever shall ask a petition of any God or man for thirty days, save of thee, O king...shall be cast into the den of lions."[3026]

9. The heart of the king was overcome through such manipulation, and by like-subtlety the elders of a certain institution will work in favor of themselves by the heaven above their earth. The earth beast is the product of its father Satan and its mother the Papacy, yet he will bear the flavor of its heritage in an unsavory manner. The Watcher said, "Leave the stump of his roots in the earth, even with a band of iron and brass,"[3027] for as the spirit of Babylon was not to escape the earth, or any empire that should come after it, so too it is not likely that the two-horned beast will stray from its foundation, but being governed and overpowered by ministers without the mind and Spirit of the LORD's Priest, the great traditions and values that made the United States such an incredible force will be abused to create an artificial union among professed believers of the same new faith.

10. It was said of Christ at one of His hearings before His sentence, "We found this fellow perverting the nation, and forbidding to give

---

3024　Song of Solomon 1:4
3025　Daniel 6:8
3026　Daniel 6:7
3027　Daniel 4:15

tribute to Caesar."[3028] Caesar is a figurative representative of civil power, and this power is defined by what Pilate said to Christ: "I have power to crucify thee, and have power to release thee."[3029] Civil and legislative powers exist only to enact civil and legislative regulations and solutions. When a civil entity becomes forefront in religious matters, or when a religious institution desires civil authority to act on its behalf, it marks the decay of the society under which such events occur, and the loss of mental and moral health of the individuals in higher ranks who belong to the situation, which loss trickles down to the innocent and ignorant citizens of various classes. This is why Christ said, "He that delivered me unto thee hath the greater sin."[3030]

11. The greater sin rested on the Jews because they could not hear, "Is it so, that there is not a wise man among you? no, not one that shall be able to judge between his brethren? Brother goeth to law with brother, and that before the unbelievers."[3031]

12. Religious issues and controversies belong within the church for internal resolution, for Christ was brought before such as knew not God by them that professed to honor Him, yet their actions spoke against the very nature of Christ who did not care to entertain matters of unlawful or unnecessary friendship with Caesar. For this same Man, at one occasion, when He "perceived that they would come and take him by force, to make him a king, he departed."[3032] Why should He not embrace the secular adoration of the public? The Christ of the living God could not welcome the title of king, for since He came bearing the words of His God, He Himself was laying the foundation of a church for that God, therefore when we see His Minister, in reality He is the physical embodiment of "the general assembly and church of the firstborn, which are written in heaven."[3033] As the Chief Apostle and High Priest over the Spirit's Church, He will not overstep the boundaries of the Government that He serves, which throne is in heaven and is ruled

---

3028 Luke 23:2
3029 John 19:10
3030 John 19:11
3031 1 Corinthians 6:5,6
3032 John 6:15
3033 Hebrews 12:23

by the LORD His God. Should any professed church of God receive an earthly kingdom, the authority of the heavenly Kingdom and Building of God would be found without that church. Thus, this Christ and His congregation confess, "I love the Father."[3034]

13. It should be noted that the only way to get *Christ* into any seat of any kingdom or government is by force, for it says, "They sought Him by force."[3035] It is not likely that this issue of Him as the king of the oppressed did not come up before Him while He was alive. The fact that individuals had to apply force and agitation speaks to the fact that Christ had to continually fight off such confrontations on a regular basis. Nevertheless, one man sought to force Christ to expose Himself as a King and Beloved Avenger of God, and Christ calls this man, "The son of perdition,"[3036] for it says, "The devil having now put into the heart of Judas Iscar'iot, Simon's son, to betray him."[3037] Judas sought to force Christ to display the perceived Jewish image of *Christ*; which image was of a chief of the host of the army of *God* set to physically free His covenanted people from the yoke of Rome; but Christ would not yield to such ignorance, even suffering death for the loyalty He had for the living Government of the LORD His God and the spiritual dominion that should appear by His labor.

14. It should also be noted how that such actions to deliver Christ to the State; for "the chief priests and Pharisees came together unto Pilate";[3038] is called, "Betrayal," for it says of Judas, "To betray Him."[3039] Any attempt to place any thing of Christ within any government is therefore utter falsehood. It is an express revelation of "perverse disputings of men of corrupt minds, and destitute of the truth, supposing that gain is godliness."[3040] Such a perverse spirit filled Judas, for the thoughts of his heart surrounded the question, "Who is the greatest in the kingdom

---

3034   John 14:31
3035   John 6:15
3036   John 17:12
3037   John 13:2
3038   Matthew 27:62
3039   John 13:2
3040   1 Timothy 6:5

of heaven?"[3041] But Christ answered the question: "To sit on my right hand, and on my left, is not mine to give, but it shall be given to them for whom it is prepared of my Father."[3042] His answer speaks to the fact that He is but a Prince or Priest in the presence of His God and is no thing more, therefore He himself cannot decree any thing unless it is given Him of that King, His LORD and God, which is why He today says, "Him that overcometh will I grant to sit with me in my throne, even as I also overcame, and am set down with my Father in his throne."[3043]

15. The fact of the matter is that, as long as "the kingdom of Christ and of God"[3044] exists, the saying should reverently be observed, "The Lamb which is in the midst of the throne."[3045] Christ Himself says that He is joined to the Throne or Government of His LORD and Father, therefore the precepts of the doctrine of Christ are undeniably found at the center of the ten immutable precepts of God. To long for Christ to take any political seat on earth would mean to lead the doctrine of Christ down that same path of death and crucifixion of old, therefore those modern chef priests and Pharisees who have such hopes for *Christ* to have any political seat are in reality betrayers of the Spirit, preaching "another Jesus,"[3046] and are actuated by "another spirit"[3047] to enforce "another gospel."[3048] This is not a reflection of the image and spirit of God's Son. This Christ currently cares to respect and revere His Father's throne, to certify the perpetual dominion of His Ten Commandments, and to also offer mankind a second probation before His God to exist in those commandments by maintaining themselves through the precepts and ordinances offered by the blood of His ministry. The religion of heaven's right will is centered upon a justified heart and mind in the presence of God and of men. The Faith of Jesus is chained to the ten laws of the LORD's Government; to place Christ

---

3041 Matthew 18:1
3042 Matthew 20:23
3043 Revelation 3:21
3044 Ephesians 5:5
3045 Revelation 7:17
3046 2 Corinthians 11:4
3047 2 Corinthians 11:4
3048 2 Corinthians 11:4

into the government of men is an open rejection of His Man as both the appointed Prince and High Priest of the living LORD God.

16. That beast which comes up from out of the earth works "in the sight of men,"[3049] and these men are at this time ingratiated within the government of the State of the earth so that the State can act as a religious conscience for the people of that earth. A false doctrine of *Christ* will be forcefully placed into the mind of the laws and lawmakers of the land of the earth, for these chief elders and Pharisees will bear an image that reads, "JESUS OF NAZARETH THE KING OF THE JEWS."[3050] But the Godhead is not ignorant of their endeavor. "I know the blasphemy of them which say they are Jews, and are not, but are the synagogue of Satan,"[3051] says the Spirit.

17. Them that will initiate a national reform movement to have a land and government for the *Christ* of their gospel will be the Jews of the institution of Satan, for this same Satan will put into their heart what he put into Judas, which ambition is his own, and that mind states, "I will exalt my throne above the stars of God: I will sit also upon the mount of the congregation...I will be like the most High."[3052] To exalt a throne, and to sit at the forefront of a congregation, or a church, is the exaltation of an ecclesiastical government. Such a spirit confesses, "I sit a queen,"[3053] for this religious faction will pick up the philosophy of her mother to say, "I shall be a lady for ever."[3054] Such a spirit is born from her that did once sit "upon a scarlet coloured beast, full of names of blasphemy, having seven heads and ten horns,"[3055] and this image will be reproduced, for it says, "They should make an image to the beast, which had the wound by a sword, and did live."[3056]

18. The actions of the two-horned ram against Daniel display the spirit and nature of the two-horned beast, and as this ram appeared on

---

3049 Revelation 13:13
3050 John 19:19
3051 Revelation 2:9
3052 Isaiah 14:13,14
3053 Revelation 18:7
3054 Isaiah 47:7
3055 Revelation 17:3
3056 Revelation 13:14

the scene after the fall of the glory of all kingdoms, so this deformed creature of the Revelation will rise up after the earth has been shaken into a division from its former glorious estate. Great perversion will occur within the Conscience of the earth by "them which glory in appearance, and not in heart."[3057] The First Lady of the earth will be violently manipulated by a woman of a strange and foreign tongue. Betrayers of Christ's instruction will forcefully accomplish their will against His LORD by violating the very word and character that He received from His God, and this is why the apostle wrote, "Whosoever transgresseth, and abideth not in the doctrine of Christ, hath not God."[3058] "Who is a liar but he that denieth that Jesus is the Christ? He is an'tichrist, that denieth the Father and the Son."[3059]

[3057] 2 Corinthians 5:12
[3058] 2 John 1:9
[3059] 1 John 2:22

37

Judas and The Chief Of The Jews

1. "Jesus answered them, Have not I chosen you twelve, and one of you is a devil? He spake of Judas Iscari'ot the son of Simon: for he it was that should betray him, being one of the twelve."[3060]

2. The image that we have of the devil given us by Christ is of no fancy illustration, but is of the frame and character of a certain religious minister. Such a character bears the name, "The Jews: who both killed the Lord Jesus, and their own prophets, and have persecuted us; and they please not God, and are contrary to all men."[3061] Such individuals that desecrate the spirit and manner of the LORD's men and prophets accomplish the saying, "Satan hindered us."[3062] Thus we have the Devil and Satan rendered for us as a priest who is volatile, a man that "will speak villany, and his heart will work iniquity, to practise hypocrisy, and to utter error against the LORD."[3063] Such a man who

---

3060 John 6:70,71
3061 1 Thessalonians 2:14,15
3062 1 Thessalonians 2:18
3063 Isaiah 32:6

is an embodiment of the disposition of Satan's religion warrants the charge, "Ye are of your father the devil, and the lusts of your father ye will do. He was a murderer from the beginning, and abode not in the truth."[3064]

3. The Jews and Judas are one denominated people strengthened by a spirit of deception and persecution. This denomination is that same house called, "The false prophet that deceives them that couch on the earth."[3065] These are them actuated by that mind "concerning Judas, which was guide to them that took Jesus."[3066] "This man purchased a field with the reward of iniquity,"[3067] "ran greedily after the error of Ba'laam for reward,"[3068] and these that will come from Judas will be "them that hold the doctrine of Ba'laam, who taught Ba'lac to cast a stumblingblock."[3069] Such a sect "are the synagogue of Satan"[3070] existing "where Satan's seat is,"[3071] and will unlawfully uphold the philosophy, "Shew thyself to the world."[3072] This philosophy the Spirit's own disciples cherished while in their ignorance, yet the Jews also confessed, "How long dost thou make us to doubt? If thou be the Christ, tell us plainly."[3073]

4. Both the Jews and Judas wanted Christ to live up to their imaginative expectations. It is then no surprise that it was fulfilled, "Judas then, having received a band of men and officers from the chief priests and Pharisees, cometh."[3074] There would come "Judas, one of the twelve, and with him a great multitude with swords and staves, from the chief priests and the scribes and the elders,"[3075] and the desire is to place Christ in such jeopardy that He would have no choice but to

---

3064 John 8:44
3065 Revelation 13:14
3066 Acts 1:16
3067 Acts 1:18
3068 Jude 1:11
3069 Revelation 2:14
3070 Revelation 2:9
3071 Revelation 2:13
3072 John 7:4
3073 John 10:24
3074 John 18:3
3075 Mark 14:43

declare His name in glory. Christ had already confessed, "The works which the Father hath given me to finish, the same works that I do, bear witness of me,"[3076] yet these works made no impression on the heart of the majority because they had no living relationship with their LORD and no tender regard for His character. "Ye therefore hear them not, because ye are not of God,"[3077] says this Christ even today of them that deny Him entrance into the chambers of their heart, for the spirit of Judas and the leaders of the Jews was of him that "is a liar, and the father of it."[3078]

5. Such a lying spirit will constrain perverse men and women to force *Christ* to reveal *Himself* to them through their proselytes, their laws and lawmakers, and their institutions. Because they are not of the living God, these *Jews* will fraudulently apply themselves for the glory of the kingdom of God's Son, and because they are bearing the image of that great Dragon and Devil and Satan, because there is no "place found any more in heaven"[3079] for them, they will join hands with the State of the land to abuse his power for the appearance of their authenticity. The kingdom of their *Christ* is of "Jewish fables, and commandments of men, that turn from the truth,"[3080] and such will "constrain you to be circumcised";[3081] as they did Christ; for He has told us, "Whosoever killeth you will think that he doeth God service. And these things will they do unto you, because they have not known the Father, nor me."[3082]

6. The devil is an ecclesiastical figure longing for religious reform in worship, and refusal to submit to that reform involves a civil mandate. The devil and the dragon are representative of an amalgamation of church and State, for this union is exemplified by the fact that "Herod, and Pon'tius Pilate, with the Gentiles, and the people of Israel, were

---

3076   John 5:36
3077   John 8:47
3078   John 8:44
3079   Revelation 12:8
3080   Titus 1:14
3081   Galatians 6:12
3082   John 16:2,3

gathered together"[3083] "against the Lord, and against his Christ."[3084] Notice that when the powers of the devil are formed, two, and not one, are violated. Such Jews put the LORD God and His Christ to death; "the commandments of God, and the faith of Jesus"[3085] are come under attack by such gross negligence. This is why the Father and the Son acknowledge such apostate individuals that would fulfill the word, "Who shall ascend into heaven? (that is, to bring Christ down from above:),"[3086] as "them of the synagogue of Satan, which say they are Jews, and are not, but do lie."[3087]

7. The lies of these people are contained in the fire of the miracles enacted by the State of the land at their command. At that time, "the people that do know their God shall be strong, and do exploits,"[3088] for these pretenders of the Faith do not have the experience of the instruction and law of the self-effacing love of God in them. Like Judas, who was found in the sea of Christ's disciples and not among the Jews of Moses, there will be an apostate universal band where one half longs to enforce their ideology of the dominion of *Christ*, and the other half longs to kill the voice of the LORD's Christ to save and preserve the stability of the nation. When "certain of the sect of the Pharisees which believed"[3089] should join hands with their State, these Jews will obtain power to "speak great words against the most High,"[3090] and that by "a great sword"[3091] with "a pair of balances"[3092] when it should be fulfilled, "He had power to give life unto the image of the beast."[3093]

3083 Acts 4:27
3084 Acts 4:26
3085 Revelation 14:12
3086 Romans 10:6
3087 Revelation 3:9
3088 Daniel 11:32
3089 Acts 15:5
3090 Daniel 7:25
3091 Revelation 6:4
3092 Revelation 6:5
3093 Revelation 13:15

8. This "great multitude both of the Jews and also of the Greeks"[3094] will "change times and laws"[3095] that it should be fulfilled, "Shew thyself to the world,"[3096] yet they will fulfill the image of "that Egyptian";[3097] even of certain Pharaohs within the early church of Christ; "which before these days madest an uproar, and leddest out into the wilderness four thousand men that were murderers."[3098] Judas and the Jews were inwardly a great beast "full of names of blasphemy, having seven heads and ten horns,"[3099] which is why it says of that nation born after the image of them and their mother, "He spake as a dragon."[3100] The doctrine of unity that these preach will be but a betrayal of all things relating to God and His High Priest, for the dominion that they are after is falsehood, the desire that they have is error, and these warrant the saying, "Ye seek to kill me, because my word hath no place in you."[3101]

9. The precepts and ordinances of the doctrine of Christ will be strangled and manipulated to death. The heart of Christ's living commandment exclaims, "Who gave himself for our sins...according to the will of God and our Father."[3102] According to whose will? Is it Christ's will? "My meat is to do the will of him that sent me, and to finish his work,"[3103] He says. Again, whose work and whose will is it? Says Scripture, "This Jesus hath God raised up."[3104] "Him hath God exalted with his right hand to be a Prince and a Saviour, for to give repentance to Israel, and forgiveness of sins."[3105] For this cause, "he which was ordained of God"[3106] even once told Paul, "I send thee, to open their eyes, and to turn them from darkness to light, and from the

---

3094 Acts 14:1
3095 Daniel 7:25
3096 John 7:4
3097 Acts 21:38
3098 Acts 21:38
3099 Revelation 17:3
3100 Revelation 13:11
3101 John 8:37
3102 Galatians 1:4
3103 John 4:34
3104 Acts 2:32
3105 Acts 5:31
3106 Acts 10:42

power of Satan unto God, that they may receive forgiveness of sins, and inheritance among them which are sanctified by faith that is in me."[3107]

10. When once the eyes are turned to God; "the eyes of your understanding";[3108] what is to occur? It says, "Forgiveness of sins and sanctification,"[3109] and this is the will of our LORD who placed into the mediation of His Christ the law of His Spirit's redemption. "As my Father hath taught me, I speak these things,"[3110] says His Priest, "for he whom God hath sent speaketh the words of God."[3111] Every thing that any one professing Christ loves about Him is derived from the LORD His Father. Yet hear Him: "None can come to me, except the Father which hath sent me draw him."[3112] No one can approach an education in the sayings of Christ unless they surrender to the power of the Spirit of God the Father, for every believer is to be "sanctified by God the Father,"[3113] that is, "sanctified by the Holy Ghost," "by the power of the Spirit of God."[3114] But Christ says, "Sanctified by the Faith in Me,"[3115] for the Faith of Jesus announces "sanctification of the Spirit and belief of the truth."[3116] Thus, the one submitted to the Spirit's educational process will say, "That I may know him,"[3117] to the end it may be confessed, "I know him, and keep his saying."[3118]

11. Both the Father and His Son have a saying that is to be kept by them that would know Them, and they are kept and upheld through His Spirit. Sincere faith on the end of the Spirit's law will cause God Himself to send "forth the Spirit of his Son into your hearts,"[3119] which

---

3107 Acts 26:17,18
3108 Ephesians 1:18
3109 Acts 26:17,18
3110 John 8:28
3111 John 3:34
3112 John 6:44
3113 Jude 1:1
3114 Romans 15:16,19
3115 Acts 26:18
3116 2 Thessalonians 2:13
3117 Philippians 3:10
3118 John 8:55
3119 Galatians 4:6

is why it says, "He that hath the Son hath life,"[3120] for "the Spirit is life."[3121] The Spirit is life because He is a teacher of righteousness' law, and because the Spirit of truth proceeds from the Father, and because the doctrine of Christ also confesses, "I proceeded forth and came from God,"[3122] all things that come from God the Father do lead right back to Him. This is why the gospel of Christ is the power of God unto salvation bearing witness of the LORD's righteousness,[3123] and why it says, "All thy commandments are righteousness."[3124]

12. The end of the gospel is the fulfilling of the saying, "My righteousness shall not be abolished."[3125] Now, if the righteousness of God is abolished, why not then dissolve the glory and virtue of Christ? "He that honoureth not the Son honoureth not the Father,"[3126] says His Priest. "I honour my Father, and ye do dishonour me,"[3127] He continues. It is not said in vain, "Our fellowship is with the Father, and with his Son,"[3128] for them that maintain such a conversation with both God and Christ His Son are members of that Church "which is in God the Father and in the Lord Jesus Christ."[3129] Such an assembly will hear, "God blessed the seventh day, and sanctified it,"[3130] and knowing that such a law upholds the other nine precepts given of God, and that such laws are magnified by "the light of the glorious gospel of Christ, who is the image of God,"[3131] "the fulness of the blessing of the gospel of Christ"[3132] is not given to them in vain, for they confess, "That I may know him."[3133]

3120 1 John 5:12
3121 Romans 8:10
3122 John 8:42
3123 Romans 1:16,17
3124 Psalms 119:172
3125 Isaiah 51:6
3126 John 5:23
3127 John 8:49
3128 1 John 1:3
3129 1 Thessalonians 1:1
3130 Genesis 2:3
3131 2 Corinthians 4:4
3132 Romans 15:29
3133 Philippians 3:10

13. Scripture plainly confesses that it is the law of Christ that is the image of God, and this image is without doubt the full character within the Ten Commandments of God. When the word of Christ is put in jeopardy, respect to the precepts and the Spirit of God will vanish from the conversation. This is what compelled the apostle to write, "Every one that loveth him begat loveth him that is begotten of him."[3134] This is why Christ said, "Born of water and of the Spirit";[3135] that is, "Ye are clean through the word which I have spoken";[3136] for by the "fellowship of the Spirit"[3137] it is fulfilled, "He saved us, by the washing of regeneration, and renewing of the Holy Ghost."[3138] It should be observed that regeneration takes place only in sinful flesh by active faith on the law of inward revival and reformation through the wisdom of the LORD's Holy Spirit. Such a process is to "make you perfect in every good work to do his will, working in you that which is wellpleasing in his sight, through Jesus Christ."[3139]

14. Faith in the virtue of the merits of Christ and in the power of the Spirit is to place one in a proper manner to accomplish the will and labor of the Spirit, for it says, "The tables were the work of God, and the writing was the writing of God."[3140] Without surrendering to the order of God's purification, the inward person will receive no recovery to have God Himself write His laws within it, for the end of the Spirit's Faith is "that the righteousness of the law might be fulfilled in us."[3141] Because *Christ* is magnified as an idol, because superstition and tradition reign in the heart of unconverted individuals, those who comprise the sect of Judas and the Jews will force a false image of an illegitimate *Christ* into civil affairs and into the public arena. If Christ were celebrated then both He and His Father would be exalted in their proper context. Because these ministers are not of God and neither possess

---

3134   1 John 5:1
3135   John 3:5
3136   John 15:3
3137   Philippians 2:1
3138   Titus 3:5
3139   Hebrews 13:21
3140   Exodus 32:16
3141   Romans 8:4

"the honour that cometh from God only,"[3142] they will commit confusion and surrender to the political power of man. For this cause their actions warrant the saying: "The wrath of God is revealed from heaven against all ungodliness and unrighteousness of men, who hold the truth in unrighteousness."[3143]

15. Them that will hold the revelation of the LORD's Son and Spirit in unrighteousness are them that maintain the power of the gospel not in God through His Spirit, but through the State and by flesh. This is why it should now be heard, "If any man worship the beast and his image, and receive his mark in his forehead, or in his hand, the same shall drink of the wine of the wrath of God, which is poured out without mixture into the cup of his indignation."[3144] The warning against the worshipping of the image of the beast; the image of Judas and the Jews approaching the Roman State to accomplish their will with Christ, or the image of the leopard beast before this two-horned republic; is a warning for every one professing some level of love and appreciation for God and His Minister to go personally "seeking for Jesus."[3145] This is why it says of His sincere followers, "They took him as he was."[3146]

16. The doctrine of Christ is the sun of the LORD's ten laws for our seed of faith, and the blessings of His Spirit are the drops of rain pouring down upon our character from His clouds of precious promises for our consistent growth. If any one would have the benefit of His Christ's intercession, they cannot know His name until they abandon the self-righteous demeanor that is naturally cultivated from birth. Is this false? Hear Him: "Except your righteousness shall exceed the righteousness of the scribes and Pharisees, ye shall in no case enter into the kingdom of heaven."[3147] The kingdom of God is not future, for it is yet a present will and science for every faithful soul, which is why it is counseled, "Our conversation is in heaven."[3148] Them that do not stand

---

3142   John 5:44
3143   Romans 1:18
3144   Revelation 14:9,10
3145   John 6:24
3146   Mark 4:36
3147   Matthew 5:20
3148   Philippians 3:20

under the name, "Thou heaven, and ye holy apostles and prophets,"[3149] will violate "them that dwell in heaven."[3150] All that honor the spurious faction and the imaginary kingdom of prescription will be cast out of heaven with them to receive the just wages that they have earned.

17. Because the voice of Christ is not studied and accepted; and as it should be in its proper context; base passion and crude sentiments will reign in them who "profess that they know God; but in works they deny him."[3151] Them that honor this image of falsehood as a conception of the will of *God* will be them that never knew Him or His Priest, and therefore will register their names beside them who should receive the Spirit's wrath. And as scripture will fulfill itself; God has spoken it; we who have a positive thought and a determined will to know His Son's voice, now is the time to know His name above what we hold on to. The hour is at hand when the LORD should sanction all things that are already set in order by Judas and the Jews with their State. "Let us walk honestly, as in the day; not in rioting and drunkenness, not in chambering and wantonness, not in strife and envying. But put ye on the Lord Jesus Christ, and make not provision for the flesh."[3152] Let us "account that the longsuffering of our Lord is salvation."[3153]

[3149] Revelation 18:20
[3150] Revelation 13:6
[3151] Titus 1:16
[3152] Romans 13:13,14
[3153] 2 Peter 3:15

38

With Respect Of Persons

1. "My brethren, have not the faith of our Lord Jesus Christ, the Lord of glory, with respect of persons." "If ye fulfil the royal law according to the scripture, Thou shalt love thy neighbour as thyself, ye do well: but if ye have respect to persons, ye commit sin, and are convinced of the law as transgressors."[3154]

2. There is only one way by which it should be accomplished, "He maketh fire...in the sight of men,"[3155] for in those men by whom fire is concocted, it is fulfilled, "These are murmurers, complainers, walking after their own lusts; and their mouth speaketh great swelling words, having men's persons in admiration because of advantage."[3156] These men who have their desires given to them by the earth beast, as we are introduced to them, encourage themselves in "giving themselves over to fornication, and going after strange flesh,"[3157] for they have fulfilled

---

3154 James 2:1,8,9
3155 Revelation 13:13
3156 Jude 1:16
3157 Jude 1:7

the word, "Upon a lofty and high mountain hast thou set thy bed: even thither wentest thou up to offer sacrifice."[3158]

3. The LORD once said, "I am against thee, O destroying mountain,"[3159] for it was said, "Every purpose of the LORD shall be performed against Babylon."[3160] Babylon was the empire that was "the glory of kingdoms,"[3161] for a mountain is figurative language denoting a kingdom, even as it says, "Woe to them that are at ease in Zion, and trust in the mountain of Sama'ria, which are named chief of the nations."[3162] In the Revelation, an apostate church within the earth beast has fixed its situation upon a mountain, her movements rest within the State of a kingdom, and it is in, and by that State, that she constructs and performs every sacrifice for the advancement of the god of her religion. For this cause, the Spirit says of her, "Thou wentest to the king with ointment, and didst increase thy perfumes, and didst send thy messengers far off, and didst debase thyself even unto hell."[3163] Thus, this woman and these men; the priests of her political religious tradition; have reproduced the image of what is recorded: "I saw a woman sit upon a scarlet coloured beast."[3164]

4. It is because of the political advantage within him; the State of the earth; that causes her; his apostate bride; to fulfill the saying, "Thou didst wash thyself, paintedst thy eyes, and deckedst thyself with ornaments, and satest upon a stately bed, and a table prepared before it."[3165] She left the few foundational principles of the Spirit's Faith that she cherished, and that held her in check from further debasing herself, to lay for another power; at the chief of the mountains she "stood at his feet behind him weeping, and began to wash his feet with tears, and did wipe them with the hairs of her head, and kissed his feet, and anointed

---

3158 Isaiah 57:7
3159 Jeremiah 51:25
3160 Jeremiah 51:29
3161 Isaiah 13:19
3162 Amos 6:1
3163 Isaiah 57:9
3164 Revelation 17:3
3165 Ezekiel 23:40,41

them with the ointment."[3166] As it was done for Christ, and Christ told this certain woman, "Thy sins are forgiven,"[3167] so when this apostate sect should band together around that red beast, which is that red dragon; a symbol of a perversely religious civil and legislative power; she too will receive the favor of her *Christ* that she may receive a new constitution with power therein to regulate herself and all who will not recognize the authority given to her.

5. These things will occur within the nation that once fulfilled the saying, "Nation shall not lift up sword against nation, neither shall they learn war any more,"[3168] because of a blatant violation against the Spirit's commandment. The man of the Spirit counsels, "Have not the faith of our Lord...with respect of persons,"[3169] for the law of Jesus reveals within the obedient, "Love thy neighbour as thyself,"[3170] yet there is an open rejection of the Faith of Jesus when placing favor within any one of, and for, advantage. Obedience to Christ's doctrine will always lead one to fulfill that royal law not out of any base prescription, not out of any fleshly stimulus for any inwardly vain presumptuous gratification, but it will be fulfilled, "Thou doest faithfully whatsoever thou doest to the brethren, and to strangers; which have borne witness of thy charity before the church: whom if thou bring forward on their journey after a godly sort, thou shalt do well."[3171]

6. Notice that the men of the LORD's Priest; James and John; both end the definition of godly charity and soul refreshing benevolence with the same saying, that is, "Ye do well." This doing well, it is the doing of good, and this "good" work is defined as: "Let us not be weary in well doing: for in due season we shall reap, if we faint not. As we have therefore opportunity, let us do good unto all men, especially unto them who are of the household of faith."[3172] This is what it means to do

---

3166 Luke 7:38
3167 Luke 7:48
3168 Isaiah 2:4
3169 James 2:1
3170 James 2:8
3171 3 John 1:5,6
3172 Galatians 6:9,10

well and to "love," for the counsel is, "Love one another,"[3173] but the reality is that this counsel means, "Comfort yourselves together, and edify one another."[3174] For this reason it is counseled, "Let us therefore follow after the things which make for peace, and things wherewith one may edify another. For meat destroy not the work of God,"[3175] and, "Let every one of us please his neighbour for his good to edification. For even Christ pleased not himself."[3176]

7. The apostle counsels, "Destroy not the work and foundation of God for meat," or rather not for meat, but for "divers and strange doctrines,"[3177] that is, "with meats."[3178] This is the reason why such a gross error has been made, and has succeeded, in the earth beast of the Revelation. Ministers sought the magnification of their strange and diverse doctrines; the meats of their belly; and because they would not wait on the voice and power of that One of God; of whom it is said, "There is no beauty";[3179] they have banded themselves together with the arm of man to create confusion. In reality, they love neither the LORD nor His Lord. Because they do not have the structure of the Spirit's law of self-sacrificing benevolence in their mind and character, they will not wait upon the knowledge of His Chief Priest to receive His power to fulfill His will, but in their heart they fulfill the condemnation, "Thine eyes and thine heart are not but for thy covetousness, and for to shed innocent blood, and for oppression, and for violence, to do it."[3180]

8. Therefore "if there come unto your assembly a man with a gold ring, in goodly apparel, and there come in also a poor man in vile raiment; and ye have respect to him that weareth the gay clothing, and say unto him, Sit thou here in a good place; and say to the poor, Stand thou there, or sit here under my footstool: are ye not then partial in

---

3173 1 Thessalonians 4:9
3174 1 Thessalonians 5:11
3175 Romans 14:19,20
3176 Romans 15:2,3
3177 Hebrews 13:9
3178 Hebrews 13:9
3179 Isaiah 53:2
3180 Jeremiah 22:17

yourselves, and are become judges of evil thoughts?"[3181] "If ye have respect to persons, ye commit sin, and are convinced of the law as transgressors."[3182]

9. These men, who stand in the presence of the State, represent before us transgressors of the doctrine of Christ and of the Spirit's law. The man of this Faith openly explains that one of the principles of our Priest's doctrine is an abhorrence of commendation towards the outward appearance for the inflammation of vanity. "Do not maintain Jesus' law with respect of persons," he says, but why? Because it is written, "For even Christ pleased not himself."[3183] "Ye know the grace of our Lord Jesus Christ, that, though he was rich, yet for your sakes he became poor, that ye through his poverty might be rich."[3184] This is the law of Jesus that we are to comfort one another's spirit with.

10. The fact that the Spirit reduced Himself to dwell with the pathetic members of flesh, and that this flesh passed away and then resurrected on behalf of that human flesh for the divine regeneration of that flesh's constitution through the commandment of that same Spirit, is proof that every soul is loved as equally as God loves His own Son and Christ. Therefore when the man says, "Love as I have loved you,"[3185] the notion is that because the Godhead so loved me, and because I have recognized that love to the degree that I have recognized it, I too want to love me as my LORD loves me, therefore I will hear the command, "Be ye transformed by the renewing of your mind, that ye may prove what is that good, and acceptable, and perfect, will of God."[3186] As I prove His will and as I receive health towards my constitution from obeying that will by His power and charge, then I will want to do for others as God has done for me, even encouraging them to know the same Place of rest and health that God Himself has brought me.

3181 James 2:2-4
3182 James 2:9
3183 Romans 15:3
3184 2 Corinthians 8:9
3185 John 13:34
3186 Romans 12:2

11. This is the love of God and the fulfillment of life's royal law. This is the education that only the humble student in the classroom of Christ will receive, for God's Priest counsels, "Be willing and obedient."[3187] "Learn to do well,"[3188] He says, but what is doing well? He says, "Seek judgment, relieve the oppressed, judge the fatherless, plead for the widow."[3189] The willing mind and the obedient child "trembleth at my word,"[3190] says the Spirit, for these are the only souls that He can help. Them that care to seek His judgment, that care to dig, to beg, to plead, and to distress themselves over understanding some thing of His voice, are them who will have it said of them by the witness of many souls, "They have refreshed my spirit and yours."[3191] This is what it means to love others as you love yourself, for to refresh the spirit of another as you your own self have been refreshed by the LORD's Spirit, this is the acceptable work of charity, which work fulfills that law comprising the last six of the Ten Commandments, bearing witness to the fact that we do absolutely honor the first four.

12. This is the spirit that these perverse men of the earth's new beast lack, and because they lack this mind, they cannot hear how it is said, "Thou shalt love the Lord thy God with all thy heart, and with all thy soul, and with all thy mind, and with all thy strength: this is the first commandment."[3192] If this charge is not heard, then it cannot be heard, "Love and edify one another." Because they lack that spirit within Christ's law, these individuals have no respect or honor for the LORD or His Spirit, and this is why it says, "Whosoever transgresseth, and abideth not in the doctrine of Christ, hath not God."[3193]

13. To violate the doctrine and "law of Christ,"[3194] one must inevitably put into jeopardy "the law of the Spirit of life in Christ."[3195] The

---

3187 Isaiah 1:19
3188 Isaiah 1:17
3189 Isaiah 1:17
3190 Isaiah 66:2
3191 1 Corinthians 16:18
3192 Mark 12:30
3193 2 John 1:9
3194 Galatians 6:2
3195 Romans 8:2

law of the Spirit teaches, "No man can come to me, except the Father which hath sent me draw him."[3196] A refusal to acknowledge the LORD and Father of Christ will deny access to the knowledge of the Faith of His Son, and this is why it says, "Every one that loveth him that begat loveth him also that is begotten of him."[3197] John wrote these things because he lived in a time when the counsel against the church was, "Thou hast left thy first love. Remember therefore from whence thou art fallen, and repent, and do the first works."[3198]

14. The early Christian church once existed under "men that have hazarded their lives for the name of our Lord Jesus Christ."[3199] Such men suffered not for doctrine, not for philosophical persuasions or superstitions, not for policy or tradition, but for the revelation of the pure work of both the Father and the Son within their person. In the beginning, "distribution was made unto every man according as he had need,"[3200] for "all that believed were together, and had all things common; and sold their possessions and goods, and parted them to all men, as every man had need."[3201] But the time would come when men would grow unsatisfied with "the apostles' doctrine and fellowship,"[3202] and it would be told them, "I know the blasphemy of them which say they are Jews, and are not, but are the synagogue of Satan."[3203]

15. John lived in the time when the word was fulfilling, "The time will come when they will not endure sound doctrine; but after their own lusts shall they heap to themselves teachers, having itching ears; and they shall turn away their ears from the truth, and shall be turned unto fables."[3204] Within the professed churches of Christ "there sat women weeping for Tam'muz,"[3205] and this is why the Spirit counseled John,

---

3196   John 6:44
3197   1 John 5:1
3198   Revelation 2:4,5
3199   Acts 15:26
3200   Acts 4:35
3201   Acts 2:44,45
3202   Acts 2:42
3203   Revelation 2:9
3204   2 Timothy 4:3,4
3205   Ezekiel 8:14

"What thou seest, write in a book, and send it unto the seven churches which are in Asia."[3206] John was seeing the religious filth of heathen societies mixing with the sayings of Christ, for a new ambition was rising into the heart of the elders of Christian churches, and this is why the Spirit said of them, "Thou hast there them that hold the doctrine of Ba'laam, who taught Ba'lac to cast a stumblingblock."[3207] The Christian church wanted a certain and peculiar power and authority to be given and bestowed upon her, and because the LORD's throne religion was not supplying it according to her fashion, she sought it on her own.

16. These same events of old will again find place in a new history of people, for this same spirit that enflamed the Roman churches will again find its ways into modern society. Them of old, who committed such villainy against the name of God, only managed to do so because they lacked Him that begat the *One* whom they professed to admire. It was God the Father that raised His Christ from the dead,[3208] and "being by the right hand of God exalted, and having received of the Father the promise of the Holy Ghost, he hath shed forth this"[3209] gift that every believer may know that "he saved us, by the washing of regeneration, and renewing of the Holy Ghost."[3210] The believer is saved or rescued; inwardly recovered or regenerated; only by that contained within the Spirit of God. Without this process of purification, none will see or know Christ's new name, and because of a failure to submit the personal religion to God that He may sanctify it, a mind inclined towards *righteousness* by works of the flesh, and of *salvation* through the institution of the church, took hold of the spirit of the early church.

17. As the Spirit of God continued to be forgotten, *Christ* was heavily worshipped as an idol of wood and stone. This is why John wrote to the churches, "Our fellowship is with the Father, and with his Son Jesus Christ."[3211] When the Father is rejected, His first four commandments will mean nothing to the natural conversation. The elders of the

---

3206 Revelation 1:11
3207 Revelation 2:14
3208 Galatians 1:1
3209 Acts 2:33
3210 Titus 3:5
3211 1 John 1:3

churches began to idolize *Christ* as a divine philosopher of *God*; the doctrinal errors within the church were prescribed by men who sought to harmonize platonic philosophy with the superstitions of many religions, along with that of the apostles' doctrine; and because they lacked the only Teacher of heaven's throne religion; as Christ says of the Spirit, "He shall teach you all things";[3212] they fulfilled the word, "They have caused them to stumble in their ways from the ancient paths, to walk in paths, in a way not cast up."[3213] The apostle's doctrine became just that, their doctrine, and not the belief of the elders and of the majority of professed converts, and this occurred because they loved not Him that begat, as it says, "They return, but not to the most High."[3214]

18. Without the Holy Spirit, these ministers were not restrained from their base indulgences. The effect of the religion of heaven's Christ on the soul is a temperate demeanor; a spirit employed to encourage self-denial and self-development for proper knowledgeable self-government; therefore without the Spirit, without faith on the doctrine of Christ, and without an actual experience in that faith by faith, it is no surprise that these mocked the name and the order of the LORD God by seeking the name and the order of another. Of such individuals it is said, "These be they who separate themselves, sensual, having not the Spirit,"[3215] and, "They taught my people to swear by Ba'al."[3216]

19. Can these, therefore, in the presence of the State of the earth beast, be of Christ's law any more than them of old in Rome? Are them that would compel a State of the earth to enact their fire born of heaven's Faith? The Spirit's man rejects individuals who would join themselves to ones of advantage for advantage. Nevertheless, history will repeat itself, for the vision given to John was but "to testify unto you these things in the churches."[3217] The same spirit of error that crept into the early church will again work inside men who "would pervert the

---

3212 John 14:26
3213 Jeremiah 18:15
3214 Hosea 7:16
3215 Jude 1:19
3216 Jeremiah 12:16
3217 Revelation 22:16

gospel of Christ."[3218] Their perversion will be known when they extend their hand to the then king of the land, for their actions are but an open condemnation against them and are a full exposition of their natural ambition. Their upholding the State's person for political prowess is in direct violation of the Spirit's Faith, and this is why all joined to them will suffer the end of that violation. This is why the Spirit today warns, "If any man worship the beast and his image, and receive his mark in his forehead, or in his hand, the same shall drink of the wine of the wrath of God."[3219]

20. That image of worship is of the spirit of the power before it. The construction of this ecclesiastical government will be founded upon spiritual lies. It serves every one professing Christ to personally know His voice, for false elders will call themselves *Jews* and stand by the name of a *Jew*, but will openly deny the living LORD; "through covetousness shall they with feigned words make merchandise of you"[3220] who do not have heaven's refinement. So then, let all acknowledge the counsel, "My brethren, have not the faith of our Lord Jesus Christ, the Lord of glory, with respect of persons."[3221]

3218 Galatians 1:7
3219 Revelation 14:9,10
3220 2 Peter 3:2
3221 James 2:1

39

By A Statute For Ever

1. "This shall be a statute for ever unto you: that in the seventh month, on the tenth day of the month, ye shall afflict your souls, and do no work at all, whether it be one of your own country, or a stranger that sojourneth among you: for on that day shall the priest make an atonement for you, to cleanse you, that ye may be clean from all your sins before the LORD. It shall be a Sabbath of rest unto you, and ye shall afflict your souls, by a statute for ever."[3222]

2. A statute is an act of the legislature of a state extending the binding force of a decree to all citizens or subjects of that state. A statute is an act of the legislature commanding or constraining some thing by a law or a decree; the supreme power of the land has declared a principle of binding force to its nation for public and private justice. "One law and one manner shall be for you, and for the stranger that sojourneth with you,"[3223] says the LORD, for He says of this manner concerning the day of atonement, "This shall be an everlasting statute unto you,"[3224] "and it

---

3222 Leviticus 16:29-31
3223 Numbers 15:16
3224 Leviticus 16:34

was so from that day forward, that he made it a statute and an ordinance for Israel unto this day."[3225]

3. We should at once ask, "Since Moses spoke these things to a certain people under a certain rule and at a certain time, who now falls under the government of the living God?" Says Christ to His Father: "All mine are thine, and thine are mine; and I am glorified in them."[3226] "My sheep hear my voice, and I know them, and they follow me."[3227] "My Father, which gave them me, is greater than all; and no man is able to pluck them out of my Father's hand. I and my Father are one."[3228]

4. The one professing Christ finds himself or herself in a bind, for the LORD of the Ten Commandments belongs to the Savior of the regeneration of the flesh's sinful form, and this same Savior belongs to that same LORD, for He confesses, "I proceeded forth and came from God,"[3229] and, "I love the Father."[3230] Should the believer of Christ exist without His LORD and Father? The apostle John found the churches abandoning pure principles of worship and service, for they idolized a figure of *Christ* without surrendering to the power of the experience of that Faith in His name, and for this he wrote, "Truly our fellowship is with the Father, and with his Son Jesus Christ."[3231] This Christ does not say, "O Father, all that I have gathered are Yours," but He says, "My Father that gave Me My assembly, even they are Yours. 'Holy Father, keep through thine own name those whom thou hast given me.'"[3232]

5. No one may hear Christ's voice if they are not willing to acknowledge the Author of that voice. It is true how it is said, "Jesus the author and finisher of our faith,"[3233] for "he became the author of eternal salvation unto all them that obey him,"[3234] yet He confesses, "I

3225   1 Samuel 30:25
3226   John 17:10
3227   John 10:27
3228   John 10:29,30
3229   John 8:42
3230   John 14:31
3231   1 John 1:3
3232   John 17:11
3233   Hebrews 12:2
3234   Hebrews 5:9

have not spoken of myself; but the Father which sent me, he gave me a commandment, what I should say, and what I should speak."[3235] The instruction that Christ spoke was "the glorious gospel of Christ, who is the image of God."[3236] God is represented by the words and works of His Son and High Priest, for these sayings and deeds originated first with His LORD and found expression through the limbs of His Minister, which is why His Faith is called, "The gospel of the grace of God."[3237] Them that obey the doctrine of Christ will receive divine health to recuperate their mental and moral faculties. Such gifts are manifested by "the Holy Ghost, whom God hath given to them that obey him,"[3238] for the reformer has to first believe on the commandment of the Spirit of God in order to receive the benefits bestowed from His Son's mediation.

6. Is this false? "Believe on him that raised up Jesus our Lord from the dead,"[3239] we are counseled. If the gospel could have a body, its flesh would be the sayings of Christ, but the bones and its organs holding the substance of its flesh, and the thoughts and feelings actuating proper movement of that flesh, would consist of that found in the law of the Spirit of God. To accept the person of *Christ* by any tradition, and to maintain that tradition as it is, or to be moved by God to love His Son, but to stall the growth of that movement by refusing to admit self to God for intimate sessions of health and recovery with His Spirit and doctrine, is but to capture a frail understanding of heaven's Faith. Herein the saying is fulfilled in such an individual, "A dispensation of the gospel is committed unto me."[3240] There is no life or benefit in uplifting religious error to fit some mold of an imagined reality. The believer needs to first personally contend within him or herself by the Spirit's wisdom to believe on Him that raised up His Christ, for Christ being dead and resurrected is the example that needs to be understood.

3235　John 12:49
3236　2 Corinthians 4:4
3237　Acts 20:24
3238　Acts 5:32
3239　Romans 4:24
3240　1 Corinthians 9:17

This is why we are counseled, "Earnestly contend for the faith which was once delivered unto the saints."[3241]

7. If Christ lived as a man, and carried within Him every thing as an erroneous human being, if it is true, "As the children are partakers of flesh and blood, he also himself likewise took part of the same,"[3242] then it is true that Christ died as a human being, therefore as a human man He could not have resurrected Himself. This is a fact, for "there is no work, nor device, nor knowledge, nor wisdom, in the grave."[3243] So then, if Christ raised not Himself; for the believer is counseled to believe on Him that did raise Christ up;[3244] who lifted up Christ from death? Says Scripture, "Christ was raised up from the dead by the glory of the Father."[3245] What then is the glory of the Father that lifted Him up, which glory is to lift us up also? It says, "If the Spirit of him that raised up Jesus from the dead dwell in you, he that raised up Christ from the dead shall also quicken your mortal bodies by his Spirit."[3246] It is then a fact that resurrection begins when once the spirit is allowed to examine and do "the law of the Spirit of life,"[3247] for "we have received a commandment from the Father."[3248] This is why Paul wrote, "I am not ashamed of the gospel of Christ: for it is the power of God unto salvation to every one that believeth...For therein is the righteousness of God revealed from faith to faith."[3249] This is why His Priest counsels, "True worshippers shall worship the Father in spirit and in truth."[3250]

8. The glory, or the righteousness of God, is seen in the fact that He Himself, and by the voice of His own Spirit, will resurrect the heart and mind of the sincere doer of His Son's law to a new estate. Christ being raised from the grave is an illustration of what the Spirit will do

---

3241   Jude 1:3
3242   Hebrews 2:14
3243   Ecclesiastes 9:10
3244   Romans 4:24
3245   Romans 6:4
3246   Romans 8:11
3247   Romans 8:2
3248   2 John 1:4
3249   Romans 1:16,17
3250   John 4:23

for every humble and sorrowful soul that falls prostrate before Him because of what they have heard concerning His Son. God sent His Christ and accepted His sacrifice "to declare his righteousness"; the righteousness of His Christ; "for the remission of sins," to the end "that he"; He God the Father; "might be just, and the justifier of him which believeth in Jesus."[3251] "God, having raised up his Son Jesus, sent him to bless you, in turning away every one of you from his iniquities."[3252] Only by "the washing of regeneration, and renewing of the Holy Ghost,"[3253] may this blessed reformation of the natural and hereditary conversation of the human being find correction.

9. The doctrine of Christ is but the road to that Sanitarium of recovery, and that recovery is found in the House of God wherein rests the Minister and Spirit of God, which is why it is says, "Our conversation is in heaven; from whence also we look for the Saviour."[3254] The Savior of the living God is at no other place but that Building of that great LORD His God, which is why it is said, "We have such an high priest, who is set on the right hand of the throne of the Majesty in the heavens; a minister of the sanctuary, and of the true tabernacle, which the Lord pitched, and not man."[3255] The Spirit's good tidings are seated at the right hand of His LORD's Government, for the voice of God has declared two laws for the religion of the believer: the ten binding immutable laws of God and the law and doctrine of His Christ. The doctrine of Christ magnifies the authority of the LORD's ten precepts, and because this is so, only a priest of God can put in order all of these things within His jurisdiction for His congregation. It is for this reason that the LORD anointed His Christ to be "a merciful and faithful high priest in things pertaining to God, to make reconciliation for the sins of the people."[3256]

10. Being the author of salvation, the knowledge of Christ's voice is the means whereby every blessing falls onto the heart of every member

---

3251 Romans 3:25,26
3252 Acts 3:26
3253 Titus 3:5
3254 Philippians 3:20
3255 Hebrews 8:1,2
3256 Hebrews 2:17

within His heavenly assembly. When once the soul faithfully believes on their personal reconciliation to God by His Man, they are immediately transferred into the hand of the Spirit for their faith in the virtue of His sacrifice. This is why it is wrong to keep the soul bound to tradition or constrained within itself to the teachings of men; "ye were not redeemed with corruptible things, as silver and gold, from your vain conversation received by tradition from your fathers."[3257] The soul and spirit touched by the Spirit needs to search after the One that moved their heart. Flesh cannot do what needs to be done for the soul's health and the spirit's recovery. Presumption and an ascent to truth will never impregnate the body of devotion to care for "the knowledge of his will in all wisdom and spiritual understanding."[3258] The understanding of heaven's High Priest must find place in the religion, for there is no other way to obtain inward recovery. If there is a refusal to learn of the Father and to receive an education by His Spirit, there will be no communion with His High Priest.

11. These things are important to consider because they return us to the beginning of our thought, as it says, "On that day shall the priest make an atonement for you, to cleanse you."[3259] The one professing devotion to Christ's law must know that no man on earth is his or her soul's priest. It is now a fact established by God "which he wrought in Christ, when he raised him from the dead, and set him at his own right hand":[3260] "The Son, who is consecrated for evermore."[3261] The Christ of God is not just Christ, but He is the Son and Minister of God over all things concerning the return of the soul temple to the moral image of the heavenly Temple. It belongs only to this Christ "to save them to the uttermost that come unto God by him, seeing he ever liveth to make intercession for them."[3262] Because the fact of His high priestly office is true, it is a fact that He has taken the order of that ministration blessed

---

3257 1 Peter 1:18
3258 Colossians 1:9
3259 Leviticus 16:30
3260 Ephesians 1:20
3261 Hebrews 7:28
3262 Hebrews 7:25

to Aaron, leaving it for us also to know, "The priest, whom he shall anoint, and whom he shall consecrate...shall make the atonement."[3263]

12. In this Christ, the saying was fulfilled, "To anoint the most Holy."[3264] "The precious ointment upon the head, that ran down upon the beard, even Aaron's beard: that went down to the skirts of his garments,"[3265] occurred when God anointed His Christ "to be the head over all things to the church,"[3266] that is, "the general assembly and church of the firstborn, which are written in heaven."[3267] Since it is true that God has now transferred His priesthood from earth to His true and living heavenly Courts, it cannot be forgotten that that institution on earth maintained "ordinances of divine service, and a worldly sanctuary. For there was a tabernacle made; the first, wherein was the candlestick, and the table, and the shewbread; which is called the sanctuary. And after the second veil, the tabernacle which is called the Holiest of all";[3268] wherein rested the ark of His testament. Since Christ and His office have replaced that of Aaron, the times and seasons, and the particular laws and manners of that ministration, do also follow after Christ's mediation in their own way.

13. For more than eighteen hundred years; from the time of His ascension to the LORD until when the end of the twenty three hundred year prophecy, as spoken by the angel, did expire;[3269] Christ executed the first portion of His ministration in the first Room of the LORD's heavenly Temple. At the end of those years it would be fulfilled, "Then shall the sanctuary be cleansed,"[3270] which is a direct fulfillment of the word, "The Lord, whom ye seek, shall suddenly come to his temple."[3271] Such a prophecy marked the fulfillment, "The hour of his judgment is

---

3263 Leviticus 16:32
3264 Daniel 9:24
3265 Psalms 133:2
3266 Ephesians 1:2
3267 Hebrews 12:23
3268 Hebrews 9:1-5
3269 Daniel 8:14
3270 Daniel 8:14
3271 Malachi 3:1

come,"³²⁷² and this counsel emphasized by how it is said, "He shall sit as a refiner and purifier of silver,"³²⁷³ for it says of this time, "The judgment was set, and the books were opened."³²⁷⁴

14. God has translated every thing concerning Aaron to His heavenly Courts to be executed by His Christ, to the end that the subjects of His ministration would find harmony with the LORD's voice and order. By the witness of His own blood, He pleads for His Church in the presence of His God, and because He is no longer in the Room where He once was; the first house of the Temple; it should not be forgotten, "My sheep hear my voice, and I know them, and they follow me."³²⁷⁵ Christ's ministration moves, just as Aaron's did. No one can reach this Christ and benefit from His ministration, and no one can ultimately be found of Him, if they do not follow Him where He is. He is in the second Room of heaven's Temple. The second Room is constrained by a law and a statue regarding the day of its commencement, and since "the law is spiritual,"³²⁷⁶ and since every believer must abide by that spiritual House and Kingdom "to offer up spiritual sacrifices, acceptable to God by Jesus Christ,"³²⁷⁷ so the statute of God concerning Aaron is binding for us if we confess His Christ and accept Him as that Minister not only over the Temple of God, but as that Physician also over our soul's temple.

15. Now is the time to know the LORD through His Son's name, that He is a living God, and that His name is true and faithful, for we are counseled, "Know ye that the LORD he is God."³²⁷⁸ Atonement is the satisfaction or reparation made by giving an equivalent for an injury, or by doing or suffering that which is received in satisfaction for an offense or injury. Atonement is the work of reconciliation after damage or injury has been suffered and acknowledged, and this is the right work to accomplish after the believer has allowed the value of

---

3272　Revelation 14:7
3273　Malachi 3:3
3274　Daniel 7:10
3275　John 10:27
3276　Romans 7:14
3277　1 Peter 2:5
3278　Psalms 100:3

their atonement to the Spirit by God's Christ to conquer them. As Christ is pleading His blood on behalf of His congregation in the second Room, it is emphasized that His host is to be made clean, for "judgment must begin at the house of God."[3279] It falls on His assembly to examine and to correct themselves by His wisdom and power in confidence of the virtue of the merits of His sacrifice. While Christ yet ministers on behalf of His penitent, "to them who by patient continuance in well doing seek for glory and honour and immortality, eternal life"[3280] is promised.

16. God Himself is judging; among the many souls in His House confessing love and devotion to the charges and ordinances of His Son; who will be faithful despite feeling or inclination to dare to bring self to Him in faith. "He that cometh to God must believe that he is, and that he is a rewarder of them that diligently seek him,"[3281] for an unintelligent faith lacking the right form of spirituality will not suffice. Every thing of the LORD God is held in check by the spiritual laws of His spiritual reign, for even from the beginning of creation the laws of God were to be first assimilated into the spirit of the mind to find right use from out of man's physical frame. The believer must have an experience whereby their atonement to the ministry of God's Spirit by the death and resurrection of His Christ is impressed on the heart of their conscience, for it is from this experience that godly sorrow will fill the heart to have "a readiness to revenge all disobedience."[3282] When once the mind is apprised of its violation against the character of God, it will turn to His Christ to learn humility by the adoption of temperate restraints to allow proper digestion of what is heard.

17. No work or effort to unlawfully produce this experience is allowed at this time, but rather a full consecration of heart and mind to the LORD our Father's commandment. It is our faith's learning that will prove to be valuable when the saying is observed: "Take heed unto thyself, and unto the doctrine; continue in them: for in doing this

---

3279 1 Peter 4:17
3280 Romans 2:7
3281 Hebrews 11:6
3282 2 Corinthians 10:6

thou shalt both save thyself, and them that hear thee."[3283] This is the hour of judgment for pruning and refining the personal and religious character to match that of our Father's Son. If one would "be found of him in peace, without spot, and blameless,"[3284] "despise not thou the chastening of the Lord, nor faint when thou art rebuked of him."[3285] "No chastening for the present seemeth to be joyous, but grievous: nevertheless afterward it yieldeth the peaceable fruit of righteousness unto them which are exercised thereby,"[3286] which is why the Spirit says, "As many as I love, I rebuke and chasten: be zealous therefore, and repent."[3287]

3283 1 Timothy 4:16
3284 2 Peter 3:14
3285 Hebrews 12:5
3286 Hebrews 12:11
3287 Revelation 3:19

40

The Times Of Refreshing

1. "Repent ye therefore, and be converted, that your sins may be blotted out, when the times of refreshing shall come from the presence of the Lord; and he shall send Jesus Christ, which before was preached unto you: whom the heaven must receive until the times of restitution of all things, which God hath spoken by the mouth of all his holy prophets since the world began."[3288]

2. The language used by Peter is the same language that John heard from the angel: "In the days of the voice of the seventh angel, when he shall begin to sound, the mystery of God should be finished, as he hath declared to his servants the prophets."[3289] Both Peter and that angel end their speech on the same point, that is, whatever God had spoken of some event to come, this event is to mark the restitution, or reconstitution, or final restoration of all heavenly things when the mystery of God is finished. Peter's language tells of the fact that neither the full times of refreshing or the full times of restitution had begun in his day, for in his voice he uses the word, "shall," for the tone of his voice is yet prophetic. When the times of refreshing do come, the preaching

---

3288 Acts 3:19-21
3289 Revelation 10:7

of Christ should be sent some where from some place, and this sending and this coming means a blotting out of sins, which work of removing sins must continue until the restitution of all things commences. Peter says, "The heaven must receive Christ, but the LORD will send the voice of His Christ to you again, and until all things are yet restored to Himself."

3. Peter already made it a point to say earlier, "He," God the Father, "would raise up Christ to sit on his throne."[3290] "Therefore being by the right hand of God exalted, and having received of the Father the promise of the Holy Ghost, he hath shed forth this."[3291] Peter emphatically explains that Christ is already caught up to God to some Place, and that His ascension has resulted in the outpouring of some thing. Christ is by the right hand of the throne of God as a Minister over the House of God, and because of His new placement, "the washing of regeneration, and renewing of the Holy Ghost; which he shed on us abundantly through Jesus Christ";[3292] began at His ordination after His crucifixion, and has not ended. If the true times of refreshing were yet falling in his day, why does Peter mention them as falling again? Why does he mention this rain in connection with a special ministerial work? And why define this special work by another coming of the Spirit's anointed High Priest?

4. The heaven receiving Christ a second time is a clue of the new dispensation that should arise until the full restitution. It is true that in Peter's day "the Spirit gave them utterance"[3293] and "they were filled with the Holy Ghost."[3294] On this group that was gathered together fell an "abundance of grace"[3295] as of "abundance of rain";[3296] it was fulfilled, "There shall be showers of blessing."[3297] But Peter's speech tells of the fact that this rain was tempered and that heaven had not

---

3290 Acts 2:30
3291 Acts 2:33
3292 Titus 3:5,6
3293 Acts 2:4
3294 Acts 2:4
3295 Romans 5:17
3296 1 Kings 18:41
3297 Ezekiel 35:26

"opened her mouth without measure."[3298] As rain does first naturally begin to lightly fall from the clouds onto the earth, and then after a short while does pick up itself to fall harder, so the rain and power of the Spirit fell lightly in the days of the first apostles, but Peter confesses that when the heaven receives Christ again, these times should bear an increase in that rain shed on us from the presence of His God. And this is quite interesting, that from the presence of the Father the years of refreshing commence, for the word, "The heaven," tells of the Place where this rain and presence of God falls out from.

5. The LORD's direct presence is found only in one Place. He says, "I will meet with thee, and I will commune with thee from above the mercy seat, from between the two cheru'bims which are upon the ark of the testimony,"[3299] for of old, whenever Moses or Aaron went in before the LORD, many "heard the voice of one speaking unto him from off the mercy seat that was upon the ark of testimony, from between the two cheru'bims."[3300] Because His throne is in that Place containing the ark of the testimony, it is then plain to understand why the times of refreshing should pick themselves up at another specific time, and why at that time the counsel should be greatly received, "Come boldly unto the throne of grace, that we may obtain mercy."[3301] A greater refreshing will come from the Father's presence because of that Place of refreshing, seeing as how, at this time, the Place of rain and of grace and of mercy "and abundance of peace"[3302] is officially open to spirits. What is called, "Heaven," is that Building of worship holding the LORD's throne religion, as it says, "The LORD is in his holy Temple, the LORD throne is in heaven."[3303]

6. The heaven thus mentioned has doors, even as it says, "The doors of heaven."[3304] When Stephen said, "I see heaven opened,"[3305] he

---

3298 Isaiah 5:14
3299 Exodus 25:22
3300 Numbers 7:89
3301 Hebrews 4:16
3302 Psalms 72:7
3303 Psalms 11:4
3304 Psalms 78:23
3305 Acts 7:56

saw a certain place opened; "the first, wherein was the candlestick, and the table, and the shewbread; which is called the sanctuary. And after the second veil, the tabernacle which is called the Holiest of all."[3306] Christ must come to the Place called the Holiest, for in the first Room of the first veil, or in the first door of heaven, it is false to say, "Your sins shall be blotted out."[3307]

7. The ancient priest allocated all sin to the Sanctuary from the one confessing their error through the blood of their sacrifice. It is said, "The priest shall dip his finger in some of the blood, and sprinkle it seven times before the LORD, even before the vail. And he shall put some of the blood upon the horns of the altar which is before the LORD, that is in the tabernacle of the congregation, and shall pour out all the blood at the bottom of the altar of the burnt offering, which is at the door of the tabernacle of the congregation."[3308] When it says, "The priest should sprinkle it before the LORD," because there was a veil separating the Holy from the Most Holy; the first Apartment from the second; the priest sprinkled the blood on that veil that hid the second room. Blood of the sacrifice filled the Sanctuary for a full year; it was gross with religious error within and without the first Room without any sure removal of that blood; howbeit "there is a certain remembrance again made of sins every year."[3309]

8. Sin was placed on the Sanctuary, and this means that religious error was kept in suspense and not removed or handled, yet, "into the second went the high priest alone once every year, not without blood, which he offered for himself, and for the errors of the people."[3310] This is why Peter said, "Repent and be converted that your sins may have chance for removal," for he could not say that they lived in the time of the removing of sins, for he would tell a lie; "the way into the holiest of all was not yet made manifest, while as the first tabernacle was yet standing."[3311] Peter said what he said and went no further because, being

---

3306   Hebrews 9:2,3
3307   Acts 3:19
3308   Leviticus 4:17,18
3309   Hebrews 10:3
3310   Hebrews 9:7
3311   Hebrews 9:8

a Jew, he knew of the ministration of Aaron and the yearly changing of that course. He knew the correlation between the Rooms and the times and the seasons on earth and in heaven by the ancient priesthood. Therefore, being alive when Christ ministered in the first Room of heaven, he commissioned them then alive to experience repentance by active and experimental faith on Christ's doctrine, that when the Father again sends this same law preached, their sins may be handled and blotted out by this same Priest at the time appointed.

9. The times of refreshing picked up in weight and fervor when the heaven received its Christ for a second time. Today, Christ is no longer in the first Room of heaven. The saying, "The Lord, whom ye seek, shall suddenly come to his temple,"[3312] tells of a scene where a new door of hope in heaven is receiving that Christ into it. Christ has long since entered "the temple of the tabernacle of the testimony in heaven,"[3313] for at this time the saying is fulfilled, "Then shall the sanctuary be cleansed."[3314] Says the Spirit of this blessed season: "I will cause you to pass under the rod, and I will bring you into the bond of the covenant: and I will purge out from among you the rebels, and them that transgress against me: I will bring them forth out of the country where they sojourn, and they shall not enter into the land of Israel: and ye shall know that I am the LORD."[3315]

10. From the time that Christ begins to cleanse His House and that Place of God, until "he hath made an end of reconciling the holy place, and the tabernacle of the congregation, and the altar,"[3316] the restitution of "all things in Christ, both which are in heaven, and which are on earth,"[3317] will be finished. Such a restitution bears the necessary fulfillment of the promise, "In that day will I raise up the tabernacle of David that is fallen, and close up the breaches thereof; and I will raise up his ruins, and I will build it as in the days of old: that they may possess the remnant of Edom, and of all the heathen, which are called by my name,

---

[3312] Malachi 3:1
[3313] Revelation 15:5
[3314] Daniel 8:14
[3315] Ezekiel 20:37,38
[3316] Leviticus 16:20
[3317] Ephesians 1:10

saith the LORD that doeth this."[3318] Such a reconstitution hinges on the fulfillment of the saying, "I will bring forth a seed out of Jacob, and out of Judah an inheritor of my mountains: and mine elect shall inherit it, and my servants shall dwell there."[3319]

11. This fallen house of David is that seed within the house of Jacob, for when this seed is perfected it will be fulfilled, "The mystery of God should be finished."[3320] The mystery of God is a two fold work accomplishing one act: for it says, "Christ in you,"[3321] and, "The Gentiles should be fellowheirs, and of the same body, and partakers of his promise in Christ by the gospel."[3322] Because Scripture says, "The mystery should be," and not, "The mystery will be," there is an expression of time until the mystery will be finished. When the mystery should be finished, then will the mystery finish, for the "the light of the knowledge of the glory of God in the face of Jesus Christ"[3323] will be so perfectly reflected by His then host that them that know not God will in turn be converted to His name. It will then be fulfilled, "Strangers shall be joined with them, and they shall cleave to the house of Jacob."[3324]

12. Before the living House of God may play their part in sealing up the Spirit's dispensation, they must be recovered or regenerated after the LORD's name by the name of His Son. The great and anticipated marvelous happenings on earth cannot begin until the Father is ultimately satisfied with the inheritors of His scattered sons and daughters. This is why when Christ entered that second Room holding the ark of the Spirit's will, it was counseled, "The hour of his judgment is come: and worship him that made heaven, and earth, and the sea, and the fountains of waters."[3325] Christ's entrance before the presence of our LORD tells of an investigative judgment among His "general assembly

---

3318 Amos 9:11,12
3319 Isaiah 65:9
3320 Revelation 10:7
3321 Colossians 1:27
3322 Ephesians 3:6
3323 2 Corinthians 4:6
3324 Isaiah 14:1
3325 Revelation 14:7

and church of the firstborn, which are written in heaven."[3326] The ones who pass this judgment when the divine sentence on the House of God closes will comprise that restored House of Judah who "shall be in the midst of many people as a dew from the LORD."[3327]

13. "Zion shall be redeemed with judgment, and her converts with righteousness."[3328] The Spirit's judgment is to prepare His host for the judgment that the LORD will sanction against them by priests fulfilling the saying, "Whosoever killeth you will think that he doeth God service."[3329] This judgment will be marked by the union of "Herod, and Pon'tius Pilate, with the Gentiles, and the people of Israel."[3330] When "the senate of the children of Israel"[3331] should find themselves before the State of the ecclesiastical kingdom of the earth, and when the king of that earth works from out of "the presence of the council"[3332] of those elders, it will be said against this peculiar people, "And were filled with indignation. And laid their hands on the apostles, and put them in the common prison."[3333] The then apostles of the Spirit must suffer an open "sentence of judgment"[3334] "that they might be judged according to men in the flesh, but live according to God in the spirit."[3335] At first, the elders of the new State-friendly religious sect will say, "Let us straitly threaten them,"[3336] but after their power becomes official, and after that official wisdom finds itself challenged by "the people that do know their God,"[3337] it will be fulfilled, "Certain of the Jews banded together, and bound themselves under a curse, saying that they would neither eat nor drink till they had killed Paul."[3338]

3326 Hebrews 12:23
3327 Micah 5:7
3328 Isaiah 1:27
3329 John 16:2
3330 Acts 4:27
3331 Acts 5:21
3332 Acts 5:41
3333 Acts 5:18
3334 Deuteronomy 17:9
3335 1 Peter 4:6
3336 Acts 4:17
3337 Daniel 11:32
3338 Acts 23:12

14. Because the LORD knows the intention of men in high places and the spirit with which they are filled, He has issued forth the present decree: "Hurt not the earth, neither the sea, nor the trees, till we have sealed the servants of our God in their foreheads."[3339] This period that we now live in is that period of great and terrible refreshing from the presence of the LORD by His Son and Spirit. Every coarse thing against His band is in order, and to help gather a people to Himself to stand under the fire that men will enact from their heaven, He has presently increased the volume and strength of His rain for the reformer to better overcome him or herself by the name of His Son. This fairly quiet time of peace on earth is reserved for the fulfilling of the saying, "And shall have purged the blood of Jerusalem from the midst thereof by the spirit of judgment, and by the spirit of burning."[3340] The believer is to come into full contention with their own self by the light of the Spirit's judgment so that their eyes may experience the counsel, "They shall look upon me whom they have pierced, and they shall mourn for him, as one mourneth for his only son, and shall be in bitterness for him, as one that is in bitterness for his firstborn."[3341]

15. Because no one can unlawfully administer this high experience from within themselves, the Spirit says, "I will pour upon the house of David, and upon the inhabitants of Jerusalem, the spirit of grace and of supplications."[3342] "In that day there shall be a fountain opened to the house of David and to the inhabitants of Jerusalem for sin and for uncleanness."[3343] It is because of this word that Christ counsels, "The Spirit and the bride say, Come. And let him that heareth say, Come. And let him that is athirst come. And whosoever will, let him take the water of life freely."[3344]

16. Notice who says, "Come," for it is the Spirit and the Bride, or, the Father and "that great city, the holy Jerusalem."[3345] The Father

---

3339 Revelation 7:3
3340 Isaiah 4:4
3341 Zechariah 12:10
3342 Zechariah 12:10
3343 Zechariah 13:1
3344 Revelation 22:17
3345 Revelation 21:10

gives this counsel by His Christ because He at this time is in the Room where rain and grace pour out in an unlimited fashion from that Temple within His heavenly City, for it is now required of every believer in that Room to be "sanctified by God the Father,"[3346] that is, to be "sanctified by the Holy Ghost."[3347] The grace of God poured out in a great measure when Christ ministered in the first Apartment, but now, at this hour, we are come to the Place of the seat of mercy, wherein rests the Faith of our High Priest and His LORD's ten immutable precepts. The Spirit of God is to transform the believer into the image of the LORD's High Priest that they may know and keep His will and commandments. The Spirit and the Bride are the means whereby the believer may receive the name, "Reformer," and being blessed during this present "time of reformation,"[3348] they may be kept safe in the knowledge of God's Man "until the times of restitution of all things, which God hath spoken by the mouth of all his holy prophets since the world began."[3349]

17. Therefore, allow the instruction of His Spirit to lead your experience that you may sincerely learn repentance to find the hope of all strength to quit persistent personal and devotional error. Know this God's High Priest that you may daily embrace conversion to heaven's benevolent will. Now is the day when sins are not only being removed from the records in heaven, but also from the conscience of the inward person by the law of life and regeneration; now is the hour when showers of understanding are pouring out from the presence of heaven's throne to help us help our own self. "Let us therefore come boldly to the throne of grace, that we may obtain mercy, and find grace to help in time of need."[3350]

3346 Jude 1:1
3347 Romans 15:16
3348 Hebrews 9:10
3349 Acts 3:21
3350 Hebrews 4:16

41

The First To Be Rewarded

1. The Spirit has given His host the privilege of understanding that the times in which they live will not always remain as they are, for a disruption in the earth will cause a new kingdom to arise. At that appointed time, "the fashion of this world passeth away,"[3351] for a new republic under a new mind will govern the earth, and its voice will inevitably stretch out across its entire surface. This new entity will fulfill the word, "When he cometh, he must continue a short space,"[3352] for his primary ambition is to cause "the earth and them which dwell therein to worship the first beast."[3353] This new republic is the seventh kingdom of a line of eight, for it arises from the sixth. Its aim is to cause all to reverence the eighth, for he that should be healed, "he is the eighth, and is of the seventh, and goeth into perdition."[3354]

2. Because "the son of perdition"[3355] knows no other pattern of existence, he will latch on to the apostate republic, and not too long

---

[3351] 1 Corinthians 7:31
[3352] Revelation 17:10
[3353] Revelation 13:12
[3354] Revelation 17:11
[3355] 2 Thessalonians 2:3

after this perverse amalgamation will them that have rested under the united shadow of this power receive the reward for their errors. Scripture teaches, "The wrath of God is revealed from heaven against all ungodliness and unrighteousness of men, who hold the truth in unrighteousness."[3356] Because the professed of God rejected a full experience with Him, because many refused to investigate, and endure in, a true heaven-appointed education, the word is fulfilled, "Through deceit they refuse to know me, saith the LORD."[3357] Because of a period of open error against the LORD's name, from the time the earth gives birth to its new ecclesiastical force until that beast should magnify its "idol shepherd"[3358] to full strength, the revelation of God was held in terribly gross unrighteousness. But then suddenly "a great voice out of the temple saying to the seven angels, Go your ways, and pour out the vials of the wrath of God upon the earth,"[3359] is heard in the ears of heaven's faithful. The impenitent and irreverent then come up before God's throne, but there is a link missing from this chain of judgment before this event of wrath takes place that must be mentioned.

3. The first of seven last plagues falls on them "which had the mark of the beast, and upon them which worshipped his image."[3360] This is all well, except that it makes no sense why seven last plagues should pour out without first considering the fact of three first plagues. The number ten is a number connoting judgment. The seven last plagues are judgments of God against them that uphold an appearance of His science through a lie. The word, "Seven last," provokes the mind to consider the fact of three first plagues, and herein is that link to complete the chain of judgment, for the three first plagues must fall, and they do not consume the world of the ungodly.

4. Placing ourselves in that future environment under the new religious republic, we are alive during a time when the chief minister of Great Confusion "maketh fire come down from heaven on earth in

---

3356 Romans 1:18
3357 Jeremiah 9:6
3358 Zechariah 11:17
3359 Revelation 16:1
3360 Revelation 16:1

the sight of men."[3361] The statesmen of the land are church elders, and their elders are princes of churches, and these princes subscribe to their king and bridegroom, his bride, and their nobles. Every individual of a perversely patriotic heart is under the wings of this power, and it is to their heaven; the presently endorsed celestial religious powers of the sun, the moon, and the stars; that worship and service is given and derived.

5. At the appointed time, the word will be fulfilled, "Take the wine cup of this fury at my hand, and cause all the nations, to whom I send thee, to drink it."[3362] Who is first to receive heaven's wrath? It says, "To wit, Jerusalem, and the cities of Judah, and the kings thereof, and the princes thereof, to make them a desolation, an astonishment, an hissing, and a curse."[3363] Why is this so? We read, "The time is come that judgment must begin at the house of God."[3364] Again, why is this so? Seeing as how it is evident that His host misrepresented His name to receive a correction, the impenitent must suffer the end of their error in judgment "because that which may be known of God is manifest in them; for God hath shewed it unto them."[3365] And while being the recognized primary depositaries of His will and character, "because they have forsaken the covenant of the LORD their God, and worshipped other gods, and served them,"[3366] they must first suffer according to their blatant disobedience. "Because my people hath forgotten me, they have burned incense to vanity, and they have caused them to stumble in their ways from the ancient paths, to walk in paths, in a way not cast up...I will scatter them as with an east wind before the enemy; I will shew them the back, and not the face, in the day of their calamity,"[3367] says the Spirit.

6. The house of God, them whom He anciently ransomed from modern Pharaoh and Egypt, them that have "come forth out of the

---

3361 Revelation 13:13
3362 Jeremiah 25:15
3363 Jeremiah 25:18
3364 1 Peter 4:17
3365 Romans 1:20
3366 Jeremiah 22:9
3367 Jeremiah 18:15-17

waters of Judah";[3368] for the LORD, "with two lines measured he to put to death, and with one full line to keep alive";[3369] this is that house called, "The house of Jacob,"[3370] which will first suffer three plagues against them for their religious negligence. It is fair to call this house of Jacob "the house of God, which is the church of the living God, the pillar and ground for truth,"[3371] because it says of His Son, "He shall reign over the house of Jacob for ever."[3372] Because the host where God's name rests, and because the people sectioned out by God, willingly forgot His name to inevitably subscribe join forces with Satan's new nation, "Thou, even thyself, shalt discontinue from thine heritage that I gave thee,"[3373] says the Spirit.

7. The Christ of God obtained this people for His God, and they obtained the heavenly religion of His LORD and Father, when the saying was fulfilled, "The Lord, whom ye seek, shall suddenly come to his temple."[3374] His entrance within "the temple of the tabernacle of the testimony in heaven"[3375] secured, for those then disciples who were joined to His movement in to the second Room, a message not only to live by, but to also spread to them that had no knowledge of His moving mediation. Them that joined Christ in the second Room of His intercession were told, "Thou must prophesy again before many peoples, and nations, and tongues, and kings,"[3376] and their message was, "Keep the commandments of God, and the faith of Jesus."[3377] The living God, before this time, dwelt with a people for twelve hundred and sixty years without a true consecrated seed, nevertheless it was fulfilled, after this period of time, "I will purge out from among you the rebels, and them that transgress against me."[3378] It was after such a period that God's

---

3368 Isaiah 48:1
3369 2 Samuel 8:2
3370 Luke 1:33
3371 1 Timothy 3:16
3372 Luke 1:33
3373 Jeremiah 17:4
3374 Malachi 3:1
3375 Revelation 15:5
3376 Revelation 10:11
3377 Revelation 14:12
3378 Ezekiel 20:38

Priest again fulfilled the word, "Forty and six years was this temple in building,"[3379] for at the end of these years the word was fulfilled, "I will bring you into the bond of the covenant."[3380]

8. Concerning this house, the Spirit says, "Then washed I thee with water; yea, I throughly washed away thy blood from thee, and I anointed thee with oil. I clothed thee also with broidered work, and shod thee with badgers' skin, and I girded thee about with fine linen, and I covered thee with silk. I decked thee also with ornaments, and I put bracelets upon thy hands, and a chain on thy neck. And I put a jewel on thy forehead, and earrings in thine ears, and a beautiful crown upon thine head. Thus wast thou decked with gold and silver; and thy raiment was of fine linen, and silk, and broidered work; thou didst eat fine flour, and honey, and oil: and thou wast exceeding beautiful, and thou didst prosper into a kingdom."[3381]

9. But as it happened, they did "swear by the name of the LORD, and make mention of the God of Israel, but not in truth, nor in righteousness. For they call themselves of the holy city, and stay themselves upon the God of Israel,"[3382] but the Spirit reported of them, "Thou didst trust in thine own beauty, and playedst the harlot because of thy renown, and pouredst out thy fornications on every one that passed by; his it was. And of thy garments thou didst take, and deckedst thy high places with divers colours, and playedst the harlot thereupon: the like things shall not come, neither shall it be so. Thou hast also taken thy fair jewels of my gold and of my silver, which I had given thee, and madest to thyself images of men, and didst commit whoredom with them, and tookest thy broidered garments, and coveredst them: and thou hast set mine oil and mine incense before them."[3383]

10. "Thou hast also built unto thee an eminent place, and hast made thee an high place in every street. Thou hast built thy high place at every head of the way, and hast made thy beauty to be abhorred, and

---

3379 John 2:20
3380 Ezekiel 20:37
3381 Ezekiel 16:9-13
3382 Isaiah 48:1,2
3383 Ezekiel 16:15-18

hast opened thy feet to every one that passed by, and multiplied thy whoredoms. Thou hast also committed fornication with the Egyptians thy neighbours, great of flesh; and hast increased thy whoredoms, to provoke me to anger."[3384] "How weak is thine heart, saith the Lord GOD, seeing thou doest all these things, the work of an imperious whorish woman; in that thou buildest thine eminent place in the head of every way, and makest thine high place in every street; and hast not been as an harlot, in that thou scornest hire; but as a wife that committeth adultery, which taketh strangers instead of her husband!"[3385]

11. Because this house of our High Priest honored that which was contrary to His God, when this people should fill up the cup of their iniquity, the Spirit reports, "Thou, even thyself, shalt discontinue from thine heritage that I gave thee."[3386] His LORD did counsel, "Be not dismayed at the signs of heaven,"[3387] and because they subscribed to the powers of heaven, and did choose to "make cakes to the queen of heaven, and to pour out drink offerings unto other gods,"[3388] it will be fulfilled, "The breath of our nostrils, the anointed of the LORD, was taken in their pits, of whom we said, Under his shadow we shall live among the heathen."[3389]

12. Thus, "I will cause to cease out of this place...the voice of mirth, and the voice of gladness, the voice of the bridegroom, and the voice of the bride."[3390] "I will consume them by the sword, and by the famine, and by the pestilence,"[3391] says the Spirit. Nevertheless it is promised, "I will bring the third part through the fire, and will refine them as silver is refined."[3392]

13. Such a woeful decree of God fulfills the word, "I will make void the counsel of Judah and Jerusalem in this place; and I will cause them

---

3384 Ezekiel 16:24-26
3385 Ezekiel 16:30-32
3386 Jeremiah 17:4
3387 Jeremiah 10:2
3388 Jeremiah 7:18
3389 Lamentations 4:20
3390 Jeremiah 16:9
3391 Jeremiah 14:12
3392 Zechariah 13:9

to fall by the sword before their enemies, and by the hands of them that seek their lives: and their carcases will I give to be meat for the fowls of the heaven, and for the beasts of the earth. And I will make this city desolate, and an hissing; every one that passeth thereby shall be astonished and hiss because of all the plagues thereof."[3393] The professed denomination of God will at this time exist no more. Nevertheless, "I will bring a seed out of Jacob,"[3394] says our LORD. "As a shepherd seeketh out his flock in the day that he is among his sheep that are scattered; so will I seek out my sheep, and will deliver them out of all places where they have been scattered in the cloudy and dark day."[3395]

14. Before the revelation of the Spirit's sword should appear to rescue His faithful and ravage their adversaries, and before the seven last plagues should consume the economy of Falsehood, the house of God must first endure a series of advancing deprivations. Says the Spirit, "This is thy lot, the portion of thy measures from me, saith the LORD; because thou hast forgotten me, and trusted in falsehood."[3396] This is that house "turned back to the iniquities of their forefathers,"[3397] in that they not only "burn incense unto Ba'al";[3398] meaning that "with their backs toward the temple of the LORD, and their faces toward the east,"[3399] "they worshipped the sun toward the east"[3400] as if it was God; but they do so while also unlawfully handling the seventh-day Faith of the living God, moving Him to say, "Will ye steal, murder, and commit adultery, and swear falsely...and come and stand before me in this house, which is called by my name, and say, We are delivered to do all these abominations?"[3401] Because they have forsaken the only law of God that holds every other precept of His heritage together, and have honored *that* image and the spurious *sabbath* of the two-horned

---

3393   Jeremiah 19:7,8
3394   Isaiah 65:9
3395   Ezekiel 34:12
3396   Jeremiah 13:25
3397   Jeremiah 11:10
3398   Jeremiah 11:13
3399   Ezekiel 8:16
3400   Ezekiel 8:16
3401   Jeremiah 7:9,10

republic, the Spirit says, "Therefore pray not thou for this people, neither lift up a cry or prayer for them: for I will not hear them in the time that they cry unto me for their trouble."[3402]

15. Them that subscribe to the house of Jacob, without having their name secured within the books of the Church in heavenly Places, will be them that get to this point in ecclesiastical history to sadly confess, "The crown is fallen from our head."[3403] Says Scripture, "The Lord hath a mighty and strong one, which as a tempest of hail and a destroying storm, as a flood of mighty waters overflowing, shall cast down to the earth with the hand. The crown of pride, the drunkards of E'phraim, shall be trodden under feet."[3404] Concerning this crown, which is but the staple of the confidence of the house of Jacob, and the edifice of their many sub-structures, "I will give it into the hands of the strangers for a prey, and to the wicked of the earth for a spoil; and they shall pollute it. My face will I turn also from them, and they shall pollute my secret place: for the robbers shall enter into it, and defile it,"[3405] says the LORD. The spiritual king and leader of the coming ecumenical faction will rise up first against the professed house of God, for the LORD Himself has instructed him, "Begin at my Sanctuary."[3406]

16. These events against the house of Jacob cannot occur until she who should arise to offend enters onto the scene of action. Again, these things cannot occur until the foundation of the earth has so shaken that it gives way to a new religious dominion and economy, which economy supplies the balm to forward that spirit of the currently wounded institution. Because it is not known when this new republic will reach its full capacity, while it is not fully known when the earth should give birth to this strange enemy of all that concerns liberty of conscience and justice of soul, at this present hour every believer should hear, "Thus saith the LORD, Let not the wise man glory in his wisdom, neither let the mighty man glory in his might, let not the rich man glory in his

---

3402 Jeremiah 11:14
3403 Lamentations 5:16
3404 Isaiah 28:1-4
3405 Ezekiel 7:21,22
3406 Ezekiel 9:6

riches: but let him that glorieth glory in this, that he understandeth and knoweth me, that I am the LORD which exercise lovingkindness, judgment, and righteousness, in the earth: for in these things I delight, saith the LORD."[3407]

17. Because there is a failure to count the living God as a faithful Savior, to the end the heart may trust Him not just to lead the experience but to also provide and replace what that experience calls for in loss and gain, all will stand under the same banner of spiritual negligence and rebellion. "The time of evil and the time of affliction"[3408] are yet held in check by God because today is an ordained appointment of atonement. After there is belief that "we have now received the atonement"[3409] of "the communion of the Holy Ghost"[3410] by faith on the virtue of the death, resurrection, and priestly vocation of His Christ, God Himself says, "Take knowledge of me,"[3411] because after this time allotted for a divine education, that house claiming to be the assembly of Jacob will find herself under "four kinds, saith the LORD: the sword to slay, and the dogs to tear, and the fowls of the heaven, and the beasts of the earth, to devour and destroy."[3412] Individuals "whose house joined hard to the synagogue"[3413] perished of old because they refused to hear the Spirit's instruction. "To day if ye will hear his voice, harden not your hearts."[3414]

18. The Spirit currently says, "Because thou art lukewarm, and neither cold nor hot, I will spue thee out of my mouth."[3415] Many during the anticipated time of hard mental and physical persecution, because they have failed to personally cultivate the habitation of their heart according to "the word of reconciliation,"[3416] will say, "We are greatly

---

3407 Jeremiah 9:23,24
3408 Jeremiah 15:11
3409 Romans 5:11
3410 2 Corinthians 13:14
3411 Ruth 2:10
3412 Jeremiah 15:3
3413 Acts 18:7
3414 Hebrews 3:15
3415 Revelation 3:16
3416 2 Corinthians 5:19

confounded, because we have forsaken the land, because our dwellings have cast us out."[3417] Being erased from the mind of God, these no longer have a place with Him or among His preserved and sanctified host. This is why He says, "I will bring evil upon them, which they shall not be able to escape; and though they shall cry unto me, I will not hearken unto them. Then shall the cities of Judah and inhabitants of Jerusalem go, and cry unto the gods unto whom they offer incense: but they shall not save them at all in the time of their trouble."[3418]

19. Now is the time to personally know the doctrine of heaven's High Priest. Today's counsel is, "Afflict your souls, and offer an offering made by fire unto the LORD,"[3419] and because He has given this charge, He has further counseled, "Buy of me gold tried in the fire."[3420] That great offering to be made is the affliction of the spirit of the mind by "the Holy Ghost, and with fire."[3421] That which is tried in the fire of an experimental faith will procure a living religion grounded in a "faith which worketh by love."[3422] Because the Spirit's charge is, "Ye shall do no manner of work: it shall be a statute for ever,"[3423] the willing reformer must hear, "God imputeth righteousness without works."[3424] Complete exercising of faith in the virtue of Christ's name is the prerequisite to obtain the fire needed to purify our inward parts, for it is this fire that is to reform and continually regenerate our personal religion. All that may have before been thought to account for devotion should presently cease, for it is counseled, "Learn to do well."[3425] All should become dumb to obtain a right spirit from silence, for the Spirit is currently securing to Himself a people to usher in to His kingdom of glory.

20. The fate of the house of Jacob is spoken by God and cannot but come to pass, but this does not mean that the souls within the house

---

3417 Jeremiah 8:19
3418 Jeremiah 11:10,11
3419 Leviticus 23:27
3420 Revelation 3:18
3421 Matthew 3:11
3422 Galatians 5:6
3423 Leviticus 23:31
3424 Romans 4:6
3425 Isaiah 1:17

have lost the opportunity to presently honor their God. The apostle counsels the faithful on the religiously negligent by saying, "We have an altar, whereof they have no right to eat which serve the tabernacle."[3426] Them that care for the government of the church, and her doctrines, her letters of degrees and certifications, and her comfort of position, will not find any right inheritance among the Godhead, or among them found in "the general assembly and church of the firstborn, which are written in heaven."[3427] Therefore "cursed be the man that trusteth in man."[3428] "Cease ye from man"[3429] and hear, "Behold your God!"[3430] There is a different diet given of the Spirit for His own pure and living creatures from the religious world, a diet differing from them who subscribe to *Him* while honoring the condemnation, "Thou hast a name that thou livest, and art dead."[3431]

21. There is a heritage of God and a Place for the obedient soul to rest in. This heritage no man or woman can fully teach in its entirety, which is why "we have received, not the spirit of the world, but the spirit which is of God; that we might know the things that are freely given to us of God."[3432] The spirit of God owns the mind of the Spirit, and because "the Spirit searcheth all things, yea, the deep things of God,"[3433] every right believer after this same mind, and open to the reception of this same Spirit, will faithfully obtain and perfect the philosophy, "I applied mine heart to know, and to search, and to seek out wisdom, and the reason of things, and to know."[3434]

22. The heart of the one drawn out to the LORD and to His Christ will say, "We would see Jesus."[3435] Such an industrious faith will be rewarded with the opportunity to hear, "Handle me, and see."[3436] This

---

3426 Hebrews 13:10
3427 Hebrews 12:23
3428 Jeremiah 17:5
3429 Isaiah 2:22
3430 Isaiah 40:9
3431 Revelation 3:1
3432 1 Corinthians 2:12
3433 1 Corinthians 2:10
3434 Ecclesiastes 7:25
3435 John 12:21
3436 Luke 24:39

handling of the body of Christ's name is that work assigned by God that it may not be forgotten, "Give diligence to make your calling and election sure."[3437] For a right study concerning "the excellency of the knowledge of Christ"[3438] will open the heart "to the acknowledgement of the mystery of God, and of the Father, and of Christ."[3439] Such an acknowledgment is but the revelation "of the truth which is after godliness,"[3440] which revelation is utterly necessary to experience so that the soul may be hid during the fury of the LORD's Spirit, which will pour out on them that have held His name unlawfully.

3437 2 Peter 1:10
3438 Philippians 3:8
3439 Colossians 2:2
3440 Titus 1:1

42

Of Thieves And Robbers

1. "And when he was demanded of the Pharisees, when the kingdom of God should come, he answered them and said, The kingdom of God cometh not with observation: neither shall they say, Lo here! or, lo there! for, behold, the kingdom of God is within you."[3441]

2. The Pharisees were looking for the One who should physically fulfill the saying, "He put on the garments of vengeance for clothing, and was clad with zeal as a cloke,"[3442] and in all their looking they missed that One who was so blatantly before them. They misconstrued the prophecies concerning Christ because the foundation of their understanding rested a belief that taught, "The Romans shall come and take away both our place and nation."[3443] When Christ said, "The kingdom is not physical, nor will any one ever honestly say, 'It is here,' or, 'It is there,'" Christ was simply saying, "My kingdom is not of this world."[3444] Because they did not accept the fact of a spiritual kingdom headed by laws and ordinances of a spiritual nature, after His death

---

3441 Luke 17:20,21
3442 Isaiah 59:17
3443 John 11:48
3444 John 18:36

and resurrection and ascension into the LORD's heavenly Building, "there rose up certain of the sect of the Pharisees which believed,"[3445] whose seed would later aligned themselves to the same Romans that they feared.

3. In this sect the prophecy is fulfilled, "Of whom hast thou been afraid or feared, that thou hast lied, and hast not remembered me, nor laid it to thy heart?"[3446] "Ye have sent for men to come from far, unto whom a messenger was sent; and, lo, they came: for whom thou didst wash thyself, paintedst thy eyes, and deckedst thyself with ornaments, and satest upon a stately bed, and a table prepared before it, whereupon thou hast set mine incense and mine oil."[3447] "Thou hast discovered thyself to another than me, and art gone up; thou hast enlarged thy bed, and made thee a covenant with them; thou lovedst their bed where thou sawest it."[3448] "Thou wentest to the king with ointment, and didst increase thy perfumes, and didst send thy messengers far off, and didst debase thyself even unto hell."[3449]

4. A branch of the sect of the Pharisees, professing belief in the Christ of God, began their own sect and branded their own faith, and because the implanted heritage of their ancestry imbibed their current practice, they inevitably joined themselves to the ones that they feared, even protecting themselves by eventually resting under the shadow of the Roman State. Their leadership approached a man with the pretended glory of their majesty, and with polluted proverbs concerning the hope of communion with them. The product later became what is called the Papacy. This was that kingdom that manipulated the conscience of his citizens to believe the *kingdom* of *God* had come and was fulfilled on earth, and that to reach *God*, one must go through this institution. Therefore, being joined to the State of Rome, the church taught, in relation to her dogmas, "Whosoever therefore resisteth the power, resisteth the ordinance of God."[3450]

3445 Acts 15:5
3446 Isaiah 57:11
3447 Ezekiel 23:40,41
3448 Isaiah 57:8
3449 Isaiah 57:9
3450 Romans 13:2

5. The church longed for political prowess so that she could do for herself what God's Christ ultimately was not going to do for her. In order to get to the point where she desired to be, she must rest "even where Satan's seat is."[3451] The seat of Satan is not literal, but is rather figurative language depicting the throne, or the mind, or the purpose, of Satan. The mind of Satan is found in the condemnation that Spirit spoke against these same individuals: "Thou hast there them that hold the doctrine of Ba'laam, who taught Ba'lac to cast a stumblingblock."[3452]

6. We should ask, "What is the doctrine of Ba'laam?" The king Ba'lak once told Ba'laam concerning Israel, "Curse me this people."[3453] "I will promote thee unto very great honour, and I will do whatsoever thou sayest unto me."[3454] Although he at first struggled within himself, eventually "Ba'laam rose up in the morning, and saddled his ass, and went with the princes of Moab."[3455] Thus, when the seed of the Pharisees which believed are connected to Ba'laam in spirit and in practice, they are but fulfilling the character of one "having eyes full of adultery, and that cannot cease from sin; beguiling unstable souls: an heart they have exercised with covetous practices; cursed children: which have forsaken the right way, and are gone astray, following the way of Ba'laam the son of Bo'sor, who loved the wages of unrighteousness."[3456]

7. The doctrine of Ba'laam is the throne of Satan, where a king, or a kingdom, exalts the dominion of a false prophet because of his feverish spirit against the LORD God's true host and religious foundation. In this we see the mind and purpose of Satan revealed, for this same Satan says in his heart, "I will be like the most High."[3457] It is therefore only natural that the son, or the chief priest of the religion of Satan, and his religious institution, should follow after their father. Thus, "Thou hast said, I am of perfect beauty,"[3458] says the Spirit concerning the child of

---

3451 Revelation 2:13
3452 Revelation 2:14
3453 Numbers 22:6
3454 Number 22:17
3455 Numbers 22:21
3456 2 Peter 2:14,15
3457 Isaiah 14:13,14
3458 Ezekiel 27:3

Satan. "Thine heart is lifted up, and thou hast said, I am a God, I sit in the seat of God,"[3459] the Spirit continues. This is "the son of perdition; who opposeth and exalteth himself above all that is called God, or that is worshipped; so that he as God sitteth in the temple of God, shewing himself that he is God."[3460]

8. The only way that a minister over a church can gain such a seat is through a State, and it was the pretended *apostolic* church of Rome that achieved such a thing in the name of *Christ*. In this institution the violation is accomplished, "Thou shalt not take the name of the LORD thy God in vain."[3461] How was His name and character violated by them? Before this church officially and openly apostatized from heaven's benevolent will, the saying needed to be fulfilled, "That day shall not come, except there come a falling away first."[3462] The falling away was accomplished when the church seduced the then king Ba'lak into her bed, that it might then be told to her, "What is thy petition? and it shall be granted thee: and what is thy request? even to the half of the kingdom it shall be performed."[3463] Her petition was as the Spirit revealed: "To cast a stumblingblock before the children of Israel, to eat things sacrificed unto idols, and to commit fornication."[3464] "To teach and to seduce my servants to commit fornication, and to eat things sacrificed unto idols."[3465]

9. With the church of Rome depicted as spiritual Jez'ebel, and her husband Ba'lak; that spiritual Ahab; together they fulfill the word, "There was none like unto Ahab, which did sell himself to work wickedness in the sight of the LORD, whom Jez'ebel his wife stirred up. And he did very abominably in following idols."[3466] Ahab should not be viewed as simply a man, but rather as a civil government or kingdom. This is that Jez'ebel, "the daughter of Eth'baal king of the

---

3459 Ezekiel 28:2
3460 2 Thessalonians 2:3,4
3461 Exodus 20:7
3462 2 Thessalonians 2:3
3463 Esther 5:6
3464 Revelation 2:14
3465 Revelation 2:20
3466 1 Kings 21:25

Zido'nians,"[3467] by whom the king of Israel "went and served Ba'al, and worshipped him."[3468] Spiritual Jezebel was no different from the literal, for when Catholicism became the law of the land in Rome, it was fulfilled, "They worshipped the dragon which gave power unto the beast."[3469] The dragon is but a symbol for the pagan religion of Rome. Paganism was at this time clothed with a garb of pretended *Christ-like righteousness*, and the services directed to *God* and *Christ* inevitably fulfilled the saying, "Their backs toward the temple of the LORD, and their faces toward the east; and they worshipped the sun toward the east."[3470]

10. Not only was God's character abused by this institution, in them was also found violence against the laws, "Thou shalt have no other gods before me,"[3471] and, "The seventh day is the Sabbath of the LORD thy God."[3472]

11. The ancient practice of sun worship was ascribed to Ba'al, the sun god. He came in many names, such as Apollo, Hercules, Tam'muz, or Mo'loch. When the Spirit says of Israel, "Ye have borne the tabernacle of your Mo'loch and Chi'un your images,"[3473] and, "There sat women weeping for Tam'muz,"[3474] the LORD is saying that even while they professed to serve Him, His congregation honored a lame and foreign entity that was not Him. This is why He told His man, "Hast thou seen what the ancients of the house of Israel do in the dark, every man in the chambers of his imagery?"[3475] This is why when the Christian church, in the beginning of her birth, began to observe the same deities as pagans, Paul counseled, "Have no fellowship with the unfruitful

---

3467 1 Kings 16:31
3468 1 Kings 16:31
3469 Revelation 13:4
3470 Ezekiel 8:16
3471 Exodus 20:3
3472 Exodus 20:10
3473 Amos 5:26
3474 Ezekiel 8:14
3475 Ezekiel 8:12

works of darkness, but rather reprove them. For it is a shame even to speak of those things which are done of them in secret."[3476]

12. Under a garb of a pretended devotion to the LORD's name, these unconverted Pharisees honored the sun god, and his sun day, by ascribing that deity to the Christ of God, thus claiming *Christ*; their sun god; above all other gods that should be observed. Because they observed Tam'muz, and the heritage of Tam'muz, they in turn had no conversation with the living God, which is why John wrote to these individuals, "Our fellowship is with the Father, and with his Son Jesus Christ."[3477] Because every thing concerning Christ was made to perfectly fit into to every pagan doctrine, these individuals who were but pagans themselves, took the sun god of their heritage to be fully revealed in the man born of *Mary* and sent from *God*. She who was known beforehand by the name of Isis, "the queen of heaven,"[3478] or "Diana of the Ephe'sians,"[3479] and her son Horus, or who to others was known as Tam'muz or Apollo, became *Mary* and *Jesus* for the now philosophical sect that called themselves *servants* to *heaven's will*. Therefore when she had obtained the power she longed after, being joined to her State, the word was fulfilled, "Through his policy also he shall cause craft to prosper in his hand."[3480]

13. The hand is but a figure of speech denoting power, thus the word is fulfilled, "His power shall be mighty, but not by his own power."[3481] The church made herself pretty for king Ba'lak, and being seduced by the power contained within her eyes, by his legislative power, every ordinance and tradition of the church was set as law so that the conscience of the citizen may be governed by the imaginary magnificence of the empire. There was even a law administered for Christian worship concerning the sun god by king Ba'lak, or Constantine. Sunday was reserved for a day of family and the cessation of every thing where every thing could rest, and in the name of *Christ* it was

---

3476 Ephesians 5:11,12
3477 1 John 1:3
3478 Jeremiah 44:19
3479 Acts 19:34
3480 Daniel 8:25
3481 Daniel 8:24

forced on the citizens of the empire. This Sunday law became a means of persecution for the ones who maintained true faithful worship to the true God and to His Christ. Thus, by the continued relationship with the State, this church added fabrication upon fabrication, and was even given power that as many as would not worship their god through their institution, and the man of their institution, should be killed.

14. These things have been briefly reviewed because the question asked by the Pharisees is a highly dangerous one. Because of a foul heart, because their religion was not purified by the means that God ordained, terrible error occurred under the guise of truth. Christ said that His kingdom had no outward visage or appearance, it had no public or open exhibit, yet the mind of the Pharisees was centered on just that, a physical dominion swallowed up with earthly pomp. Christ said, "No; no one will be able to say, 'Here it is,' or, 'God save the king,' for My kingdom is not physical, and even more than this, its beginning is first in you." The eye of faith is the first prerequisite necessary to pass into the priestly reign of God's Christ. This is why He said, "Except ye be converted, and become as little children, ye shall not enter into the kingdom of heaven."[3482] The kingdom is only of heaven. By the death of Christ, after the Father accepted His sacrifice, He personally "opened the doors of heaven"[3483] to us, and this means that "we have a building of God, an house not made with hands, eternal in the heavens,"[3484] for the development of our faith and spirit.

15. Only in this Place rests the kingdom and communion of the Spirit. For because "a spirit hath not flesh and bones,"[3485] Christ confessed, "My kingdom is not of this world."[3486] No religion of the LORD's Christ can be connected to any State and continue to call itself pure or honorable. Her power thus procured is accomplished by her State. The entrance of the church into the halls of legislative courts is not from heaven's God, despite what victory may be given to *God* on

---

3482 Matthew 18:3
3483 Psalms 78:23
3484 2 Corinthians 5:1
3485 Luke 24:39
3486 John 18:36

behalf of such things, for it is but the perverse self-willed spirit of the church that magnifies herself above the appointment of God. It was not ever the will of God that man take the place of God on things relating to God, and it is most blasphemous for man to call himself and his economy that country proceeding from God, to then sit himself in the room of *Judge* over strange violations as director over the moral and mental intentions of man. These things the Pharisees expected Christ to do and to establish, and because His answer confessed a contrary stance to their unsanctified heart, "she despised him in her heart."[3487]

16. Because the kingdom is in heaven and is of God, and because "God is a Spirit,"[3488] the kingdom of God is in reality the government of the Spirit. To know God now means to humble the soul to enter into personal "fellowship of the Spirit."[3489] There is a reason why John did not say, "Our fellowship is with the Son and the Father," but rather he wrote, "Our communion is with the Father and the Son."[3490] There is a reason why John did not say, "Every one that loves the begotten loves Him that begat," but rather he wrote, "Every one that loveth him that begat loveth him also that is begotten of him."[3491] The Father is He who begat, and it is Him who, "of his own will begat he us with the word of truth, that we should be a kind of firstfruits of his creatures."[3492] What should stand out is the fact that birth comes from mentally learning of and doing the Spirit's will, and also from His own hands over our spirit from our diligent belief on the instruction of His Faith. Faith on the science of the redemption and reconciliation of man to the LORD will place the believer into the hand of His Spirit that the will of His Son's intercession may commence in the heart of their person.

17. This is the entire reign and kingdom of God and of His Christ. This is why "we have such an high priest, who is set on the right hand of the throne of the Majesty in the heavens; a minister of the sanctuary,

---

3487 2 Samuel 6:16
3488 John 4:24
3489 Philippians 2:1
3490 1 John 1:3
3491 1 John 5:1
3492 James 1:18

and of the true tabernacle, which the Lord pitched, and not man."[3493] Christ is not simply seated by the right hand of the throne of God, He is not at the right hand, but He is most emphatically ON the right hand of throne of God. "Christ sitteth on the right hand of God,"[3494] and for any religious institution to take the right hand of man to accomplish her ambition only exposes a terrible "schism in the body"[3495] of her elders; the report is confirmed against them that says, "There must be also heresies among you."[3496] Because God does not sanction these heresies, she must seduce one who is ignorant and foreign to heavenly things in his own understanding – her State.

18. "He that entereth not by the door into the sheepfold, but climbeth up some other way, the same is a thief and a robber."[3497] Who is the door to the kingdom of heaven? "I am the door of the sheep,"[3498] says the Spirit's Priest. And how can one first receive the privilege of entering into that door? "No man can come to me, except the Father which hath sent me draw him,"[3499] counsels our High Priest. "Every man therefore that hath heard, and hath learned of the Father, cometh unto me."[3500]

19. The means to enter into the door; that is, to have "boldness to enter into the holiest by the blood of Jesus...through the veil, that is to say, his flesh";[3501] is but a fulfillment of the saying, "They shall be all taught of God,"[3502] which is but pointing us back to the LORD's new will and covenant for penitent man. "I will put my law in their inward parts, and write it in their hearts; and will be their God, and they shall be my people. And they shall teach no more every man his neighbour,

---

3493 Hebrews 8:1,2
3494 Colossians 3:1
3495 1 Corinthians 12:25
3496 1 Corinthians 11:19
3497 John 10:1
3498 John 10:7
3499 John 6:44
3500 John 6:45
3501 Hebrews 10:19,20
3502 John 6:45

and every man his brother, saying, Know the LORD: for they shall all know me,"[3503] He promises.

20. Every thing begins and ends with the Majesty of the heavens, which is why He devised a new and more powerful covenant for individuals who should care to feel after Him. The Faith of Jesus is but the means whereby mankind may know the LORD of heaven and earth to be transformed into the image and likeness of His Son, which is why our Father placed the law and knowledge of His Son's mediation at the center of His Faith. But there will arise a new sect of the seed of the Pharisees to work as did their mother, causing their Ba'lak to enact their own will by fulfilling the word, "He maketh fire come down from heaven."[3504] These men in the sight of the king of the State, having found no place or rest in our Father's presence, have climbed up another way to become the supposed door of *God's* flock. They are the thief and the robber of the LORD's heritage, "and through covetousness shall they with feigned words make merchandise of you"[3505] who are without a living membership to the Church within His heavenly Country.

21. Today, and especially at this time, the Spirit says, "Lay not up for yourselves treasures upon earth, where moth and rust doth corrupt, and where thieves break through and steal: but lay up for yourselves treasures in heaven, where neither moth nor rust doth corrupt, and where thieves do not break through nor steal."[3506]

22. Let us then ask, "Why, Lord, cannot any one desecrate that which is now under Your possession and authority in heaven?" "Behold, a king shall reign in righteousness...and a man shall be as an hiding place,"[3507] even "the Son, who is consecrated for evermore,"[3508] it is written. "My people shall dwell in a peaceable habitation, and in sure dwellings, and in quiet resting places,"[3509] it says. For this cause, "look upon Zion, the city of our solemnities: thine eyes shall see Jerusalem

---

3503 Jeremiah 31:33,34
3504 Revelation 13:13
3505 2 Peter 2:3
3506 Matthew 6:19,20
3507 Isaiah 32:1
3508 Hebrews 7:28
3509 Isaiah 32:18

a quiet habitation, a tabernacle that shall not be taken down; not one of the stakes thereof shall ever be removed, neither shall any of the cords thereof be broken. But there the glorious LORD will be unto us a place of broad rivers and streams; wherein shall go no galley with oars, neither shall gallant ship pass thereby."[3510]

23. The intention of the new apostate sect of the new State of the earth is after the same ambition of her mother. The Spirit is warning us against the doctrine of these thieves and liars, and we cannot know to stay from them unless consistently found at the door of the House of God and in the arms of the Minister of that Temple. The current purpose of the One found within "the temple of the tabernacle of the testimony in heaven"[3511] is translated as, "Bind up the testimony, seal the law among my disciples."[3512] To keep them from the errors of this gross period of ecclesiastical history, our Father would have His will finished in His host before that time. Because these robbers will fulfill the vision of themselves in reference to the image of their mother, "Afflict your souls, and offer an offering made by fire unto the LORD,"[3513] counsels our High Priest.

3510 Isaiah 33:20,21
3511 Revelation 15:5
3512 Isaiah 8:16
3513 Leviticus 23:27

43

Deprivation's Compromise

1. "And when he had fasted forty days and forty nights, he was afterward an hungred. And when the tempter came to him, he said, If thou be the Son of God, command that these stones be made bread."[3514] "The devil said unto him, If thou be the Son of God, command this stone that it be made bread."[3515]

2. When absolutely and totally famished, the heart within man will serve as a great betrayer to his higher faculties. That spirit of error against every human being knows this. He knows that appetite begins and ends with direct influence over the mental and moral powers of the human being. He knows that a lapse in discretion, or that an overindulgent stomach, will influence the moral portions of the human being to quiet the voice of the mental. When man is thus overcome by his or her diet, he knows that, although he can physically cause no man to sin or to commit error, the persuasion of his coercion upon the spirit of man in a weakened state will not be objected to. And he knows this to be a fact because his experiment with both Adam and Eve proved to be a complete success.

3514 Matthew 4:2, 3
3515 Luke 4:3

3. An intemperate heart caused the pair to choose irrational disobedience over sober reason. "The woman saw that the tree was good for food"[3516] only because she did not have a right constitution to believe otherwise. Her strength and counterpart had slowly abandoned himself to his own defects, not recognizing what was ultimately happening within him. From the time the LORD said, "Do not eat from that tree," Eve was immediately enflamed with a desire to understand why they could not rest under it. Instead of investigating her environment, instead of boldly approaching the God of the garden to prove that this God was the God of creation, her appetite quenched every avenue of reason, leaving her to abandon every point of loyalty to inevitably apostatize from God. And as for Adam, he found no reason to gather around someone that was hard to teach and to convince. Because he saw her spirit, and because she did not have his mind, and because he would not overexert himself to study his environment along with his God's voice to help her, he separated from her altogether. He sat alone overeating the then secret frame of his natural disposition.

4. Seeing the discord and the disunity between the two, the serpent understood that his time to strike was right. "The serpent said unto the woman, Ye shall not surely die."[3517] "If thou be the daughter of God, turn this meat into stone." Heaven's enemy minister saw in man what man could not see in their self. He saw how deranged the eye of the heart became when it willingly detached from its Creator. Their stubborn human nature had caused them to starve for communion with God, for a new and strange substance within them would not allow them to humble themselves to be taught by Him. This nature compelled them to believe that they were more independent than ignorant, and as the serpent saw this taking place, doubtless the dragon was amazed. Being a creation of God himself, and being an eye witness to the formation of man, hearing the angels of God personally review the act of the Father and Son in the Courts above and on the good earth beneath, when he saw that strange portion of man rear up in him, and when he saw that it was the same mind that he too carried, he turned to God and

---

3516 Genesis 3:6
3517 Genesis 3:4

said, "Hast not thou made an hedge about him"?[3518] "Thou hast blessed the work of his hands, and his substance is increased in the land. But put forth thine hand now, and touch all that he hath, and he will curse thee to thy face."[3519]

5. "The LORD said unto Satan, Behold, all that he hath is in thy power."[3520] Thus began the great controversy for the heart and mind of man on the basis of appetite, which is why the Christ began His ministry where the fall originally occurred. He entered into the wilderness by His Father's side, but eventually, just like with the pair in the garden, His Father and the host of His Father left Him for a time. Christ was alone. Nothing but the memory of the warmth of the intercourse between Him and His Father, and the sound faith that He upheld in the power of His Father's voice, joined Him during and after His fast in a dry place. Again, the times and the seasons were right. "What a victory would it be if I could actually have the Son of God?" said the same contrary spirit of Eden while observing the thin and sickly looking man. "Adam was not that Man, and my voice was secured in Eve, but it is yet imperfectly cultivated. If I could have this Man, then I may be like the most High."

6. "And Jesus being full of the Holy Ghost returned from Jordan, and was led by the Spirit into the wilderness, being forty days tempted of the devil. And in those days he did eat nothing: and when they were ended, he afterward hungered. And the devil said unto him, If thou be the Son of God, command this stone that it be made bread. And Jesus answered him, saying, It is written, That man shall not live by bread alone, but by every word of God."[3521]

7. Christ here gained the victory for every human appetite, no matter which passion should irritate the person. Adam and Eve thought that the literal word of God was to be literally held without any mental labor to comprehend and digest that counsel. The pair believed the creature of God to be above the Creator of the work. While Adam

---

3518 Job 1:10
3519 Job 1:11
3520 Job 1:12
3521 Luke 4:1-4

stubbornly held to the tradition given him, never examining the fact of that religion, and while Eve did not count the religion of God as factual, but longed to know its fact by placing faith on a tree that contained no understanding to relay that science, the two fell victim to intemperate thoughts and feelings, causing their separation from God's voice. As a result, Eve turned bread into stone, and because it says, "Gather out the stones; lift up a standard,"[3522] and, "Breaking bread from house to house, did eat their meat,"[3523] we see that Eve turned meat into a standard. Eve turned what had no life into something made to be perceived as full of life, thus coercing Adam by the fraudulent standard of her testimony. The devil now sought to constrain the LORD's Christ, now deeply famished, to turn a stone into bread, or rather, a standard into meat.

8. Christ would not turn something that had no power, or that already had a set structure, into something else according to His mind, and to serve His own self by that proceeding from His self. Man does not exist, and is not expected to subsist, on bread or meat. Christ fully knew the saying, "Meats for the belly, and the belly for meats: but God shall destroy both it and them."[3524] This is why He says, "Think not that I am come to destroy the law, or the prophets: I am not come to destroy, but to fulfil. For verily I say unto you, Till heaven and earth pass, one jot or one tittle shall in no wise pass from the law."[3525] God's Christ would not be shaken, and no matter how poor His state was, He would not compromise to alter any thing for some temporal benefit.

9. Christ could have done any thing to whatever thing was around Him to quench both hunger and thirst. Even when faced with death, and being protected by Peter, He said, "Thinkest thou that I cannot now pray to my Father, and he shall presently give me more than twelve legions of angels?"[3526] This in fact was the Spirit and power of the living God's wisdom functioning in the flesh's members, but it was not the

---

3522   Isaiah 62:10
3523   Acts 2:46
3524   1 Corinthians 6:13
3525   Matthew 5:17,18
3526   Matthew 26:53

position of the Christ of God to turn a stone into bread. He didn't appear to fulfill His own will, but rather He says, "My meat is to do the will of him that sent me, and to finish his work";[3527] and again, "I have not spoken of myself; but the Father which sent me, he gave me a commandment, what I should say, and what I should speak."[3528] In this confession, Christ exemplifies the relationship that His believer should have with Him and His God. This is why He says, "If ye keep my commandments, ye shall abide in my love; even as I have kept my Father's commandments, and abide in his love."[3529]

10. Christ is that Savior of the defective human nature, of the unstable human spirit, and of the negligent human disposition. "Of him"; by the will of the LORD God our Father; "are ye in Christ Jesus, who of God is made unto us wisdom, and righteousness, and sanctification, and redemption: that, according as it is written, He that glorieth, let him glory in the Lord."[3530] As He existed in His Father's name and Spirit, so His faithful must examine His voice that they too may rest in the same name and Spirit that kept Him. And because He confesses, "I also overcame, and am set down with my Father in his throne,"[3531] being joined to the throne of the living God, "truly our fellowship is with the Father, and with his Son Jesus."[3532] Christ changed no thing of the Bible's LORD, but His victories through His Father ensure every victory for us by His current mediation, and through the same Holy Ghost that led and kept Him while He hungered, that we too may keep both the commandments of God and the precepts of the Spirit's Faith. If the believer abides in the benevolence of heaven's confidence, which love is better understood as being the hope of the Spirit's will concerning soul regeneration in sinful flesh, then the believer will also rest in the same joy as His Christ, even the joy of keeping every word that has come from out of His Father's mouth, and will also live in

---

3527   John 4:34
3528   John 12:49
3529   John 15:10
3530   1 Corinthians 1:30,31
3531   Revelation 3:21
3532   1 John 1:3

the same Spirit for health and for continual newness od thought and feeling.

11. The devil could not cause Christ to turn stone into bread, to ordain a self-cultivated standard to be meat, for He sought to overcame man's natural heretical spirit to prove that He was the Son and High Priest of man. When Christ was among His men, "he said unto the disciples, The days will come, when ye shall desire to see one of the days of the Son of man, and ye shall not see it."[3533] Christ was letting His disciples know that there would come a time, in every age, when they would encounter famine, sword, and pestilence. When the saying should again be fulfilled, "All the disciples forsook him, and fled,"[3534] then should the season of hunger begin. This saying occurred as Christ was sentenced to death, and in every age when Christ is openly before the judgment seat of a king, this is that time when the illicit affects of hunger are best honored.

12. The time after the death of the first apostles, and even during their lives, was a time "of false brethren unawares brought in."[3535] "There rose up certain of the sect of the Pharisees which believed"[3536] who "would pervert the gospel of Christ."[3537] Thus the servant of salvation's science was constrained to write, "There are certain men crept in unawares, who were before of old ordained to this condemnation, ungodly men, turning the grace of our God into lasciviousness, and denying the only Lord God, and our Lord Jesus Christ."[3538] Notice that both the LORD God and the Lord Jesus Christ are cut off from the conversation of certain men. Because this false manner of worship and service was taking over Christian churches, John wrote to Christian elders that true fellowship is with both the Father and His Son.[3539] Persecution by peers and by colleagues, by the Roman State, by the emperor of the times and his colleagues, and by the priests of pagan

---

3533 Luke 17:22
3534 Matthew 26:56
3535 Galatians 2:4
3536 Acts 15:5
3537 Galatians 1:7
3538 Jude 1:4
3539 1 John 1:3

priesthoods, along with the citizens of Rome, caused the Christian church to long for her Captain to walk on the earth again. Daily she cried, "They have taken away my Lord, and I know not where they have laid him."[3540]

13. The Christian church was desperate to see one of the days of her Priest, but that time had passed. Even before Rome had sought an issue with this new sect, there was a persecution in Jerusalem against the Spirit's flock, of which Paul, then Saul, was in charge of. "He made havock of the church, entering into every house, and haling men and women committed them to prison. Therefore they that were scattered abroad went every where preaching the word."[3541] Even at this time, the ones who professed faith in the Father's doctrine "were all scattered abroad throughout the regions of Judaea and Sama'ria, except the apostles."[3542] Only the apostles remained strong in the Faith of their LORD, staying put in Jerusalem, while others that disbursed from them kept what they learned from the apostolic church of Jerusalem, but also added on strange things to the speech of their mother church. Because Paul saw the evidence of this heinous work against heaven's good will, he wrote to the elders of the churches, "Have no fellowship with the unfruitful works of darkness, but rather reprove them. For it is a shame even to speak of those things which are done of them in secret."[3543]

14. Church doctrines that were once pure were becoming tainted, and things that had no weight of authority were being translated to hold authority. When Paul saw this among Christian ministers he wrote, "Hath not God made foolish the wisdom of this world? For after that in the wisdom of God the world by wisdom knew not God."[3544] The elders of the churches, because they were before servants to rites and rituals, were finding it hard to leave off their coarse heritage to honor the counsel, "Be renewed in the spirit of your mind."[3545] Therefore "in those days, when the number of the disciples was multiplied,

---

3540 John 20:13
3541 Acts 8:3,4
3542 Acts 8:1
3543 Ephesians 5:11,12
3544 1 Corinthians 1:20,21
3545 Ephesians 4:23

there arose a murmuring of the Grecians against the Hebrews, because their widows were neglected in the daily ministration."[3546] This daily ministration is the continual offering of sin by physical sacrifice. This that existed, both in Jewish and Gentile circles "in meats and drinks, and divers washings, and carnal ordinances, imposed on them,"[3547] was suffering as "they continued stedfastly in the apostles' doctrine and fellowship."[3548] The ignorance of the religious world that their heritage valued passed away by the knowledge of Jesus that Chief Minister of the Spirit's law, but these would not let their tradition go.

15. Because the elders of the churches would not fully surrender to a diligent and personal examination of the Spirit's voice, commandments and traditions were established by them. Meanings of the religion of *Christ* were being placed into rites and feasts and days and physical images backed by a developing body of ecclesiastical laws. What should have remained a stone was turned into bread by men that fulfilled the rebuke, "They would none of my counsel,"[3549] moving Paul to write, "If righteousness come by the law (the law of a traditional religion), then Christ is dead in vain."[3550] Again, at the sight of this error by Christian ministers, Peter was moved to counsel faithful men against the new approach to faith by saying, "Unto you therefore which believe he is precious: but unto them which be disobedient, the stone which the builders disallowed, the same is made the head of the corner, and a stone of stumbling, and a rock of offence, even to them which stumble at the word, being disobedient: whereunto also they were appointed."[3551] For Paul, protesting them that held their law as being from *God*, and who taught, "Righteousness come by the law,"[3552] said, "For meat destroy not the work of God,"[3553] which opened up their heart to receive Peter's

---

3546 Acts 6:1
3547 Hebrews 9:10
3548 Acts 2:42
3549 Proverbs 1:30
3550 Galatians 2:21
3551 1 Peter 2:7,8
3552 Galatians 2:21
3553 Romans 14:20

counsel: "Know that ye were not redeemed with corruptible things, as silver and gold, from your vain conversation received by tradition."[3554]

16. The translated meat of Eve destroyed the conscience of Adam, and the meat of unconverted elders was destroying the work of the will of God in the heart of the spirit of men and women. Paul saw this spirit while he was alive and up until his death, and one of the last things he wrote to heaven's faithful was, "Be not carried about with divers and strange doctrines. For it is a good thing that the heart be established with grace; not with meats, which have not profited them that have been occupied therein."[3555]

17. The work of God was being destroyed by a sect who "profess that they know God; but in works they deny him, being abominable, and disobedient, and unto every good work reprobate."[3556] This is why Paul had to tell them, "The name of God is blasphemed among the Gentiles through you, as it is written."[3557] The apostles saw Jewish and Gentile Christian churches draw back into their unprofitable lineage, and it was this work of transgression that caused them to no longer differentiate themselves from the polytheistic religion of the then times. This is why Paul wrote to them, "If I build again the things which I destroyed, I make myself a transgressor."[3558]

18. Their religious symbols, such as their symbol of the cross, and their idolatrous regard for other men and women, their set day for worship being the same pagan Sunday festival of pagan Roman ancestral upbringing, and their other days and feasts being synonymous with the other pagan festivals, but being replaced with new names for their new faith, and yet their strange refusal to regard the pagan religion of Rome, even though to the reasonable mind they actually magnified and praised that religion, cast a hypocritical shadow over their practice, and disqualified the *God* they espoused to their fellowship as being any God at all.

3554   1 Peter 1:18
3555   Hebrews 13:9
3556   Titus 1:16
3557   Romans 2:24
3558   Galatians 2:18

19. The misery they suffered against themselves was self-inflicted because they would not listen to the counsel given to them by the first apostles. "The darkness is past,"[3559] said one, and, "Ye were sometimes darkness, but now are ye light in the Lord: walk as children of light,"[3560] advised another. The state of their affairs took its shape according to the state of their heart and according to their own independent effort to reform that heart. If they did consent to hear and do the doctrine of Christ, then they would have heard the voice of God to obtain the Spirit's meat. "The fruit of the Spirit is in all goodness and righteousness and truth,"[3561] but the production of these unsanctified men produced hatred, envying, hypocrisy, and evil thinking. One servant of God's commandment saw this foul spirit emerging to supplant the right spirit of His Christ's voice, and counseled, "If ye have bitter envying and strife in your hearts, glory not, and lie not against the truth. This wisdom descendeth not from above, but is earthly, sensual, devilish. For where envying and strife is, there is confusion and every evil work."[3562]

20. This is that "spirit of error"[3563] producing the spirit of confusion, for only by confusion may a stone find itself turned into bread. What is confusion? Says the LORD, "Neither shall any woman stand before a beast to lie down thereto: it is confusion."[3564] Herein we have the full image of the institution of confusion, for it is written, "I saw a woman sit upon a scarlet coloured beast."[3565] The seed of them that cried after the daily ministration of their heritage are them that, because of their state of hunger, joined themselves to the Roman State of their land to exist in both their ancestral heritage and the doctrine of *Christ*. Years of disobedience and apostasy developed a child of Satan to work the will of his father as Christ did concerning His Father. "The son of perdition; who opposeth and exalteth himself above all that is called God, or that

---

3559 1 John 2:8
3560 Ephesians 5:8
3561 Ephesians 5:9
3562 James 3:14-16
3563 1 John 4:6
3564 Leviticus 18:23
3565 Revelation 17:3

is worshipped";[3566] was inevitably conceived by this apostate church and spirit.

21. Thus, when the time of famine became hot upon the professors, Christ reported of them, "I know the blasphemy of them which say they are Jews, and are not, but are the synagogue of Satan."[3567] When once the church sanctioned the confusion that the Christ of God would not consent to, and when she filled up the place "where Satan's seat is,"[3568] bearing "the doctrine of Ba'laam, who taught Ba'lac to cast a stumblingblock,"[3569] then was it fulfilled, "His power shall be mighty, but not by his own power... Through his policy also he shall cause craft to prosper in his hand; and he shall magnify himself in his heart, and by peace shall destroy many."[3570]

22. The religion of deviation from the LORD now had his own son, and he was this practice's god and savior. For this cause, Christ's rebuke of this foul creature echoed when this False Wicked sat upon the seat of the Roman world: "Ye are of your father the devil, and the lusts of your father ye will do. He was a murderer from the beginning, and abode not in the truth, because there is no truth in him."[3571] From the time of his official birth until this day, the spirit of this persuasion has in his heart to "speak great words against the most High,"[3572] to "wear out the saints of the most High,"[3573] and longs "to change times and laws"[3574] "which the Father hath put in his own power."[3575]

23. Christ will not change or alter any thing that has come from His God, for every word of Christ did first pass through the mind of the LORD His God. "Whatsoever God doeth, it shall be for ever: nothing can be put to it, nor any thing taken from it: and God doeth it, that

---

3566 2 Thessalonians 2:4
3567 Revelation 2:9
3568 Revelation 2:9
3569 Revelation 2:13,14
3570 Daniel 8:24,25
3571 John 8:44
3572 Daniel 7:25
3573 Daniel 7:25
3574 Daniel 7:25
3575 Acts 1:7

men should fear before him."[3576] Nevertheless, it remains a fact that certain elders will honor the laws of them who beforehand "changed the truth of God into a lie."[3577] It will be encouraged "that they should make an image to the beast, which had the wound by a sword, and did live,"[3578] therefore we can know that before this occurs, there will be a terrible famine in the land due to the appearing of the body of Christ at the judgment seat of men. The beast that suffered a wound was even that institution headed by that son of perdition, and it is in the likeness of its mother that a new republic will emerge. After certain ministers become hungry, after they are wearied from whatever should blast their soul to death, a compromise will inevitably take place in their religious palaces, and the earth will again find herself jeopardized by certain stones turned into bread.

24. Because these things are certain, the counsel is ever applicable, "Man shall not live by bread alone, but by every word of God."[3579] The Spirit's counsels may be that bread for the soul, but unless that bread is properly tasted, chewed, digested, and then infused within the life-current of the spirit of the mind and person, no good thing will come to the personal religious experience. This is why Christ didn't just say, "I am bread," but also, "My blood will refresh your inwards when you drink it." The drinking of Christ's blood is the experience of the Spirit's will and wisdom by active and experimental faith. Eating and drinking the Faith of Jesus will leave the reformer saying with the apostle, "We both labour and suffer reproach, because we trust in the living God, who is the Saviour of all men, specially of those that believe."[3580] Belief does not come from simply eating meat, but belief is born when that sustenance is allowed to enter into the members of the heart and mind, that the limbs of the body may verify its authority.

25. While the early church was allowing her intemperate and impatient spirit to draw her from the law of heaven's will, she forgot

---

3576   Ecclesiastes 7:14
3577   Romans 1:25
3578   Revelation 13:14
3579   Luke 4:4
3580   1 Timothy 4:10

how it was once said, "He humbled thee, and suffered thee to hunger, and fed thee with man'na, which thou knewest not, neither did thy fathers know; that he might make thee know that man doth not live by bread only, but by every word that proceedeth out of the mouth of the LORD doth man live."[3581] What is apparent hunger and agitation is but the Father sealing the knowledge of Himself within the soul temple. Because the early church did not care to prove the LORD's will, the saying was fulfilled, "The time will come when they will not endure sound doctrine; but after their own lusts shall they heap to themselves teachers, having itching ears; and they shall turn away their ears from the truth, and shall be turned unto fables."[3582]

26. The time will come when apparent leaders of the *Faith* of *Jesus* will move in a way most contrary to His name, and because none have endured the self-denying religion of heaven's throne, they will apostatize with them "whose judgment now of a long time lingereth not, and their damnation slumbereth not."[3583] "Many shall follow their pernicious ways; by reason of whom the way of truth shall be evil spoken of;"[3584] but "ye therefore, beloved, seeing ye know these things before, beware lest ye also, being led away with the error of the wicked, fall from your own stedfastness."[3585] The goal for the ministers of the new republic is to turn stones into bread, that "through covetousness shall they with feigned words make merchandise of you."[3586] This is not the character of the LORD's Christ, but it is of a form contrary to His intention. Now is the time to know the LORD and His Son that we may receive a right revelation of the Godhead's will and science.

3581 Deuteronomy 8:3
3582 2 Timothy 4:3,4
3583 2 Peter 2:3
3584 2 Peter 2:2
3585 2 Peter 3:17
3586 2 Peter 2:3